KILLING KENNEDY

Also by Harrison Edward Livingstone

High Treason
High Treason II
Killing the Truth

KILLING KENNEDY
And the Hoax
of the Century

Harrison E. Livingstone

Carroll & Graf Publishers, Inc.
New York

Copyright © 1995 by Harrison Edward Livingstone

First edition 1995

Carroll & Graf Publishers, Inc.
260 Fifth Avenue
New York, NY 10001

Library of Congress Cataloging-in-Publication Data is available.

ISBN 0-7867-0195-1

Manufactured in the United States of America.

97 96 95   5 4 3 2 1

To Judy Schwabacher

and to Herman Graf and Kent Carroll,

to Professor William Alfred at Harvard,

to Dean John Adams at Harvard,

and to Jacqueline Bouvier Kennedy.

Take no part in the worthless pleasures of evil and darkness,
but instead, rebuke and expose them.

—Ephesians *5:11*

ACKNOWLEDGMENTS

As ALWAYS, many people helped out with my research and this book. There are those who helped me personally, and for all who cared, I am eternally grateful.

I AM MOST INDEBTED to Judy Schwabacher, for her caring, her understanding, her help, and her art. She came to my assistance at a crucial moment, sensing that I needed help. Judy is a sculptress who made what I consider the finest bronze portrait of John Kennedy I have seen.

I am particularly indebted to Donald Siple, M.D., David Mantik, M.D., Kathy Cunningham, R.N., Robert Livingston, M.D., James Folliard, Gary Rowell, Peter Dale Scott, and Bob Cutler.

David Mantik has made an enormous breakthrough in his study of the X-rays, and like Doug Mizzer and Daryll Weatherly, will be ranked among the key people who broke the JFK case to pieces by exposing the forgery of the key evidence—a study pioneered by me.

Anna Marie Kuhns-Walko deserves special thanks not only from me but from all. She has devoted a period of her life to obtaining from the National Archives copies of many, if not nearly all, of the secret documents and interviews conducted over the years in the Kennedy case. According to Steve Tilley of the JFK collection in the Archives, Anna Marie spent fifty-nine hours at one stretch. Anna Marie obtained these documents through requests under the JFK Assassination Records Act.

In particular, I'd like to thank Bradley Kizzia and Dr. Charles Crenshaw not only for their provision of court documents, but also for their great contribution to this case.

Then, there are the many readers who write letters to me, so many that I'm no longer able to answer them all. I want to thank all those who write. At times, the letters help me to get through the dark nights. That is, as a writer, much of my time is spent isolated from human contact, and it is very pleasant to receive feedback and praise. Even criticism is welcome, because writers (some of us, anyway) learn from it. I take this opportunity to thank those who write and apologize to those I'm unable to answer.

I appreciate the support of Dale Hawkins-Elliott in particular over the years and the many letters she has written.

Very many letters have come to me from England and from the rest of the world, offering praise, encouragement, and ideas.

I would especially like to thank Officer Marco Miranda of the Baltimore City Police, for the many hours of work he has put in and the many trips we have made to Dallas. Marco has been a bulwark of support and help, and I appreciate it more than he knows. The same goes for Officer Richard Waybright, who survived the best they could throw at him and "culled the herd!" He's got the quickest reflexes around.

Special thanks also to Martin Shackelford who has been supportive through a great deal of new work. Martin is unfailingly helpful when I have a question and understanding when I am under too much stress and working too hard. Martin is one of the many unsung heroes of this case whose expertise and character is eclipsed by those who get the accolades and publicity, but whose work is nothing when compared to his.

Richard Trask and the Yeoman Press have provided us with the finest work in the photographic evidence that has been or will be produced. It is regrettable that Yeoman could not print the best color reproductions due to a lack of financing, and that greatly inferior books have gotten the financial backing, coopting the public recognition Mr. Trask and Yeoman deserve.

Doug Mizzer found many doors slammed in his face, but he had the courage to risk rejection and try again. With encouragement, I watched him blossom as I tried to integrate him into the new team I was building. He traveled to New York, Washington, D.C., and California with me and met some of the most prominent people in the new research I was stimulating or conducting. Doug has turned out to be a good friend, and his proximity to me in my own city has given me support and friendship as well. But the wonderful fruit of his own thoughts and work began to make breakthrough after breakthrough in the work that we do, and he has provided some of the most important keys to decoding the forgeries in the case.

Daryll Weatherly has also blossomed, writing a steady stream of articles and research papers that I assigned him, plus his own. He has provided without doubt the basic research that will someday be shown permanently to destroy the many lies surrounding the assassination of John Kennedy. Daryll's fundamental research in the National Archives on the Zapruder film and his work with the documentation of the FBI and the Secret Service reconstruction of the assassination show that those few researchers who flirted with it in the past were merely little boys and girls in short pants. Weatherly's brilliance in this work will take hold and will be recognized by future historians. Chapters 3, 4, and 5 of this book rest heavily on his research. My house was his base for the expeditions to the National Archives, and I will remember his visits fondly.

Edgar Tatro has been especially helpful and supportive, and I want to thank him for all his kindness and materials.

Madeleine Brown has been unfailingly helpful to me, and I will always be grateful for her friendship and assistance. She is a great dinner date, and I'll never forget her. She has written a wonderful and beautifully written book about her love affair with Lyndon Johnson that we pray will find a publisher. The book is quite a slice of history and many famous names walk through its pages.

Vince Palamara, Patricia Dumais, Mark Oakes, Richard Bartholomew, Steve Barber, Earl Golz, Robert Johnson, Angela Parker, Suzanne Dunlevy, Larry Lentol, M.D., Douglas Weldon, Ron, Linda Newman, Casey Jack Thornburg, Todd Tucker (Vaughan), John R. Woods II, Tom Purvis, Richard Gates, Perry Adams, Fred Newcomb, Patrick Boyles, Lara and Joan, Charles R. Stone, Dr. Joseph L. Thimes, Dr. Michael D. Morrissey, Arend Kistemaker, Chuck Marler, Dennis Bishop, Mark Ballen, Karl Salisbury, John Nagel, Emory Brown, Karen Wright, Joanne Braun, Tim and Janet Kehoe have all provided steady support, research, contacts, and other forms of help. Deanie Richards deserves special mention for her magazine, *JFK Honor Guard,* and her constant effort to expose the truth of 1963. Peggy Davidson has also provided a great deal of help and information.

Bob Campbell is another who wrote letters of praise to me to which I fortunately responded. Years after I had gotten to know him through the mail and finally in person, Bob, a fireman on a military base in California, pulled a pilot from a crashed plane. The pilot was saved and received only minor injuries, but Bob injured his back so badly that he was immediately retired and began a series of painful operations. The pain he has lived with from the moment he rescued the pilot was acutely on my mind as the weeks and months went by, listening to his distress over the phone. Bob Campbell is a *true hero* and a son of the state of California and this nation.

Also, thanks to those conscientious people at the National Archives, who were very patient with my forays there, tolerating me, often when I was too tired to be there in the first place. In particular, thanks to Dale Connelly, Fred Purnell, Matthew Bynum, Betty Hill in the Still Pictures Branch, and Steve Tilley.

I would like to thank author George O'Toole. His book, *The Assassination Tapes,* remains one of the better books written about the mystery and tragedy of John Kennedy's death. *The Assassination Tapes* is a fine resource, and O'Toole's original thinking and analysis stand as a great achievement.

Professor Jerry Rose is to be commended for the completion of ten years at the helm of what has become one of the most important journals of research into the assassination of JFK, *The Third Decade.* When another ten years passed in November 1993, he changed the name to *The Fourth Decade.*

Equally important is *The Investigator,* a first-class journal of research and news edited by Gary Rowell.

Kevin Brennan, our attorney, deserves a medal for heroism. And I'll have one struck off, because I probably can't pay him for all that he does. He deserves more than that, having to deal with me. . . .

Katarina Witt provides me with powerful inspiration through her wonderful ice-skating and ice dancing. Her personal campaign against war and violence in general, the violence of the war in Bosnia and what it is doing to Sarajevo in particular, and the horror of Auschwitz and other death camps perpetrated by her own country is equally inspiring. Katarina has used her great artistry in competitions to make very powerful statements against many of the nightmares of our century, and I relate to what she is doing with deep emotion. I only wish I knew her. I have gone about attacking violence in our political process. That is what these books are about, in addition to keeping the memory of John Kennedy alive. As an artist, I identify with her statements, because they are also mine.

Last but not least to thank are my publishers, Kent Carroll and Herman Graf. Their constant support and encouragement through thick and thin have kept me in there, fighting.

—Harrison E. Livingstone

CONTENTS

PREFACE

When you have eliminated the impossible, whatever remains, however improbable, must be the truth.

— Sherlock Holmes

WELL, HERE WE ARE AGAIN. I never thought when I wrote the original volume *High Treason* in 1979–80 that I would be writing four books on the JFK case. It certainly was not my intention. Repeatedly, I have tried to go back to my artistic writing. And I have been able to work steadily, if sporadically, on a major novel I undertook in September 1993 throughout the writing of the book you now hold in your hands.

But on the train ride back home to Baltimore after our historic press conference in New York City on November 18, 1993, and after a few heavy-handed hints from others, the necessity of a fourth book became very clear in my mind. I had to tie up the loose ends, answer my critics, and present new evidence.

In fact, new evidence rapidly developed from the moment we went to press with *Killing the Truth*, my last book. It was clear that there was no end to my work. The calls from many researchers praising that book encouraged me. I had expected to be crucified for coming out publicly against the old crowd, the *establishment* or Old Guard among the "critics," who I had come to believe were actually blocking the solution to the case.

As Vince Palamara told me on November 25, 1993, Thanksgiving Day, "They don't want the case solved. They want to keep it going at all costs because it gives them a reason to live, and it's money in the bank. Harry, you want to solve it. You want to end it. That's what separates you from almost everyone else."

A letter from Germany expressed a deep understanding of my writing. Jochen Hemmleb wrote me:

> For me the Kennedy case proved to be a room with a hundred doors. The more I read about it, the longer I tried to understand

its meaning, the more doors I seemed to open—even if it was just for a brief glance.... The moment when you leave the point of reading something matter-of-fact, instead reading it between the lines and thus peering deeper and deeper into what's really behind all this. These are fundamental things like psychology, emotions, thoughts—the true nature of human behavior and existence.

There's one big difference. In other books, about my sport of mountaineering, for instance, you read mostly about similarity, not controversy. You learn about people who think like you do, feel like you do, have the same goals in life—reading this brings a lot of self-confidence and understanding. Reading the books about the Kennedy assassination, I found myself caught in a mess of opinions, theories and criticisms—sometimes it was a mental struggle, really! "Don't fall for the lure of Kennedy case, this is too big for you!" ... But then your books pushed me over the edge, finally closing the little back door through which I hoped to bail out. There are chapters in them which are so dense with emotion that I couldn't help but wonder what you have been through. You probably peered deeper into the case than anybody had done before—which is, in some respects, another way of exploring the limits of what is possible.

Congratulations! Although it leaves me somewhat frustrated that I can't grasp all the feelings and thoughts I have when I'm reading these books, I hope I have expressed a few of them. I am 22 and probably should care about other things—but as long as I feel that people like you have a better and deeper understanding of human character and behavior, of what's "real" in this world, I will see a true sense in the life I'm leading now. Because you are the ones who break the indifference and superficiality which is so much a disease of today's society—so why shouldn't I take time and listen to your words?

If it is possible to solve this case, as I believe we are now doing, yes, I want to end it. I am heartsick over the fact that a virtual industry has been made out of it. There are those who will say that whatever it takes to keep the case going and in the public eye is valuable, but I have always maintained that publicity for publicity's sake makes it doubly difficult, if not impossible, for serious evidence to come forward.

I have always felt that the Oliver Stone movie *JFK* set in motion the terrible wheels of the media to close this case, with the official story beginning all over again in *The Journal of the American Medical Association*'s articles in 1992 and ending with the terrific onslaught of the media in the fall of 1993: Gerald Posner's *Case Closed,* the *U.S. News* issue of August 30–September 6, 1993, and the CBS docu-drama *Who Killed JFK, The Final Chapter?* My original perception has proven to be correct.

Stone made a circus of the case, and from that moment on, the die was cast—the media would gang up and try to kill it. Meanwhile, I was publicly disassociating myself from the group that did it and trying to launch the definitive history of the case based on the hard physical and medical evidence that would prove it. We attempted to do so at our press conference in New York City just before all of this reached a peak in November 1993.

THE NATIONAL ARCHIVES

There are quite a few researchers making the pilgrimage to the new National Archives II, which is located in Maryland at College Park. The new structure is a nice-looking space-age glass building of silver and white covering a lot of ground. Inside, you feel like a bug on a plate under a microscope where surveillance cameras in the ceilings watch your every move.

But the surveillance was much worse than that and may be a lot worse still. Graduates of the National Security Agency and other intelligence agencies staff the place and run the JFK materials. Longtime researchers have experienced intense provocation. In one case, the researcher lost it and exploded at "Einstein," a surveillance person who later explained to me that he was only doing his job. The victim was brought on the carpet and warned that if she did it again, she would lose her privileges and be thrown out. This is the grossest sort of provocation, in my opinion, and when I closely questioned the staff person responsible, he denied that he had anything whatsoever on the researcher. He said that he was just keeping her alert so that she did not forget that she was handling part of the national history and make a mistake by putting a document back in the wrong box.

Certainly, such close watching will force mistakes. Four of us were looking at materials when the a surveillance supervisor moved in within one foot of us and would not go away. I finally had to stop what I was doing and ask him what he wanted. This initiated a very long discussion that took up much of our time and set aside our reason for being there. He was able to learn a great deal about what we were doing.

I then learned that this information was being passed on to em-

ployees of the Defense Intelligence Agency and other intelligence
and Pentagon operatives, some of whom have infiltrated the JFK
research community and become quite prominent, though most
researchers have the wool pulled over their eyes and either don't
realize they are dealing with the real intelligence agencies of
America or could care less, wishing to trust their newfound friends.

What fools we all are.

I also learned that the great amount of money researchers contin-
ually pay Henry Zapruder (Abraham Zapruder's son and heir) for
the copying of slides from the film by the National Archives is paid
over and over, since Zapruder's lawyer, Jamie Silverberg, does not
return the slides to the Archives. The Archives staff told me that
they were surprised to hear this and that none of the slides had
ever been returned.

In December 1994, we informed Steve Tilley, a chief archivist at
the National Archives, that certain materials seemed to be missing
from Secret Service notebooks and that other materials we wanted
to see were missing from their boxes. The notebooks lack any text
or explanatory material to accompany the pictures of the reenactment of the assassination. Only the pictures that appear in CE
875 are in the notebook. Tilley told Daryll Weatherly: "They should
be there, but they aren't." I know Tilley personally. I can't imagine
him removing materials from our reach, so there has to be some
other explanation. Tilley later gave an opinion that the pictures
had never been deposited in the Archives.

The box that holds Warren Commission Executive Session transcripts is missing many pages and in some cases entire transcripts.
This fact is noted in the 1973 inventory of Commission records
compiled by the Archives.

With regard to this, it is appropriate to note the introduction to
the book *The Secret War Against the Jews* by John Loftus and Mars
Aarons (St. Martin's Press, page 3) which tells us that it is customary
for government agencies to misplace articles that they don't want
people to look at. Evidently, this could be the means whereby full
disclosure of the records in John Kennedy's murder and the act
that was passed to make that possible will be circumvented.

We are also detecting a pattern of different evidence for different
folk. We now have several instances of being shown different things
each time we go to the Archives to study one item. We are certain
that there are different reference sets of Zapruder frames in the
Archives. In mid 1994, Steve Tilley gave me a print of CE 399. I
obtained another print six months later from him, and it is a different photo or exposure and lacks any identification or Commission

Exhibit (CE) number, which the other print had, but the same print was published elsewhere.

The vast assassination literature features many different pictures of the single bullet, the alleged bullet fragments, and other evidence, which are not identical to the Warren Commission or HSCA photographs. The authors credit the pictures to the Archives, of course, but the photos almost never include identifying information or other authentication. Who is really providing them? This has caused major confusion as to how many grooves the bullet really has.

On January 9, 1995, researcher Daryll Weatherly asked Archivist Steve Tilley about an apparent conflict between the Warren Commission and the House Select Committee on Assassinations (HSCA) pictures of the single bullet. Tilley indicated that he knows of no Archives-produced photograph documenting their possession of CE 399.

It would seem perfectly reasonable for them to have taken a picture of the bullet next to a marker with the Archives symbol and a date, but apparently, the Archives did not do this when CE 399 was deposited there, or later when the HSCA examined it. This lack of organization makes it easy for someone to switch evidence. We know of Texans who handled this bullet in the Archives decades ago, when the archivist in charge of the JFK collection was a Texan and the President was a Texan.

Tilley asserted that an Archives photo of the bullet would be unnecessary, since the Archives is in possession of the bullet itself. He told Weatherly he would not consider trying to resolve the discrepancy himself by looking at it, since it would be inappropriate for a nonexpert to make such a determination. An outsider who tries to look at the bullet is directed to the published official photographs.

The original autopsy documents are unavailable to researchers wishing to examine them for any reason. Suspicions of forgery or alteration of these documents and those dealing with the autopsy photos and X-rays over the next few years cannot be dealt with, because all of the key evidence, such as the autopsy photographs and X-rays, cannot be seen. FOIA and the new Assassination Records Act are useless.

The Archives' boxes of Commission and HSCA documents contain mostly copies or copies of copies. It is understandable that they would want to protect original documents, but the refusal to allow examination of the originals invites suspicion that they are not in the Archives at all. There have been several instances of researchers

finding subtly different versions of the same document. Is it, perhaps, a game designed to keep people focused on minute details?

In fairness to the College Park personnel at their new facility,
Archives II, they have had to deal with the confusion created when
this material passed through the old Archives in Washington, D.C.,
the Warren Commission, and the HSCA investigation.

The National Archives is not just a repository of documents and
materials. In my view, the Archives has a responsibility perhaps
much broader than the mission they probably define for themselves,
and that is to ensure the integrity and authenticity of the treasures
protected there. Granted, it is not an investigatory division of the
government, but even the Post Office has inspectors, and most agencies, if not all, have security operations that include investigation.
It seems to me that we could have expected better than what I
think we have with the Archives: a repository of a major amount of
bogus information represented to us as authentic just because it
is there.

I don't know what the answer is to the problem with the materials
we find in the Archives that have been featured in investigation after
investigation over the years since John Kennedy's murder without
acceptable authentication. I believe the Archives must rethink their
mission as custodian. I think the common law probably covers a
case when custodians accept bogus goods or materials that are then
sold to others or misrepresented. The legal theory that must be
involved would therefore apply.

It is unfortunate that the very integrity of the National Archives
is at stake in these issues.

GILBERT ALEJANDRO WAS IMPRISONED for a felony in 1990 on the basis
of false testimony by Texas county lab technician Fred Zain. "Dr.
Vincent DiMaio, the Bexar County medical examiner, said the case
was the first in an ongoing review of Zain's Texas work that indicates his trial testimony conflicted with tests of the evidence. 'Mr.
Zain implicated this guy, but the test results excluded him,' DiMaio
said. 'Essentially, the DNA tests were done correctly, but the results
reported by Mr. Zain were incorrect.' "

An investigation in West Virginia concluded that the technician
committed perjury and falsified evidence in numerous cases as a
state police technician before coming to Texas (Associated Press,
El Paso Times, July 13, 1994).

The entire political complexion of the nation was changed by the
assassination of JFK, which essentially went unpunished. Letting it

go by in the states of Texas and Maryland and letting the federal government fake an investigation gave a green light to the forces of reaction and repression in the United States.

We are becoming a very real example of George Orwell's *1984*.

For those people who think they so dearly love America, they had better take a close look at what we have become: a nation of violence and ruthlessness, a nation with nothing better than its pop culture and shrines to the past, museums for the art that was created long ago.

Karen Wright wrote the following and sent it to me: "Numerous books on the tragedy in Dallas have been published as answers to the questions of Who, Why, and How. What is so disheartening is that for John F. Kennedy, who admired courage, displayed it, and wrote about it, the country and subsequent administrations have not shown courage in resolving the true facts of his murder. Consequently, the nation has left him and the principles he espoused down."

I believe in human dignity as the source of national purpose, human liberty as the source of national action, the human heart as the source of national compassion, and in the human mind as the source of our invention and our ideas.

—John F. Kennedy

KILLING KENNEDY

Introduction

The conclusion seems inescapable that at least some of the people who framed Lee Harvey Oswald were members of the Dallas police.
                                                              —George O'Toole,
                                                         The Assassination Tapes

WE HAVE SEEN the national media, Gerald Posner, Norman Mailer, and others make a massive effort to focus the public on Lee Harvey Oswald and his alleged psychohistory, deflecting attention away from recent breakthroughs in the physical evidence in the assassination of President Kennedy showing a conspiracy at high levels. Powerful forces have been quite aware that the autopsy doctors, along with every other witness to the President's wounds, strongly reject the official autopsy photographs. At all costs, the doctor's statements, along with all the rest of the evidence presented in this book showing a completely faked case against Oswald, must be kept down.

This book contains explosive new evidence concerning the assassination of President John F. Kennedy of the United States. I may not have all the pieces, but this book will be a road map for future investigators to get to the bottom of what really happened to President Kennedy, filling in the pieces that I may not have. I will demonstrate the following:

1. This book will put forward definitive new evidence *that the famous Zapruder film is the biggest hoax of the twentieth century.* The story is so big, it should blow this case off the map forever.

The alleged film of the assassination, which has controlled everybody's perception of it for most of these years and which is supposed to be a "clock" of the assassination—to give us those crucial timings—is fake. The timing and placement of the shots were

3

changed, and for those who fell for this clever but sloppy animation, one can only take a good hard look at those who pandered it. Our attention was being directed elsewhere.

2. This book will present definitive new evidence *that the images seen on the X-rays in the National Archives were altered to cover up the large hole in the back of the President's head.*
The Kennedy family lawyer, Burke Marshall, authorized Dr. David Mantik to enter the National Archives in October 1993 with a sensitive, light-measuring instrument—an optical densitometer—and examine the X-rays taken at the autopsy of President Kennedy. It was the first time the test was ever conducted, and it will be replicated by other scientists. Mantik has since made more trips, and on the most recent, brought an astrophysicist, an historic first. That is, it was the first time a nonmedical doctor was allowed to examine the X-rays, the autopsy photographs, the President's clothing, CE 399—the "magic bullet"—not a part of an official investigation.
Dr. Mantik found beyond any question that the X-rays are altered images intended to hide the position of the large defect as described in the autopsy report itself. This means that an exit wound from a shot that hit JFK's head from in front was hidden by the fake X-rays. We can see the unusual whiteness on this area of the X-rays with the naked eye. Dr. Mantik, both a radiologist and a physicist, outlines his findings in this book. He irrefutably proves the independent research of other scientists and radiologists, which I publish here for the first time and have maintained in all of my previous books: The autopsy X-ray images are altered.

3. I present information from the heretofore secret documents that *the autopsy doctors all but screamed at investigators from the House Select Committee on Assassinations that the autopsy photographs did not show the wounds that they had seen,* and that the X-rays and photographs are wrong in that respect.

4. Drawings and descriptions made by those present at the autopsy for House investigators and kept secret for more than fifteen years show that *the body was not altered between Parkland Hospital and the autopsy at Bethesda Naval Hospital.* The large wound in the back of the head was identical at the two hospitals.

5. *From the secret documents,* conflicting evidence is apparent, and we will discuss what it may mean. My study represents a major advance in our historical understanding of the evidence. The secret documents demonstrate conclusively that the House Assassinations Committee lied and covered up what the autopsy doctors had tried to tell them. They didn't dare reveal the truth of what the doctors said because it put the lie to the Warren Commission and FBI's official story. This book shows *the desperate attempt made by the autopsy doctors* to get out the truth about where the bullet's entry hole was on the head, and how this information was suppressed.

6. *The conflicts in the evidence* demonstrate a *trail* through the official evidence, giving us a clue to what the truth was. I postulate an entirely new theory from my study of all the available interviews with the autopsy personnel and the conflicts in the physical and ballistics evidence. The conflicts are so severe on each issue in the evidence that there is an entirely different meaning than what was supposed—that is, federal agents and autopsy personnel were forced to lie and fabricate evidence in the face of a conspiracy, then sabotaged it by switching evidence or otherwise planting conflicts that would tell us that something was drastically wrong. That is why this case never came together.

7. *The Cover-up.* This book contains powerful evidence of how the Warren Commission, the House Assassinations Committee, and other investigations covered up the case.

8. *This book refutes the Warren Report point by point* in the most powerful manner yet published.

9. I show that *Gerald Posner's book* **Case Closed** *tricked the public and the media with false scholarship.* His propaganda blitz was intended to head off the scholarship of myself and my team, and he did not interview all of those he claims to have interviewed. Posner distorted and selectively ignored evidence, and had one intent: to trick the public and President Bill Clinton.

10. I present a major analysis of the heretofore secret interviews conducted by the HSCA with the autopsy personnel that show beyond a shadow of a doubt that *no bullet passed through President Kennedy's body or neck, and that the entry into his head was far below where it is claimed to be in the photographs.*

11. For the first time, I present *an entirely new proof of a shot to the President's head from in front.* The 6.5mm fragment seen on the X-rays (and mentioned in the FBI report) on the back of the head appears to be on the inside of the skull and not on the outside. Therefore, it was not noted in the autopsy report or by the Warren Commission and had to be covered up.

AT SOME POINT, the people in charge are going to have to face the fact that the public and the professional class in this country have become alienated from their government. This process began with the assassination of President John Kennedy and step by step— cover-up after cover-up—has smashed our faith in the government. The *only* way this country can become whole again is to return to square one and to tell the truth about the murder of the President. Most young people have little concern about government or knowl- edge of current events because the popular culture they are ex- posed to turns them away from it. This is a deliberate form of brainwashing. It is deliberate because there is a lot to hide among the criminal or borderline criminal elites who run some of the world's nations, and they don't want people to be too conscious of their activities.

To bring the power of the media to bear on the real facts in John Kennedy's murder is to tamper with the fundamental forces of nature. The fear is so great that we may have no hope of ever seeing a hard-hitting series of articles in the daily papers spelling out what you will find in this book.

The media are tools of those criminal forces, and above all, the media are there to protect the establishment, which condones and covers up some of the biggest crimes because it is often a part of them. The media could break this case apart in a few days with what we have already, but they aren't going to do it. They aren't here for a good story, good journalism, or any other altruistic in- tent. They are here to keep things going around, and they are here above all not to stir things up where real power is involved. The members of the press pick handy targets to investigate and ruin when it suits them, but they are not going to talk about anything that involves the real nature and realpolitik of this country. Such is the case in most if not all nations in the world. The press is often paid, influenced, or run by the very forces it needs to investigate.

The forces at work in this nation to control the public and the government are so great that it would seem all but impossible to resist them. Whatever hope we once had for democracy as an ideal and practical means of government is quickly being destroyed in the modern world.

Yet, the massive propaganda attempts by elements of the establishment's power structure in 1992–93 to tell once more the big lie about John Kennedy's murder to this nation and the world failed to change more than a few minds. The endlessly repeated official story will never overturn the basic facts of the evidence that long ago demonstrated a conspiracy to assassinate Kennedy. But some facts have gotten through to the nation's collective consciousness from those persons in 1963 who saw what happened.

The bottom line in this case is that the autopsy was unable to scientifically determine much of anything, and the report of the doctors had to be changed within hours to conform to the needs of the conspirators. Then, the autopsy doctors were, to a certain extent, sacrificed, just as the Parkland doctors had already been sacrificed—because the needs of the cover-up could not accept everything that had already been written in the autopsy report. The entry wound in the head was in the wrong place in order to fit with the faked photographs and X-rays shown to those who would officially cover up the murder: President Lyndon Baynes Johnson's Warren Commission. The doctors already had been gotten to say that a bullet had passed through the President from back to front, and that was the primary lie the new administration under Lyndon Johnson had to have in order to survive. Every single person at the autopsy knew that bullet never perforated the wall of Kennedy's chest in the back.

The autopsy report, pictures, and X-rays had to be faked in order to cover up the truth.

When *The Journal of the American Medical Association* (JAMA) told its readers that the bullet wound in the throat of the President was scientifically measured and photographed, they lied because officially the autopsy doctors didn't know about it. The doctors *couldn't* admit that *they did* know about it because they would have had no way to excuse the fact that they had no evidence that a bullet transited the body from the back to the front and went through Connally. They lied. They made it up. They were forced to lie about a few things.

Dr. Robert Livingston told Dr. James J. Humes before the autopsy started that the Dallas medical witnesses saw an entry bullet wound in the throat.[1] But they didn't dare officially know there was a bullet hole in the throat. The doctors were caught between a rock and a hard place from the start, and no matter which way they turned, they were forced to lie.

If the autopsy doctors lied about this, how can we believe anything else they said? We have to sort through their statements and *weigh* the evidence to find the truth.

*   *   *

EVERYONE IN AMERICA and the rest of the world knew that the same type of bullet that broke up upon striking a skull would not remain whole after striking two men and breaking a lot of bone.

And everyone knew that one man could not inflict this amount of damage on three victims in the middle of massive police and Secret Service protection as Lee Harvey Oswald was supposed to have done. It was unreasonable.

The trajectories that came from the window are impossible as well.

But what is ultimately most unreasonable in this case are the facts of the minutiae of the evidence, which many don't want us to look at closely.

The brilliant researchers who had control of this case were not just amateurs but were there all along to throw us off. What we got all those years from the leading medical critic in the case was a theory based on trajectory analysis, on wild suppositions for which he would have been thrown out of any medical examiner's office. For instance, Michael Kurtz writes that Dr. Cyril Wecht "believes that based on his computation of the angles of the bullet wounds in President Kennedy and Governor Connally, that the shots were fired from a lower floor of the Book Depository building and from the roof of the Dal-Tex building. Wecht's theory is valid only if the precise instant in which the President and Governor were struck is known. . . ."[2] In my opinion, the media left the case alone because the leading amateur critics who led the investigation never had much credibility or competence.

SOMEBODY IN THE GOVERNMENT wanted us to know the facts! They printed enough of them to let us know that the evidence on every score was being switched and planted. Everyone, from the autopsy doctors to the FBI lab agents, was trying to leave a record for posterity, since it was clear that our government would never tell us the truth. Individuals found a way to subtly sabotage the conspirators who were either known to them or who had very forcefully caused these individuals to fabricate evidence. Those who were forced stuck a knife in the conspirators who used and perverted them, piercing the lie in the case.

They don't want to admit that Oswald might have been an FBI informant or provocateur. I have it from a former Dallas FBI man that both Oswald and Jack Ruby were paid by the FBI. That is one huge reason why the connection had to be covered up after Oswald was supposed to have shot Kennedy. And this leads to J. Edgar Hoover's possible involvement in the murder. It would be easier for me to give in and write, well, Oswald did it, and he was part of a conspiracy—to save myself having to argue his innocence as well as trying to prove a conspiracy. I'm not, however, going to do that because Oswald killed no one, and he was killed to silence him forever.

The conspiracy was sloppy and major mistakes were made. The conspirators did not worry too much about how it came down as long as they controlled the key people: the Dallas cops in the criminal lab, the Dallas FBI agents who would then conduct the investigation, and, above all, the Commission that would be set up to control, shape, and lie about or bury the evidence—cleaning up mistakes as best as it could. If there was evidence of a conspiracy, it was a foregone conclusion that a committee would have to cover it up for political reasons.

WE ARE DAVID V. GOLIATH

We Davids against Goliath are dealing with hard physical and medical evidence as opposed to the speculation and theories the Warren Report put out. That's all the Warren Report was—a theory—and that is all the autopsy report was—a theory. It was *not* scientific. A vast edifice, like a house of cards, was constructed upon outright lies and fabricated evidence, and it will all collapse. It is collapsing now.

There has been an attempt by the most powerful forces in the media since 1992 to have the last word and close this case. We are in an uphill struggle to get the news out.

The case is cracked. What you are about to read is hard criminal evidence in the assassination of President John F. Kennedy. It is enough to go into a court of law—a criminal court.

It is reasonable for you to doubt what you hear from me and other critics of the Warren Commission and the official story, and to suspect a trick in what I have to say. It is reasonable for you to want to accept the combined utterances of Random House and their "Wall Street" lawyer-author, Gerald Posner, *The Journal of the American Medical Association, Newsweek,* CBS, and the Warren Commission. Incredible as it sounds, their words are all fabrications. None of them is facing the facts. In its massive cover story called "The JFK Cover-up: It's Not What You Think" (titled inside: "The Real Cover-up") in the fall of 1993, *Newsweek* sought to explain that the government covered up Kennedy's murder (which they now admit) because it was "at odds with itself, almost comically scurrying to disguise its own nefarious plots, bureaucratic miscues, and personal vendettas,"[3] or that the people covering it up were "more concerned with safeguarding their own agenda,"[4] warding off demands for revenge and a possible third world war called for by the public. What could be more preposterous an explanation: If the public demanded revenge, the government would instigate a war that we could not possibly survive?! The *Newsweek* conception of a cover-up does not explain the falsification of the autopsy evidence at Bethesda Naval Hospital. It does not explain the obvious set-up of Lee Harvey Oswald as the patsy weeks before the murder.

We know that the media often have tried to treat this story in a straightforward way, but it rapidly becomes obfuscated by the authorities and media executives.

The plotters controlled everything after the assassination, and it was easy to contrive this malarkey. They covered it up to bury their own mistakes in not monitoring Oswald, or to prevent a world war!

WHAT IS WRONG WITH THE MANNER in which *Newsweek* and so many other official apologists tend to dismiss conspiracy evidence? (They call it "conspiracy *theories*.") They do it by omitting facts that conflict with the result they want. *Newsweek* attempts to dismiss the possibility of a coup d'état in 1963 by writing as follows: "With so many people ready to help—from hit squad to autopsy team to Warren Commission—why a Rube Goldberg scheme in view of a plaza full of witnesses?"[5]

Was the autopsy in view of a plaza full of witnesses? The plot was highly compartmentalized by then, and one hand did not know what the other was doing. There were plenty of witnesses in Dealey Plaza who reported evidence of conspiracy. The FBI insisted for a long time that the bullets that hit Kennedy and Connally were separate, and three years later, the FBI men who had been at the autopsy insisted that the autopsy doctors had evidence contrary to a bullet passing through JFK. All this was *ignored*. The Dallas medical witnesses were kept apart from what was actually done at the autopsy, and they were later told their observations were mistaken and they really hadn't seen what they thought they saw. The military and the FBI controlled that autopsy in no uncertain terms, and no family member was present in the room.

People are simply *paid* or otherwise encouraged to cover up the case. There is a large component of intelligence operatives posing as critics, and there are many agents of right-wing interests. In the 1960s the Pentagon admitted to placing at least fifty thousand agents on college campuses, some of whom infiltrated the Students for a Democratic Society and are active in the JFK case today as provocateurs and misinformation specialists.

The statement in *Newsweek* is so irrational as to be almost beyond comment. There have been many conspiracies in history. Anyone who doesn't acknowledge them or coups d'état is mistaken. Those who don't think that there was enough money in Dallas to buy the murder of John Kennedy, to pay people to stand in Dealey Plaza and quickly report to the conspirators how the murder played out so they would know how to cover it up and fake the evidence— having the money or power to get people to take films and photographs, and then to alter film—are vastly unrealistic. The earlier statement by *Newsweek* is false because it assumes that the witnesses did not report what they in fact insisted upon: other gunmen in the plaza.

When there is a coup d'état, the winners and their media allies control the evidence and to a great extent, the media. Lyndon Johnson created the Warren Commission, and it did what he and his allies wanted it to do: calm things down and make it all go away, at least for a time—*cover it up.*

Those who deny that a conspiracy existed because it would be too complicated, deny the history of many coups d'état, and they assume that the cutouts or middlemen would not be killed, that unreliable hit men would not be killed, and that the way that criminal acts and criminal conspiracies are normally committed would be ignored in a presidential assassination. It would all be done cleanly.

Try to pretend that the facts aren't there, that there aren't crazy things in the evidence, that evidence wasn't faked, wasn't planted, and wasn't stolen from the National Archives. All this happened. The autopsy doctors are trying to tell us something: They had a gun, figuratively, at their heads in that autopsy room. That's how the conspirators got the result they wanted. We know this from the pattern of severe conflicts in the record of the autopsy. Nobody can keep his story straight. The big lies they're hiding are the facts that no bullet passed *through* JFK's body; that the X-rays and photographs of the body are fake; and that a bullet hit JFK in the front of his head. Also, the doctors knew that a bullet had struck JFK in the throat from in front, but ignored it.

The failure of the media to cover hard news stories presenting breakthroughs in the investigation of President Kennedy's death is a crime against America. In fact, the media are pursuing a course of action intended to close the case with no further discussion of the evidence.

"In 1981, Secretary of State Alexander Haig presented a State Department *White Paper* to Congress, US Allies, and the public that supposedly 'proved Soviet and Cuban sponsorship for the FLMN guerrillas in El Salvador. Haig later had to admit to Congressional committees that the names of the Soviet 'masterminds' in the paper were fabrications."[6]

"While director of the CIA in 1976, George Bush teamed with William Casey, then a member of the President's Foreign Intelligence Advisory Board, to form a study group to counter the CIA's assessments of Soviet military spending. Thus began the politicization of key CIA intelligence estimates. The inflated Soviet spending estimates became the basis for huge increases in US military spending during the Reagan administration. But in 1984, the CIA, even with William Casey as director, admitted that these estimates were heavily inflated."[7] This is like all the claims made for the B-2 bomber.

Another example of bogus documents in history were Richard Nixon's "Pumpkin Papers," which were used to frame Alger Hiss and send him to jail. Then, there is the phony evidence that led to the Gulf of Tonkin Resolution which got us and President Johnson into the Vietnam war.

There was great suspicion abroad and in the land in 1964 that Lyndon Johnson had something to do with John Kennedy's murder. Named after Lady Macbeth and Lady Bird Johnson, the popular play *MacBird* told that story. And there was great suspicion surrounding J. Edgar Hoover as well.

We have had massive organized mind control at work in the amateur investigation of JFK's death, and we have had the same thing at work in the official presentation of the government's case for the public.

My job is to get people focused on the big picture of a faked case. Once seen from that perspective, there is a chance of unraveling the whole thing by decoding the forgeries and seeing how the rest of the evidence was faked and planted.

Many researchers and the leading critics originally had strong resistance to the idea that the basic evidence in the case was fake or altered. Too often they needed that evidence to prove this or that among their pet theories, and their attitude is nothing but suspicious, unless indicative of mere mental deficiency. But when there is in fact considerable proof of extensive alteration of that evidence—of the autopsy X-rays and photographs, of the films in the case, of switched evidence such as the "magic bullet," and of many other pieces having been planted, stolen, or faked—then that is far more important than any of their pet theories. Acceptance of the idea of a faked case gives us a window into the true nature of the conspiracy.

THE OFFICIAL EVIDENCE IN THE CASE is completely fake. Gerald Posner, the author of a recent text on the case, distorted evidence that I personally dealt with. He is no scholar, as NBC's Tom Brokaw was led to believe. Posner distorted evidence that conflicted with his and the Warren Commission's conclusions. He did not interview some of the people he claims to have interviewed. The lie was believed long enough to do vast damage to the truth, the real facts, and those of us bringing out that truth.

There is now hard criminal evidence in the murder of John Kennedy. For the first time, we have enough for a grand jury investigation.

It is my belief that some of the primary players in the investigations of the assassination of John Kennedy, along with the autopsy doctors, know the truth, but everyone is too afraid to speak. It remained for a few of us to come out with more of the story.

The tragedy of November 22, 1963, is not going to go away. The core of the problem lies in the failure to either solve the mystery or deal with it in the national consciousness. We have become hostage to our own lies and propaganda, and the case is not closed.

1

The Official Story

The Liberal Society is a free society, and it is at the same time and for that reason a strong society. Its strength is drawn from the will of free people committed to great ends . . .

—John F. Kennedy

THE WARREN COMMISSION was constituted by President Lyndon Johnson shortly after President John Kennedy's murder. Johnson was suspected in the popular mind as a possible conspirator in the killing of Kennedy, and he benefited from the murder more than any other person. His Commission, headed by the Chief Justice of the Supreme Court, Earl Warren, had the intent of calming things down and making it look like they understood what had happened. The Commission deflected attention away from the chief suspect: the new President of the United States. Truth was not their client, because the pillars upon which the Warren Report rested were based upon false evidence, false findings, and false witnesses.

The Commission found that there was only one assassin and no conspiracy. What were those pillars upon which the findings rested? How did they try to establish the history of those terrible events of November 22, 1963?

In order to have one assassin, the government had to limit the number of bullets to an amount one man could fire during the time alleged. They had to arbitrarily establish the time limit between the first and last bullets, and they had to test the rifle to see how fast it could be loaded, aimed, and fired. It would look bad if an assassin fired too many shots while the driver of the limousine looked around to see what was happening, moving along at only ten miles an hour or so. The driver didn't step on it until the last shots were fired.

They needed a film—conveniently taken by Abraham Zapruder, who had just bought his first movie camera—and the film had to

14

show the timing and number of the shots, or better yet, be ambiguous enough to support alternative versions of the story.

They needed a rifle. They needed a bullet that had markings linking it to the rifle that was found at the Texas School Book Depository Building.

In order to do all this, it was necessary to plant false evidence.

Before we go on, let me point out that the focus of my work (and that of many others) brings out facts demonstrating a conspiracy in the case: that there were more gunmen firing, and that there was a deliberate premeditated cover-up at a high level, which required the framing of the patsy—Lee Harvey Oswald.

But the government's official story and its apologists ignore the evidence of conspiracy. The cover-up artists or apologists for the Warren Commission's official story engage in the logical fallacy of trying to build a case based on what was found at the scene of the crime and later "learned." We maintain that the entire edifice of their case is fake.

A careful reading of the findings of the Warren Report indicate that the Commission avoided the real questions. For thirty years, we have been tricked by the most famous evidence in the case: the film. We were tricked by clever writing and propaganda to think that their conclusions represented a true investigation. The language was devious, and the conclusions really have nothing to do with the questions. It is like some recent writers in the case who ask a witness a question, and when they get an answer they didn't want, attach a different question to it that fits the answer. The witness can't say he wasn't accurately quoted.

THE RIFLE MAY OR MAY NOT have been used in the assassination, but no evidence was ever presented showing that it had been fired.

The government had to prove that Oswald was the shooter, and to do that, they had to find his fingerprints on the rifle. Nobody ever did. A partial print of a palm turned up sometime later—though not seen by the FBI because it was lifted "too completely" by the Dallas police. Fingerprints would be somewhere in the official evidence if required.*

* Dallas police lab detective R. W. (Rusty) Livingston claims in Gary Savage's *JFK First Day Evidence* that there were sufficient remnants of parts of fingerprints on the trigger housing that the police lab technician recently assembled an identifiable fingerprint belonging to Oswald. No one heard of this thirty years ago, and it proves nothing at all—other than Oswald might have handled what is claimed to be his own rifle (he denied ever owning it). It is highly unlikely that the FBI laboratory experts who examined the gun could not have found such prints and assembled them. The Warren Report

In order to prove Oswald did it, they had to place him in the window of the sixth floor of the Texas School Book Depository, where the rifle and three empty shell casings were found. Since he was seen only ten or fifteen minutes before the shooting on the second floor of the building, the government had to establish that he had a propensity for violence—something that could be said about any soldier or Marine trained to kill.

Bonnie Ray Williams was eating his lunch on the sixth floor of the building and neither saw nor heard anyone else there before he left at 12:20 P.M. to go down to the fifth floor. Williams noticed no one coming up as he went down, which would put the time even later. Certainly, Oswald would have been in the window ready to do his deed by then, since the motorcade should have come by at 12:25 P.M.

To prove that Oswald did it, they had to get corroboration on several points from his widow, and for this, she was threatened with deportation.

The autopsy of the President had to come up with unlikely findings. Conveniently, no bullets were found in the body. Inconveniently, it was found that the bullet that struck him in the back did not pass through the body, so it later became necessary to lie about this—to make the autopsy doctors say that the bullet came through the body and exited the throat.[1]

They had to say this because their theory demanded that one man shot both Kennedy and Connally, plus a third person wounded far down the street by debris from a missed shot. With only three shots fired, one of them, therefore, had to hit both Kennedy and Connally, since a third shot struck JFK in the head. The Warren Report states, "The weight of the evidence indicates that there were three shots fired." They found three empty shells by the Book Depository window. They didn't know or were afraid to admit contrary evidence.

Most importantly, they had to ignore evidence of another shot that struck Kennedy in the head from almost directly in front of the car, taking out the back of his head. To prove that the back of his head was not missing, they had to fake autopsy photographs and X-rays.

To conceal evidence that an additional bullet had struck JFK in the throat from in front, as the Dallas doctors and nurses insisted, that wound had to be converted to an exit wound. To accomplish this, the Secret Service visited the Dallas witnesses and told them

---

(p. 122) says there were no fingerprints.

that a scientific autopsy had found that they were wrong and what they saw did not happen.

They had to lie to the Dallas medical witnesses because the Secret Service knew very well that no bullet had passed through Kennedy's neck or back.

Another lie was the claim that the autopsy was "scientific" and that the throat wound had been "scientifically measured and photographed." This didn't happen either, because the autopsy doctors did not know that there was a wound in the throat. All the autopsy doctors saw was a tracheostomy incision that extended the original entry hole in the throat.

FOR A GUNMAN TO WAIT while the limousine carrying Kennedy came toward him for a full block all the way down Houston Street, watching it turn the corner just below him when he could have dropped a brick or a grenade on the car, then to wait until the car went well down Elm Street before taking deadly aim at this much more difficult target is preposterous. This is what the official story would have us believe.

The alleged trajectories from the window never happened. The gunman was across the street in another building, and they made up the angles and distances. The computer graphics models seen on the PBS show *NOVA* and in Gerald Posner's book are false because they are based on false figures from the Warren Commission.

The FBI figures printed in small boxes along with reenactment photographs, certain frames from the Zapruder film, and photos taken from the firing position in the window with a telescopic lens are clues that were deliberately given us by the FBI to show that Kennedy and Connally do not line up at any time for them to both be shot with the same bullet.

Now comes one of the biggest lies of the case. This lie told us what the angle of trajectory was for the shot that struck Kennedy and Connally with one bullet. "Viewed through the telescopic sight of the C2766 Mannlicher-Carcano rifle from the sixth-floor window during the test, the marks that simulated the entry wounds on the stand-ins for the President and the Governor were generally in a straight line. That alignment became obvious to the viewer through the scope as the Governor's model turned slightly to his right and assumed the position which Governor Connally had described as his position when he was struck."[2]

"A surveyor then placed his sighting equipment at the precise point of entry on the back of the President's neck, assuming that the President was struck at frame 210, and measured the angle to the end of the muzzle of the rifle positioned where it was believed to have been held by the assassin. That angle measured 21 degrees 34'. From the same points of reference, the angle at frame 225 was measured at 20 degrees 11', giving an average angle of 20 degrees 52'30.''[3] The lie is that the bullet struck both men between frames 210 and 225, which is just after the car emerged from the tree. According to the Warren Commission, the first available shot over the top of the tree, which they say struck Kennedy in the back of the neck between frames 210 and 225 of the Zapruder film, was at frame 210.

In fact, they did not achieve alignment of the two men and a trajectory from the window until well past the place where Connally had turned his back away from the window.

THERE WERE TWO SURVEYS of Dealey Plaza made after the assassination. One was on December 5, when the Secret Service reenacted the crime. The second survey and reenactment was in May 1964 and changed the findings of the first survey. The results of this new survey were also changed. Frame numbers were moved on the street, and the shots were fired earlier and farther up the street. Both maps, though poor and hard to follow without proper scales, were printed by the Warren Commission. The December 5, 1963, map was CE 585,[4] and the May 31, 1964, survey map with the frame numbers on the street and with elevations is CE 883.[5]

THE OFFICIAL STORY IS THAT three shots were fired—since three shells were found in the sniper's window—and one missed. The missed shot, in order to line up with both the limousine and the man, James Tague, who was struck in the face with debris at the underpass on Main Street, had to have been fired from the Dal-Tex Building. The trajectory is far from the Book Depository window. See the last color photo in my book, *Killing the Truth*, for a view from the window of the Dal-Tex Building. The fatal car is moving straight away from the window down the center lane for one hundred feet or more, with no variance, and is the easiest of shots for a shooter. The car is also pointed directly at the storm drain on the left side of the overpass, where a sniper had to have been concealed.

Let's take it from the top. The Warren Report suggests that a shot could have been fired before the car was obscured by the tree below the window, at the corner of Elm and Houston, before frame

166 of the Zapruder film. In other words, someone could have shot almost straight down on the car before it disappeared from the view of the shooter at frame 166, but such a shot could not pass through Connally and Kennedy. For "a fleeting instant, the President came back into view in the telescopic lens at frame 186 as he appeared in an opening among the leaves."[6] There is evidence that a shot was fired at about this time.†

If a shot was fired then, it would not pass through both Kennedy and Connally because they were not aligned. The *only* way they could get that to happen was to create a false model: They postulated where the rear bullet holes were in both men and at what point on the street they could line up with the window, *instead* of giving us the first available true angle down from the window over the top of the tree to the car.

No tree came up to the fourth floor of the Texas School Book Depository, meaning that the trees were no more than three stories tall. We had two floors unobscured by trees. The height over which the gunman fired to hit targets in the car was at a maximum of 3/5 of the 60 feet, or about 36 feet. The windowsill is one foot above the floor and his rifle could have been another foot above it. I think the trees were actually about four feet shorter than this, which gives us a steeper angle at the first available shot.

I noticed this years ago when standing in the sniper's window and looking down over the tree. The first available shot after the car emerged from under the tree is very steep and all but goes through the floor of the car. It could not have lined up with both men and made the wounds that were seen. I thought that the long, low trajectory that we have from the Warren Commission would place the gunman back in the next block, at the very least in the Dal-Tex Building on the third floor—if one shot hit both men.

The Warren Commission's entire scenario went at the problem backward: by drawing a line between the two men, connecting the alleged positions for their wounds to the window. This actually placed the shot far down the street from where it could possibly have happened, and this was akin to a child playing with blocks and moving model cars down a play street, seeing how it all lines up.

The correct method was to determine between two points on the street where the shots had to have occurred and then to see what the angles were back to the window, accounting for the tree being in the way part of the time or closing off further possibilities. The authorities didn't dare do that because the only conclusion would

† For a good discussion of the first shot, see Josiah Thompson, *Six Seconds in Dallas* (New York: Berkley), pp. 32–70.

be that there had been more than one gunman. The whole deal is predicated upon premises that are false. It depends on a set of figures that don't add up, and perhaps, deliberately so.

THE ENTIRE EDIFICE OF THE CASE is the largest mountain of lies and fabrication in American history. That says a lot, considering some other massive government cover-ups in the past. After all, look who they are afraid of: *The public.* That's why it has to be controlled.

The clever wording of the reports show the uncertainty of the evidence and findings. So, why not just lie? Here is an example of what I alluded to above: "Although it is not necessary to any essential findings of the Commission to determine just which shot hit Governor Connally, there is very persuasive evidence from the experts to indicate that the same bullet which pierced President Kennedy's throat also caused Governor Connally's wounds."[7] Here we have an enormous official lie right in our face. For, if the bullet that they claim came out of Kennedy's throat (instead of entering the throat from the opposite direction as witnesses in Dallas reported) did not strike Connally, then what bullet did? It has to be a fourth bullet, a shot one man could not have fired in that timespan.

The Commission was deathly afraid of being implicated in a treasonous collaboration with the assassins. They were covering for themselves, since the dead President's brother was still the Attorney General of the United States, and they were afraid of what he might do. Sadly, Robert Kennedy was effectively neutralized.

The plain fact is that the Commission simply did not know what the truth was, but they had to come up with something to give to the public and the world. Those who now state as fact their suppositions and who assume the certainty of what could never be proved or known overlook the fact that the investigators at the time really did not know what had happened. Worse, their vision was seriously clouded by the need to not find a conspiracy, which meant having only one gunman. That meant torturing the evidence.

The media and Warren Commission apologists, such as Gerald Posner, are trying to prove the unprovable and are ignoring the facts.

The autopsy report itself plays word games when it terms the wound in the back "presumably" the wound of entrance.[8] It calls a small, partial hole (where the remainder of the bullet struck the skull and exited, taking with it large pieces of bone) on the skull "presumably" of exit.[9] We have a vast dispute between the doctors and the suspect photographs and X-rays as to just where the entry was in the skull. The doctors completely reject what the pictures seem to show which moves the wound of entrance some inches from where it was in the autopsy report, thus changing the trajectory.

Why would Dr. Humes not allow a forensic examination of the brain by a neuropathologist, as Dr. Pierre A. Finck (one of the autopsy doctors) reported to his commanding general? Because it wasn't JFK's brain at the supplemental autopsy two weeks later.[10]

ANOTHER EXAMPLE OF CLEVER WORDING is this: "The Commission has found no evidence that either Lee Harvey Oswald or Jack Ruby was part of any conspiracy, domestic or foreign, to assassinate President Kennedy."[11] If Oswald didn't do it, he could not be part of a conspiracy. The Commission had adequate reason to know that Oswald could not have done it, because he could not be placed at the window. The rest of the case against Oswald was circumstantial. But the Commission had to know there was a conspiracy because the evidence demonstrated it. Knowing there was a conspiracy, they cleared Oswald of being involved in it. Same for Ruby. The punch line in their finding says they could not link Oswald to a conspiracy, which they publicly claim did not exist.

The Commission found no evidence of a conspiracy because they didn't look for it. They did very little investigation, and instead relied on the FBI.

OSWALD IN THE WINDOW

The chief of police of Dallas, Jesse Curry, had serious doubts about the case. For this, he was hounded from his job and broken. "Curry always maintained that he couldn't say with absolute certainty that it was Oswald who killed the President because Oswald was never physically placed in the room where the shots were fired."[12]

Curry wrote that "the physical evidence and eyewitness accounts do not clearly indicate what took place on the sixth floor . . . the testimony of the people who watched the motorcade was much more confusing than either the press or the Warren Commission seemed to indicate."[13]

Curry, a decent and studious man, found himself in a death struggle with FBI Director J. Edgar Hoover after the assassination. The chief had publicly embarrassed the FBI and Hoover never forgave him for it. Hoover took strong action against the Dallas Police Department and cut them off from the FBI Academy until Curry was forced into retirement. He also intervened directly in the affairs of a city over which he had no authority. Ultimately, Hoover forced Curry from his job because Curry resisted Hoover's handling of the case. We now know that Hoover did more to cover up the facts in the Kennedy case than anyone else. He had condoned the same organized crime groups in America that the Kennedy brothers had tried to eliminate.

But then, Hoover was close to the wealthiest men in Dallas, such as Clint Murchison. He was in Dallas the night before Kennedy died.

This is not a criticism of the FBI. My stepfather was an FBI agent and I cannot believe that the agency as an institution participated in Hoover's crimes, although elements, of course, did, as they may have helped kill Martin Luther King, Jr.

BUT WHAT OF THE CONCLUSION of the Commission that "on the basis of the evidence before the Commission, it concludes that Oswald acted alone"? The circumstantial case against Oswald is not credible. What evidence did they have, and was their conclusion correct?

I REPORTED IN MY FIRST BOOK on the case that *every single medical witness ridiculed the official photograph of the back of the President's head.* Take it to heart. Gerald Posner can try to distort this all he likes, but he will never overturn the truth of it because my information that the photograph is fraudulent came from Jacqueline Kennedy through her staff in 1979 and from representatives of the Kennedy family. My last book, *Killing the Truth,* details the further testimony of the witness who knows better than anyone else what that body looked like when it left Parkland Hospital, Nurse Diane Bowron. She ridiculed all of the autopsy photographs. "This is not the back I saw," she wrote beneath one of the photographs. Posner's only way to deal with it and me is to distort facts, distort interviews, and smear me and the doctors who disagree with him. Well, Posner *did not conduct* at least some of the interviews he claims.

The drawings of the wounds made by those at the autopsy make a mockery of the photographs claimed to be those of Kennedy.

Posner has got to overturn the autopsy doctors' insistence that the photos and X-rays of the body have the entry hole in the head far from where they saw it. He insists that these fake materials are authentic when *all* the key witnesses question them. Posner and

JAMA, therefore, impugn the credibility of the very autopsy doctors they need to prove their case.

The intrinsic bias of the media prevents a fair presentation of the facts. The hard facts are not being faced and examined.

There were many eyewitness reports of gunmen in front of the car, including a statement by the sheriff of Dallas. It was obvious the head shot came from in front. There was credible evidence from witnesses that there was an entry hole in the throat, and no amount of twisting can change what they originally said they saw. These witnesses have *never* changed their story. I repeat, the Dallas doctors have *never* changed their story. Look at who these doctors were and are and the experience they had with gunshots, when the autopsy doctors (who never saw the throat hole) were hospital pathologists and had no gunshot experience. The regular autopsy doctor at Bethesda who should have performed the autopsy, Robert Frederick Karnei, was relegated to the sidelines.

The most important conflict in the evidence is that the position of the entry hole in the back of the head moved four inches. The autopsy doctors insisted to the House Committee that the entry hole is not in the right place in the photos or in the X-rays. This is the key to the case. Those who performed the propagandist function of telling us what "best evidence" is (photographs and X-rays) derailed this case when they ignored clear evidence of forgery. They got us to *assume* the autopsy photographs and X-rays were authentic. Nobody questioned *any* of the basic assumptions in this case.

How can we have a liver that weighs too little to sustain human life, as is listed in the autopsy report? How can we have a brain that weighs more than the average male brain, *after* having lost much of its mass on the street? The autopsy doctors were trying to tell us something. The brain at the supplemental examination two weeks later was not John Kennedy's brain. The brains were switched in the "dead drop" in the admiral's closet.

The facts were covered up at the autopsy for one reason and one reason only: to protect the perpetrators of this terrible crime. *Forty-two credible witnesses* in Dallas described the right rear scalp and skull as missing, and don't forget this: The same area is described as missing in the autopsy report. It's not missing at all in the X-rays or the identifiable photographs.

The autopsy doctors have repeatedly tried to alert us to the real nature of things. They were trying to tell us that they had a gun to their collective heads.

*   *   *

I DID NOT THINK that the release of the documents being kept secret in Washington would amount to much. I couldn't believe that anything of substance would be found there—certainly, no smoking gun. What we did find through Kathy Cunningham's FOIA requests and the dogged work of Anna Marie Kuhns-Walko in the National Archives were a number of interviews with important witnesses that contain small but important pieces of the puzzle. These bits of information add to our knowledge of the case. *What comes through loud and clear* in these interviews is the near scream of each autopsy doctor that the autopsy photos and X-rays *don't show what they saw.* Listen, media and history. Yet, these interviews seem to be doctored or edited. This book presents an extensive exposition of what we found.

THE CASE WOULD HAVE BEEN SOLVED years ago were it not for the situation left by Lyndon Johnson's Warren Commission. I believe the confused and unsettled result was an intentional goal of Lyndon Johnson and J. Edgar Hoover and their allies on the Warren Commission: Allen Dulles and John J. McCloy, "The Chairman" of the establishment.

The state of Maryland, which by law has concurrent jurisdiction in the case, should pursue it. Texas is faced with a conflict of interest between the need to protect its reputation and investigating a homegrown treasonous conspiracy. Texas had its chance, but was deliberately preempted by the FBI's takeover of evidence that had been gathered by the Dallas police. Secret Confederate societies, the Ku Klux Klan, Texas Republic organizations, and Citizen's Counsels, are all dedicated to the preservation of their twisted way of life, were enough to do the job.

KENNEDY REPRESENTED MODERNITY. He and his wife were the essence of culture and intelligence, beauty and grace. The ruthless destruction of the hope they embodied was a terrible blow to the country, plunging us into the disorders of the sixties, war, riots, more assassinations, near bankruptcy, the national debt, the nightmare of Watergate—which may have been intimately related to the assassination of Kennedy—and the runaway crime of today.

The murder of John F. Kennedy represented the death of democracy as we knew it, where we elected a leader who was free of entangling alliances, who was his own man, who answered ultimately to his own heart, to the people, and to God, who was no puppet, neither owned nor controlled by the rich financial interests of Texas or of anyplace else.

Those murderous interests that oversaw the tumultuous years that followed left a legacy of a nation's affairs out of control, forever robbed of anything but conspiratorial government beyond the will of the people, governed only by the few for the few.

We've had one conspiracy after another since 1963: Cambodia, Watergate, Honduras, Guatemala, Noriega, Desert Storm, Iran Contra . . .

ON NOVEMBER 18, 1993, in New York City, highly qualified scientists presented hard criminal, forensic evidence sufficient to prosecute this case.

There is no trick in the research that I and our team are putting forward. I don't blame others for being wary after so many false stories have infected this case with misinformation. The John F. Kennedy case is deeply political, and those with an interest in smearing forever the memory of President Kennedy are making sure that the facts are distorted.

The team of physicians, scientists, and researchers who are at work on this case with me are up against an attempt to kill the real evidence. I wonder why those who are trying to bury evidence of conspiracy are doing it? How much money is out there from the special interests that don't want the truth to come out? How much stock do they own in these media giants? Or is it just the fear of the liberal impulse Kennedy represented?

The medical evidence is the key to the case. The case is broken; yet, the hard medical, scientific evidence we are trying to present is being ignored.

What nobody can face is that the photographs and X-rays are fake and were used to trick Earl Warren. The meaning of this is too horrendous for the media and the public. It means that people in power were able to fake this evidence and force the autopsy doctors to lie, and to pay off segments of the media to cover up this case.

The media are afraid to put me on head-to-head with Gerald Posner and other fakes, and they are afraid to let me make my case nationally. Gerald Posner and Norman Mailer are no scholars. They misrepresented the evidence, ignoring many facts. They have *no* understanding of the physical evidence.

There is a serious credibility problem among all parties on both sides of the dispute. I believe that my interviews are unbiased and truthful, but I know for a fact that many of those in the media who claim to have investigated this case lied about their interviews. Many other authors put their own twist on important evidence, clouding many people's minds.

The body was not stolen or altered. This theory has done more to retard the solution of the JFK case than any other hoax. I believe that some of the leading critics of the Warren Report are wittingly or unwittingly part of the cover-up and don't want the real medical facts to be made clear. Many of the principal critics in the case have put forward false information, or sought to coopt the case and exclude legitimate investigators.

The establishment critics of the Warren Report have watered down or stifled criticism in the past, enforcing a rigid conformity or party line on the evidence. These critics are fundamentally weak, shallow in their research, and stooges of powerful forces in the United States. Now, we have a new team of doctors and Ph.D.'s coming into the case, credentialed in 1992 by the *JAMA* affair, co-opting the medical evidence and testimony and wrecking the JFK case in the process. They come bearing gifts of credible research in one hand, and with the other hand, they deliver a blow at the very evidence that explains the case. In other words, these doctors are here to tell us the autopsy evidence is authentic, when such a theory contradicts all of the testimony. Much of the evidence they support often cannot stand scrutiny. This has been the game from the time John Kennedy was murdered: having the evidence both ways.

WHEN A SNIPER IS SETTING UP A SHOT, he has to take into consideration the time of day and the weather. The temperature, angle of declination, and the wind affect the shot, as does a cold barrel. The scope has to be sighted in.

"Lee Harvey Oswald," wrote Carlos Hathcock—billed as "the most successful American military sniper"—was supposed to have made a head shot at a moving vehicle at a range of almost a hundred yards, from a six-story-high angle to street level, using a crude 6.5mm Carcano carbine with a worn barrel and a defective scope. And I doubt, since he was not a trained sniper, that he knew of the downward trajectory formula. Add to this fact that he supposedly fired three rounds in 5.6 seconds, through the leaves on a tree that partially obscured the car almost half of those 5.6 seconds—dropping the rifle from his eye to work the bolt after each shot. And all of this time the limousine that carried President Kennedy and Governor Connally was moving on a curve. If one is to believe the Warren Commission Report, these were three remarkable shots indeed."[14]

When a case does not come together, there is something basically wrong with the evidence. In *this* case, it has all been fabricated.

A reader, Howard F. Benner, Jr., wrote me a note thanking me for one of my books. He said, "JFK was of my generation—sort of like an older brother. He was an inspiration and a beacon of hope to all of us. He tried to correct some of the injustices, and they killed him for it." I must have hundreds of letters saying nearly the same thing.

In the old warehouse district two blocks from where Kennedy died, Dallas created a huge and glitzy tourist mecca—nightclubs, restaurants, rock concerts, taverns, mounted police, horses and carriages. It's sex, an overtone of violence, and standard American fun. Just amusements and rock and roll for the tourists come to see where Kennedy died. That's entertainment Dallas-style, sports and circuses. Nothing is sacred, especially the killing ground turned into a carnival.

2

The Fake Autopsy Photographs from the Secret Documents

Silence and concealment are the mothers' milk of conspiracy theories. . . . If we have learned anything in the twenty-nine years since the President was shot, it is that silence and concealment breed theories of conspiracy . . .
—Earl Rose, M.D.
JAMA, 1992, 267:2806

"PROSECUTOR APOLOGIZES for bogus photos" read the lead of an Associated Press story in 1993. A big trial was in progress in Boise, Idaho, and the government was desperate. "For weeks, prosecutors have proceeded meticulously, even tediously, in the trial of two extremists accused of killing a deputy U.S. marshal in a deadly shootout at a mountaintop cabin. They have been dogged with difficulties from the start, and lately, the problems seem to have gotten even bigger.

"Prosecutor Ronald Howen apologized in court yesterday after admitting he was told in early April that investigators had fabricated photographs of evidence from the deadly gunfight August 21.

"On Friday, the judge abruptly adjourned the trial."[1]

LET'S FACE IT, AMERICA, faking evidence is old hat, not only in this country, but all across the world. We just aren't brought up to think in these terms.

When I was a boy on the way to school in Baltimore one morning, I found that every telephone pole had a new poster tacked to it. They were fake photographs of Maryland's distinguished United States Senator Millard Tydings arm in arm with the chief of the American Communist Party, Gus Hall.

There was an investigation and it found that the composites emanated from Senator Joseph McCarthy. Tydings, known as "the Judge" in the Senate, had been asked by the Senate to head up an investigation into McCarthy's charges of communism in government, and McCarthy's own misuse of campaign funds. McCarthy hated Tydings for his straightforward and honest decency, something McCarthy did not understand. So he faked the pictures to try to defeat Tydings in an election in Maryland.

Former CIA man E. Howard Hunt of Watergate fame admitted that he forged a cable implicating President Kennedy in the assassination of Diem, the president of Vietnam.

Faking evidence is an old tradition in the world. The truth is that medical examiners too often obtain such jobs because they are bought and paid for, because they can be counted on to cover up through faked autopsy evidence political murders, and illegal police murders.

Gary Aguilar, M.D., writes: "The photographs and X-rays have taken on a central position in the controversy, as they have been determined by subsequent physician reviewers to be authentic and reliable representations of JFK's wounds. These pieces of evidence thus comprise the 'best evidence'—evidence more reliable, according to some, than human recollections."[2] Of course, as Aguilar believes, the photos and X-rays are false.

As for the questions swirling around their authenticity or lack of it, and the fact that the pictures do not show the wounds in the same places where they were in 1963, the autopsist Dr. Pierre Finck "believed strongly that *the observations of the autopsy pathologists were more valid than those of individuals who might subsequently examine photographs* (emphasis mine)."[3] Humes and Boswell repeatedly made strong statements saying that *their personal observations and testimony should govern what and where the wounds were, not the photographs.* There is a massive difference between what they saw, recorded, and say versus what the photographs seem to show. And Humes, Boswell, and Finck conducted the autopsy on President Kennedy's body.

CALL IT "EXPERIENCE"

Shortly after my last book on the Kennedy case, *Killing The Truth*, went to press, I traveled to Florida to see an expert on photo retouching, Veronica Cass. Ms. Cass was a close friend of Gary Rowell, the publisher of *The Investigator*, a magazine devoted to inquiry into the assassination of John F. Kennedy. Rowell was a former police officer, and a fellow police officer had been married to Cass.

I showed her the autopsy photographs, and she had an immediate response to them. Cass picked up each photograph, with one exception, and put it into a pile, while stating in a very strong voice, *"This is fake!"* With each picture, she announced, *"This is fake!"*

Cass had had no previous knowledge of the pictures. She knew nothing about the photographs and had read not a word about the assassination or the controversy surrounding the autopsy photographs (a controversy I brought to national attention through my writing and efforts.) In addition, she had no recent contact with Rowell, her old friend, and my visit came as a surprise.

The difficult problem was to find some scientific backup for her findings of fakery. My deduction that the pictures were fake came primarily through reason, through the problems in the pictures pointed out by all autopsy personnel, and through personal contact with witnesses with whom I had shared the photographs. Every single witness who saw the body had the same response when they first saw the photographs: *"This isn't the way it was!"* This is what Jacqueline Kennedy Onassis told me through her staff, and it's what all of the doctors and nurses have said.

How could Cass find that the pictures were fake without knowing that they didn't show any of the wounds described by the medical witnesses? She stated that it was "experience." She was perhaps the most experienced retoucher in the world, someone who had invented the very dyes used to retouch photographs in modern times, and she was able to pick out such tampering with her trained eyes.

In addition, she was able to see that several of the pictures showing the face and the top of the head were composites, just as Richard Tobias had been the first person to tell me. Remarkably, the composites she spotted were not the ones showing the back of the head that we had originally suspected as fake in 1978 when they were shown at the House of Representatives.

Tobias was a medical worker at Parkland Hospital, and along with others who worked in the photographic lab there or at the university medical center, believed the material to be entirely fake.

ALONG WITH THE GUT FEELING that the autopsy photographs I saw in 1979 were paintings—though I may have been seeing retouching or painting on the prints rephotographed—I had got onto a trail that would lead to unraveling much of the case. The arguments advanced that the photos maintain their integrity when viewed in stereo does not negate their obvious falseness, for the reasons advanced in my synthesis.

As some have suspected, notably Houston lawyer Cindy McNiell, some of the photographs may not even be of Kennedy. Some may show a wax dummy. Others appear to be made up from photos of the assassinated Robert Kennedy. There seems to be something seriously wrong with each photograph.

We know from the statements of the autopsy doctors that a number of pictures are missing. The only picture showing the large defect in the head cannot be oriented for certain or identified with Kennedy's head. Nothing shows but the large hole, with no part of the face or other photos that would help connect it to the body of Kennedy.

"If simple and accurate wound descriptions are unavailable, who can trust any theory of the wounding?" Gary Aguilar, M.D., asks.[4]

My feeling is that the entire inventory of photographs, or at least those that have crept out into the public domain, is a hoax that goes back many years, before the House Committee. We know that the autopsy photographs that I and others have published are similar or identical to those that are in the National Archives, as has been stated by all those doctors who saw them at one time or another in the Archives.

MICHAEL BADEN, former medical examiner for New York City and member of the forensic panel for the House Committee on Assassinations, wrote: "Proper photographs were not taken," and "certain things didn't happen . . . [such as] the kinds of documentation, *pictures*, measurements, that the forensic pathologist does automatically. . . ."[5] (Emphasis added.) Dr. Gary Aguilar adds: "Is this the best that the United States could do for its slain President? The problems with the photographs do not end there, however."[6]

JOHN THOMAS STRINGER

In 1977, Andy Purdy and Jim Kelly of the House Committee had a talk on the phone with John Stringer, the civilian director of medical photography at the Naval Medical School at Bethesda. The following material is from their interview, which had not been published by the Committee, and which was obtained by Kathy Cunningham with FOIA requests.

Dr. James Humes, the man chosen to perform the autopsy (over Dr. Robert Karnei), called Stringer at dinnertime on November 22, 1963, and asked him to come in to work. Stringer used a four inch by five inch graphic "view camera" with a standard lens, and he used film holders with one film on each side. He "probably" used floodlights, which again poses a problem since the backgrounds of the photographs are often quite dark. Some of that might be explained by the "enhancement" process described in my previous book by the critic who obtained the photographs from the government, and possible use of the "burn and dodge" process which controls the amount of light reaching various parts of the print paper in the reproduction process.

"He said Dr. Humes was the one who primarily told him what pictures he wanted taken during the surgery. Stringer said the operation was like a three-ring circus with so many people present, including a number of flag-rank military men. Some of these military men (possibly Admiral Galloway) talked of bringing metal detectors to help in the search for any bullets or bullet fragments in the President's body."[7]

"Stringer said that there was a school of Medical Photography there and one of the corpsmen was on duty there that night. It was his film which was destroyed by a federal agent. He believes the man's name was *RIEBE*, who had a designation of HM-3. He said Riebe was a student there whose job it was to help Stringer. Riebe had a small camera that the agent opened and exposed. Stringer does not believe the student was going to take any pictures or had taken any pictures."

"Stringer said he does not remember how many pictures he took, but he is sure that he exposed each of the two sides of each film holder used. He said (following Stover's orders) that after each film holder was exposed he gave it to a Secret Service man standing by. He said that Secret Service man later signed a release to Stover." He kept a copy of the receipt.

James K. Fox, a Secret Service man, took the pictures to the Anacosta Navy Base where they were developed a few days after the autopsy.[8] Stringer did not see the pictures he took until 1966, when he and the autopsy doctors viewed them when they were transferred into the control of the National Archives.

Stringer told Purdy that at the time he viewed them in the National Archives "it was his recollection that all the photographs he had taken were not present in 1966. He noted that the receipt he had said some of the film holders had no film in one side of the cassettes. He said the receipt said this happened in two or three of the film holders where one side only was allegedly loaded. He said he could understand it if the film holders were reported to have poorly (sic) exposed or defective film but could not believe that there were any sides of the film holders which were not loaded with film."[9]

The point of this is that the present inventory of the photographs he is supposed to have taken does not balance with his inventory at the time. As the following shows, all participants recall photographs being taken of the interior of the chest, and these pictures are not present. Perhaps for obvious reasons. "Stringer said that his recollection that all the photographs he took were not present in the materials he viewed in 1966 was based on the receipt."[10]

He said the Kellerman receipt indicated that Kellerman received "one or two empty film holders." "Stringer explained that the film in the film holders were silver on the one side when the picture was unexposed and black when exposed. He remembers explicitly that when the film holders were turned over, both sides were black. He said he did not personally examine the film holders to see if there was actually film within them. In other words, the fact that both sides were black and while indicating the exposure was made, did not speak to the question of whether or not there was film in there. Stringer remembers taking 'at least two exposures of the body cavity.' "[11]

Regarding the possibility that he took interior chest photographs, Purdy writes that Stringer said, "I believe some pictures were taken of the body cavity." He indicated that he "exposed a film holder" of that area. *The other doctors have repeatedly commented upon the fact that they are missing.*[12]

In addition to the indications of evidence-tampering, there is the fact that "Stringer said he did not take any black-and-white photographs and that those that were made must have been from the color transparencies in the two-step process."[13] The HSCA asked James K. Fox who developed the autopsy film. Fox told Andy Purdy that he developed the black-and-white photographs at the Secret Service lab. The color prints were done at the Naval Processing Center; White House photographer Knudsen was in the drying room. Fox said that he checked and there was color film on both sides of the film holders. He said some of the black-and-white prints were missing.[14] Obviously, some of the color prints are missing as well, and this lends credence to the "burn party" that Fox described to Mark Crouch.*

*High Treason 2, by the author, p. 322.

Stringer took some photographs of the brain in the morgue two or three days after the autopsy. He said he was there with Doctors Humes and Boswell. He said he gave this film to Humes and received no receipt. He believes he took at least six color transparencies. He indicated he wasn't sure if he viewed these photographs when he saw the materials in 1966.[15] Stringer's recollection of a brain exam or photographs of the brain at that time seriously conflicts with the other dates for the brain exam of either one full week or two full weeks later. Once again, the clear indications of an exam of a brain that wasn't Kennedy's but claimed to be, may be exposed as a lie by this conflict.

With regard to the orientation of photograph #44 (F 8) which shows a large hole in somebody's skull—allegedly Kennedy's—Purdy wrote that there was considerable discussion regarding the direction of the face in the picture of the large hole in the head with the brain removed. In this picture, we cannot see the face or anything else that tells us which part of the head we are looking at or even whose head it is. "Mr. Stringer felt the face was going in a different direction than Dr. Baden's impression. The piece of skin area was likely a shoulder, while Dr. Baden thought it was the cheek."[16]

And, could the brain have come out of that particular small hole?

Baden was the chairman of the HSCA forensic panel and the medical examiner of New York. Baden had a track record of stating the official government story in most of the evidence, even if it contradicted what the autopsy witnesses and other evidence indicated.

Stringer did not take photographs of the organs. He said the photographs of the back were taken when the body was held up and the photographs of the open head were taken while the head was held up.[17]

Stringer again repeated in his interview that "in the general autopsy, he only took color photographs." This fact creates a massive problem in that the black-and-whites of somebody's head alleged to be Kennedy's show some long whitish matter hanging from the top of the head (F 6 and F 7). This white matter is red in Groden's color Right Superior Profile but turns to black, as red always does, when the color pictures are printed in black and white. If the white matter or brain matter was originally red, it would turn to black.

How can the brain matter be white in the black-and-white photographs, red in Groden's color version,[18] and black in his black-and-white version? Are we looking at an example of "enhancement"? I suggest that the top-of-the-head photographs, as Veronica Cass and others say, are fake, because if no black-and-white photographs were taken at the autopsy, then the color photographs would show this material as red, which would darken toward black if reprinted as a black-and-white photograph.

In addition, that area of the head on top was not missing. The surface of the brain could not be showing at the top of the large defect as it is in the photograph because it had been blown out of the head.

Therefore, F 6 and F 7 have to be of someone else's head, or are composites made up partly from the pictures Stringer took.

DOUG MIZZER HAS WORKED LONG AND HARD studying the Zapruder film. He believes that the film does in fact show clearly that there is a fist-sized hole in the back of the head without any scalp or bone, visible in multiple frames. The best example is frame 367. Mizzer has produced fairly clear videographs demonstrating this. He will continue to try to obtain clearer photographic prints of the film.

His discovery is possible additional corroboration that the official autopsy photographs are forgeries.

What do the autopsy doctors think of the photographs and X-rays? The doctors are highly critical of them and Boswell told the HSCA investigators that they were of poor quality.[19] Boswell said that the "material is not ideal. . . ."

The most loaded query in the secret documents dealing with authenticity was asked Dr. Pierre Finck by Dr. James T. Weston for the House forensic panel: "Pierre, can I ask you a question. When you got the chance to look at the pictures and were indexing them into the Archives, so to speak, and assigning numbers to them and looking at the pictures and the X-rays, did it occur to you independently or anybody else that when you looked at the picture of the back of the head that perhaps the location of the wound as it was described in the report was not the location of the wound as it was depicted in the photo? Was there any conversation about that by you or anybody else in the group?"

"I don't recall. I don't recall."

Andy Purdy then asked him, "Was there discussion where the entry was in the head specifically when you examined the photograph?"†

†To study good copies of the official autopsy photographs, consult my second book, *High Treason 2* (Carroll & Graf, 1992, 1993). For the color autopsy photograph of the back of the head, consult my last book, *Killing The Truth*, (Carroll & Graf, 1993).

"In January 1967, I would say there was, but have to refer to the memorandum of the Department of Justice. In that respect for January 1967, the record will be better. Do I answer the question?"

Purdy asked; "When you examined the photograph in 1967, did you consider or was it pointed out to you the red spot in the higher portion on the head that we pointed out to you?"

"I don't remember. If it is not in the memorandum, I cannot remember."[20]

Finck struggled with the pictures, trying to place the wound of entry on the back of the head: "Well, I would say that this was the wound of entry to the right of the external occipital protuberance. It is more accurate to determine an anatomic location when you have the wound itself on the dead body. On the photographs it is embarrassing, it is distorted as far as the angle of shooting is concerned, so you feel much more at ease when you have the dead body and the wounds to establish a location than when you have photographs."[21] I don't think he would say this if he was not looking at a picture that bore no relationship to what he either saw or claimed to have seen during the autopsy. The statement, taken together with his and the other doctors' very strong questions about what these pictures show or do not show, tells us only one thing: They do not show the wounds, and are fakes.

When Finck states that whatever is on the cowlick is not an entry wound, he asks a startling question: "I don't know what it is. How are these photographs identified as coming from the autopsy of President Kennedy?" *He doesn't recognize the pictures!*

"They are initialed. No. 43 here is a copy made from the original which is initialed by Dr. Boswell. They were initialed at the time of the review and they were turned over to the Archives."[22] This was during the reign of Lyndon Johnson, Kennedy's successor, a prime suspect in the case, when his ally in the Justice Department, Barefoot Sanders, made the doctors look at the pictures, apparently initial them, and then sign a statement provided by the Justice Department. But then look at what is said next in the interview with Finck, when Dr. Petty asks, "If I understand you correctly, Dr. Finck, you wanted particularly to have a photograph made of the external aspect of the skull from the back to show that there was no cratering to the outside of the skull."

"Absolutely."

"Did you ever see such a photograph?"

"I don't think so and I brought with me a memorandum referring to the examination of photographs in 1967 when I was recalled from Vietnam. I was asked to look at photographs and as I recall there were two blank four-by-five transparencies; in other words, two photographs that had been exposed but with no image, and as I can recall I never saw pictures of the outer aspect of the wound of entry in the back of the head and inner aspect in the skull in order to show a crater although I was there asking for these photographs. I don't remember seeing those photographs."[23]

Dr. Finck had a strong statement to make about the usefulness or lack of it of these photographs and X-rays. This came up in his examination by the House Committee's Forensic Panel of doctors when he was asked if he was familiar with Dr. John Lattimer's work and Lattimer's claim that the autopsy doctors were greatly mistaken about the position of the entry wound in the back of the head which they dissected and measured. Finck said: "I am impressed by his background experience. He has combat experience. He was a combat surgeon. I am impressed by the thoroughness of his work. My comment on what he wrote regarding the anatomic location of wounds stating that on the basis of the photographs such a wound seems to be higher than described in the autopsy report, my opinion is that the man who can see the wound itself on the dead body is in the best position to establish an anatomic location as compared to others who refer to drawings, photographs, X-ray films. Again, we need those, that is the only thing left, but when you have the choice in those various types of evidence, my first choice is the examination of the wounds in place on the dead body to see where they are."[24] It is then pointed out in the next question that none of the doctors saw the photographs for several years after the autopsy—a very suspicious situation, considering that they would have wanted to review them before writing their autopsy report.

Do the autopsy doctors agree with the photographs and X-rays? Along with the other doctors, Pierre Finck seemed to question strongly the value of the fake pictures. Nobody came right out and said that they were fake, at least not on the record, but there are indications that each of them must have blurted out something of that nature to investigators and other doctors at their various meetings.

For instance, this is how Dr. Finck started off an interview with House investigators, striking first at the question of the photographs: "My only wish now is to help you as much as I can and to try to add clarity and not confusion. In particular I'd like to refer to the photographs shown to me, not seen in 1964, taken in 1963, at the time of the autopsy, not seen at the time of the Warren Commission hearings, and seen for the first time in January 1967. [Author's note: Finck was not present during the November 10, 1966, examination by the other autopsy doctors.]

"I think that the doubts and the controversies now arise from the fact that the people used these photographs as a basis for interpretation, saying they don't fit the autopsy report. And that's what bothers people and that's why I came back—to clarify that situation as well as I can after all that time. At the time of autopsy, I palpated the scalp of President Kennedy, I examined it. Outer and inner surfaces of the scalp in the back of the head."[25]

Why is he saying all this? The day before he had looked at the autopsy pictures and they were obviously deeply troubling him, so he came back for another talk, and asked to see them again. He wanted to see photograph no. 42, a photograph of the back of the head which is supposed to show the entry through the scalp. Finck goes on, and not only just goes on, but powerfully denounces this photograph with its fake entry hole in the cowlick where there was no bone or scalp at all. Does he just come out and say it's a fake picture? No, but he might as well. They must have edited these interviews because we have none of what was undoubtedly said about the pictures being fake. Just their reasoning. That leaves it up to us to sort out what they really said.

"I have now in my hands [a photograph which] is made from that four-by-five color transparency. And I was asked several questions regarding two areas in this eight-by-ten print, and going back to the questioning, going back to my answers, try to summarize my opinion about this photograph, *having examined the scalp myself, I don't think there is much point in arguing about the so-called wound seen high in the scalp* [author's emphasis]. . . . There is not much point in arguing about this, when asked the question, 'could that be a wound of entry, is that the penetrating, or a perforating wound?' for the good reason that, at that level I did not see in the scalp of President Kennedy, a perforating wound of the scalp. [Author's note: Finck and the other doctors *could not* see a perforating wound through the scalp there because there was no scalp there.] Again, there was only one . . . perforating wound of entry of the scalp in the back of the President's head, and that was the wound low in the photograph with a wide center in contrast to the previously described area which has a red center on the photograph. What I'm referring to now is the wound in the lower, lower portion of the photograph, near the hairline, and this is what corresponds to the perforating wound of the scalp, a wound of entry in the back of the head, unequivocally being a wound of entry because it corresponds to the hole in the bone I have described with no beveling on the outer aspect of the skull and with beveling on the inner aspect of the skull. Again, here we have to remember the differences between what you palpate with your fingers at the time of autopsy and what you see on a flat photograph.

"The external occipital protuberance is not clearly seen on a photograph like this, so I have to trust my measurements, my locations at the time of autopsy. So my conclusion regarding this photograph is that I saw only one perforating missile wound of the scalp, wound of entry in the back of the President's head.

"When asked about these photographs, 'how deep is the wound?', 'is this penetrating?', which means it is not through and through, or 'is it perforating?', which means it is through and through—I don't think is a fair question, because on the basis of a photograph—flat photograph—you cannot say with certainty how deep the wound is. We see here the white area in the wound near the hairline as being a wound where, with apparently some tissue protruding out of the wound so it's in favor of a deep wound, but the photograph is so flat, it's not too sharp, that you cannot give exact measurements, exact depth."[26]

Again and again on the next page Finck repeats that he held the head in his hand and indicates that anyone who did not do that can't tell him the wound was somewhere else.

Dr. Humes stated categorically that his physical measurements are correct and emphasized that he had access to the body itself and made the measurements of the actual head region. In addition, he said that the photographs and X-rays *have inherent limitations which are not present when one is examining the subject.*[27]

It seems to me that the great vehemence and what the House of Representatives called "the rigid tenacity with which the prosecutors maintained that the entrance wound was at or near the external occipital protuberance" is so strong as to preclude lying on this point. Their insistence has become their means of questioning the Warren Commission's perversion of the doctors' findings and their means of salvaging dignity and integrity after being forced to lie on other points: that is, sign an autopsy report and sign the documents put in front of them by the Department of Justice in January 1967 with which they disagreed.

As disturbed as some are with the manner in which the autopsy doctors treat aspects of the evidence and issues in the case, they are also trying to tell us that they were coerced in a political case, and are leaving a trail for us to follow.

What they aren't saying is that the wound low down on the back of the head could not have come from that window and blown off the top of JFK's head. Instead, the bullet either came out of his throat or traveled down the spinal column into either the chest or the pelvis. If true, certainly this means that the only direction the bullet that blew off the back of his head could have come from was in front. The bullet that hit him low on the back of the head came from somewhere else behind him and shot from a much lower height.

FURTHER INFORMATION WAS ELICITED in Finck's exchange with Dr. Rose, having to do with what exuded from the apparent small hole near the hairline just above the back of the neck. "Would you say beneath that wound, or that white tissue is, that there would be injury into the deep tissue beneath that area as well? So that it would extrude back out through the hole?"

"Probably. Yes. That wound being a perforating wound of the scalp, there was soft tissue coming out of that wound, if it's your question."[28] Then comes another loaded question from Dr. Petty: "At that level I'm not entirely clear that it would be brain. I just wonder what portion of the anatomy of the President that inshoot wound near the hairline would actually penetrate. I'm just asking if that's ... " (and we have no more from him in the transcript here on this key issue of where did that bullet go?). Finck seems to interrupt Petty and say "I said perforate because it was through and through. Unquestionably it's through and through so it's not penetrating. It's a perforating wound of the scalp and what came through that wound I really don't know, what that white area is [Author's note: brain, cerebellum, or tissue]." Finck repeatedly jumped on the slightest misuse of a word or slightest manipulation by the panel of forensic doctors.

"The beveled wound was beneath that wound, then," Petty asks or states.

"Sir?" Finck asks.

"The beveled, inward beveled skull injury was beneath that wound as far as you could see."

"Yeah. What we see here is the outer aspect of the scalp, and the beveling you are referring to is in the bone in the inner aspect of the scalp, corresponding to that soft tissue wound in the back of the head in the scalp."[29] The issue of whether or not there was beveling in the bone corresponding to where he says there is a perforation through the scalp comes up again and again.

Finck tells them: "It bothered me, yesterday's session bothered me very much, you know, to answer 'I don't know' and to, to . . . I don't want to add doubts to this, and I think now I understand why there are doubts. It's the difference between the interpretation of photographs and the autopsy wounds, and this is why I can help."[30]

The next question in this interview for the House of Representatives dealt with how close the wound Finck said was the inshoot into the back of the head was to the hairline, which is very close, perhaps below the EOP, ". . . the question arises in my mind as to an estimate . . . of how far up from the lowest portion of the hairline are we, with that white material that appears in the photographs. . . ."[31] There is then an implication in the text that Finck signaled that they measured that distance at the autopsy. "You did? Somebody did? Oh." This important transcript ends in mid-sentence and mid-page with Dr. Weston querying Finck as follows: "Do you think it's possible that that measurement relative to the occipital protuberance that's contained within the. . . ."[32] And there is nothing more.

Both Humes and Boswell at one point stated to this same panel of doctors a few months earlier that the entry was actually *below* the external occipital protuberance.[33]

DR. EBERSOLE WAS SHOWN color photograph no. 42 of the back of the head and asked the following: "Do you remember or have any independent recollection of that condition of the President when you were in the autopsy room?" "You know, my recollection is more of a gaping occipital wound than this but I can certainly *not* [author's emphasis] state that this is the way it looked. . . . But had you asked me without seeing these or seeing the picture, you know, I would have put the gaping wound here rather than more forward."[34]

Neither the doctors in Dallas nor the doctors at Bethesda find that the wounds in the photographs agree with what they saw at the time. The autopsy doctors strongly disagree with the position of the entry hole in the back of the head, and the Dallas doctors find that there is no large gaping wound in the occipital area, just as Dr. Ebersole said above in private to House Committee investigators in 1978. The doctors are unanimous on this. All those who seek to discount this information betray not only their country but something very sacred in human affairs—history itself.

Ebersole is again asked a similar question: "When you compare those two photographs (42 and 32), what inference do you draw now about the nature of the gaping wound to the President's head in terms of where it was located? Earlier, you said it was in the back of the head. Looking at these two views, how would you characterize the location of that gaping wound?"

"More lateral. Much more lateral and superior than I remembered."[35] He is saying that the photograph shows the wound in a different place—on the right top of the head—"than I remembered."

Ebersole makes it clear that he would have seen such a hole on the right top side of the head: "I would have been more familiar with this aspect in positioning the head for the X-rays. I mean, this requires a forward effort to show this portion of the head on the part of the prosector, right?"[36]

Ebersole is then asked: "Is there a point in that photograph on the head which you take to be a bullet wound?"

"[Number] 42? No, I would not want to make a statement on that basis."[37]

Why were the photographs and X-rays reviewed by the autopsy doctors in 1966–67? Dr. Boswell said that their reviewing was at the behalf of the Archivist of the United States and to some extent the Justice Department. He said their purposes were twofold: to identify the materials and to catalogue them. This they did in November 1966. He said he had received a lot of pressure from critics of the Warren Commission, and it was in response to this that he suggested to the Justice Department that they conduct an independent review of the material. He thinks that his letter led to the creation of the Clark Panel which studied the materials in 1968. Dr. Boswell indicated that he didn't think there were any inconsistencies between the Clark Panel findings and their own, though he said the "material is not ideal . . ."[38]

The first viewing on November 10, 1966, was for the purposes of inventorying and initialing the material. Then there was an examination by the autopsy doctors on January 20, 1967.

Who first received the autopsy film and X-rays? Thomas Stringer, the Navy civilian photographer, said that as he took each picture and used up film holders, he handed them to a Secret Service man standing close by. He said the Secret Service man later signed a release to Captain Stover. Stringer said he has a copy of that receipt.[39]

Roy Kellerman said that he recalled getting the photographs and X-rays "in a big cardboard box . . ." but doesn't know from whom he got the box. Kellerman said neither he nor Greer, to the best of his recollection, handled the photographs or X-rays at any time during the autopsy, prior to the time they were put into the cardboard box. In other words, Kellerman does not believe that the FBI agents were the individuals to whom the film holders and X-rays were handed as soon as they were ready. Kellerman said he took the cardboard box with the films and the X-rays from the hospital and went to the White House by ambulance, after the casket had been taken in. Kellerman said he was "about to forget them when someone said 'here's all your film.'" Kellerman said he believed he had copies of the receipts he handled that night. Kellerman said he had "no reason to think he had everything" when he took the cardboard box with the films and X-rays. When asked why the Secret Service wanted this material, he said, "The point is, he was our man, everything belonged in the White House." (Author's note: It was Lyndon Johnson's White House by then.) Kellerman noted that the photographs were not developed before he took them.[40]

Kellerman produced a copy of the receipt for the photographs that he received from the hospital. This receipt includes the changes made and initialed by Captain Stover. Kellerman was not sure where he got his copies or where he got the corrected version of the receipt which had his name typed in. Mr. Kellerman had only the corrected version of the receipt for the X-rays which had his name typed in. He didn't have the one with his signature on it. . . . He said that he believes that he "signed the receipts after the changes were made." He said that prior to signing the receipts "everyone counted them. . . . I think I even counted them . . . I would think so (Note: The day before, Mr. Kellerman said he never counted the films and X-rays.) Mr. Kellerman also had a receipt dated 12–2–63 which was for the transmittal of the windshield to the Archives. This was signed by Marion Johnson."[41] The date on the latter has to be wrong, since the Archives was probably not authorized to receive such material at that time. The Warren Commission had only just started its work. True, cracks in glass spread rapidly, especially when the glass is moved about, and the Secret Service might have wanted to store the windshield quickly, as Martin Shackelford pointed out in a letter to me.

Vice Admiral Calvin Galloway signed the retyped receipt for the autopsy films.

Why were the autopsy photographs and X-rays not officially shown to the Warren Commission? Dr. Finck has this comment: "We were told at the time by I believe Arlen Specter, who was a counsel for the Warren Commission, that Robert Kennedy, Attorney General, did not want the X-ray films and photographs introduced in the hearings of the Warren Commission."[42] Here we have one more enormous lie and can thank Dr. Finck for his answer. Various people on the Commission, including Warren, did see the photos and X-rays. But there was no official examination of the material, no questioning of it. The material was undoubtedly faked just to trick them. No one thought to question it, but they had to put out the above story in order not to have to show the doctors the material and face what might have been their strong shock. That is, if the doctors were not being used already, and forced to lie on key evidence.

Did the photographer fail to expose some of the film? Stringer said that he does not remember how many pictures he took, but he is sure that he exposed each of the two sides of each film holder used.[43] Stringer did not see his pictures until 1966 when he and the autopsy doctors inventoried them and found numerous unexposed negatives.

Are some of the photographs missing? There are a number of photographs missing from the inventory and it was thought that they had left blanks on one side of the two-sided film holders for the view camera. "Stringer said it was his recollection that all the photographs he had taken were not present in 1966. He noted that the receipt he had said some of the film holders had no film in one side of the cassettes. He said the receipt said this happened in two or three of the film holders where one side only was allegedly loaded. He said he could understand it if the film holders were reported to have poorly exposed or defective film but could not believe that there were any sides of the film holders which were not loaded with film," wrote House investigators.[44]

"Stringer said that his recollection that all the photographs he took were not present in the materials he viewed in 1966 was based on the receipt. However, Stringer also said that he thought he had taken some interior photographs of the President's chest ('I believe so'). He said he didn't recall if these photographs were taken before or after the vital organs were removed."[45] Stringer said he was present in the autopsy room from about six or six-thirty P.M. on the night of the twenty-second until about three or three-thirty in the morning.[46] Stringer does not recall if in 1966 he viewed the color transparencies (at least six) he took of the brain "two or three days after the autopsy, with Humes and Boswell present."[47]

Regarding the interior photographs, Stringer said he believes he took at least one from the neck down and said he thinks he saw it in 1966.[48] It's not there now. Again he said, "I believe some pictures were taken of the body cavity . . ." He indicated that he "exposed a film holder" of that area. Stringer remembers taking "at least two exposures of the body cavity."[49]

Were interior chest photographs taken? Dr. Boswell told the House investigators that at least one was taken. He did say he didn't believe the track of the missile through the body could be seen. He said that if a photograph was taken of the apex of the lung and of the apex of the chest, this would have demonstrated the track better than not having such a photograph. Dr. Boswell did not state that such a photograph was not taken, saying instead that he "thought a photograph was taken of the lung."[50] Dr. Humes told House investigators the following: "We described a contusion in the apex of the lung and the inferior surface of the dome of the right pleural cavity, and that's one photograph that we were distressed not to find when we first went through and catalogued these photographs, because I distinctly recall going to great lengths to try and get the interior upper portion of the right thorax illuminated—you know the technical difficulties with that, getting the camera positioned and so forth, and what happened to that film, I don't know . . . we never saw that photograph."[51] Along with the photographs Finck had taken, these were probably the most important, so the fact that they are missing cannot be put down to a technical failure of camera or film, but to theft. Taken together with the fact that some of the remaining photographs are probably of some other body, the picture clarifies greatly for us.

As stated above, the photographer, John Thomas Stringer, remembered taking at least two exposures of the body cavity.

Dr. Humes has been emphatic on several occasions that Kodachrome photographs were taken of the President's chest, one of which, according to him, showed a relatively significant part of the track of the first missile, but is conveniently missing.[52] Having something they can get away with criticizing, after which no one listens, gives the doctors a saving grace: credibility where they have so little.

Admiral George Burkley, the President's physician (now deceased), who was present at both the shooting in Dallas, the emergency room at Parkland Hospital, on *Air Force One* with the body, and in the autopsy room, *stated that there were no photographs taken of the interior of the chest.* He indicated that he had possession of the brain and the tissue sections at the White House and that he took them to the National Archives. He said the only thing of interest among the materials was the tissue sections, which were taken of every major organ. He expressed grave concern about the misuse of these materials, particularly the adrenal glands. He said he felt it would be permissible to examine the tissue sections of the wounds.[53] Since Burkley was not in the autopsy room the whole time, how could he know if chest photographs were not taken? This is the same character who forgot to describe the throat wound on the death certificate.

One possibility is that Burkley, who drank a lot, was not competent. He stayed on with Lyndon Johnson as his physician, and in his oral history given to the presidential libraries, he has nothing more than one sentence or so to say about the assassination, to which he was such an important witness. He was not interviewed by the Warren Commission, which seems crazy.

We can also say that he might be a prime suspect for Liar Of The Case. He's either lying or someone else was. Maybe a lot worse. He was giving the orders in the autopsy room, and he had custody of the brain and the rest of the autopsy materials. His statement that no interior chest photographs were taken appears to be an outright lie, if not a mistake. Taken together with several other statements above, it appears to be a lie. To say that nothing was of interest among the rest of the autopsy materials is false. As my research found, there were no adrenal glands found in Kennedy, and that is why they were not listed in the autopsy report.

Were photographs of the entry hole in the skull taken? Yes. Statements and testimony of Dr. Pierre Finck: "I remember positively that a Navy photographer took pictures and I wanted pictures of the crater in particular because this is a positive finding for a wound of entry in the back of the head. So I wanted a picture showing no crater from the outside and a clear-cut crater from the inside, but I don't know."[54]

The photographs are listed in the 1966 inventory.

Whose photos were destroyed by Secret Service men or FBI at the autopsy? Stringer said that they destroyed the film from the camera belonging to, he thought, Floyd Riebe, a student medical photographer who assisted Stringer. Stringer did not believe the student was going to take any pictures or had taken any pictures.[55]

Were there black-and-white photographs taken during the autopsy? Stringer denies it,[56] although we originally thought that

Stringer and Riebe each used different film and two cameras. The FBI report lists eighteen 4 × 5 black-and-white photographs and 22 4 × 5 color photographs as having been delivered to the Secret Service undeveloped.[57] "Stringer said he did not take any black-and-white photographs and that those that were made must have been from the color transparencies in the two-step process."[58]

Stringer said he only took color photographs at the autopsy.[59]

How should the photograph of the large defect in a head be oriented? This is in great dispute. Regarding this picture (number 44, or F 8) Stringer said he was focusing on the bottom part of the picture. There was considerable discussion regarding the direction of the face in this picture of the top of the head with the brain removed. Mr. Stringer felt the face was going in a direction different from Dr. Baden's impression. The piece of skin area was likely a shoulder, while Dr. Baden thought it was the cheek.[60] One of the others present at the autopsy, Paul O'Connor, placed it squarely in the right rear quarter of the back of the head, and drew a picture for me which I published in *High Treason 2*. The drawing is in the autopsy photo section.

Were other photographers present who took photos and films at the autopsy? Admiral Calvin Galloway said that various enlisted men took photographs and X-rays throughout the autopsy.[61] The FBI claims they prevented anyone but Stringer to take pictures, who was assisted by Floyd Riebe. But there are reports of other films, such as a film by Commander William Bruce Pitzer,[62] and still more reports of photographs of the body taken by others in the morgue and at Parkland.[63]

CONCERNING THE SEPIA-COLORED ALLEGED AUTOPSY "stare of death" photograph put out in a video about the case (Wavelength Video's *Assassinations of the Twentieth Century*), and printed in color in my last book, *Killing the Truth*, Dr. David Stern of Torrance, California, performed a computer study of the photograph and determined that it was a colorized black-and-white photograph.

"This illustrates that the 'color picture' is really a *colorized* picture, where all apparent color is really hue. That is, it is all a mix of white, black, and a single color. The entire process, from black-and-white print to colorized screen image, took less than three minutes. These results could have been greatly improved on, if it was desired.

Different areas can be selected and tinted to a level of accuracy to where telling a colorized forgery from a black-and-white 'authenticated' photo is virtually impossible. In the final analysis, there are two conclusions that can be drawn from this exercise:

1. The 'color' photograph is a cheap forgery.
2. No photographic evidence produced in the last few years can be taken at face value. It is *impossible* to differentiate a well-done forgery from a genuine article. Hollywood provides perfect examples of that fact on a regular basis.[64]

EARL RUBY AND THE AUTOPSY PHOTOGRAPHS

Jack Ruby's brother Earl was interviewed by the Secret Service on December 6, 1963, when the Ruby's sister related quite a story to the Secret Service. "Earl Ruby interviewed relative to alleged photographs portraying President Kennedy's head wounds."[65]

The *Saturday Evening Post* magazine writer Peter Moss had been approached with an offer to purchase some confidential photographs of the assassination of President Kennedy. These photographs were alleged to show the large head wound with parts of the skull missing. Ruby understood that this offer was made to Moss by either attorney Tom Howard or his representative. No figure was mentioned for the cost of these photographs.

Tom Howard died of a "strange" heart attack not long after, in 1964. He was one of three men who died rather soon after meeting with George Senator, Ruby's roommate, in Ruby's apartment on the weekend Kennedy and Oswald died (see p. 118 of *High Treason*, Conservatory Press edition).

Ruby said he understood that these photographs **were apparently in the possession of law enforcement officials in Dallas.** Earl Ruby, who had flown to Los Angeles to meet with his friend Mike Shore, and a writer, Billy Whitfield, about the photographs, then returned to Dallas and talked to his sister, Eva Grant, his brother Jack Ruby, and Tom Howard (Jack Ruby's lawyer). Howard denied any knowledge of the pictures.

What we are hearing here is that the Dallas police had copies of photographs showing the President's wounds. They are either photographs taken on the street during the shooting, photographs taken at Parkland Hospital, or photographs taken at Bethesda Naval Hospital at the autopsy. I had reports from several independent sources stating that photographs were taken at Parkland.‡ I also knew that copies of the autopsy photographs were spread around Washington soon after the autopsy.

The possibility exists that Tom Howard was killed because of this. His death was certainly connected to whatever he learned about the assassination. Even more curious was the death of a Dallas morti- cian. John Melvin Liggett was buried in a part of Restland Memorial Park, the cemetery where he last worked, called "The Field of Honor." Liggett was believed to have killed several women, and was arrested the year he died, 1975, for the attempted murder of Doro- thy Peck.[66] The only reason he was caught was that his victim sur- vived to identified him. Liggett was said to be part of the witness elimination program, and was directed or forced to kill several wit- nesses.[67] He also worked at Laurel Land, which was close to where one of the women was killed at a nightclub.[68]

The MO of the murders was the same in several deaths: Bludgeon or stabbing, mutilation, then the bodies were burned. Dr. Mary Sherman died this way in New Orleans.

Liggett was arrested in 1974 for the attempted murder of Dorothy Peck, who was beaten. Her husband, Bert Peck, I am told, is the key to why they tried to kill her. He had told her too much. Peck was a deputy sheriff and worked as a security guard at the Mercan- tile Building in Dallas, where Lamar Hunt's offices were. Peck died on July 4, 1969.[69] He was a cousin of President Lyndon Johnson and was an identical lookalike for him.

John Liggett didn't just die, but was shot down by Sheriff's Deputy Joe Crawford when he fled from a jail chain while being returned to the old county jail, February 14, 1975.[70] "He was the best guy in Dallas who could build wax on JFK's face," someone in the know tells me. From this they might have made the official "autopsy" photographs we now have, allegedly taken at the autopsy. Houston lawyer Cindy McNeill and others insist that the photos are of wax dummies. But why? There is no known damage to Kennedy's face in the shooting . . .

Kyle Brown, a mortician in Copperas Cove, Texas, and his friend, Billie Sol Estes, know about this whole story, which they were shop- ping around. Brown says that the reconstruction work was done on *Air Force 1*.

Possibly, he made a "death mask" of wax and then cast a wax head, which was used for the false photographs we now have.

Larry Howard, now deceased, was looking into this in the Austin

‡*Killing the Truth*, H. E. Livingstone, p. 511.

area in 1993, when he had the first of two strokes. The second, in Arlington, killed him soon after. Larry Howard was the director of the Assassination Information Center, which closed upon his death. Howard had a great fear of certain close members of Liggett's family. But why are the others looking at it still around?

Howard told me that Liggett was at the funeral of his wife's aunt when Kennedy was shot. He was called to Parkland shortly after Kennedy died, and stayed there until late. At 11:00 P.M. the next day, he went home, apparently very frightened, and loaded his family into a car and drove to Austin, getting a speeding ticket in Waco on the way.

Howard said Liggett became close to Roscoe White, a Dallas police officer, soon after John Kennedy was killed, and was thought by some to have been one of the shooters on the Grassy Knoll. White was a fixture in Liggett's home. "He was very respected by Liggett," Howard said.

There is an indication that Liggett was working for the government and maintained his rank in the US Air Force of Airman 1st Class when he died. The story is that he did some reconstructive work on JFK.

These stories always throw one when you first hear them, and they are difficult to confirm. Larry Howard, now deceased, and my informant on the above, was investigating the deaths of a number of Dallas police officers and other law-enforcement types: Nick Christopher, Maurice "Monk" Baker, Lt. George Butler, Lt. H. M. Hart, Bill Biggio, Clint Peoples, John Liggett, and the death of Henry Wade's former investigator, Clarence Oliver. The need for book and movie deals by some of the wanna-bes sometimes leads to fantastic claims. Like the other strings of strange deaths in this case, the above unknowns are more than strange, when you know something about them.

I'm not saying it didn't happen.

SUMMARY

It should be clear that the autopsy doctors do not agree with what the photographs of President Kennedy's body show. They made far stronger protests to the staff of the House Assassinations Committee investigating the murder than we understood at the time. Another great crime was committed by keeping their interviews secret fifteen more years.

The doctors could not be mistaken about what they saw, and there is a prima facie case for the forgery of the photographs.

The matter should be investigated before the witnesses leave this earth. The forgery of the autopsy materials is one of the keys to the case.

3

The Reenactments and
the Trajectories

If the reenactments relied on the films, and if the films do not show today what was in the reenactments, then the films changed as the Official Story evolved.
—Daryll Weatherly

ARLEN SPECTER DIRECTED THE MAY 1964 reenactment of the assassination from the sixth-floor window at the Texas School Book Depository, according to the FBI's Lyndal Shaneyfelt. "Mr. Rankin and Mr. Specter were in the sixth-floor window of the TSBD, which was referred to as our control point, where we had the master radio control for other units," Shaneyfelt said.[1] This was the culmination of a six-month process in which shots were moved and made to disappear, films were doctored and suppressed, and the record was altered beyond recognition. What emerged was an "official story" that had no connection to the way in which the assassination happened.

There were at least three official reenactments of the assassination, involving various combinations of FBI, Secret Service, and Dallas Police Department personnel, plus a survey done for *Life* magazine before those. Each reenactment coincided with a survey of the Plaza by professional surveyors. Dallas County Surveyor Robert West supervised the drawing of survey plats to accompany at least two of the reenactments. These are greatly significant maps because they show where the government first had evidence of shots according to still-suppressed films, and these shots did not survive the politically motivated official story.

According to West, the first survey was done for *Life* magazine within a few days of the assassination.[2] His assistant, Chester Breneman, also recalled in detail the *Life* survey on November 25, saying later that the official findings changed some of the facts.[3] West made a survey plat, marking the angles and distances.

Official reenactments were held on (or before) November 29, December 5, and finally on May 24, 1964. Documentation for the two earliest reenactments is obscure, and much material seems to be missing from the Commission files. Each reenactment was based on the scenario of three shots from the TSBD window, and each reenactment used one or more films of the shooting. Remarkably, the reenactments differ substantially in their placement of the one thing that should be easiest to identify in the films: the fatal shot to Kennedy's head.

The credibility of the figures needs to be carefully established. Ideally, to follow the argument below, one should have a large-scale copy of one of the Warren Commission's Dealey Plaza plats, which are printed as Exhibits 585, 882, and 883. CE 882 and CE 883 are nearly identical, six feet in length, and have more detail than CE 585. All three maps are reproduced in this book, and copies of CE 585 can be obtained from the National Archives. Due to the lack of a special copy machine necessary for large maps, CEs 882 and 883 cannot be copied at the Archives.

Long ago, Robert West provided copies of his six-foot map to researchers, and a copy has been made available by Robert Cutler. Some researchers have produced quite accurate maps of the Plaza from this material.* The Commission exhibits include data such as elevation contours and distance markers every twenty-five feet down Elm Street. Very small photographs of the plats can be seen on page 262 (CE 585) and page 901 (CEs 882–83) of vol. 17 of the Warren Commission books, and reproduced in this chapter (hopefully!). Microscopic examination of the tiny pictures in those volumes reveal where they had actually placed shots 2 and 3. Maybe that is why they are so small.

One might ask why the Warren Commission reproduced them at all? Or, why not alter the drawings themselves? Again, my theory is that along with the official story, we often get contradictory facts telling what really happened. Either they want those facts out so the more intelligent will know to keep their mouths shut, or those officially charged with lying to the public were tricked by those they made to lie, and some facts slipped in between the cracks. It's also politics.

Martin Shackelford comments that the Warren Commission may have reproduced the maps because suppressing them would too easily point to the truth. When something is suppressed, attention

---

*Contact Craig Ciccone, 419 E. Saratoga, #B, Ferndale, MI 48220 for a map with placement of the many witnesses, and architect Robert Cutler, Box 1465, Manchester, MA 01944, for a copy of the official plat, CE 882.

is drawn to it. The easiest way to conceal damaging information is to bury it in a pile of trivia, which seems to have been the Commission's approach. Printing the maps so tiny would also help, without actual "suppression."[4]

CD 298 AND THE EARLY REENACTMENTS

Commission Document 298 is an FBI-bound memorandum presented to the Commission on January 20, 1964, to accompany its Dealey Plaza scale models and other visual aids. The photographs of the scale model in this chapter were made at the National Archives without removing them from the bound presentation.

The document gives the following as the distances from which the shots were fired: Shot 1 from 167 feet; shot 2 from 262 feet: shot 3 from 307 feet. It is made explicit that each shot "hit the target" and that shot 3 hit the President. There are no missed shots in this scenario.[5] These measurements are from the street to the window.

CD 298 also gives the following distances from the limousine to Zapruder's position as he filmed the shots:

A. Shot 1 was photographed from 123 feet away, 10.5 feet below eye level.
B. Shot 2 was photographed from 77 feet away, 18.0 feet below eye level.
C. Shot 3 was photographed from 85 feet away, 20.5 feet below eye level.

The differences between this account and the Warren Report are major. The Report gives 265.3 feet from the window as the distance for the head shot, and allows only the possibility of a later missed shot.[6] The CD 298 scenario has a shot at about this distance, then says that another one hit the President in the head forty-two feet farther down the road.

THESE NUMBERS WERE NOT PULLED FROM THE AIR. They describe specific locations on the street and for each location; the three figures are internally consistent. A shot of 307 feet would hit the street about six to seven feet to the west of the mark "5+00" on the Dealey Plaza plats (refer to the maps in this book labeled CE 585 or CE 882). Measured on one of those plats, the point where the shot hit is about eighty-five feet from the concrete pedestal. The elevation above sea level at that point on the street is about 416 feet (elevations are given on all the plats).

Zapruder's eye level can be approximated by adding the pedestal's height of 430.8 feet above sea level (given on CE 883) to the height of about five to six feet at which he would have held his camera. This comes out to 435.8 to 436.8 feet, which is very close to 20.5 feet above the elevation of the point on the street.

The figures given here can be verified, but the materials are hard to find. They should be studied in conjunction with a large-scale copy of one of the Commission Exhibits (585, 882, or 883) made from Robert West's survey plats, and reproduced in this chapter. By measuring the horizontal distances on the map, and taking differences of elevation into account, it is possible for a given station on the street to calculate the distances to the TSBD window and the concrete pedestal. A table of such calculations is provided for the reader.

Similar calculations can be done for the other two shots, and help establish that the FBI data came from an actual survey conducted at the site, using the Zapruder film in some form, probably still pictures from individual frames. The fact that the measurements below eye level go all the way to the pavement indicate that this survey probably measured distances to a point under the rear bumper of the car, as did the December 5 Secret Service survey.

The shot trajectories are similar to those of the December 5 survey, to be discussed later, in that they have two of the shots much farther down the street than where they seem to happen in today's Zapruder film. CD 298 has these shots even farther west on Elm Street. The 307 feet distance for shot 3 would put the limousine at about where it appears in Zapruder frames 365–370, and the 262 foot distance for shot 2 would put the limousine at about where it appears in frames 310–315.

THERE MAY BE AN EXISTING FILM RECORD of this reconstruction, which is the source of information for the FBI's Dealey Plaza scale model exhibits. Three photographs from the Commission's Secret Service file, taken from the concrete pedestal, show an apparent reenactment in progress. They were taken by either Dallas Police Department or *Dallas Morning News* personnel, according to a memo in the same file from Inspector Kelly of the Secret Service. The memo is dated December 5, 1963.[7]

Three traffic cones are placed on the north curb of Elm Street

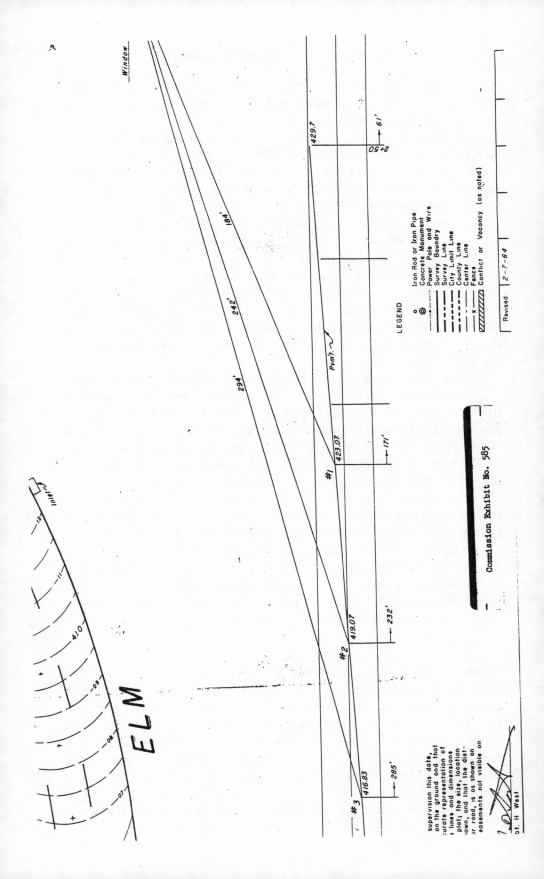

Commission Exhibit No. 585

DL 89-43

2
—

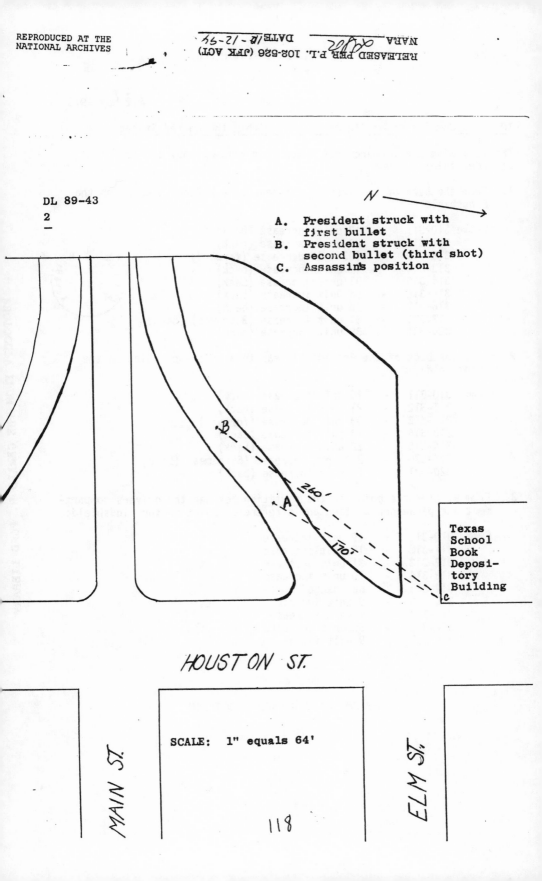

N

A. President struck with first bullet
B. President struck with second bullet (third shot)
C. Assassin's position

B

260'

A

170'

Texas
School
Book
Deposi-
tory
Building

c

HOUSTON ST.

SCALE: 1" equals 64'

MAIN ST.

ELM ST.

12 May 1975

<u>TO: The Commission on CIA Activities Within the United States</u>

The following are measurements taken from a 16-mm copy of the
Zapruder film:

1. From the back of the President's head to a reference point on the
    windshield:

    Frame 310-311 -   13 unit increase (back)
          311-312 -   23 unit increase (back)
          312-313 - 103 unit decrease (forward)
          313-314 -   42 unit increase (back)
          314-315 -   31 unit increase (back)
          315-316 -   86 unit increase (back)
          316-317 -   60 unit increase (back)
          317-320 -   89 unit increase (3 frames) (back)
          320-321 -   38 unit increase (back)

2. From the back of the President's ear to a reference point on the
    windshield:

    Frame 310-311 -   10 unit increase (back)
          311-312 -   21 unit increase (back)
          312-313 -   93 unit decrease (forward)
          313-314 -   74 unit increase (back)
          314-315 -   22 unit increase (back)
          315-320 - 204 unit increase (5 frames) (back)
          320-321 -   25 unit increase (back)

3. From a reference point on the <u>partition</u> between the driver's compart-
    ment and passenger section and a reference point on the windshield:

    Frame 310-311 -   19 unit increase
          311-312 -   15 unit increase
          312-313 -   31 unit decrease
          313-314 -   10 unit increase
          314-315 -   no change
          315-316 -   9 unit increase
          316-317 -   4 unit increase
          317-320 -   60 unit decrease (3 frames)
          320-321 -   9 unit increase

STATEMENT OF ALFRED G. OLIVIER

in these photographs, and their positions are in agreement with the placement of the shots in CD 298. The cone for shot 1 is partly obscured by the Stemmons sign.

Prints of two of these photographs are in the Secret Service investigative file. One of these, and the third, which was not in the file as of 10/94, were published by Harold Weisberg in *Whitewash II* (p. 248). We print the others in this book.

Another document in the same file dated December 4, 1963, (CR 87) is a descriptive list of films of reenactments of the assassination. Of the twenty films listed, one is described as follows:

> The next sequence shows a simulated motorcade during the same route as at the time of the assassination. 17 millimeter lenses on 16 millimeter film was used. Immediately after the motorcade passes out of view, Lt. Day of the Dallas Police Department walks onto the street from the right-hand side and places a traffic cone at the point of impact of the third shot. He then walks forward and places a traffic cone at the point of impact of the second shot and continues forward to place a traffic cone at the point of impact of the first shot and exits to the left. The 17 millimeter lenses were then zoomed to 85 millimeters keeping the three points of impact in view.[8]

THE FBI's SCALE MODEL has cars placed to indicate the positions of the limousine at shots 1 to 3. Many of the photos clearly show the model car representing shot 3 adjacent to the stairs leading down from the pergola, and the model for shot 2 at the point on Elm Street closest to the pedestal. The Warren Commission published only one of these pictures.[9] I print several more in this book.

CD 298 gives the interval between shots 1 and 2 as 4.4 seconds to 5.5 seconds for the car to move 96 feet, and the interval between shots 2 and 3 as 2.0 seconds to 2.5 seconds for the car to move 45 feet.[10] These figures are apparently based on the presumed speed of the limousine of 12–15 mph, and not on the speed of Zapruder's camera. The interval between the second and third shots thus could have been less than the minimum time for firing Oswald's rifle twice. Even keeping in mind the likelihood that the limousine was moving substantially slower than 12 mph, this would be a very short time for two wounding shots, and may account for the different positioning of shot 2 in later reenactments.

Contrary to what decades of propaganda have made us think, *the so-called "timing problem" involved the fatal shot and never had anything to do with the single bullet.*

The single-bullet concept may have originated as a way to explain four hits in three shots. Keep in mind that the government could not have the lone gunman fire more than three shots, as he could not fire more than that in the amount of time and distance available. If we try to correlate the CD 298 data with the films, as we see them now, we have a shot hitting Kennedy at or before Zapruder frame 225, another hitting him at frame 313, and yet another hit at a point 45 feet down the street, at about frame 370. To fit a three-shot scenario, one of these would have to hit Connally as well.

How do we know that the FBI didn't simply fabricate their data? They could have run a false reenactment, using the films as a guide, but choosing their own locations for the shots, ignoring any information they didn't want. If so, what does this say about their willingness to play with the films?

As mentioned before, the FBI materials other than CD 298 contain no mention of an extensive reenactment of the crime. The massive November 30, 1963, FBI report to the President (CD 5, commonly called the "Gemberling Report." Robert Gemberling was the head assassination investigator in the Dallas FBI office) has two pages on this subject, one a crudely drawn diagram of the Plaza. The accompanying memo states that Secret Service agent John Howlett, with the aid of a surveyor and movie films of the assassination, determined the distances of two shots hitting Kennedy as 170 feet and 260 feet, and was unable to determine where Connally was hit.[11]

This sounds like either the CD 298 scenario with the problematic 307–foot shot taken out, or the eventual Warren Report shot placements. Conveniently, the memo speaks of Kennedy being struck in the *neck* with the first shot, whereas all contemporaneous FBI accounts call this a shot in the back.

There is no attached survey plat or detailed figures, or any other documentation to back up this memo. Its credibility can best be assessed by viewing this item in the Archives copy of Gemberling's report, which has many pages devoted to the crime scene and other physical evidence. The pages are hand-numbered, so there is no way to tell how much material may have been taken out or switched.

The Gemberling Report was the first official story and the public solution to the case. Nothing much that the Warren Commission reported changed after that, except that the three separate wounding shots (the FBI strongly held that Kennedy and Connally were first hit with different shots) to the two victims in the car were combined into two shots, and the third became a wild shot that caused a man far down the street to be hit with debris. They otherwise could not explain that shot.

SHELL GAME WITH THE FILMS

The reconstruction of the assassination upon which CD 298 was based used an unknown film of the assassination wrongly attributed to Orville Nix. Daryll Weatherly discovered the document—and the wrong film attribution—by using simple mathematical calculations. I find it hard to believe that the FBI's mistake in the name of the photographer and the rest of what follows is a mistake or coincidence.

The document gives the locations of "Nix" as follows, in the form of an answer to the question of where Nix was standing:

> On the Plaza grass across the Parkway, approximately 125 feet from the abutment upon which Zapruder was standing at the time of the shooting. Nix was approximately 95 feet from the presidential car when he photographed the President being hit by Shot 3 and a man jumping on the rear left foothold of the car.[12]

This point can be located to within a few feet by placing two rulers on a 1" = 20' scale plat. Start one ruler at the pedestal and the other at the "shot 3" point you found earlier. Locate the point on the Plaza lawn where 125 feet from the pedestal coincides with 95 feet from "shot 3." (There are no elevation data given for points off the pavement, so these distances might be off by a few feet from the horizontal measurements you are making.) You will wind up with a point directly across Elm Street from the Stemmons sign, and fifteen to twenty feet from the curb.

This is not the location from which Nix filmed. He was standing on the south curb of Main Street, a few feet directly in front of Charles Bronson who was also taking pictures, at least 150 feet away from this location—according to CE 883. (He is marked on the official map. You need a microscope to see this in the Warren Commission picture.)

Nix, therefore, was filming from much farther away, near the Houston and Main corner, a full block from the action. However, 125 feet from Zapruder and 95 feet from shot 3 (as located in CD 298) is precisely the location of the bystander known to assassination researchers as the "Babushka Lady," who can be seen filming the motorcade in many pictures.

Beverly Oliver has claimed for a long time that FBI agents took her camera away from her and she never saw her film again. Certainly someone played a shell game with her film and that of Orville Nix, which was returned to him "cut to ribbons." Somebody wanted her film out of circulation—if it was used in the *real* investigation to place the shots. When the Warren Commission, and specifically Arlen Specter, perverted the FBI and Secret Service investigations for their own political purposes, Oliver's film had to disappear. Somebody changed Oliver's name to Nix as the person who took the film they relied upon to perform their reconstruction of the crime.

The document also says of this film:

> Nix . . . photographed the motorcade as it approached the tri-
> ple underpass. Nix photographed the left side of the Presidential
> car with Mrs. Kennedy in the foreground waving when the Presi-
> dent's head suddenly snaps to the left and the car picks up speed
> as a man jumps on the left foothold. The Nix film runs about
> 8 seconds.[13]

This is clearly *not* the Nix film, whose head shot sequence began long after Jackie stopped waving, and is six and a half seconds long.

We have once again the trail through the evidence left by FBI agents and others who were made to change the facts by Hoover. By giving us the precise placement of whomever took the film they are calling the "Nix film," **they are telling us that it wasn't Nix.** It was up to Daryll Weatherly, a mathematician, to make the measurements on a six-foot copy of the map on my office floor. Anyone with a ruler and a copy of the map could do it, but no one did it before because no one ever took a look at the document—once it was mentioned by the leading critic of the time. Everyone thought that he had handled the problem, so there must not be anything there. No one questioned what this meant.

Are there other switches and shell games at work? If you look closely at CE 882 or CE 883, there is a small detail included in the lower right, the concrete pedestal on the south side of Main Street where Charles Bronson stood when he shot film and still pictures. The duplicate structure on the north side of Main Street is not depicted. Is it a hint that Bronson's pictures were used in some way?

There appears to be a nearly straight line through the locations of the Stemmons sign, Beverly Oliver, Orville Nix, and the pedestal that Bronson used at the time of the shooting. The sign's entire length defines a vector or arrow pointing at the three camera operators. Is it coincidence, or were landmarks used to guide people to certain parts of the Plaza? Were some of the camera people unwittingly led or placed where they were? This alignment of the sign and camerapersons can be seen on the inside front cover of Richard Trask's book *Pictures of the Pain.*

Perhaps at least two of the three cameras in a straight line with each other, almost perpendicular to the shooting area, could yield film that might later be used to perfectly determine where shots happened and when. It could be evidence of conspiracy, since such a product from these films would make it possible to alter another film—the very public Zapruder film—and cover up the truth.

There are too many coincidences in this case, coincidences which might be called the hallmark of the case.

The Bronson film allegedly has a twenty-six-frame head-shot sequence, shot at twelve frames per second. Nix was standing directly under Bronson's line of sight. Could the Nix head-shot sequence come from a blowup of Bronson frames? Could the intention have been at one time to pass off one film as the other? An objection would be that Nix's camera ran at 18.5 frames per second, according to FBI tests, but who knows what has been done with the Bronson head-shot sequence in terms of stretch framing or other tricks? Nix originally told the FBI that he was filming at forty (sic) frames per second,[14] or maybe the FBI made that up. Except for variable speed cameras, they did not work that fast.

I personally believe there is even more of a trick concealed in this, since Bronson is insistent that he did not get his movie camera going, after taking a snapshot with his Leica, until Jackie and Clint Hill were on the trunk of the car. The time span of a second or two between the first frames of his alleged film and the point of his last snapshot would seem to preclude his having got the camera in position and started sooner than when he says he did. Therefore, there is a strong indication that the film now said to be his is a fake. (See pages 78 and 313–19 of my last book, *Killing the Truth.*)

As fast as Hoover got people to lie, the victims of this hated man and boss shot him down by switching evidence, or planting data in the figures that give us the truth.

THE DECEMBER 1963 REENACTMENT

An extensive reenactment was held on December 5, 1963. The Dallas surveyor, Robert West, calls this an FBI reenactment,[15] although it may also have involved Secret Service agents. An album of photographs from the reenactment was presented by the Secret Service to the Commission, and its contents, more or less, became CE 875. An accompanying survey plat locating three shots became CE 585. The plat has a notation saying "revised 2–7–64."

The December 5, 1963, map, Commission Exhibit 585, shows a third shot hitting the limousine from a distance of 294 feet, not the 265 feet given for the alleged fatal shot shown in Zapruder frame 313 and not the 307 feet given in CD 298. The accompanying Secret Service reconstruction photos (CE 875) support the placement of the limousine at a distance of 294 feet from the window at the third shot. A distance of 294 feet would put the limousine directly in front of where James Altgens was standing during the shooting and where he testified he was, relative to the car, at the moment of the head shot. This would put the limousine at about where it appears in Zapruder frames 353–58, well past the present head shot.

Note that the Warren Report trajectory distances are all from the assassin's window to the President, and the Secret Service reenactment trajectories are from the window to the rear bumper of the car. An approximate distance of six feet separates the rear bumper from the President's seat.

Since there is no mark on the CE 585 map or trajectory drawing for a shot of 265 feet, we should ask what the officials directing the reconstruction thought of the obvious head explosion and "halo" in Z 313 and the "blob" visible in the following frames. Did they choose to ignore these features in the film, or were they not yet in the film? What evidence were they looking at to determine that a shot struck the President at a distance of 294 feet plus about six more feet?

The next problem: Why is this shot so much farther down the street than it ended up the following May in CE 882? The Zapruder film shows the fatal head shot to strike when the limousine is perpendicular to Zapruder's line of sight to the President, which is where the head shot was placed on the street in the May maps. Did they see the film in December and was it then changed by the following May?

How do we know that the last "X" marked on Elm Street on Commission Exhibit 585 represents the location of where Kennedy was struck and not a missed shot—not at the manhole cover on the left side of the car toward the bridge, which they believed was struck by a bullet?† The map, made in December 1963, and revised in February 1964, shows three trajectories drawn from the TSBD window, and the measurement of the last of these is 294 feet. The Plaza was five hundred feet from the County Records Building on the east side of the overpass. The overpass does not cross the streets in a perpendicular to Main Street, but at an angle.

Kennedy at frame 313, or the fatal head shot, is 265.3 feet from the TSBD window, according to the May 1964 Warren Commission reenactment. The manhole cover, at approximately 380 feet from the window, is more distant than the last "X" or trajectory, at 294 feet, so if the cement around the manhole cover or the cover itself was struck, as many believed, it does not correspond to the last shot marked in the middle of the street on the map as "3."

J. EDGAR HOOVER AND PRESIDENT LYNDON JOHNSON

A major point is the possibility that John Connally was in fact struck three seconds after President Kennedy was hit in the neck.

Indications of a late Connally hit might have caused alteration of the film to cover it up, since there would be too many shots from the rifle for one man to have fired. Newcomb and Adams suggested that the Zapruder film was reframed on an optical printer at this point.[16]

Connally is clearly turning all the way around to look at Kennedy long after Kennedy is hit, even as late as frame 290. Connally appears to have taken a major wound at about frame 286, rather than at frame 225 as the government claims. At this point the Kurtis version of the film so greatly enlarges the scene in the back of the car that Connally's body is entirely out of this picture and the succeeding frames so that it is impossible to see which way he is turned. We cannot see the driver and Kellerman in the front seat. Essential information is therefore out of the picture. Connally falls back into his wife's lap after the fatal head shot to Kennedy.

Certainly, if Connally had received what ordinarily would have been a fatal wound, he could not have done all the twisting and turning we see in the film after he was thought to be shot by frame 225 or even as late as 235. The odds are that Connally took a minor wound earlier, such as through his wrist, for which there may be a

†CE 2111.

visible reaction. But his vigorous movements after that seem to indicate that he has not yet been shot through the chest.

Observers of the film the day after the assassination, such as Dan Rather, saw Connally hit in the chest with a shot when he was turned far around and looking at Kennedy.

During the discussion between President Johnson and J. Edgar Hoover a few days later, Hoover makes it clear that Connally got in the way of a shot that would otherwise have hit the President, clearly implying a shot from in front. Hoover tells Johnson that Kennedy was not hit with the second shot. "No, the President wasn't hit with the second one ..."

"I say, if Connally hadn't been in his way?"

"Oh, yes ... yes ... The President would no doubt have been hit ..."

"He would have been hit three times ... ?"

"He would have been hit three times ..." Hoover tells him.[17] But when was Connally really hit? If he was really hit while turned around, that certainly had to be changed if the shot that wounded him was to have come from the TSBD window.

CE 585, again consistent with CE 875, shows a second shot hitting the limousine from a distance of 242 feet. This would put the limousine about where it appears in Zapruder frames 285–90. Those frames show Governor Connally turned around, looking into the backseat. Only his head is visible, since, starting at about frame 275, the field of view in the Zapruder film shifts upward.

It seems to me that when Connally was struck in the back, he was turned around far enough for the bullet meant for Kennedy to have hit him from ahead of the car—the storm drain on the bridge to the car's left.

DAN RATHER DESCRIBES THE SAME THING

Dan Rather, after viewing the Zapruder film the day after the assassination, broadcast two descriptions of what it showed. The following are both descriptions of the shot that hit Connally:

"Governor Connally, whose coat button was open, turned in such a way as to extend his right hand out towards the President ... and as he turned he exposed his entire shirt front and a shot very clearly hit that part of the governor. He was wounded once with a chest shot, this we now know."[18]

"The governor's coat was open. He ... he reached back in this fashion, back as if to, to offer aid or ask the President something. At that moment, a shot clearly hit the governor, in the front, and he fell back in his seat."[19]

Rather was describing Connally turned around, facing the Depository, at the instant he was hit, which is exactly his position in Zapruder frames 285–90. What did he see, and what did those in charge of the reconstruction see, to place a shot there?

Something not in the film as we are allowed to see it.

At that time, they did not know the point where Connally should be hit because the official story had not been assembled yet. The story, when it came, was that *both men were hit with the same bullet, an idea the FBI has never officially accepted.* It came from the district attorney of Philadelphia, Arlen Specter. Specter is now a United States Senator and presidential hopeful.

THE DECEMBER 1963 MAP—CE 585—is notable for all the landmarks that are missing from it, but it is copied from the map made by the Dallas County surveyor, Robert L. West, two days earlier.

EACH PHOTO IN COMMISSION EXHIBIT 875 shows the car in the December 5 Secret Service reenactment moved 25 feet farther down the street. The car's position on page 890 (volume 17) shows the car 35 feet farther down the road than the May 24 placement of the head shot, and the text says that "A picture was taken at each point from 0+00 to the 6+25 mark, except no picture was taken at the 5+00 mark as this was about 4 feet from impact of the third shot."[20] This is very strong evidence that the government's professional criminal investigators had every reason to believe that the fatal shot was quite a bit farther down the street.

Weatherly discovered that the picture on the next page in the Warren volume shows the car moved 50 feet toward the underpass. The following page shows the car back up the street toward Houston by 25 feet. The fourth picture on page 893 shows the car fifty feet down the street toward the overpass. This switching of the two pictures following the one representing the fatal shot is exactly like the switching of Zapruder frames 314 and 315 in the next Commission volume. Could it have been someone's attempt to leave a hint that something was seriously wrong? One mistake can be supposed to be just a mistake. Two identical mistakes brings the switching up to the level of questionable coincidence. I think this is another example of the trail in the evidence left for us and history by the professional investigators who found a way to direct our attention at the clues.

Both mistakes draw attention to both the fatal wounding and the position of the car at that time. The position of the car at the moment of the fatal head shot during the December 5 Secret Service reconstruction is 35 feet past where it is today in the Zapruder film. They could not have made a mistake about this, as the current film shows that the car is directly opposite Zapruder. The roll bar on the convertible is in a line with his camera at the time of the shot.

By switching the two pictures following the photograph that shows their placement of the fatal shot, they are telling us that the car's position is what we have to concentrate on.

The shots are marked on the map by x's beneath the rear bumper of the car, on the street, six feet behind Kennedy's actual position farther down the street.

WE DISCOVERED SOMETHING ELSE. In July 1994, Officer Marco Miranda and I measured various aspects of Dealey Plaza. We stood in the middle of Elm Street at just that point where we could look over the top of the tree to the "Assassin's Window" in the TSBD. We then ran a tape measure down the street to the closest point to Zapruder in the middle of the street. The distance was 62 feet. It would be less, had I gotten down lower, to the level Kennedy sat in the car.

In volume 18, page 89, of the Warren books, the data block gives the distance from "Station C" at the juncture of Houston and Elm to the same point on the street (frame 210) as 138.9 feet. On page 95, the distance to the point of the fatal head shot is 230.8. Therefore, the official distance (for public consumption) down the street in which all three shots had to happen is 91.9 feet. This is 30 feet more distance (*and time to load, aim, and fire the weapon*) than we think was available, based on my own measurements in the street.

That 30 foot difference is alarmingly similar to the 35 feet farther down the street marked as the moment of the fatal head shot by the Secret Service.

Since the Warren Report was issued, apologists trying to explain these discrepancies decided that maybe there was another shot long before frame 210 of the Zapruder film, ignoring the impossibility of firing such a shot either through the branches of the tree or through the floorboards of the car straight down from the window. They claimed that there was an earlier shot from that window. Indeed, there probably was an earlier shot, but not from the window. At the time, the Warren Commission knew it had a problem with this, since they were forced to admit to three shots with one of them missing, so it seems to have lengthened the distance on the street in which the shots were made by 30 feet.

This invented 30 feet which is supposed to take us as far as the point opposite Zapruder's pedestal where his film tells us the fatal head shot was is not the additional 35 feet (approximately) past that point to where the criminal investigation actually had the shot. The wide discrepancy in the figures is another clue left for us.

Still another clue lies with the strange yellow marks painted on the curbs in the kill zone. There are three sections of curb about two feet long and painted yellow, which can be seen in the Zapruder film. Why? Why would the city of Dallas do this, if they did it? These yellow marks are also present on the survey maps for both December (CE 585) and May (CE 882–83). The yellow marks are visible in the Zapruder frame stills or slides, so they were put on the map to coordinate their information.

If the plotters got Zapruder wittingly or unwittingly to make his movie, one possible explanation is that they are marks used by those who needed to know if there was something in the film that they would have to take care of and cover up. With the zoom lens on full, there is no background in the film at the time of the head shot to tell us where the car really is on the street. The three yellow stripes are the only possible means of determining where the car is, and they would have known where they were.

Some feel that they are marks for the long-range snipers to make their shots. The stripes might also have been there as a signal to Greer to that if Kennedy was not dead yet, slow down.

How did the Secret Service, which so many feel was involved in the cover-up of John Kennedy's murder, *arrive at the positions in their reenactment where they thought the shots landed or struck the victims?* It is clear that *they could not have learned this from the versions of the film which we now have.*

Surveyor Chester Breneman, working with Robert West, the surveyor of Dallas County, helped survey Dealey Plaza, lining up the landmarks as seen from Zapruder's perch with where the film showed the shots. They worked from *Life*'s slides made from the Zapruder film frames. He told reporters that on November 25, 1963, he had still photos which were made from all frames of the Zapruder film by *Life* magazine. Much later he said that the numbers of the frames were changed. He described things in the frames that are no longer there, such as globs of blood and brain coming from the head to the rear of the car.[21]

Did they have a different Zapruder film then? One that showed the shots much farther down the street than where they are now?

THIS POINT SHOULD BE MADE CLEAR: in offering this analysis, I am not endorsing the credibility of the FBI (CD 298) or Secret Service placement of the shots. These reconstructions were part of the effort to build a case against Oswald by limiting the number of shots to three. Thus, their data are as suspect as the rifle and other apparently manufactured evidence. They are part of the emerging pattern of official fabrication and contradictory evidence.

The thing to keep in mind at all times is that *all* of the evidence comes from official sources. The inherent contradictions point to an official mindset in which physical evidence can be altered to fit changing circumstances. The reconstructions damn each other just as much as they damn the Zapruder film. Certainly there can be no inherent credibility in a reconstruction such as the one underlying CD 298, in which a film was misidentified and then discarded.

One must look at all the reconstruction evidence and then carefully weigh it. For instance, CD 298 gives a very short time interval between the second and third shots. If the Zapruder film they were using then was identical to the one we have now, why would they create this problem for themselves by placing shot two and shot three so close together? It seems far more reasonable that they were forced into this placement by the film record as it then existed. They decided that the interval between the shots was just too short, and the reconstruction data were buried in an obscure document. The Oliver film was suppressed and never seen again, and the Zapruder film was rearranged.

The December 5 Secret Service reenactment reflected in CE 585 and CE 875 placed three evenly spaced shots *on the street,* including a head shot 35 feet from where we now see it in the films. This arrangement of shots improved on the CD 298 data by eliminating the too-close spacing of shots two and three. It is entirely possible that the positions were made up for this purpose—but what does that say about the official view of the films? They were subject to change as circumstances dictated.

In this case, circumstances dictated that yet another reenactment take place, since those three nicely spaced shots could not account for the bullet strike on the south curb of Main Street, or for Kennedy's throat wound. So the December 5 were also buried.

The records of this reenactment are incomplete in both of their locations in the Commission files. The photographs in the actual folder handed over to the Commission are numbered 1 to 26, with 19, 24, and 25 not included. The Commission published all twenty-three remaining pictures in CE 875. The photographs are also part of Commission Document 88. There, the same twenty-three pictures appear, numbered 1 to 30 with 8, 13, 15, 19, 22, 23, and 24 not included. Were these once pictures from the various locations where people were filming, to compare with what their films actually showed? According to Archivist Steve Tilley, the National Archives does not know who originally inventoried these photos or what happened to the missing ones. They may never have gone to the Archives.

THE MAY 24 REENACTMENT

There was a core group of key people from the FBI, Secret Service, and the Warren Commission who analyzed the Zapruder film along with 35mm slides made for them by *Life* magazine. They met for at least seven full days, and Specter, Gauthier, Shaneyfelt, Kelley, and John Howlett were the principal players.[22] Chuck Marler wrote me that "these are the same people who conducted the reenactments and introduced the only documents with 'precise' measurements of the crime scene via the survey plats. They also 'reenacted' the James Altgens photo which was taken at Zapruder frame 255. John Howlett, Secret Service agent from the Dallas office, is also the same individual who contacted Dallas Surveyor Robert West for measurements of the Stemmons Freeway sign."[23]

THE WARREN COMMISSION changed three key frame numbers (168, 171, 208 to 161, 166, 210) in exhibits 882 and 884,* as the Stem-

---

*"Comparing Mr. West's field notes with CE 884 will prove significant alterations," Chuck Marler writes. "CE 884 is a data block containing Zapruder film frame numbers, elevations, and distances from the reenactment. It was drawn on the survey plat (CE 883) but apparently was introduced as a separate exhibit due to the difficulty in reading it. When one examines Mr. West's field notes of the fourteen Zapruder frame locations, there are no measurements made for frames 161, 166, and 210 as contained in CE 884. However, Mr. West did make measurements for frames 168, 171, and 208, which are not included in CE 884. The distances and elevations he made for these frames have been used for frames 161, 166, and 210 respectively. . . ." (Chuck Marler, "Questioning the Warren Commission's Evidence in JFK Assassination

mons Freeway sign was moved almost a foot, and raised and turned toward where Zapruder was standing shortly after the assassination. "The consequence of the alteration," Marler writes, "caused the first two frames to be positioned more west on Elm Street and frame 210 slightly more east. Using the measurements that the limousine traveled from CE 888 through CE 902, a calculation of speed between frames 168 to 171 indicates the vehicle traveled 3.7 miles per hour and 28.7 miles per hour between frame 207 and 208. Altering the 208 to 210 would reduce the 28.7 mph to 9.6 mph. However, the speed calculation between the altered frames of 161 to 166 is 2.2 mph. These calculations demonstrate how erroneous the Warren Commission reenactment was, as neither the original nor the altered data frame references are consistent with the speed of the limousine during these sequences. The alteration of the data block raises questions as to what other information may have been changed but is still undetected today."[24]

Tom Purvis, a surveyor, is the source of the information about the alteration of the numbers in the data block on CE 882, and discovered this through his own observation that the numbers had been changed. We then found that they had been crossed out on the original map.

Marler has one final comment that is appropriate here, since the subject or perpetrator is at this time a proclaimed candidate for the presidency of the United States: "Arlen Specter's single-bullet theory reenactment was equally insulting. His Connally stand-in is leaning to the right and slumping in a position Connally assumed in Zapruder frame 240 (well after he was hit). The rod Mr. Specter is holding doesn't align with the wound locations and demonstrates a left to right trajectory, although a trajectory from the Texas School Book Depository would have been right to left. These re-creations are so far removed from the truth, it makes a mockery of the entire investigation."[25]

None of the photographs from the assassin's window during the reenactment actually show an alignment of the two men and their alleged wounds until long after Kennedy is hit and Connally is down, both obviously hit with different shots.

Reenactment"). Daryll Weatherly's and my observation in the National Archives of the plats showed that the three old frame numbers were crossed out and renumbered as above on the old paper copy (folded like a road map) of CE 882. In the published version, the old frame numbers were erased and new numbers carefully put in, but not so carefully that it cannot be detected.

* * *

AERIAL PHOTOGRAPHS TAKEN of the Plaza on the day of the tragedy by Squire Haskins[26] give a good view of Elm Street, and show twelve traffic lines on Elm Street. The two plats made by Robert West for the December and May reenactments have a differing number of lane dividers: The December plat (CE 585) has 13 pairs of traffic lines, and the May plat (CE 882) shows 12. Chuck Marler has pointed out that the difference in traffic stripes places the fifth pair of lines farther west on Elm Street in CE 883 than the earlier reenactment. "The fifth pair are critical clues since the uncropped photograph taken by AP photographer James Altgens clearly identifies the location of the limousine on Elm Street with its left tire aligned with the fifth traffic line ... and are an important crime scene reference. If the location of these lines in CE 883 is in error and placed too far west (downhill) on Elm Street, then all other prior Zapruder frame references would have been affected. *This issue is important in determining the Zapruder frames in which the oak tree blocked an assassin's view of the motorcade from the sixth floor window.*"[27] The CE 882 road stripes in fact appear to be correctly placed wherever it is possible to use known landmarks to locate them. More work will be necessary to determine whether they are all in the places they occupied on November 22, 1963. The end result of these problems with the reenactment was a significant difference in the placement of the car and "how far off the reenactment was from the true location of the limousine in Altgens's photograph. ... It is therefore obvious the reenactment vehicle is too far west and needs to be backed up approximately seven to eight feet."[28] The Zapruder film shows Altgens standing just east of the second (middle) yellow stripe painted on the curb on the south side of Elm Street.

The city of Dallas was diligent in tidying up the crime scene—moving the freeway sign, removing some signs entirely, moving all the lampposts on the north side of the street—but they did not repaint the traffic lines before the aerial photo was taken the day of the murder. Lampposts give us something with which to gauge the speed of the car. Daryll Weatherly finds the front wheel of the car on the fifth traffic line in the Altgens photograph by lining up background objects and parts of the car in the picture, which places the car on the street without making reference to any traffic lines.[29] After doing this, the exact location of the car can be placed on the aerial map.

After explaining that he had been farther from the car when he was preparing for his next photograph when the President was hit,

and that fragments fell at his feet at some point, Altgens writes that
he did not see Kennedy moving backward—probably because he
was right in front—not that it did not happen. The implication of
his statement about bodies moving toward the direction from which
a bullet comes, after an initial movement backwards, clearly implies
that the fatal head shot came from in front, although he does not
say this.

Altgens lives in Dallas today, and adds what seems to be a stock
statement by many Dallasites who don't want trouble: "There is
absolutely no evidence to support claims that shots came from front
and side of the limo. . . ." Yet, he gave very good reason to believe
that the fatal head shot came from in front when, four paragraphs
back in his letter, he describes animals being shot and moving towards the direction of the shot.

He says, "I am not a ballistics expert, but this sounds reasonable
to me."

IN THEIR CHAPTER, "The Filmed Assassination," Newcomb and
Adams (*Murder From Within*, unpublished) showed an awareness of
these changing shot placements, although they did not express
themselves clearly (and their book was suppressed in any case).
They wrote:

"Again, on December 5, 1963, the Secret Service held another
reenactment. At that time, the car, according to photographs, was
positioned at 207, 330, and 375. When this was put on a map, they
coordinated with frames 207, 285, and 330 [CE 585, 17 H 262].
[Author's note: This is confusing because Newcomb and Adams use
frame numbers for positions on the street. It creates a large semantic problem when they try to talk about alteration of the film.]

"A final version of the hits further compressed the time. The
Warren Commission stated that the President was first hit between
frames 210–25, and (the last occasion when Governor Connally
could have received his injuries was between frames 235 and 240
Warren Report p. 106). Connally was hit between frames 235–40.
Frame 313 was the final hit.[30] In short, the timing of the shots was
compressed. This solved the problems of time that the film
created."[31]

BY "PROBLEMS OF TIME," Newcomb and Adams mean the slow movement or even stopping of the limousine, and the inaction of the

1

Positions of presidential car when SHOTS ONE, TWO, and THREE were fired, as viewed from the south side of the parkway looking toward Pergola (line of fire indicated by string leading to each car.)

The following eight photographs are visual aids for the FBI scale model. In each picture, note that the car representing the third shot is positioned with the front bumper at about the point where the stairs from the pergola meet the sidewalk. Note also that the car representing the second shot is positioned to the west of the lamp post nearest to the pedestal where Zapruder stood.

Approximate location of presidential car when SHOT TWO was fired from a distance of 262 feet, measured downward along an 18° angle. The target had moved forward about 96 feet (indicated by string leading to white car).

3

Close-up view locating the presidential car when shots ONE, TWO, and THREE were fired from the 6th floor (lines of fire indicated by strings leading to cars).

4

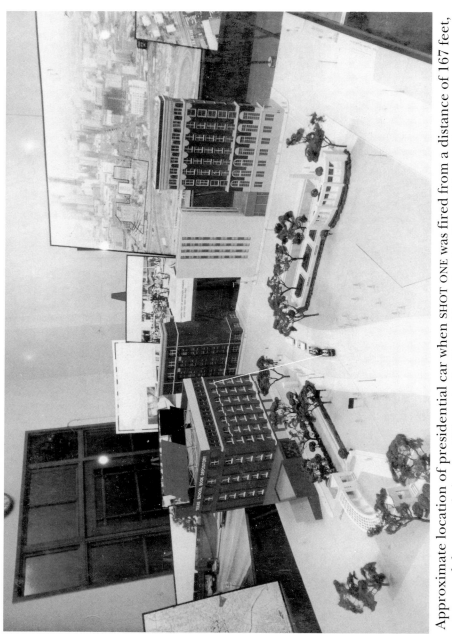

Approximate location of presidential car when SHOT ONE was fired from a distance of 167 feet, measured downward along a 23° angle (indicated by string leading to blue car).

Approximate location of presidential car when SHOT TWO was fired from a distance of 262 feet, measured downward along an 18° angle. The target had moved forward about 96 feet (indicated by string leading to white car).

5

6

Motorcade viewed from assassin's position. Aiming pattern of SHOTS ONE, TWO, and THREE indicated by strings.

Locations of presidential car when SHOTS ONE, TWO, and THREE were fired, indicating that the target was moving away in a downward direction and to the right from the point where SHOT ONE struck the president. (Strings at ground level show target movement to right of assassin.)

8

Approximate location of presidential car when shot three was fired from a distance of 307 feet, measured downward along a 15° angle. The target had continued to move forward for about 45 additional feet (indicated by string leading to first white car).

9

CE 585: This map was drawn during the Secret Service re-enactment in December, 1963, and frames from the Zapruder film were used. Three shots are marked on this map and the succeeding maps (CE 882, 883) as hitting in the car. This was changed by the Warren Commission to two, with a third shot striking down the bridge. Note how far down the street the shots are. The second shot is opposite Zapruder, where his film now shows the head shot.

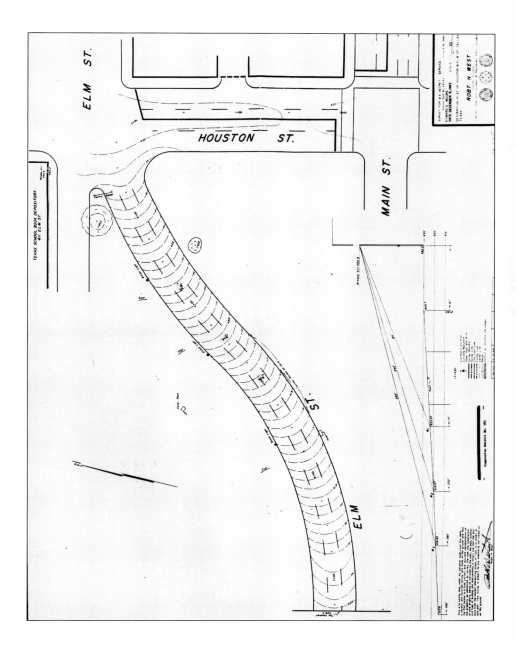

10

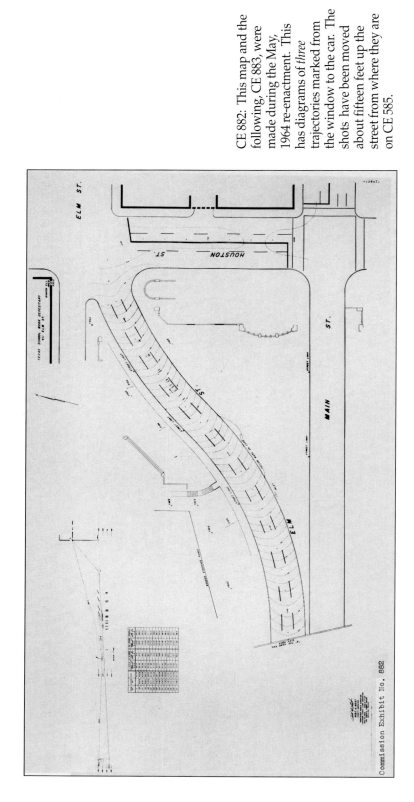

CE 882: This map and the following, CE 883, were made during the May, 1964 re-enactment. This has diagrams of *three* trajectories marked from the window to the car. The shots have been moved about fifteen feet up the street from where they are on CE 585.

Commission Exhibit No. 882

11

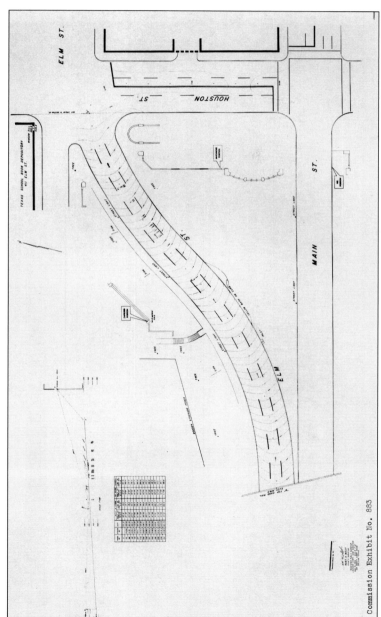

TEXAS SCHOOL BOOK DEPOSITORY
411 ELM ST.

ELM ST.

HOUSTON ST.

ELM ST.

MAIN ST.

Commission Exhibit No. 883

CE 883: The difference in this map and 882 are a few more landmarks and people placed in it.

12

FIRST SHOT

Photographs (three) made from the assassin's window by the Secret Service showing each shot marked on the street and cones marking them. Compare the placement with the photos taken from Zapruder's pedestal. Note the handwritten notations made by the Secret Service showing each shot, and how drastically this differs with the Official Story.

SECOND SHOT

14

THIRD SHOT

Two of the three unidentified photographs found in the Secret Service records at the National Archives. Each of the three photographs was taken from Zapruder's pedestal, and each shows a shot marked on the street according to their reconstruction. The placement of the three shots coincides exactly with the photographs of the reconstruction made from the assassin's window.

16

Secret Service agents over an extended firing sequence. Compressing the timing of the shots and speeding up the car (removing frames) in the film would solve this problem but create a new one by making the shots too close together.

Robert L. West, the surveyor, told Daryll Weatherly that he saw the limousine nearly stop at the time of the fatal head shot.[32] West stood about one block away at the time, at the corner of Main and Houston streets. He also told Weatherly that when he learned the Stemmons Freeway sign had been moved before the reenactments had been completed, he went back and measured it after his reports and surveys had been handed in to the government in 1964, and found that the sign had been moved more than ten feet, possibly fifteen feet.

"But the altered film still left major problems unexplained by the single-bullet hypothesis: (1) the lack of reaction by the President's guards, who were supposed to protect him; (2) the backward movement of the President's head after he was struck at frame 313; and (3) Mrs. Kennedy crawling across the trunk of the car," Newcomb and Adams wrote.[33]

This was written in 1974. Analysis of this type, however flawed, was too dangerous for the big-name critics, and so had to be suppressed.

IT HAS BEEN VERY UNFORTUNATE FOR HISTORY that the reenactments did not utilize an identical car to the Lincoln limousine Kennedy rode in. Instead, they used a Cadillac convertible, and this not only lessened the length of the car considerably, but changed the height the President was sitting at. One would think that if the government was going to go to so much trouble to reconstruct what happened, they would have used the same car.

Tom Purvis obtained West's notes stating that in March 1964, additional measurements were made for the carefully planned May 24 reenactment. On March 16, West wrote, "Distance to window ... 265 feet." It had to be this calculation used in the March 27, 1964, rifle tests, according to Chuck Marler.[34]

Purvis strongly believes that the Zapruder film is a fabrication. "It's a joke," he told us.[35]

Chuck Marler, who has so strongly maintained the Zapruder film is fake, asks this: "The December 5, 1963, survey was used for setting up targets in the rifle tests using the Carcano rifle. Why was the last target set up at 265 feet[36] instead of 294 feet? Since the rifle test was conducted on March 27, 1964, how did they know to use the precise distance of 265 feet for the reenactment since this figure was not calculated as the frame location of frame 313 until the May 24, 1964, reenactment."[37]

MARLER WRITES, referring to the longer (294 foot) trajectory: "A final shot occurring in this area may be why Zapruder frames past frame 334 were not printed in the Warren Commission exhibits. Wouldn't it be ironic that Dan Rather, the only newsman present at a private screening of the Zapruder film the day after the assassination, was partially correct when he told a nationwide radio audience that Kennedy's head 'went *forward* with considerable violence'?"[38]

The plain facts are that the reenactments were a fraud. Identical cars were not used and were not aligned with the precise locations in the photographs in evidence, as Marler says. The survey measurements were altered to conform to the landmarks in the film, and even today, we don't know where the Stemmons Freeway sign was, after it had been moved.

Marler writes, "In the sixth-floor window of the School Book Depository at the master radio control unit for the reenactment personnel was Arlen Specter.[39] It is difficult to understand why Specter used the sixth-floor window as the control unit for the reenactment when all photographic evidence to conduct a precise reenactment was made from the street. It is also apparent that while he was up there, Specter didn't correct the Connally stand-in position to coincide with his single-bullet reenactment illustrated in CE 903." The photographs of the Secret Service men in the car clearly show that there was no alignment of the men for one bullet. Not even close.

TRY IT YOURSELF

In what follows, the reader needs a copy of the 1"=20' scale CE 585 plat, which is available from the National Archives. This will illustrate how to place the third shot from CD 298 on the map.

To get started, the document tells us that shot 3 hit from a distance of 307 feet from the window. This needs to be translated into a horizontal distance that can be measured on the map. The 307-foot trajectory can be thought of as the slanted side (hypotenuse) of a right triangle, with the vertical side being a plumb line down from the window, and the horizontal side being what is actually measured on the map.

If the vertical side is of known length A, then the length of the horizontal side can be found as the square root of $307^2 - A^2$. The survey plats give the elevation of the sixth-floor windowsill as 490.9 feet above sea level (60 feet above the street. Elevations are given above sea level), so we need an elevation for shot 3, and our vertical side A will then be the difference between these two elevations.

No precise elevation for shot 3 is given, but we can give some upper and lower extremes, using data on the maps, to see how they affect the calculations. The plats CE 882 and CE 883 have a dot labeled 313 on the street, to indicate the Report's placement of the head shot. To find this same place on CE 585, locate the three marks drawn on the south curb of Elm Street, start at the one farthest east, and follow the elevation contour out into the middle of the street. The elevation at this point is 418.5 feet. It is possible that the reconstruction involved a car and stand-in for the President, so add four feet to give 422.5 feet as the elevation of the top of the head, and that will be the upper extreme, giving a value of $490.9 - 422.5 = 68.4$ for A.

For a lower extreme, take the elevation of the pavement at a point 42 feet farther down the street from the 313 dot. For instance, the street at the storm drain just past the steps has an elevation of 414 feet, which would give $490.9 - 414 = 76.9$ as the value for A.

Using these two extremes, we find that when A is 68.4 feet, the calculated horizontal distance is 299.3 feet, and when A is 76.9 feet, the calculated horizontal distance is 297.2 feet. These are only two feet apart, and the real value of A is well within the extremes, so we can set the horizontal distance at 298 feet and be no more than a foot off.

Take a yardstick and place it on the 1" = 20' Dealey Plaza map, hold one end at the TSBD window, and swing the other end around so that the 14 and 7/8-inch mark (representing 298 feet) is in the center of Elm Street. Mark this spot on Elm Street. If you have done everything right, your spot should be on the contour line that touches the middle of the three dashes on the south curb.

Make a little scale model limousine (a cardboard rectangle 1" × ¼" is close enough), and place it on the shot 3 spot you have found. It is not clear whether the CD 298 distances are to the President or to some part of the limo, but by centering your scale model on the shot 3 spot, you will have it precisely where the FBI visual aids show it, with the front end directly across from the Knoll steps (CE 585 does not show these steps).

As a check, measure the distance between the pedestal where Zapruder stood and the shot 3 mark. It should be close to 4 ⅛", meaning 82.5 feet for the horizontal distance. The vertical distance (a plumb line from the pedestal) is given by the statement that Zapruder photographed shot 3 at 20.5 feet below eye level. The distance from Zapruder's camera to shot 3 works out then to 85 feet, as stated in the document.

In the same manner, one can confirm that the data given for shots 1 and 2 are internally consistent and represent real points on the street. So even if these shot locations are made up, they could only have been made up using data from an existing survey plat, which implies an actual survey and reconstruction in the Plaza.

The elevation for your shot 3 mark should be about 416 feet. The top of the pedestal has an elevation of 430.8 feet. (This figure appears on CE 883 and can be seen in volume 17 only under extreme magnification. I read it in the Archives on a full-size copy. CE 882 does not have the elevation of the pedestal.) It would appear that the distances given were to points on the street, and that an estimate of 5.7 feet was used for Zapruder's eye level. (416 + 20.5 - 430.8 = 5.7.)

I urge readers to obtain the necessary materials and perform these calculations. Try not to feel silly about pushing a little cardboard "limousine" up and down a Dealey Plaza map. This is the kind of work those who monopolized the trajectory issue should have done long ago.

CONCLUSION

The plain facts are that the results of the FBI and Secret Service findings of where the shots were—amply demonstrated in their records and Commission exhibits—show that they were disregarded for political reasons. The findings of the Warren Commission were clearly motivated for political reasons. The murder of the President was political. The Commissioners appointed to explain the assassination to the public were political.

And the man who possibly played the biggest single role in shaping those findings, Arlen Specter, a wolf in sheep's clothing, who changed political parties at the appropriate time after that murder, knows best why he ignored the findings of the professional criminal investigators of the FBI and the Secret Service.

4

The Forged Autopsy X-Rays and Dr. David Mantik's Historic Findings

There are many things here that seem to exist and have their being, and yet they are nothing more than a name and an appearance.

—Quevedo

THIS IS MY FOURTH CHAPTER on the X-rays, as there has been one in each of my works on John Kennedy's assassination. Wrestling with the issue has seen some mistakes, and most assuredly, I have been wrestling with a bear. Finally comes hard scientific proof that the X-rays were altered, and that is what I present to you now.*

To forge something means a number of things, among them to make *fraudulent,* to *contrive,* or to *devise.* It does not necessarily mean that an existing film *itself* is altered but that the *image* seen on it was separately altered.

There is a set of proofs contained in the evidence that shows the forgery of the X-rays independent of all that follows in this chapter. It is rather simple. Throughout the years the autopsy doctors described a small wound of entry low down on the back of the head near the hairline. They have repeatedly described the entry as being on the edge of the large defect on the back of the head. They had only half of it, and I have discussed this in great detail in Chapter 6, "From the Secret Documents: Conflicts in the Autopsy Evidence." The doctors said they had only half the hole. The other half was on a piece of bone which arrived from Dallas at the autopsy

---

*The reader is referred to the chapters on the autopsy X-rays in all three of my previous books on the JFK case, but in particular to Chapter 17 of *High Treason 2,* p. 341, and to Chapter 10 of *Killing the Truth,* p. 298 (both Carroll & Graf editions).

about midnight the night of the assassination. In other words, there was no bone above that point on the head in the back, just as was described by all witnesses who saw the wound in Dallas.

Yet, the present X-rays seem to show bone covering the entire back of the head. The Clark Panel in 1968 found that not only was there bone there, but there was a round bullet fragment stuck on the outer surface of the skull four inches above where the autopsy report placed the entry, and where there should be no bone. They also found a discontinuity (or step) at the rear of the lateral X-ray that they took to be the entry, 1 cm above the fragment on the outside of the skull. It was described again for the House Select Committee on Assassinations by Gerald M. McDonnell, a radiologist for the Good Samaritan Hospital in Los Angeles. "A metallic fragment on the outer table of the right occipital bone 9.6 cm above the mid-portion of the external occipital protuberance (EOP). 1 cm above the metallic fragment is a depressed fracture from which stellate type fractures 'radiate' into both occipital bones, the right parietal bone and the right temporal bone."[1]

We know from this same 1978 document written by McDonnell that "there have been allegations that the postmortem radiographic images have been modified or altered ('doctored') to produce misinformation and therefore improper conclusions." He then discounts alteration. Since only a few of us saw that material prior to that date, I would like to know who else besides myself questioned it.

McDonnell wrote that there was a "nearly complete loss of right parietal bone, the upper portion of the right temporal bone, and a portion of the posterior aspect of the right frontal bone." This statement begins to join the battle which we read about in this chapter and my previous work. The parietal bone is all that bone extending across the top of the head as far as the coronal suture. The frontal bone connects to it and comes down to the forehead, and the temporal bone is where the temple is. The autopsy doctors described no bone missing in the frontal area, where it clearly *is* missing on the current X-rays, and no witness described the damage to the head in that area that would be seen by anyone looking at the body and the face. Dr. John Lattimer, the first outsider to view the X-rays, wrote Joshua Rodgers on November 11, 1994, that "JFK's face and facial bones were intact. The brow broke off cleanly, up about the hairline."

The second problem with the X-rays is that the three pieces of missing bone that later arrived at the autopsy nearly filled up the area of missing bone, and none of it was from any area other than the back of the head and the skullcap. The Harper fragment, had they had it that night, would have completed the area of missing bone, as the doctors said.

I believe the X-rays are composites—altered so that part of the X-rays are not of Kennedy's head, and the part that is of his head has the hole in the back of the head covered over.

The rest of the proof of faked X-rays lies in McDonnell's statement: "A linear alignment of tiny metallic fragments is associated with the entry, path of travel, and exit in the posterior aspect of the right frontal bone." The autopsy doctors described this trail of dustlike metal in their report. "Roentgenograms of the skull reveal multiple minute metallic fragments along a line corresponding with a line joining the above-described small occipital wound and the right supraorbital ridge." The occipital wound is the small wound of entry on the back of the head near the hairline, and the supraorbital ridge is the upper portion of the eye socket.

At the rear of the skull, the two conflicting trails of metal fragments are four inches apart. Thus, the issue is, as I have screamed through four books: Where was that occipital wound? If there was no bone above the small entry hole, which was only half present on the intact skull, how could the trail of metal fragments be above it? What they saw on the X-rays taken during the autopsy is not at all what is there now.

Could the doctors have made a mistake as to where the entry was? Hardly. This book presents their own extensive testimony insisting on their measurements and placement of that wound, and they ask us not to pay any attention to these X-rays and photographs, which were produced as part of the official story.

WE ALL HAVE TO LEARN ABOUT THESE X-RAYS and the medical and anatomical language of them, because this has turned out to be the key to the Kennedy case. The case is broken because of my discovery of the forgery in 1978 and the interpretations of Dr. Donald Siple† and his staff in 1979. The follow-up work of Dr. David Mantik in this chapter proved our findings indisputably in 1993. Without Mantik's training in physics as well as radiology, the mystery of John Kennedy's murder might never have been solved. We didn't have it all right in the beginning, but I believe Mantik has nailed it down. Fifteen years had to pass.

The autopsy report described a large hole or defect in the right

†See *Killing the Truth* by the author, p. 300.

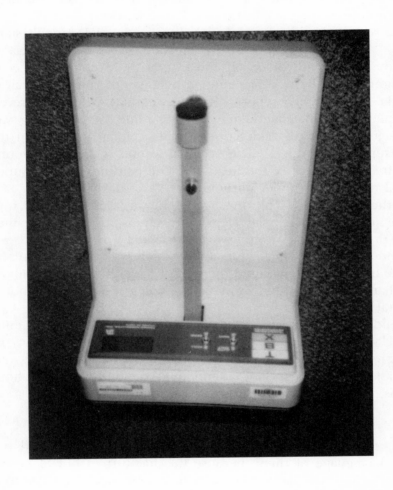

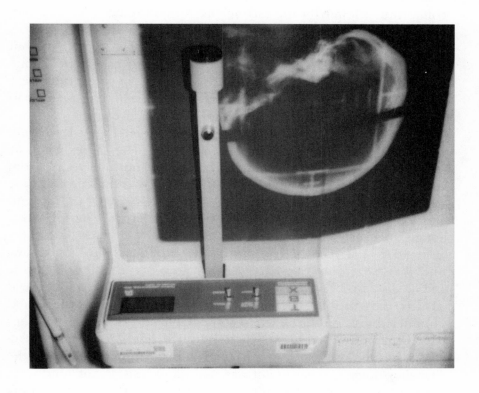

rear part of the President's head. As I wrote in my earlier books, this hole does not appear on the X-rays in the correct place. Instead, the lateral X-rays show an apparent large hole on the forward part of the head extending to the high forehead, just above the hairline, according to Dr. David Mantik. Others believe that the large hole comes much lower on the face in the X-rays the National Archives now have. Just how far is arguable, for reasons that we'll discuss later. The forward part of the real hole appears in the X-rays, but the dark area is extended further forward into the frontal bone region, which was not described in the autopsy report, and the rear part of the hole described by all witnesses is nowhere to be seen in the lateral X-rays. That is because it is covered over.

The fake X-rays were intended to show evidence of a shot from behind only, and not a shot from in front. The large exit hole described in the autopsy report and in Dallas indicates a shot from in front of the President, a shot Lee Harvey Oswald could not have fired. But the actual X-rays may very well contain proof of a second shot from in front, overlooked by the forgers who performed a rough and hasty cover-up.

In 1978, I wrote about some of the problems with the X-rays, and they were confirmed by Dr. Donald Siple, a chief diagnostic radiologist, in 1979. In late October 1993, a physicist, Dr. David Mantik, a radiation oncologist, entered the National Archives and conducted tests on the still-secret X-rays. He confirmed our findings with an optical densitometer—a sensitive light-measuring instrument—on the original X-rays in the National Archives. This was the first time such an instrument was used, and tests of any kind were conducted on the X-ray film to determine their authenticity. Mantik stated at our press conference on November 18, 1993, that there seems to be little possibility of error in his findings. More recently, his comparisons of light readings on postmortem X-rays on other cadavers (provided by Doug DeSalles, M.D.) in the area of what Dr. Mantik calls the "great white patch" over the large defect area in the back further proves that it cannot be a true feature of the skull.

My first book, *High Treason*, spoke of my consultations with a then-unnamed chief radiologist—Dr. Donald Siple—who consented to being named in my second and third books on the case, *High Treason 2* and *Killing The Truth*.

FOR THE LAYMAN, a left lateral skull X-ray means that the X-ray film is on the left side of the head and the X-ray tube is on the right, and vice versa for a right lateral view. In a left lateral, you are seeing the structural features of the left side of the head more clearly than that of the right in the picture. The JFK AP (anterior/posterior) view has, in this case, the film behind the head and the tube in front, so the damage and bone in the back of the head is closer to the film, but still obscured somewhat by facial features.

Optical densitometry measures the transmission of ordinary light through selected points of the X-ray film. If the X-ray has been altered, for instance, by putting a white patch of metal or some other substance over a wound somebody wants to hide, the additional density of the patch will stop more light, creating a whiter area on the X-ray. The following outline of the scientific theory involved in Mantik's discovery comes after a tough struggle by me to understand it.

1) The X-ray machine sends X-rays through an object (such as bone, organs, metal) to film.

2) Denser areas in the object will produce a whiter image on the developed X-ray.

3) The optical densitometer (OD) will measure the light's intensity which passes through the X-ray itself, when the X-ray is inserted into this simple instrument.

4) The readings from the densitometer give the levels of light on various parts of the X-ray image.

5) The densitometer tells you how much the X-rays were impeded or how much they got through the object to the X-ray film, depending upon how dense and how thick was the object.

6) Numerous light readings with the densitometer can be compared with other X-rays.

7) Higher OD readings mean that not much light can go through the film. At such sites the X-ray is very dark, so the object that was X-rayed was not dense or thick—or both; i.e., closer to air density.

8) Lower OD measurements mean that a lot of light passes through the X-ray film, and therefore the object that was X-rayed was more dense, i.e., more like bone.

DAVID MANTIK, M.D., Ph.D.

David Mantik majored in physics at the University of Wisconsin, where he then received a Ph.D. in physics. Five years later, he entered medical school at the University of Michigan. His medical internship and residency was at the University of Southern California at Los Angeles. He was at one time an assistant professor of physics at Michigan and also held fellowships in biophysics at Stanford from the National Institute of Health, in physics from the National Science Foundation, and held the American Cancer Society Junior Faculty Clinical Fellowship. He was formerly Assistant Professor of Radiation Science at the Loma Linda University School of Medicine, where he also directed the residency program. Mantik is at present the Director of Radiation Oncology at the Eisenhower Memorial Hospital in Rancho Mirage, California.

Only a person with training both in physics and radiology could break this case. That is what Dr. David Mantik did.

Dr. Mantik made his announcement at our November 18, 1993, press conference. In addition to his findings about the "patch," he presented evidence that two shots had struck the head, and that the magic bullet is anatomically impossible.

X-rays pass through the body and make images on film emulsion. The denser an anatomical structure, such as bone, the fewer X-rays pass through it. During processing, the silver halide granules are reduced (and then washed off), leaving a white transparent image on film, corresponding to dense organs, such as bone. Air does not absorb very many X-rays, and so this appears on the film as a black area. Where X-rays strike the film, the silver halide is converted to elemental silver after developing. This stays on the film during developing and so becomes opaque to light. The ratio of whiteness to blackness would fall within a well-defined range for a normal human skull, and "any values which lie outside of this range—and especially those which lie unnaturally far outside—would not be consistent with ordinary skulls and would raise questions of authenticity."[2]

The naked eye tells us certain things about the Kennedy X-rays even before we get to tests of this material. First, one notes that the front of the head is "unusually dark," Mantik writes, and secondly, the large white area is too white.

"When I first saw these two areas I was struck both by how extremely white and how extremely black they looked. Both areas looked very different from what I was used to seeing in my own patients. I was therefore very anxious to measure these areas for optical density to see if they were normal or not. What I found was quite astonishing. The posterior white area transmits almost one thousand times more light than the dark area!" Mantik found that this was true on both left and right lateral X-rays. He measured the light in normal skull X-rays for his patients and his measurements "showed only small differences in optical densities between the front and the back." "At most, the rear portion of the skull was slightly whiter and transmitted up to twice as much light as the anterior portion. I concluded, therefore, that the measured differences of about one thousand between the front and back of the JFK skull were too large to be explained by any ordinary differences as seen in typical patients."[3]

He says that the lucent area in the back of the head is almost as dense as the densest bone in the body, which surrounds the ear canal and which runs from the left to the right, like an axle. "In order for the white area at the rear of the skull to match the whiteness of this very dense bone, most of the brain in this posterior area would have to be replaced by very dense bone—and the bone would have to extend nearly from one side of the skull to the other. No human skull is constructed in this fashion."[4]

Mantik believes that the X-rays are incompatible with the brain photographs, which he has seen in the Archives.

Mantik compared a print made from an X-ray taken of JFK's head when he was alive and concludes, "This extreme range of whiteness to blackness is not seen in this X-ray print, as judged by the unaided human eye." The JFK Library in Boston would not allow him to compare the actual in vivo X-rays with those made at the autopsy.

"On the AP X-ray, posterior bone does appear to be missing in several areas. Because of overlapping shadows, I cannot properly evaluate all of the posterior bone. Also, note that some occipital bone must be present. The right lambdoid suture is partially visible. The more interesting question is whether this is a mobile bone flap."[5] I would add that if the bone is in fact missing in the AP view, it does not appear to be missing in the lateral view in the corresponding area of the back of the head. Mantik adds: "Most of the most posterior bone is being viewed end on from the side, so it would be hard to tell."[6] Furthermore, the posterior surface of the skull is not flat. It gently curves forward as it reaches the side of the skull. If bone were missing in areas farther from the midline it would be more difficult to detect on the lateral X-ray.

THE 6.5MM BULLET FRAGMENT

The diameter of the supposed metal object seen in the front-to-back AP X-ray of the skull in the lower part of the right eye socket has a bite taken out of the lower border of it. It is visibly twice as wide at the center as near the bottom. "On the lateral X-ray,"

Mantik writes, "using the optical density measurements, I would have expected this object to appear thicker at the center than at the bottom. To my surprise, however, the optical density measurements showed just the opposite: they implied distinctly more metal at the bottom! This fragment clearly does not behave like an object which was physically present on the body during the original X-rays."[7]

Mantik goes on to explain that "this disagreement between the frontal X-ray and the lateral X-ray was not found in other objects on the X-rays. For example, there is a 7 × 2 mm metal fragment located well above the right eye. This is seen on both frontal and lateral views. On the lateral view its optical density was quite homogeneous. That is what I would have expected from the way it looks from the front. It therefore appears to be real—that is, it was located on the body during the original X-rays. In fact, the pathologist described removing it. *By contrast, it is most peculiar that the pathologists did not remove the much larger and more obvious 6.5mm round object which should have been quite accessible at the back of the skull.*" (Emphasis author's. It is also peculiar that the very obvious circular outline of a bullet cross section was not discussed in 1977 by the large group of doctors who met with Humes and Boswell for the HSCA, in light of it having been reported by the Clark Panel ten years before. Were these the same X-rays?)

"Considering that the pathologists' main task was to find bullets, or at least large bullet fragments, it is astonishing that they did not even describe this object! Perhaps its size was smaller and its shape was different. That is, in fact, suggested by the Sibert and O'Neill report for the FBI. When I asked the autopsy radiologist, Dr. John Ebersole, whether he saw this object on the X-ray on the night of the autopsy, he refused to answer my question and he abruptly terminated what had otherwise been a reasonable conversation. *JAMA* has refused to publish my article which contained a summary of my conversation with him. Unfortunately, Dr. Ebersole has since passed away."[8]

As I wrote in my previous books, the large fragment most likely could not have been there because nobody saw it at the autopsy, and that was specifically what they were looking for: fragments or bullets. The only two fragments removed at the autopsy were found above the right eye. These two fragments are also described in the autopsy report and the FBI report as having been removed. The FBI report mentions a fragment at the rear of the skull but no mention of this having been removed. This whole issue may be a clue to something else.

AP SKULL—6.5MM OBJECT

Where metal is thicker, the optical densitometry (OD) measurements should be lower. The ODs are a means of determining relative thickness of metal. Mantik was surprised to find in October 1963, while examining the X-rays in the National Archives, that the OD of this 6.5mm object is lower than any measured OD on Kennedy's teeth. This is surprising because on the lateral skull X-ray, this object appears to be only 3 to 4mm thick (from front to back), whereas the teeth are nearly filled with dental amalgams (probably 50 percent silver, 50 percent mercury) *and* they overlap on the AP X-ray. One would therefore expect, from visible appearances, that there would be more metal in 3 to 4 overlapping teeth with amalgams; but the ODs suggest the opposite—that a rather small thickness (3 to 4mm) of lead was more effective at stopping X-rays than all the metal in these overlapping amalgams.

LATERAL SKULL—6.5MM OBJECT

Mantik thinks that because of the perspective created by the curve of the head, the fragment only appears to be on the outer table of the skull where the Clark Panel placed it.

I would like to suggest that if in fact the large fragment was lodged against the inside of the back of the skull, it would therefore seem to be proof positive of a shot from in front, and that would explain why the fragment was not mentioned in the autopsy report. It may be one of the very large things I have suspected are being hidden from us while they throw us some bones—some of the story but not all. A fragment in that area was mentioned in the FBI report of the autopsy.

Mantik points out that there is a metal fragment *above* the head on the left side which is not an artifact. So here we have metal on the outside of the left skull on the top, which is outside of the skull altogether.

Mantik was able to confirm some of the unique features of JFK's anatomy in the autopsy X-rays, as had the HSCA.

Dr. Mantik's work, while raising questions about the authenticity of the X-rays, seems to exclude the possibility that they were produced using a commercially available copier. He explains as follows (fax to the author, June 19, 1995):

"Each X-ray has an emulsion on both sides—I've thoroughly verified that. The OD of each emulsion adds together to make up the
total OD for the film, just as the total thickness of a book is the
simple sum of the thicknesses of its individual pages. The total OD
of the background air of the JFK X-rays is about 4 (very black). The
OD of one emulsion is about 2. *All* of them.

"The maximum OD that is possible for these films is about 4.
That is certain based on the Kodak curve which applies to this film.
I have gotten that from Kodak for the 1963 films. That maximum
is still in common use today; there is nothing unusual about it.

"The maximum OD that is possible for a film that is copied on
the same Kodak film (using the usual processes of a dark light) is
2. This is so because light can effectively strike only one side of the
film; the emulsion prevents its transmission to the opposite side.
The unilluminated side, when developed, will appear clear, i.e., its
OD will be very low. Therefore, any film that has a maximum OD
of 4 cannot be a copied X-ray film!"

The author believes that this implies that the X-rays in the Archives must have been made by exposing film in a cassette to X-ray
radiation. In principle, this could be a method for reproducing an
X-ray, since developed X-ray film contains metallic silver which is
radiopaque. Composites could, in principle, be created by placing
several developed films over each other and passing X-ray radiation
through them to the loaded cassette.

Dr. Mantik has asked that it be made clear that he himself does
not assert that the X-rays are composites, as he is not aware of any
process that would produce copies with equally darkened emulsion
on both sides.

Such a process might have no commercial application, but that
hardly means that it hasn't been researched and developed somewhere. Keep in mind the vast research projects conducted by the
NSA, DIA, and other intelligence organizations, that look into every
possible use of technology, on the grounds that they might need
it someday.

Methods of compositing X-rays are proposed at the end of this
chapter by Daryll Weatherly.

A Search for the Posterior Entry Site in the Skull

The autopsy report placed an entry hole on the back of the skull
near the hairline just to the right of the external occipital protuberance (the bump). Several years after the autopsy, the photographs

and X-rays were viewed by the Ramsey Clark (Clark was from Texas) panel. The photographs and X-rays showed that the entry hole had moved more than four inches above its placement at the autopsy, where part of the circumference of an entering bullet from behind was seen on the skull. The House Committee on Assassinations concluded that the bullet entered slightly above the 6.5mm object which we see on the skull X-rays.

"They based their placement of the entry hole high on the back of the head from their observations of the lateral views (X-rays). Oddly enough, they did not comment on the location of this bullet hole as seen on the frontal X-ray. On this frontal X-ray, I carefully scanned the area above the 6.5mm object looking for their described bullet hole. As judged by optical density measurements, there is no such hole anywhere in this vicinity,"[9] Mantik writes.

The "fragment" on the AP does not correspond to the fragment on the lateral in the sense of size and shape (which are inconsistent), but the placement in space is the same on both views.

Mantik insists, as I have from 1979 on and made an issue of the movement of that wound by four inches, that the lower site "was emphatically described by the autopsy pathologists in their official HSCA testimony and was recently confirmed in their interviews with *The Journal of the American Medical Association*."[10]

"IF THIS LOWER SITE IS CORRECT—and it is generally agreed that there are no other candidates for this bullet entry site—then there is no good explanation for the obvious and numerous metallic fragments near the top of the skull, at least four inches higher than the lower entry site. I have always found it odd that these fragments near the top of the head were not described by the pathologists. Even *JAMA* did not venture to ask the pathologists about these oddly located metal fragments which are so obviously inconsistent with a lower entry site."[11]

But are we all seeing the same stream of "dustlike particles"? Those who saw these X-rays in 1977, including the autopsy doctors, describe the trail of dustlike fragments through the head as coming from the lower entry point near the external occipital protuberance insisted upon by Humes and Boswell.[12] Mantik saw only a few minuscule fragments in this vicinity that barely hint at a trail, from the EOP to the right forehead. "Now the evidence for that on X-ray would be a trail of radiopaque spots which, with a magnifying lens, we can see in X-ray film No. 2 extending in an upward direction from the region of the external occipital protuberance, with the upper portion of this in an area where there's a large defect in the posterior parietal bone."[13]

This startling statement by pathologist Dr. Joseph Davis, made during the meeting of the two autopsy doctors, Humes and Boswell, with a panel of doctors for the House Assassinations Committee, is further expounded upon in the next sentence of the official record: "Now, there is radiopaque material, some of which appears to be even exterior, at least in this view, with continuation of radiopaque fragments in the vertex part of the interior of the head, and also continues straight ahead, and I think there's some more down here in the mid-posterior area. So all of us who have done a fair number of investigations like this are well aware that a bullet can split into fragments and one fragment can be deflected outward, another fragment can be deflected inward and slightly upward, and even a third fragment can go straight. There's all sorts of things can happen with bullets when they strike in this manner. I think I can see radiopaque trails going up which could reconcile the testimony and opinion of Dr. Humes that this material, this brain material, represents the loss of brain from the entrance site. . . ."[14]

Mantik comments that, "the pathologists suggested that the bullet which entered from the rear continued toward an area well above the right eye. But the dense metal objects on the actual X-rays (near the skull vertex) are so far from this path that they are impossible to explain without invoking a second bullet near the top of the skull. This was exactly the dilemma that the HSCA tried to resolve by elevating the entry site on the back of the head by nearly four inches. Since I could not find an entry site at this location in my measurements, the HSCA entry site is quite unlikely.

"The pathologists' much lower site then becomes that much more likely. . . . The numerous bullet fragments near the top of the skull, however, would then require a second bullet for their explanation. . . . This obvious conflict had never been addressed by the pathologists—no one has even asked them about it! Jerrol Custer, the radiology technologist who took the X-rays, has confirmed to me that this collection of metal debris was indeed present on the original X-rays."[15] Custer has made clear that the X-rays in evidence are not the ones he took on the day of the assassination. See my chapter on Custer in *High Treason 2* and the report of our May 29, 1992, press conference in *Killing the Truth*.

I again note that there can be no such trail of metal dust from a military-jacketed bullet, even after striking bone. It could only come from a frangible bullet which was breaking up. When a copper-jacketed bullet breaks up, it leaves fairly large fragments, but it does not leave dustlike particles. The lead core is chemically hardened to prevent just that from happening.[16]

In addition, *the trail does not even lead to the 10 cm higher, HSCA claimed entry in the head but is well above them.* This disparity was never addressed.

Furthermore, the trail is not in the shape of a cone at all, and therefore cannot be pointing at the alleged entry in the back of the head.

THE BACK AND THROAT WOUNDS AND THE SPINE

Mantik measured the width of the spine directly on the X-ray. He estimated the front-to-back distance of the body as 14 cm (typical for males of this size) and the distance of the back wound from the midline (4.5 cm to 5.0 cm) was given by the HSCA. He measured distances on the photographs as well. The wound seen in the front of the throat at Parkland was placed at the midline. "When I placed these measurements onto a cross section of the body at the seventh cervical vertebra and then connected the bullet entry and exit sites by a straight line, I immediately saw that the 'magic' bullet had to go right through the spine. This path would have caused major damage to the spine and would have been very obvious on the chest X-ray. In fact, there is no major trauma like this anywhere in the spine.

"Because of the impenetrable vertical barrier produced by the transverse processes up and down the entire cervical spine and because of the total width of the cervical spine, there is no place for the bullet to pass through anywhere in the neck and still exit through the midline of the throat. If, instead, the upper chest (thoracic spine) is considered as a possible bullet trajectory site, then another problem arises. The bullet would have to go right through the lung. But no lung damage of this type was seen by the pathologists and none is seen on the X-rays either. This 'magic' bullet simply cannot enter through the back wound and then exit through the throat wound without hitting the spine—or else causing major lung trauma!*

"It is odd that this rather simple reconstruction with exact mea-

---

*The autopsy report stated that in the apex of the right pleural cavity (supra-clavicular portion) there is "contusion of the parietal pleura and of the extreme apical portion of the right upper lobe of the lung. . . . Incision in this region reveals recent hemorrhage into pulmonary parenchyma." This could be why drainage tubes were inserted in Dallas.

surements has never been done before. Its very simplicity, however, provides direct evidence that the object which entered the back could not have exited at the front of the throat. This throat wound, which looked like an entrance wound to the Parkland physicians when they *first* described it, may indeed have been an entrance wound."[17] But where did it go? It has become obvious that the back and throat wounds Kennedy received were frozen pellets shot from close range along the street's curb that froze Kennedy in place so that the riflemen could not miss. Such a technique is also a clue to the sort of conspiracy that took the President's life. Robert Cutler previously noted, in his schematic cross-sectional drawings, that the magic bullet would have had to dematerialize while passing through the spine, and this had been testified to by Dr. John Nichols in New Orleans during the Clay Shaw trial. Nichols performed a more simplified version—without measurements.

As for the supposed "hairline" fracture of T1, the transverse process of a vertebra in the neck closest to the shoulder, which some claim that a bullet must have passed there and broke the bone, it was, according to Aguilar, a preexisting fracture, "and a very small one at that."[18] The Clark Panel's report does not mention the T1 fracture and to the contrary says that "there is no evidence of fracture of either scapula or of the clavicles, or of the ribs or of any of the cervical and thoracic vertebrae."[19]

Dr. Michael Baden asked Dr. Humes, the autopsist, if the transverse process had been struck. "There is present in the X-rays some opaque material to the right of the lower cervical spine which has been interpreted as being tiny bullet or bone fragments. Would the track, as you recall, be consistent with the missile striking a transverse process?"

"Well, I must confess that we didn't make that interpretation at the time. I'm familiar with the writings of Dr. John Lattimer . . . but as you can see from the point of entrance, it wasn't that far lateral."[20]

MANTIK ALSO DESCRIBES how a three-dimensional optical density map of the skull could be constructed. "If I had measured thousands of points I could have constructed a three-dimensional topographic map of the X-rays. The higher points on this map would represent the blackest areas of the X-ray film and would correspond to areas in the body where the most X-ray had passed through to strike the film. In a way, therefore, the information contained in the X-ray film is converted from two dimensions into three dimensions and

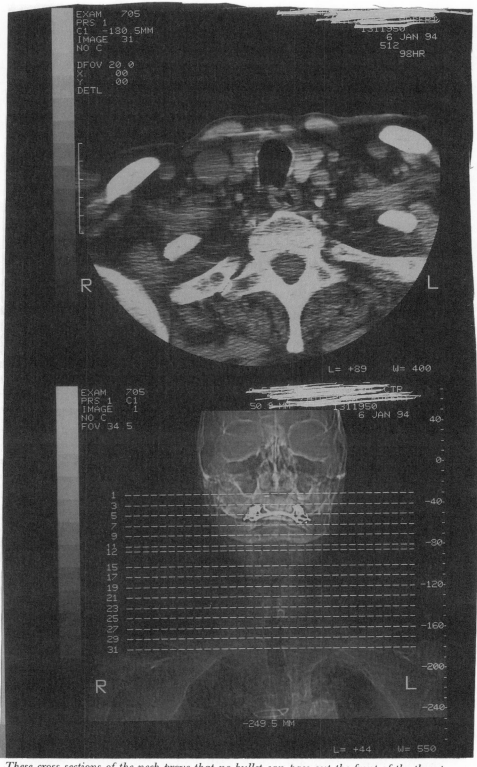

These cross sections of the neck prove that no bullet can pass out the front of the throat without doing major damage to the bone.

is that much richer in detail. The range of peaks and valleys on such a topographic map would be expected to fall within a well-defined range for a normal human skull. Any values outside of this range—and especially those which lie unnaturally far outside—would not be consistent with ordinary skulls and would raise questions of authenticity."[21]

MISSING FRONTAL BONE

I will admit that I may have been wrong to assume that more right frontal bone is missing than the published X-rays show. The autopsy report and all witnesses offer no evidence whatsoever of any frontal bone being missing. My radiological advisors and I did not have access to the actual films, which compounded the problem. Dr. David Mantik, during his viewing of the film at the end of October and early November 1993, saw some right frontal bone, as did Dr. Robert Artwohl (who also saw the original X-ray films in the National Archives), whom I treated unfairly in this regard. Artwohl overall is dead wrong and missed other aspects—such as the fact that no bone at all is missing in the area described as lost in the autopsy report. Nevertheless, frontal bone anterior to the coronal suture and bone in the temple area is missing on the X-rays and there is no report of that in the autopsy report either.

The solution to the quandary raised by the apparent missing bone in the right forward part of the head and face is that the forgers deliberately created such a puzzle. They have made it look like a great deal of right frontal bone is missing and that it is an apparent exit wound, just as the tracheostomy wound is retouched in some of the photographs to make it appear to be a large ragged exit wound. Dr. Angel commented: "It's really hard to be sure, square this with the X-ray which shows so much bone lost in this right frontal area."[22] This fooled a lot of competent people. The X-rays fooled a lot of people because they wouldn't listen to Humes, Boswell, and Finck.

Boswell's drawing seems to show a large amount of the skull missing on top. It even suggests that this defect (hole) extends into the frontal bone area which was not mentioned in the autopsy report.

The case has very cleverly planted red herrings at every turn. We could spend the rest of our lives following rabbit trails. For a compendium of documentation that there is in fact a massive amount of missing frontal bone, see the Medical Encyclopedia in the back of my book, *Killing the Truth,* p. 697, and discussions on pages 75, 79, 298, 300–302.

What X-rays *were* being looked at when the following discussion ensued with Drs. Humes and Boswell and the panel of doctors interviewing them for the House Assassinations Committee? Dr. Davis says ". . . we can see in X-ray film no. 2 extending in an upward direction from the region of the external occipital protuberance, with the upper portion of this in an area where there's a large defect in the posterior parietal bone. . . ."[23] Did he make this up?

The indications are that the composite X-rays in the National Archives may in fact be of John Kennedy, and not of someone else as I speculated in my first book, *High Treason.* The X-rays betray information that is damaging to the official story. Dr. Mantik was able to verify that Dr. Lowell Levine's identification of the teeth and sinuses were consistent with the in vivo X-rays of Kennedy. Therefore, in *High Treason 2,* my comments on Dr. Levine's authentication of the X-rays, are probably wrong. My apologies to him. The information in the composite X-rays is so conflicting that the mistakes were bound to happen, especially since I am not a scientist. This does not do much good for Dr. Levine whom I maligned, but I hope that this apology will find him willing to forgive me.

Dr. Levine could not help it if he was the stooge of the forgers. And as wrong as I have been on some of the details, these remain minor in terms of the overall rightness of my amateur interpretations of conclusions of forgery and that these X-rays are composites. There existed a possibility that at least part of the X-rays were made from someone else's reconstructed head after he was shot, and I explored that in my previous writing. My second book, *High Treason 2,* declared that the X-rays were composites, an idea explored further in *Killing The Truth.*

THERE IS SOME DISPUTE as to whether the anterior/posterior X-ray of the skull is taken in a modified Water's projection or not. Drs. Mantik and Artwohl agree that it is. That is, the X-ray tube would be looking up at the face somewhat, shooting toward the rear top of the head rather than straight back. Jerrol Custer has described it different ways at different times. It would be very difficult to remember after thirty years, and it was not documented at the time.

Robert Artwohl explains it this way: "The head is tilted back from true AP (front to back) and the X-ray beams were projected upward through the skull at an angle of around 20 degrees. This is why the missing portion of parietal and frontal bones appear to be behind the upper one-third of the right side of the face. This in itself has led to a lot of erroneous interpretations about the upper one-third of the face missing, since the relative darkness caused by the missing skull makes it difficult for the lay person to properly read the films.

"You can confirm the projection by looking at the distinctive bifurcating fracture seen just above the eye socket on the left side. Notice how it is just above the superior orbital rim on the 'AP' view, while on the lateral X-ray, it is well above the eyes."[24]

THE RADIOLOGIST AT THE AUTOPSY, Dr. John Ebersole, drew pencil lines on the original X-rays, which intersect at a fracture line on the right side of the occipital bone. That is where the autopsy doctors said the rear head entrance wound was located. Some say that "the important thing is that they intersect at a fracture line in the *right* occipital bone," which is right where Humes, Boswell, and Finck have always said an entrance wound was located.[25] Some say that Ebersole's lines are only for the bullet that entered in the rear down low and that one of the lines is horizontal.[26]

But Ebersole made clear in his newly released HSCA testimony that his pencil lines had nothing to do with trajectories.

ONE DOCTOR HAD THIS TO SAY about the insistence of the autopsy doctors that the rear head entry wound was not where the panel of "experts" was placing it, but low down on the back of the head where they had located it in their autopsy report: "How a panel of forensic pathologists could completely ignore the testimony of the autopsy doctors without even bothering to check the X-rays to see if there was any validity to their claims is beyond me. I do not envy the position they are going to be put in."[27]

The HSCA wrote: "The panel continued to be concerned about the persistent disparity between its findings and those of the autopsy pathologists and the rigid tenacity with which the prosector maintained that the entrance wound was at or near the external occipital protuberance."[28]

DR. MANTIK TOLD ME THAT THERE is a significant defect showing in the extant lateral X-rays "more near the vertex of the head." Basically, he said, the hole corresponds to the drawing published by the House Assassinations Committee,[29] and does not correspond to the drawing made by the Warren Commission. He says that the drawing made by the Warren Commission is "probably very nearly correct." Mantik wrote: "According to the AP and lateral X-rays, a large area of intact skull (and probably scalp) is present behind the right ear. This extends well above the upper edge of the ear." But that is exactly where there was no bone. It had been all blown away.

CLEARLY, THE PLOTTERS KNEW that the shots from the front were rather obvious, so they elected to cover over any evidence in the X-rays and photographs that might betray the facts.

DARYLL WEATHERLY

Daryll Weatherly is a mathematician at the State University of New York. His training and way of thinking in symbolic terms have given this case a great boost, through his examination of the Zapruder film and the alleged autopsy X-rays of John Kennedy. Weatherly found extensive evidence of forgery in both pieces of visual material and not only offers proof, but explanations of how the forgery was done. Only time will tell, and testing by those who read his work to determine if he is right or close to it.

The idea, in forging the composites, was to make them be all things to all people. That is, they show completely conflicting information, and are therefore interpreted differently by those who view them, according to their needs, or what they have been asked to look for. In late 1993, about the time we were announcing Dr. Mantik's findings at our press conference in New York, Weatherly published his historic article in Gary Rowell's *The Investigator*.

Weatherly's *primary* grasp of what was done to the X-rays involves the assembling of a composite picture through overlaying right and left lateral X-rays at the autopsy, the use of an opaque substance such as paint to retouch the composite, and the possible use of living or in vivo X-rays in the composites.

He writes: "The following is a description of how these composite X-rays (and others whose existence is inferred) could have been produced. An X-ray transparency, with opaque background and lucent areas representing bone, is placed over an unexposed film. The fresh film is then exposed by passing either light or X-rays through the original transparency. This second film, after development, will have lucent background and opaque areas representing bone. (This is called a "diapositive" of the original transparency.

Black and white areas are reversed from the original.) Two or more such films can be overlaid on another unexposed film, this arrangement exposed to light or X-rays, and after development, the last film will show a combined image.

"The missing bone in the right front of the head in autopsy #2 took some extra work. Before that piece of transparency was added to the composite, somebody painted over it with an opaque substance, obliterating the bone in the foreground, but following the outlines of the sella turcica and other internal structures so that they would still cast an image on the photographic plate. If you look carefully at the outlines of the 'saddle' and at the bone fragments in the adjacent sinus, you can see little spots that were missed. The job was not done perfectly, so there are remnants of the original images of overlying bone."[30]

In my opinion, paint was used on the AP view as well, and the same technique had the forgers paint over the frontal bone down to the right eye but left portions of the right supraorbital ridge showing to confuse the onlooker. We see those parts if we know what to look for, the way we see the sella turcica, which, as Dr. Donald Siple and I noted in my first book, is floating in mid-air. That is because it is surrounded by paint covering over the bone.

They had to paint around the sella turcica because it is necessary to compare the autopsy skull X-rays to antemortem views to authenticate them.

SOME DEFINITIONS ARE IN ORDER: AP is short for "anteroposterior," or front to back. The typical positioning would be with the patient (the deceased, in this case) lying on his back, with the photographic plate under the head and the X-ray tube above. The image produced will have features of the front and back of the skull superimposed on each other. The parts of the skull closest to the plate will seem more distinct.

There is a natural tendency, when looking at such a film, to "see" a skull viewed from the front, Weatherly notes. "When looking at the Archives X-ray, one might conclude that it depicts massive damage to the front of the head, with the right forehead and half of the right globe blown out. Keeping in mind, though, that the strongest images are cast by pieces of bone closest to the plate, in this case the rear of the skull, it is possible to interpret this X-ray as showing a large hole in the back of the head.

"I think it is possible, in this X-ray, to follow the outline of the right globe, even the part of it which is superimposed over the defect area. (For comparison, see the outline of the left globe which is more distinct.) At the top, there is a break in the continuity of this outline, and adjacent to this fracture, there is the image of a round metallic fragment.

"The official accounts, going back as far as the Clark Panel, place this metallic fragment on the back of the head, adjacent to the entry wound (which they place 10 cm above the occipital protuberance.) Fractures in the skull are also described leading away from this point. The report of Dr. David O. Davis to the HSCA Medical Evidence Panel states: 'There are a large number of fractures of the calvarium, and the linear fractures seem to, more or less, emanate from the embedded metallic fragment, and radiate in a stellate fashion in various directions.'[31] (Is this actually depicted? They appear to, but I don't believe they really do. They don't actually track in continuous trails back to the entry site. "It's an optical illusion," Mantik says.) "It seems to me that the cracks extend only to the edge of the defect and no farther."

In that case, the round metallic fragment, if it is located in the back of the head, is in the defect itself and not embedded in the skull at all. *If* it is in the back of the head.

"This X-ray correlates very well with what is stated in the autopsy report, but it is just ambiguous enough so that it supports a different interpretation. So, somebody who was involved in the autopsy, say Dr. Humes, could look at the X-ray and agree that it shows things pretty much as he remembered them. Then this endorsement of the X-ray's authenticity could be attached to interpretations of what it shows that are not his."[32]

Weatherly then points out that the published drawings of Dr. John Lattimer of his observations of the skull X-rays show the globe intact and the forehead still present in the lateral view, and the globe and all of the right frontal bone or forehead missing in the AP view. How could Lattimer do this, and what is going on? "The answer is that the first glance is deceptive. If you try to correlate this interpretation of Lattimer's AP picture with the letters and notations in the diagram (you need Lattimer's fully published drawing with notes for this), nothing is in the right place ... not even the placement of the words 'front' and 'back.' So, in fact, the correct interpretation is that he is depicting the back of the head in the foreground and the front in the background.

"If one accepts this as what Lattimer is trying to convey, then the entry wound cannot be in the position depicted in the lateral diagram."

Weatherly says that the large 6.5mm fragment which Lattimer

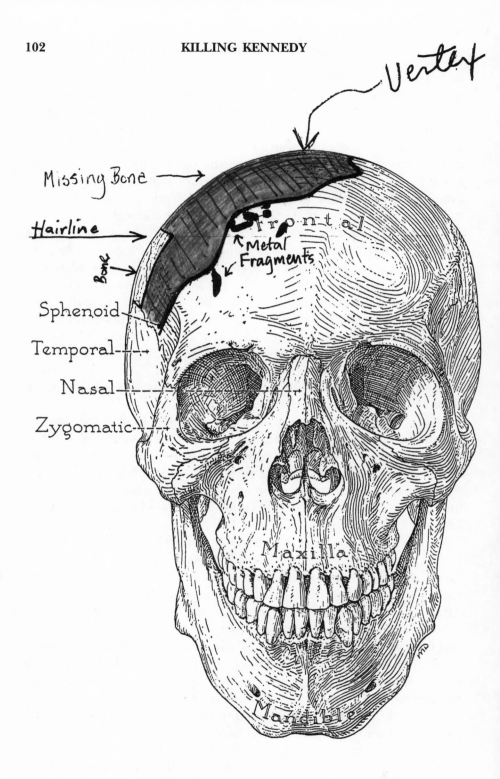

Mantik's interpretation of x-ray

drew in cannot be where it is because it is in the defect area and (referring to the lateral-view diagram) "There, the entry and associated bullet fragment are marked A and B, but nothing is so labeled in the AP diagram, and while the round fragment is drawn, it is located in the defect area, and so cannot be embedded in the back of the head."[33] Mantik agrees. I previously printed this observation myself, so it is good to hear scientists saying the same thing independently of me. But there still remains a question of these X-rays actually showing the bone either missing in the back of the head in that area, or is it missing in the front of the skull? Again, the answer seems to be that this clever forgery is trying to do both to confuse the issue, and since the bone is missing on the lateral view toward the front of the head and not in the back where it was gone when all of the witnesses saw the body, then the AP view must correspond to that, as Donald Siple, M.D., insisted long ago.

The trouble with this is that the lateral view, showing much of the frontal bone gone, has to be read with the AP view, which shows a large part of the head missing either in the front or the back. Since the lateral view clearly shows that the back of the head is intact, the missing bone has to be forward on the head. The two pictures do not correspond to each other, even when accepting that the AP view is a "modified Waters" projection—at an angle shot from below the nose somewhat upward through the skull rather than straight on. (A Waters view shows the maxillary sinuses in the cheeks. In a normal AP view, the Petrous bone is projected through the middle of the orbit.) Although there is evidence to the contrary, these may be two different skulls of two different men. The Waters views, assuming that the missing bone depicted in the lateral view was in the same place, would move that large defect, and it would appear to be higher or lower depending upon the direction the central ray of the X-ray beam was pointed.

There has been an attempt to claim that the original X-rays do in fact show the frontal bone in place on the AP view where other radiologists find it missing. I think this is proof that we are looking at composites, because it can be interpreted both ways. The laterals seem to show that frontal bone is missing in that area and not anywhere toward the rear of the head in a manner that corresponds to the large defect described in the autopsy report. Nevertheless, some of the bone has been spotted with bright lighting, in the Archives. Mantik says that, referring to the area of bone on the side of the head just above the zygoma, "the fracture lines are pretty

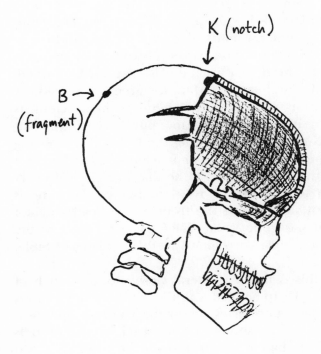

If Lattimer's AP drawing depicts the right front of the head missing, then the lateral drawing should look like this.

If Lattimer's AP drawing depicts the right rear of the head missing, then the lateral drawing should look like this. Note bullet fragment (B) not attached to skull, but in the defect itself.

good evidence that this bone is *present!*"[34] But that is only one part of what appears to be missing.

HOW DID THE HOUSE COMMITTEE DECIDE on the exact place to crop the X-rays they published? They cut out the EOP area, and the place of entry described in the autopsy report!

"I think Dr. Lattimer was fully aware of the ambiguous nature of this AP X-ray, so he drew an ambiguous sketch. However, either interpretation of his picture causes it to clash with the lateral sketch and/or printed descriptions of where the wounds were. . . . Although this X-ray contains a lot of information consistent with the autopsy doctors' account, the AP view does not show the margin of the defect reaching that far back down in the rear of the head. It would appear that, at least, the image of one of those separately received fragments has been added to the picture, making it a composite."[35]

There are two lateral X-rays in the Clark Panel's listing, and both are listed as left lateral. "The autopsy report places both the entry wound and the exit defect in the right half of the skull. Why would there be only views of the left side, obscuring the defect with a more prominent image of intact bone?"[36] Jerrol Custer, the X-ray tech at the autopsy who took the films, states that they took both left and right laterals. We have all discussed this with him many times.

Weatherly then presents an argument that one of the "left laterals" is actually a right lateral. He bases this on the large 10 cm bone fragment that seems to be displaced on the top rear of the head in the lateral view, and says that this is actually on the left side and as such corresponds to the 10 cm piece drawn on the left side of the skull by Boswell, constituting one of the three flaps of scalp and bone described by Boswell. Adjacent to it was a 10 cm piece of parietal bone missing on the right and which was recovered, arriving at the autopsy at midnight with two other small pieces of bone.

His study indicates that the X-ray penetrates the bone twice over part of its surface, making a stronger image on the X-ray—which tells one which side the X-ray tube was on. He also thinks it's a right lateral because the detached flap of scalp and bone above the right ear is not obscured by any overlapping image of bone from the left side, as it ought to be in a left lateral view.

"This is even more evident in the unenhanced X-ray, where the fragment seems to be sitting by itself.[37]

It isn't enough to say that there is confusion over whether this is a right or a left lateral X-ray. It seems to combine elements of both. In fact, I think I can see a place where one part of the head appears twice, viewed from both the left and right.

Dr. David O. Davis describes a fracture line extending from the embedded metallic fragment to the rearmost corner of the bone fragment in the right temple.[38] Dr. Davis regards this as the rear margin of the defect, and so above it one should see bone only on the left side. One can see a fracture that closely parallels the one described by Dr. Davis, but on the left side. The fracture starting near the rear of the skull and curving upward to meet the defect margin appears to be superimposed over a similar fracture on the left side.

Have bone images from a left lateral view been reversed and transplanted into what was once a right lateral X-ray? That could be the reason why one no longer sees the exit defect in the back of the skull, where numerous witnesses saw it.

This picture seems to consist of three distinct parts. Much of the rear of the skull, as far forward as the temple area and where Dr. Davis describes the edge of the defect, looks like a transplanted image from a left lateral projection, and so actually shows the left rear area. It would make sense to replace a large area of the right side, to avoid creating a composite showing identifiable features from both sides. Such a creation would not withstand comparison to a genuine premortem X-ray.

From the displaced fragment upward, and from the defect margin forward to about where the coronal suture should be, I think the images come from the original right lateral film. Forward of the coronal suture, there is apparently a huge defect with the right forehead and bones once underlying the right side of the face all missing, so that the only images are cast by structures inside the skull.

With the whole right front of the skull missing, the X-rays might have no identifiable features left that are unique to the right side of the head. The film could be compared with a genuine antemortem X-ray of the left side of the head, and be 'authenticated' as showing the President's skull."[39]

Mantik, who is looking at the actual X-rays, has an advantage over Weatherly. Mantik is also a professor of physics, as well as a radiologist. He agrees with Weatherly's interpretations for the most part, but he says there are just two different composites: (1) the left and right laterals have a patch added to cover over the large defect in the back; and (2) the AP view has a 6.5mm fragment superimposed over the small initial fragment described by Siebert and O'Niell in their FBI report of the autopsy. This is placed at the "juncture of the bone," which we assume is where there is a large displaced piece of bone in the area of what is called the "skullcap."

AUTHENTICATION BY THE HSCA

There is no way of knowing whether the pictures of teeth and the skull X-rays published by the House are from the same X-ray, as they are separate. The skull X-rays are carefully cropped so that one does not see the teeth in the published photos. The teeth were used as a primary means of identifying the autopsy X-rays.

Whether we are looking at left or right laterals become key questions because it appears in the published copies of the X-rays that part of the right front of the face is missing.

Weatherly writes, "I am proposing that the lateral X-ray combines elements of both a right and a left lateral projection. Identifiable features such as suture lines would be mirror images of each other in the two lateral films, one a left lateral and the other a right lateral with left lateral 'replacement parts.'

"If the composite X-ray needed to be compared to a left lateral premortem film to authenticate its suture lines or vascular grooves, it was called a left lateral autopsy X-ray, in which case there were officially two left lateral views. If the composite needed to be compared to a right lateral premortem film to authenticate, say, the dental work, then it was called a right lateral view.

"The HSCA consultants were compartmented, did not share information, and did not retain their materials. The key to the defective 'authentication' was that whoever was running the show could decide, for each consultant, how to represent the composite X-ray, or whether to show it to them at all."[40]

Dr. Lowell Levine, who authenticated the films by dental comparison, turned in a report to the House Committee on September 7, 1978.[41] In this report, all antemortem and autopsy skull X-rays that he had to work with were given an orientation, and the two autopsy X-rays were called right (#2) and left (#3) laterals.

At some time before the report was photographed as an exhibit, somebody went through it and scratched off all the lateral identifications for the autopsy X-rays, and most of those for the antemortem X-rays.[42] Who did this?

Levine's description of autopsy #3 indicates that it is a left lateral, as it shows the teeth on the left side of the head more prominently.

Eyeballing autopsy #2 (Levine Exhibits, pp. 62–68, HSCA, Volume VII), we determine that it is a right lateral when comparing the teeth which show most prominently superimposed on those on the left side with the teeth of the antemortem exhibit of the right side dental pictures.

Two forensic anthropologists, Drs. Ellis R. Kerley and Clyde C. Snow, helped authenticate the skull X-rays, along with Dr. Levine. There is no indication of whether they are looking at left or right laterals in their report.

The House published the findings by Dr. Ellis and Dr. Snow, and they state that the following anatomical features were used in their authentication: "The outlines of the sella turcica, the complex patterns of the cranial sutures (the joints uniting the bones of the skull), and location and arrangement of the vascular grooves (the shallow depressions on the inner surface of the skull which mark the course of blood vessels) were the same. There was also nearly exact duplication of the honeycomb-like air cells of the mastoid bone."[43]

WEATHERLY WRITES: "I think Drs. Kerley and Snow saw autopsies #2 and #3 represented as left lateral views, compared them to the left lateral Groover film, and made limited use of the right lateral White film, using it only to compare centrally located features such as the sella turcica. Since they don't say what they looked at or when, this is only an educated guess. Their report has no attached exhibits, so they were apparently not allowed to photograph anything. Why not?"[44]

Dr. David O. Davis was only allowed to see enhanced versions of autopsies #1 and #2. His job was to interpret the films and provide a description of the wounds.[45] Weatherly continues, "Similarly, Dr. Lawrence Angel studied X-rays #1 and #2 and his specific responsibility was to explain where the separate bone fragments could fit in the exit wound.[46] Their descriptions lead me to wonder whether they really saw the same films, but for the moment it is enough to point out that neither one mentions seeing autopsy #3.§

"In the August 4, 1978, report of Dr. G. M. McDonnel, there is specific mention of a right lateral autopsy X-ray.[47] Dr. McDonnel examined this along with the autopsy AP and left lateral projections, and some of the antemortem films. McDonnel found a number

§Note Dr. Davis's parenthetical comment at the bottom of p. 225 (7 HSCA) where he mentions a right lateral view "taken post autopsy."

of common features.[48] Some of the items of similarity come from comparison of AP views of the skull with antemortem, but numbers 1, 4, 5, and 6 of McDonnel's list describe structures which would be best seen in a lateral view, but which being located near the midplane of the skull, should not have distinct 'left' and 'right' lateral images. There is no mention of suture lines, air cells, or any other feature that would be recognizably different in left and right lateral projections.

"I think Dr. McDonnel was given a specific list of comparisons to make, and in case he became overly curious, his only premortem lateral X-ray showed the left side of the head. It is worth pointing out that items 4, 5, and 6 refer to structures inside the skull that are generally visible in a lateral view even if there is no damage. So the fact that he describes these features does not necessarily mean that the right front of the skull was missing from the X-ray that he saw.

"To summarize, *it is possible for the AP and lateral X-rays to be composites, in the way that I described, and yet be 'authenticated' by comparison with genuine antemortem X-rays of the President. The key elements were compartmentalization of the Committee's experts, strict control over what they saw, and strict limitations on what (if anything) they could reproduce in their exhibits.*"[49] [author's emphasis].

Weatherly then asks the hard question: "Who exercised this control?" Look out for the New York connection in the cover-up by the House Assassinations Committee. "On page 348 of the Medical Evidence Panel's report, the very last page, is a memo from Dr. Michael Baden listing the X-rays. Autopsies #2 and #3 are listed as right and left lateral respectively, and there can be no mistake since it is specifically mentioned that #2 has pencil lines on it, as does the published lateral picture. This is the only place in the entire volume where it is spelled out that the published lateral X-ray is a right lateral view. The identification is credited to Dr. John Ebersole, who supposedly marked and identified the X-rays.

"Dr. Baden, the chairman of the Medical Evidence Panel, seems to have reserved for himself the privilege of officially identifying autopsy #2 as a right lateral X-ray. Was that a state secret in 1978? If so, he could point to Dr. Ebersole as the one who let it slip. Dr. Baden is thus covered from both sides, and what does that say about his role?"[50]

Weatherly then goes for the throat: "I think the preceding not only shows that HSCA's validation methods contained a truck-sized hole, but describes the truck that was driven through it. *There are provocative indications that the various Committee consultants were, in fact, presented with several different versions of 'autopsy #2.* [author's emphasis].' This gives us some clues as to how the X-ray images may have evolved over time.

"In the report of Dr. Davis, note that he describes the defect in the bone as extending only as far forward as the coronal suture. Furthermore, he describes a fracture through the frontal bone at about the midline, and also a fracture through the roof and floor of the right orbit. There is no mention of any part of the frontal bone or orbit being missing, as the current lateral X-ray seems to depict.[51] Dr. Angel's 10/24/77 memorandum, and attached drawings, suggest a defect with a large part of the frontal bone missing, including some from the left side.[52] [Author's note: I pointed this out in my earlier books, and the whole issue of the right frontal bone apparently missing was first determined by myself and Dr. Siple in 1979.]

"I wonder how he could describe something so different from what Dr. Davis saw, if they both looked at the same thing."[53]

Weatherly then notes that Dr. Joseph Davis indicated during the medical panel's review of the autopsy materials with Drs. Humes and Boswell that there was a long trail of bullet fragments on the X-ray they were looking at which stretched from the external occipital protuberance (and corresponded to one of Ebersole's pencil lines). Dr. Davis told the others that he could actually see a trail of spots on the X-rays leading upward from the vicinity of the EOP.[54] No such thing shows in the current autopsy #2. (Mantik says that the trail of fragments does not show on the prints but that there is a "faint suggestion" on the X-rays which is partially covered up by the white patch). As was stated early in this chapter, part of the trail is visible from the EOP, but the rest is covered up by the "white patch" used to fake the X-ray.

This was quickly followed by the famous scene where Dr. George Loquvam broke it off by shouting, "I don't think this discussion belongs in this record. . . . We have no business recording this. . . . This is for us to decide between ourselves; I don't think this belongs on this record. . . . I don't think this belongs in the damn record."

Dr. Humes: "Well, it probably doesn't."

Dr. Loquvam: "You guys are nuts. You guys are nuts writing this stuff. It doesn't belong in that damn record."

Dr. Baden: "I think the only purpose of its being in the record is to explain to Dr. Humes what—"

Dr. Loquvam: "Why not turn off the record and explain to him and then go back and talk again."

Dr. Baden: "Well, our problem is not to get our opinions, but to get his opinions."

Dr. Loquvam: "All right then, keep our opinions off. Here's Charles and Joe talking like mad in the damn record, and it doesn't belong in it. Sorry."

Dr. Baden: "Dr. Humes, realizing our concerns, if there is anything that you or Dr. Boswell can say that can help clarify any further the entrance wound and track of the bullet in the head, we would be most appreciative."

Dr. Humes: "I think we're at a distinct disadvantage because, as I said, when we catalogued the photographs and numbered them, and spent half a day or day to do it, I'll confess to possibly even overlooking the area to which you gentlemen, and apparently someone else, have directed attention. I would not attempt to make an interpretation of what it represents because I can't at this point."[55] I first published this fight over the placement of the rear head entry wound in *High Treason*. It seems clear that the central issue of where the entry hole was on the back of the head was very sensitive, and when it came up during the above meeting, caused a fight. Humes questions the photos and ignores that he was supposed to have given them a much more intense examination years before, along with the other doctors, when they were asked to sign a statement prepared by the Justice Department in 1967 that the autopsy photographs and X-rays did not change their opinion as expressed in the autopsy report. The pictures sure didn't, as their report totally contradicts them! And if Humes was forced to sign a statement in 1967 that said something he didn't believe, he certainly tells us here that he cannot remember that, but goes back to square one: telling us what he saw and experienced: an entry hole some inches further down on the head. Humes, in his very next exchange in the above, says that what they are calling an entry hole in the cowlick area is a clot of blood and not the entry hole, which he tirelessly insists is near the hairline some inches away.[56]

DR. LATTIMER'S EARLY DRAWINGS made from his observations of the autopsy X-rays show the right frontal bone to be missing down to the right eye, just as I described it in my early books. Dr. McDonnel describes similar damage and missing frontal bone,[57] writing that there is a "nearly complete loss of structure of the right frontal and parietal bone."[58] *The published X-ray is supposed to indicate the entry hole above the lambdoid suture, which is the border of the occipital bone and the parietal bone.* But McDonnel wrote that the entry hole was in the right occipital bone and repeats it several times,[59] This is not consistent with the published X-rays.

Weatherly points out that the Clark Panel's report of 1969 "is rather vague on the source of their statement that the entry wound is about 10 cm above the occipital bulge . . . with no discussion of how far the plate and X-ray tube were from the head, one can only suppose this measurement was made on the film itself."[60] McDonnel measured the large metal fragment as being 9.6 cm above the EOP. It ought to be clear to us that the entry hole which Petty and the other doctors insist is at the cowlick in the X-ray is not there on the body itself if the autopsy doctors say it is not. It might be there on the X-ray, but it isn't what the autopsy doctors saw and experienced.

CONCLUSION

Some additional points that surfaced from the heretofore secret documents follow.

Were the autopsy X-rays altered? Dr. John Ebersole, now deceased, was the acting chief of radiology that weekend while the regular chief, Dr. Loy Thietje Brown, was in Chicago for the RSNA meetings. Ebersole was trained in nuclear physics at Duke University and at Oak Ridge, Tennessee, and served on the first two nuclear submarines, the *Nautilus* and the *Sea Wolf.* He started his residency at Bethesda and had just completed it in July 1963.[61] He had experience in interpreting X-rays involving gunshot wounds in "perhaps twenty to twenty-five cases."[62]

Ebersole owed his heart and soul to the Navy and probably would have done anything he was asked—including, as we know, making X-rays the next day by taping pieces of metal fragments to bone fragments that might have been used to make the composites we now have. He also claims to have operated the X-ray equipment,[63] which is highly doubtful since there were two technicians present who normally did that and who claim to have done it. Ebersole claims to have carried the films to the lab upstairs himself,[64] waited for their development, and returned them. The men claim to have done this. It seems highly unlikely that a commander in the Navy would have done those things himself, and the men say it would have been impossible.[65]

More proof may exist that the X-rays were altered which answers both the question above and that which follows in the next section: Dr. Humes described that the X-rays they saw that night "disclosed to us multiple minute fragments of radiopaque material traversing a line from the wound in the occiput to just above the right eye, with a rather sizable fragment visible by X-ray just above the right eye."[66] Dr. Mantik says that some of the line is visible but "a good portion is covered by the large white patch." This line of fragments is not visible in the present X-rays as extending from the entry wound. There is a different line of fragments across the very top of the head five or six inches above where it would have entered near the hairline, according to the autopsy report.

Are the X-rays in evidence the ones that were taken in 1963? Evidently that was in some doubt, as Dr. Michael Baden, in asking a question, put it this way: "Dr. Weston brought up the point about interpreting X-rays. Hopefully you will be able to provide us two functions. One is discussions about technically what was happening when you were taking these X-rays, *and in fact these are the X-rays you have taken* [author's emphasis] as well as any insight you might give us as a radiologist as to the findings."[67]

Ebersole: "These are the films."

Baden: "These are the films that you took?"

Ebersole: "Yes."

Baden: "And that you put into the Archives later?"

Ebersole: "Right."[68]

Baden: "And as we look at each of these X-rays, implicit in your discussion of the X-rays is that these are the X-rays that you took at the time of the autopsy and that you later labeled and put into the Archives?"

"Yes."

"Have you seen anything that would suggest any alteration of the X-rays in any way, shape, or form as you have viewed them apart from the heat artifacts (blisters) you have discussed on the skull X-ray?"

"No."[69] It sounds like Baden had grave doubts about this phony material, but perhaps not.

BOSWELL SAID THE X-RAYS WERE TAKEN "just to identify a bullet, they were not taken as clinical X-rays." He stated the photographs "didn't portray as much of the things as we would have liked."[70]

Dr. Boswell continues to exhibit the greatest contradiction in his statements, as do the other doctors on this and other issues. For instance, Boswell says that his subsequent viewing of the X-rays was consistent with his understanding of the location of the entry wound to the head. (The House here wrote: "It should be noted that the Clark Panel report of the location of the head wound was also based on the X-ray in addition to the photograph and they placed the entry wound to the head approximately 100mm higher up than the autopsy doctors.")[71]

My investigator, Richard Waybright, went to see Dr. Boswell in his home, and came away disturbed by Boswell's reaction to the X-rays. Waybright wrote that the autopsy X-rays deeply troubled the doctor. Boswell noted that the X-rays did not show the crack in the floor of the orbit of the eye at all. Waybright went on to say Dr. Boswell "appeared to be troubled by the X-rays and continued to look at them. He stated that they did not look right, but that he would have to see the originals before he could make a valid judgment."[72]

"I believe that he declined to make a judgment because they were not the right X-rays. However, he had not seen the X-rays in twenty-seven years and they may have confused him. It is my opinion that these are not the X-rays that Dr. Boswell saw on the night of November 22, 1963. His statement that they did not look right and his obvious bewilderment at viewing them tend to indicate that either they are not what he saw, or they are obvious fakes, and he did not want to commit himself at this time."[73] Boswell had seen them during his interview with the House Committee, unless those he was shown were different from the ones they published, which is what we showed him.

The X-rays may be in part authentic, yet the images seen on them have been altered in some fashion. Therefore, they may still contain subtle evidence proving a shot from in front, as doctors Robinson and Mantik argue, but this evidence is so technical and obscure that it was missed by the forgers and everyone else for thirty years.

If the 6.5mm fragment is in fact against the rear of the skull inside, as Mantik thinks, it may constitute the most tangible evidence yet of a shot from in front.

5

The Hoax of the Century: Faking the Zapruder Film

Time has been deleted from the film. With time removed, the film is useless as a clock for the assassination.

—Newcomb and Adams

IN MY LAST TWO BOOKS I questioned the validity of the films in the case. As time goes by it is becoming increasingly clear that much of the publicly known evidence in the case, both privately held and that in the National Archives, consists of stage props. My questions concerning the films have stimulated much discussion and dissent. Many who suspected—or believed—the films were altered or fake got in touch with me and shared their research, ideas, and information. The lid came off one more can of worms! I found a very large number of people who had suspected—or believed—for a long time that the famous films of the murder might be altered or fake. Each person who approached often had a piece of the puzzle different from the next. A picture began to emerge. This was the first national notice that the Zapruder film is a massive hoax and is an animation.*

The real film of the assassination was taken by someone else, and is quite different. It was taken right alongside the car and showed all that is not in the Zapruder film, which was taken from much farther away. The first film was used by the FBI to reconstruct the crime, and it's still secret.

The Zapruder film is for public consumption.

In 1967, Professor Josiah Thompson, whom I respect, was a paid consultant on the assassination and its visual evidence for *Life* maga-

* See also my chapters on the film in both *High Treason 2*, pp. 357–373, and *Killing the Truth*, pp. 319–336.

115

zine not long after the assassination. He had early access to the film and described his viewing of it there, writing that "if [the Zapruder film] is studied with the utmost care and under optimum conditions, it can yield answers to enormous questions. Where did the shots come from, and when were they fired? Limited in scope though it is, the Zapruder film is capable of answering these questions . . .[1] Quite obviously, the Zapruder footage contained the nearest thing to 'absolute truth' about the sequence of events in Dealey Plaza."[2]

That is what they want Prof. Thompson and us to think.

The one thing that has become deadly certain is that far too much of the assassination evidence that critics and the public had relied upon for many years was phony.

There is no question not only that oil man H. L. Hunt had bought and paid for the local Dallas offices of the FBI, the Secret Service, and the CIA but that J. Edgar Hoover himself was "owned" by and conspired with his friends, the Dallas oilmen. Hunt employed former FBI men as well, so he was informed of all that happened there.

A fast shell game went on at the Jamieson Lab[3] in Dallas where Zapruder had taken the film to be developed. From there it may have found its way to the National Photographic Interpretation Center (NPIC) film lab in Washington.[4] Erwin Schwartz, Zapruder's partner, said that the film did not reach Jamieson until after 6 P.M.[5]

Zapruder was asked by Wesley Liebeler of the Warren Commission, ". . . after you had the film developed, I understand Mr. Sorrels from the Secret Service came over and helped you get the films developed and you gave two copies of your films to Mr. Sorrels, is that correct?" It was at this point that Forest Sorrels, now deceased, of the Dallas Secret Service office, had to have gotten control of the film, and the film-lab game began.

"Yes. One we have sent to Washington the same night and one went over for the viewers of the FBI on Ervay Street. . . . The Secret Service—I brought one roll there and they told me to dispatch it by Army plane or I don't know what they had done with it but it was supposed to have gone to Washington, and one of them, I believe, remained here with Mr. Sorrels. He came to my office quite a few times to show them to different people."[6] Zapruder can't get his lines straight, and this shows evidence of coaching. Officially, there was only the original and three copies of the film, two of which went to the Secret Service, and one copy and the original were sold to *Life*, but no sale had occurred on the day of the assassination. The official story is that the Secret Service gave one copy to the FBI.

*   *   *

ZAPRUDER TELLS US that a copy of the film was flown to Washington that day, but it is completely unreasonable that a *copy* of a film of one of the most major crimes of the century would have been sent for study there, and not the *original.* The Dallas Secret Service and the Dallas FBI would have been working closely together and helping each other. Since Zapruder has said elsewhere that he retained a copy which was shown to the FBI, the Secret Service, and others in his offices, as he says above, there is an obvious contradiction in how many copies existed.

There are a couple of bombshells in all of this. Erwin Schwartz, Zapruder's partner, insists that *Life* never got the film until at least Tuesday, November 27. Schwartz accompanied Zapruder to the film labs and stayed with him the whole time the film was being developed and copied on November 22, and was with him also when *Life*'s Richard Stolley collected the film at the Adolphus Hotel on Tuesday, he says. The copy given to *Life* was to be used to make stills.[7] This would have given the conspirators plenty of time to alter the film before *Life* got it. However, *Life*'s November 29 edition was printed on Tuesday, November 26th, which gives damn little time that day to get plates made for the printing presses from the frames in the film. The only answer to this is that *Life* must have got the film before Tuesday, clandestinely—perhaps on Saturday, November 23. I believe that additional, officially unaccounted-for copies of the film were distributed as soon as it was developed on the day of the assassination. Initial alterations were simple and easy.

Since Schwartz himself delivered the film to Stolley, he does not believe Stolley's claim to have been looking at the film before then. "If Zapruder gave Stolley a copy to take with him, Schwartz doesn't know anything about it," Richard Bartholomew says. It makes no sense to me that Zapruder would have given *Life* the original film that Saturday without a check, and we have no knowledge of money passing until the more formal contract made on Monday, November 25. At that point, *Life* would cut a check and send it overnight to Zapruder and collect the film. On the other hand, the film Schwartz describes taking to Stolley was for making stills, and so would be a copy, not the original. Furthermore, Schwartz, whose memory could conceivably be dimmed by the intervening thirty-one years, does not think that Stolley even saw it that Saturday morning, and was gone from Zapruder's offices by ten or ten-thirty in the morning.

It would seem that *Life* did not officially have the film until Monday, November 25, the date of their contract with Zapruder. That would theoretically give them one day to prepare the photographs.

Since *Life* was a news magazine and they had a very big story, if they were willing to spend an extra million bucks or so to speed it up, there may have been no problem with the short lead time.

The deal was for a hundred fifty thousand dollars, to be paid at the rate of twenty-five thousand per year.

Schwartz confirms that all the employees of *Life* and anyone else who happened to be present were shown the film repeatedly while they were there, and he insists that he saw blood and brains come out the back of JFK's head, even though we do not see this in the film today. Schwartz said that Dallas police with shotguns were at Zapruder's office a half an hour after the shooting.

Philip Melanson argues in his *Third Decade* article, "Hidden Exposure: Cover-Up and Intrigue in the CIA's Secret Possession of the Zapruder Film," that the original film in fact went to the National Photographic Interpretation Center (NPIC) in Washington, and could have been altered there. He tells us that the technology to resize images, create special effects, and remove frames existed in 1963. The equipment was there to analyze films but not necessarily to alter them.

But Daryll Weatherly and I question whether the forgery would have happened there. It seems to me to be irrational for the film to have been altered at NPIC, unless we are looking at a blatant military coup. The alternatives are that they analyzed the film there, the film was altered somewhere else, and this is a red herring.

Researcher Paul Hoch discovered the NPIC story, when in 1976 he was able to obtain a batch of documents through a Freedom of Information Act request from the CIA. Item #450 was nine pages of documents relating to an analysis of the Zapruder film conducted for the Secret Service by the CIA's NPIC. Philip Melanson writes, "For the first time, there was evidence that CIA had possessed and analyzed the film. Apparently the CIA had gotten the film from the Secret Service. . . . Did NPIC make extra, unaccounted-for copies; or did the NPIC-produced copies somehow end up as the Dallas copies? Was NPIC producing third-generation prints; or had it somehow obtained the original?"[8] An item in this batch of documents lists the time it took to process the film. It tells us that two hours were required to "Proc. dry," which always refers to developing original film. "If NPIC had been working with a copy, the first step would have been to *print*, then process." The item then says that it took one hour to do a "Print test." Melanson writes that "print test" refers to a short piece of film printed from the original and used to check the exposure—to see if the negative is too light or too dark—before printing copies from the original.

"Thus there is strong indication that NPIC had the original."[9] The print they made may have been from one of the three negatives Schwartz mentions. If NPIC had a print, it made a negative from that, then did the print test from it, which may be more likely, according to assassination film researcher Martin Shackelford. At the very least, the film was analyzed at NPIC for the number, timing, and sequence of the shots, but it could have been altered there as well.†

Melanson suggests that Zapruder may have made a bargain with the Secret Service on the day of the assassination. "Whether someone in authority *asked* or *told* Zapruder, indications are that he did indeed relinquish it . . . If Zapruder *did* manage to strike a bargain with the Secret Service, the terms may well have been that the Service took the original for a brief time (perhaps only eighteen hours) but promised to keep the loan secret so as not to jeopardize Zapruder's chances for a deal. If potential buyers knew that the original had been out of Zapruder's hands, they might have perceived it as secondhand merchandise; if they knew the government was printing extra copies, the exclusivity of the purchase rights might be in doubt. Exclusivity was very important to the deal, and Zapruder knew it. *Life*'s Richard B. Stolley recalled that through all the chaos, Zapruder kept his 'business sense.' "[10]

"And why would the Secret Service be satisfied with a copy which was less clear than the original?" Melanson writes. "Since it seems certain that NPIC conducted its analysis on the night of the assassination, this greatly increases the likelihood that NPIC had the original."[11] But Melanson and Paul Hoch have not proved that the film was there on November 22, 1963.

Stolley also said that "if the federal government had not been in such disarray at that moment [immediately after the assassination] somebody with authority and a sense of history would probably have asked Zapruder for the original film and he probably would have relinquished it."[12]

In a letter to me, John R. Woods II, the author of an important work on the visual evidence in the case, asks, "Did NPIC create different versions of the film in order to create several different versions in which the government could decide which film would fit the scenario?"

We always have to be watchful for false trails and red herrings in the evidence. To my way of thinking, it is just as likely that the film might have been first roughly altered and a new "original" struck

† See also *High Treason 2* by the author, pp 369–371.

off that day in Dallas. Over the next days and weeks the copies were made picked up and destroyed, with altered copies substituted in their place.

I had high-level information in Dallas that the original Zapruder film (from Zapruder's camera) was first obtained by H. L. Hunt before *Life* bought what they thought was the original. The FBI, the Secret Service, and the military allowed Hunt to either control the evidence or be used as the front for control of it by those using him. The indication is that Hunt's people obtained it and passed it on to the FBI who sent it to headquarters in Washington shortly after it was developed.

In view of the close relationship between the FBI's J. Edgar Hoover and Cartha DeLoach and *Life* wherein the FBI would and did plant completely false stories on that magazine,†† we might suppose that if the FBI had the film, and if the case was being faked, then they may have fed frames from the film to *Life* as needed to fulfill the emerging official story.

And for this we have a witness. Erwin Schwartz, Zapruder's partner, is related by marriage to Richard Bartholomew, a researcher. Schwartz told Bartholomew that after the film was developed, Schwartz took either the original or a copy of the film to Hensley Field Naval Air Station the night of November 22, and it was flown to Washington about nine or 9:30 P.M. Actually, the time may have been a little later, as Schwartz has the work being finished at Kodak at this time—or the developing was done a bit earlier. This would have allowed for alteration in Washington at NPIC or somewhere else.

Schwartz told Richard Bartholomew what happened earlier that day just after the assassination. He ran over to the Dal-Tex Building where the offices of their company, Jennifer Juniors, were located— they had the entire fourth and fifth floors. Two policemen were standing in the elevator vestibule with shotguns when Schwartz got back to the office at about 2:00 P.M. As Lieutenant Day was removing the rifle from the TSBD, Schwartz walked past them going to his office, saw Zapruder, and asked him why the police were there. "I don't know. I told them to go get somebody in authority. I'm not giving that film to them," Zapruder replied.[13] Then Forrest Sorrels, head of the Dallas Secret Service, arrived with a reporter (Harry McCormack) from the *Dallas Morning News*. Zapruder told them what he had seen. Sorrels said he would like a copy of the film,

†† Detailed in Anthony Summer's *Official and Confidential: The Secret Life of J. Edgar Hoover*, (New York: Putnam, 1993), pp. 208–213.

and the reporter said that they could develop it at Channel 8, a local TV station.

Zapruder, Schwartz, McCormack, Sorrels, and the cops went to a police car, and with the siren going, drove to the TV station, where they were sent on to Kodak. There they watched the film developed through a glass partition. The film was developed about 2:45 P.M. One of the cops then called Sorrels, who had to leave because of the capture of Oswald, and told him "you can see everything."

Bartholomew says that they had told Sorrels they would go and get a copy made for him. To do that, Jamieson made them a negative which they had to take back to Kodak for developing. The first time any money was mentioned was when they got out of the car at Jamieson. "A guy came out of the shadows and said, 'I'd like to offer you two hundred dollars. I'm with the *Dallas Morning News*— for every still we use off of your film.' "[14]

According to Schwartz, they watched the copy negatives being made at Jamieson and only three were made. "The original was still intact. It had never been split. It was still on 16 mm film." They returned to Kodak where the positives were made from the three copies. About twenty or thirty people saw the film projected there several times. The two partners ate food from machines while the developing was going on. The work was finished close to 9:00 or 9:30 P.M. Sorrels then called them and asked them to come to the jail to deliver a copy of the film to him. Later, Sorrels asked them to take the film to the Secret Service office. Sorrels had not seen the film; it was to be flown to Washington that Friday night from Hensley field.

That night Schwartz was offered $10,000 just to introduce reporters from the *Saturday Evening Post* to Zapruder. By early the following morning there were many media people at their offices, and offers for the film were already at $100,000. Zapruder introduced Richard Stolley of *Life* and said he was going to sell it to the magazine. An agreement was drawn up and signed. Stolley then left. "The agreement was that Schwartz would bring the film up to him the first part of the following week. He did not leave with the film in hand."[15] The film continued to be shown to employees in Zapruder and Schwartz's offices off and on through that Saturday.

THERE IS AN UNCONFIRMED STORY that a report of the Los Alamos Scientific Laboratory found that the Kodak symbols were missing from the original film. We do not know if the Review Board has released this HSCA report. If true, that would mean that what *Life* or Henry and Abraham Zapruder thought was the original film, isn't.

On December 4, J. Edgar Hoover informed Lee Rankin of the Warren Commission that he was told beforehand that the FBI had "a copy" of the film. "The film being referred to was taken by Abraham Zapruder, who, after making a copy available to the FBI, sold the film to *Life* magazine. . . . The Central Intelligence Agency has inquired if the film copy in possession of this Bureau can be loaned to that Agency solely for training purposes." This is, of course, one copy too many. Richard Stolley of *Life* wrote his boss, C. D. Jackson, on November 25 in his contract with Zapruder, that three copies were made, one copy going to *Life* with the original, and two copies going to the Secret Service—one of these sent to Washington. The Secret Service gave a copy to the FBI, but the evidence that I've gathered shows that more copies were made, and the film began to proliferate right from the start. There is better evidence for FBI possession of the original in a memo from Cartha DeLoach at the FBI to M. Mohr[16] quoted later in this chapter.

The story is that the Dallas Secret Service was the source of the copy that went to Hoover and the FBI. Certainly the film or films Zapruder and Schwartz took to Hensley Field went to both NPIC and the FBI in Washington. The second Secret Service copy was probably sent along to the Washington Secret Service office, though we would hope in a separate plane. None of this explains how a copy, which he showed to many people over the next weeks, remained in Zapruder's hands.

The *official story* from Stolley is that he got the original film and copy on Saturday, the day after the assassination. For this and the rest of the known history, see this endnote.[17] The Chicago *Life* office had it on Saturday. C. D. Jackson saw the copy of it in New York on Sunday and decided to buy it. He had to see it on Sunday, therefore. We might theorize that the *Life* sale was being set up without Zapruder knowing that they might already have the film. A copy might have been made that Zapruder did not know about and sent to *Life*, while quick alterations had already been made in Washington or Dallas.

Schwartz is solid that the film did not go to *Life* until Tuesday, which gave them almost no time to use the film for their November 29 issue. Zapruder was not present when Erwin Schwartz gave the film to Stolley. It is possible that there was a preliminary contract made on Saturday, November 23, and either with or without cash, the deal was struck and Zapruder let *Life* have the film then, firming it up with the Monday, November 25, contract. It just seems peculiar to me that he would have given them the film without both the cash and a written agreement.

Schwartz also said that Jamieson made three negatives and no positives, so they had to return to Kodak to have copies made. He was with Zapruder throughout the processing and said that the film was shown to everyone present several times, and that half the screen was blank, as it was still in 16 mm.

Zapruder was directed to Dealey Plaza to make his film. He claimed that he did not want to do it or plan to do it, but that his wife and his secretary, Lillian Rogers, talked him into it. It sounds like he was used, like so many others. Schwartz said that Zapruder didn't care that Kennedy was coming, though another story claims that he intended to film JFK, but it looked like it might rain, so he left the camera at home.

It is relevant to look at the connections of Erwin Schwartz and Abraham Zapruder, whose son worked for the Department of Justice. If we are to talk about alteration of this film, then the background of its owner is pertinent.

Zapruder's partner, Schwartz, was tight with the Campisi brothers (owners of the Egyptian Lounge). These were the two Mafia dons who were the hands in Dallas of Carlos Marcello of New Orleans. Schwartz was also tight with Jack Ruby. They gambled together and went to the same clubs to gamble as did H. L. Hunt. Ruby and Schwartz had the same rabbi. Schwartz had a good knowledge of Ruby's activities and history without having read any books on the JFK case. And Erwin Schwartz hung out at the Carousel Club, Ruby's joint. It would seem probable, therefore, that Zapruder knew Ruby. A massive amount of investigation and research over the years has proven Ruby's connections and involvement with the mob.

A source states that "meeting Erwin's friends would make you feel like the casting director of *Goodfellas*." Schwartz loved to play golf at La Costa, a major mob hangout on the West Coast in the past. The lawyers for both Zapruder and Schwartz were Sam Passman and Shannon Jones. Passman also represented the Campisis, and Jones represented the CIA and did quite a bit of work for them in Texas.

THE CONTRADICTORY AND CONFUSING CHAIN of possession for the Zapruder film would seem to identify it with the other bogus stage props in the National Archives.

The evidence is fast developing that all this material is fake—faked by the conspirators who planned the murder of John Kennedy. None of it was ad hoc, after the fact, because somebody was trying to prevent a war, but was faked in concordance with the plot to overthrow Kennedy and all he stood for.§

ALTERATIONS OF THE ZAPRUDER FILM

In my last two books, *High Treason 2* and *Killing the Truth*, I maintained that the large blob showing on President Kennedy's face just after the fatal head shot is an impossibility, since moments later he was seen at Parkland Hospital and there was no damage whatsoever to his face. Some have offered various explanations for what we see in the film. Some people believe that the "blob" is simply the inside of a large flap of skin that has fallen down which reflects the sun. The problem with this is that no one at Parkland saw such a flap. It would have fallen down in the emergency room and been noticed. Dr. David Mantik became convinced during a visit with us to the National Archives to view the slides of the film on June 23, 1994, that the "blob" is an unnatural add-on to the film and *not a flap of scalp* hanging down over the face. It cannot come from the laceration reported by some witnesses at the autopsy because the President's hair leading down to his right forehead is clearly visible above the "blob" and undamaged, until the frames appear at about 335 when there is no evidence at all of a head above the blob.

The film is simply altered to show an apparent shot from behind. They want us to think the damage is to the frontal part of his head, backed up by fake X-rays. The blob obliterates a shot from in front.

I ALSO WROTE THAT IN SOME OF THE FRAMES following the fatal head shot, the figures of Jacqueline and John Kennedy appeared to be painted in, and in some frames appear to be cutouts. In several

---

§ Frame-by-frame study of the Zapruder film for those with access to a CD-ROM computer system may best be accomplished by use of Medio Multimedia's "JFK Assassination: A Visual Investigation," available for $39.95 by calling 1-800-237-6623. The disk contains four films of the assassination, including the Zapruder, Nix, Hughes, and Muchmore films, and an overview film with other footage included. Each Zapruder frame is numbered and can be studied frame by frame and in slow motion. Unfortunately, the poor resolution of CD-ROM obscures or eliminates details that are of great importance, and other means of study must be employed from slides or the actual film copies. The CD-ROM is also available from the Last Hurrah Bookshop (see Bibliography).

frames, the entire front half of the head is missing, leaving only a stub from the back of the neck and back of the head. Before this happens, but after the fatal head shot, it seemed clear that in some frames the back of the head is not just in shadow, but signs of the gaping open wound described by all witnesses in the back of the head have been painted out with black paint. Unknown to me, Fred Newcomb and Perry Adams had written extensively on the Zapruder film many years before my observations of the painted faces, and had said this: "Although splicing marks were undetectable about frame 313, it is likely that frames were removed and the remaining retouched. The appearance of 313 is vital to the health of the scenario. . . . To camouflage evidence of a shot from the front, the actual exit wound at the side of the head was covered with opaque."[18] A few frames in one of the sets of slides at the National Archives, such as 316 and 317, appear to show the margins of the hole. The hole itself is blackened across the back of the head. In the *Life* original slides at the Archives, that area is what might be called "reference black." It is so dark and unnatural-looking so that it is not shadow. "Above it, the hair sticks out toward the back—as we see from the side in frame 335. This appears in all sets of Zapruder frames, but the features are clearer in the Archives set," Martin Shackelford told me.

As for painted faces and figures in the fatal car (none of this is actually painted on the film itself), many have noted the apparent art effects after the fatal head shot, but not many have had the courage to talk about it in public. I found that lots of people from the Los Angeles area *assumed* or knew that the film was fake. They called it a product of "special effects." In other words, for more than thirty years people have been suspicious or disbelieving of this film, but almost no one dared say a word.

VERSIONS OF THE ZAPRUDER FILM

There are several main sources of the film. Two versions are probably the primary public source. The most widely known and publicized is the *Life* magazine version, which officially was bought from Abraham Zapruder the day after the assassination. When this film "leaked" out on television to the public, it was sold back to Zapruder for one dollar, and the Zapruder family has collected money for its use ever since, though charging researchers only a nominal fee. *Life* also made slides of the frames from the film and donated them to the National Archives. These slides have uncommonly well-preserved color values and clarity. One can view a carousel of the slides at the Archives in College Park, Maryland, in a good viewer sitting at a table about a foot or two away from the screen. The Stemmons Freeway sign, for instance, is very steady and well defined around its edges. The grass in the background after the car emerges from behind the sign is very green, and the outdoors is filled with sunlight glinting off the chrome and glass of the fatal car, the whole scene brightly illuminated.

Doug Mizzer says the cleaned-up version was made for public consumption. He put it this way: "This is how good it can look. It's the *final version*."[19] And, indeed, it appears to be not quite the same as the others. Even this has been changed in various versions.

The Secret Service version was loaned to the House Select Committee on Assassinations in 1976.[20]

There is a version known as the "Kurtis film" which is dark and gloomy and the colors nearly gone so that it almost appears to be a black-and-white film. It was first shown on national television on the Arts & Entertainment Cable Network by Bill Kurtis in 1992 in a show called *Who Killed JFK?: On the Trail of the Conspiracies*. The film has a message at the bottom of the TV screen saying that it was being shown "Courtesy: House Assassinations Committee." That it is from the HSCA may be in doubt because the program was produced in 1992. Where did he get the film? The Bill Kurtis video version is therefore not the actual film.

Films transferred to video for showing on TV are altered by machinery in order to fit the video format of thirty frames per second. Some frames may be taped twice and others combine fields from preceding and following frames. Why is the film so dark, and why would he show such a poor copy?

Unfortunately, this version stops at frame 316. The HSCA had a clear copy of the Secret Service version of the film, and it was shown on *In Search of Lee Harvey Oswald*. PBS broadcast the clear copy of the original film when it televised the HSCA's hearings.

Researchers often use the terms "*Life* version" or "Secret Service version" to refer to the publicly shown films which are derivatives of these, often heavily altered for television, or for screening with a projector with a speed different from eighteen frames per second.

Frames that are missing from the *Life* version are in the Secret Service version and "if you're trying to sync a real-time audio tape to the film, you don't want a film with splices in it,"[21] Doug Mizzer writes. The Kurtis version and many *Life* versions are reframed after the car passes the lamppost to Zapruder's left. The Kurtis version has the frames enlarged at the time of the head shot. Though there may be nothing sinister in this, Robert Groden did the reframing. In the earliest bootleg copies of the film, as in the October 1964 *Life* copy, JFK is at the bottom of the frame in Z-313. This is how the original film looked. When Groden steadied it, he also raised the frame, as the bottom is cut off by the projector during projection, thus producing the black bar effect at the bottom of the frame. That is the quickest way to differentiate a copy of the original film from a copy of one of Groden's steadied versions.

Mizzer says, "In different documentaries, the film is enlarged differently."

In addition, there is the Dallas FBI field office Zapruder film now located in the National Archives, but little is known about it at this writing. One might ask that if the local FBI had to continue to return to see the film in Zapruder's office, then how did they obtain this copy? And how, if Zapruder did not retain a copy, as was publicly claimed after the sale to *Life*, was the FBI able to see a copy in his offices for some time after? And, as explained above, if a copy or the original went to FBI headquarters in Washington, what happened to that? What happened to H. L. Hunt's copy? Why won't the Hunt family discuss this?

David Lifton, a researcher, has both a 35mm copy, and another copy obtained from other early sources. Lifton's film, said to be uncommonly clear, is being used for research. His video of the film is the same as the HSCA version that was being sold by the Assassination Information Center in Dallas.

There were bootleg copies that appeared at the time *Life* provided the film to Jim Garrison for his prosecution of Clay Shaw, which were copied and given to Mark Lane, and many copies made from that and given to researchers. There was a copy provided to Robert Groden sometime after the assassination and shown on a Geraldo Rivera show on March 6 and 27, 1975, for the first public showing. Many have felt that these men were used to show the film because the original had been altered and proved the government's case more than it disproved it. The government's case is protected by a false film that has key events removed.

John Woods, II, author of an important work on the visual evidence in the case—*JFK Assassination Photographs*—wrote me that he learned that there is a "European" version of the film which has no halo around the head at the time of the head shot (Z-313), but he was unable to verify this. Many people feel that the "halo" around JFK's head for a brief frame was added on to the film. The halo appears in the Nix (N-395) film, and the Muchmore film (M-

467–8). These films would have been altered in register with the Zapruder film—no big task.

In 1978, the documentary, *In Search of Lee Harvey Oswald,* was made as a syndicated program and sold to individual stations. Later, the Arts & Entertainment network bought the entire package. On it, Robert Groden showed an unspliced version of the Zapruder film. Where did he get it? He was a consultant to the HSCA at the time, and they were the only ones in official possession of an unspliced copy outside of the FBI and the Secret Service, unless one believes that the CIA, H. L. Hunt, or the military had it. The copy Groden showed on TV, otherwise uncut, started at frame 133, omitting the motorcycles seen in the beginning of the film, and had all the frames in it which were missing from the *Life* version at the point of the well-known splices where they claimed they "accidentally" broke the film.

Some versions have oddities that may be mistakes made by the forgers at the point of those splices: At about frame 208, the Kurtis version shows a wall in the background across the street, overhead of the Stemmons Freeway sign which in one frame has completely different sets of holes in it, separate from each other, doubling the number of holes. This is not a double image but is instead a repetition of two different images out of register with each other. We got a good video print of this forger's mistake or stretch-framing artifact. Frame 208 of the *Life* version is where there is another major splice. We also see double images in that frame of Rosemary Willis, the motorcycle helmet visible above the limo, the edge of the Stemmons sign, the corner of the wall, and other features.

"The obvious indication is that the background overlays were not perfectly lined up when the frame was rephotographed. From this frame forward is also where the sign does the most noticeable jumping around. Again, this occurs at the second splice point in the *Life* copy that starts at frame 208."[22] The "Jumping Sign" version is the Kurtis version of the film, "and the rest of the mistakes," as Doug Mizzer wrote in the same letter.

Mizzer proposes that some of the available versions of the film, incorporating stretch framing, composite frames, and other cinematic alterations, may in fact derive from early, clumsily forged versions that may have been shown to the official bodies while a better-looking, permanent version was prepared. Today these low-quality bootlegs still fool people. One of the early forgeries seems to have been shown on Dallas/Fort Worth television in 1991 and is now doing double duty as bootleg film.

The biggest single question we are faced with when talking about alteration of the Zapruder film is: Wouldn't the other films and photographs contradict it? Only three other films were claimed to show the shooting: those of Nix, Muchmore, and Bronson. The Bronson film was taken from one block away on the left side of the car and well behind it, too far, even if the camera was in fact running, to record information of any value about the shooting. As I have written in previous books, Bronson, who was taking snapshots, denies having gotten his movie camera going until Jackie was on the trunk of the car, *after* the last shot.

As for Orville Nix, his daughter stated that he didn't get the film back from the FBI in the same condition as the one he gave them.[23] This film was also taken from the left side of the car during the shooting, so that little can be learned about the wounds from it, except that it appears to show a piece of skull fragment flying from Kennedy's head and landing on the trunk. Mrs. Kennedy then crawled out to the trunk to try to retrieve it, but we don't actually see this in the Zapruder film, either.

The Muchmore film, also taken from the left side of the car, seems to have a painted-in head explosion corresponding to frame 313 of the Zapruder film and looking not even similar to the one we see in the Nix film. It is a different angle and occurs an instant apart.[24] But one sees a grayish white (pink in the original film) matter rather than the bright red we see in the *Life* version. The point of view is from behind. The Secret Service/HSCA version of the Muchmore film is very poor. Both the Nix and Muchmore films are damaged, as is the *Life* Zapruder film. One wonders how they could have become so damaged, unless the splices and burns on them cover up mistakes. How could anyone handling them do such damage to this priceless historical and criminal evidence?

We see in these visual images as-yet-unidentified people filming the murder, and know nothing of their films. One of them, possibly Bronson, is near Nix. Then there is sixteen-year-old Tina Towner, who operated a movie camera while her father took slides, standing near the corner of Houston and Elm. One would be inclined to believe that there was another film around.

The final problem to mention here is the tampering with the film by other researchers who chose to change this vast historical treasure still more—in some way other than that of the original forgers. Whether "image steadying," optical enhancement, "roto-scoping," blowups, stretch framing, or other means of alteration, this would seem yet another crime against our history when the ultimate effect is to divorce the viewer and the public from whatever would have been the most real version of the film.

ROTOSCOPING AND ENHANCEMENT

The entire concept of "rotoscoping" and "enhancement" of the priceless evidence in this case by researchers should come under the greatest scrutiny because some of the best technical people in the nation tell me rotoscoping, or rotoing as it is known, refers to animation. This may be a "researcher's" major Freudian slip of the tongue, since the technique used to alter the Zapruder film was in fact a form of animation.

"Rotoing is most commonly known from Disney films that combine live action and animation," a reader wrote me from Japan. "The live action film is enlarged to animation cell size and a cartoon drawing is prepared for insertion. This inset is the roto. The process can also be reversed to put live action into a cartoon."

Daryll Weatherly explains rotoscoping: "The rotoscope device allows a piece of film to be projected through a camera lens onto a flat surface, so that the outlines of inserted art work and/or mattes can be drawn. Later, the same camera, in the same position, rephotographs the art work. An animation camera is constrained to move along a single line, toward or away from the animation table, so the insert will appear in its proper place as long as the camera is the same vertical distance away for projection and rephotographing. The separate parts (unless the scene is all artwork) are then combined using an optical printer."[25]

A good description of rotoscoping is in Roy Madsen's book, *Animated Film—Concepts, Methods, Uses.*[26]

Madsen describes the method: "When the filmmaker plans to combine cartoons or titles with live-action footage or to matte out images in live-action scenes, he often employs a technique called rotoscoping. Using a rotoscope unit, he projects each frame of the live-action background scene from the camera onto the animation tabletop. He can thus make layouts of drawings which correspond precisely to each frame of the live-action footage."[27]

Raymond Fielding, in *The Technique of Special-Effects Cinematography*, explains how rotoscoping sometimes is used as an image steadying technique:

"There may sometimes be unavoidable occasions when valuable footage is rendered worthless because of accidental vibration or jiggling of the camera. . . . The technique involved is tedious and costly, since it usually requires that each frame be rotoscoped onto an alignment chart where changes in image position which are due to jiggling can be plotted from frame to frame. During final optical printing of the shot, the process camera's lens is moved from frame to frame so as to reregister the image, thus evening out vibration in the shot. This operation usually requires that a slightly reduced section of the master positive image be enlarged; otherwise, the correcting movement of the process camera's lens would cause it to photograph areas outside the frame."[28]

It may be that those who have misused the technical terms all of these years in many national and local public appearances were actors saying lines they did not even know the meaning of, and they were never exposed publicly. Only a few people familiar with filmmaking got their number.

Chuck Marler thinks that it is very easy to make a duplicate copy of the film that zooms in closer to the image, therefore cropping out the background. He believes this has been done in an effort to eliminate important references and visual clues. Although Zapruder testified "he got it all," President Kennedy's head between frames 273–328 is at the very bottom edge of the frame. By this close cropping, the foreground references of the two ladies who were standing next to the streetlight and the Newman family were just barely eliminated from the picture frame.[29]

"Image steadying" eliminated a certain amount of the data on the frame in order to keep it centered. That action may have served the conspirators well, because those frames where the film jerked—sometimes during a shot—contained intrinsic information showing whether or not it had been altered or moved from some other part of the film.

The "optical enhancements" of the film, or narrowing of the field of vision, eliminate a great deal of background information so that one cannot compare parts of the film to see its alteration. The "enhancement" thus is a perfect means for the conspirators to counteract the data presented in the published frames by the Warren Commission. It plays into their hands if it is not a deliberate intent to cover up.

THE RED MIST

There is a widespread belief among many who believe that the film was altered that the red mist we see in frames 313–14, when President Kennedy is struck in the head, is an enhancement painted in. I had felt it was an event from around frame 324, when we believe

Kennedy is struck in the head from in front, that was combined with frame 313 in a composite frame, but numerous others studying the film say it is merely retouched. Newcomb and Adams noted this a generation ago: "The exploding, bloody halo was manufactured on the film in the area around the President's head in frame 313."[30] The halo is only present for one frame in the current film. Shackelford says that two frames in the Muchmore film show the halo, though one of them is damaged.

"The halo, a cartoonlike, red-orange burst that nearly obscures the President's head, not only confuses the features of the head but also distorts the actual and less dramatic wounding. Furthermore, the burst occurs for one frame only—an eighteenth of a second—and does not appear on the very next frame. The film should have shown the burst developing and decaying over a sequence of perhaps eighteen to thirty frames. For example, a film made of the effect of a rock hitting a window would require a number of frames to record the moment of impact, the spidering and splintering of the glass, then the shattering effect of the rock, and the outward showering movement of fragments, and their eventual descent to the ground."[31] Perhaps a more reasonable period for decay of the halo burst is five to six frames. Dr. Luis Alvarez, a Nobel laureate in physics, filmed exploding skulls, and the effect took the equivalent of five to six frames at 18 fps to dissipate the bone and substitute head matter.

There is a major problem with the sets of slides in the National Archives. On separate trips to the Archives, one is liable to see different things in the different reference sets. There was a hole clearly visible behind Kennedy's ear in one viewing of frames 316 and 317 at the Archives,[32] for example, and it was not visible the next time. Daryll Weatherly prepared the following memo for this chapter concerning the problem:

> I have a very clear recollection that in June 1994, you pointed out one of the Zapruder slides in the head-shot sequence which had visible brush strokes darkening the back of Kennedy's head. This was during viewing of the reference set in the Archives, the one that comes in a carousel. As of January 6, 1995, there was no such frame in the reference set or in the original set. The back of the head was still unnaturally dark in these frames, but there were no brush strokes.
>
> I have a clear recollection that in June 1994, frame 336 showed a bright object coming out of the back of Kennedy's head. Doug Mizzer pointed it out to all four of us.
>
> I don't think it is in the reference set I just saw. I may have looked in the wrong place for it, but I think I looked at all the

head-shot frames and I'm pretty sure I would have spotted it if it was there.

Both of our Archives notes (from June 1994 visit) say that a 'red shift' occurs in the slides right at 312. My notes say that 313 has 'red-orange grass.' The reference set of slides that I saw on January 6, 1995, become gradually redder, but are not suddenly red at 312. At no time are they red-orange like some of the slides provided by Zapruder today, ostensibly from the Archives.

The change from green grass to red more than once in the slides in the reference set in carousels at the National Archives and on the film slides possessed by Robert Groden indicate this red shift related to the slides in the Archives, though it is not present in their "reproductive set" or the original slides. *All* the Groden slides are very red, as is the Assassination Information Bureau slide set from the 1970s.

There is no sudden shift from green to red in the reference set at the Archives. The shift toward red is gradual. At no point does the whole picture get as red as those slides that one gets if one orders slides from the Archives. This gradual shift to red (brown is perhaps a better description) may occur over time as the color wears out. The red grass is explained by saying that different film stock was used for some of the slides. But why? In other versions there is no red shift and the grass remains startlingly green.

Shackelford says that this may indicate that "the frames in the Archives sets appear to have been assembled from copies made with two different film stocks, one of which shifted over time." Weatherly just thinks that the developing solution wore out and was changed before the slides were finished.

JAMES ALTGENS'S MISTAKE AND WHAT IT MEANS

Ike Altgens, the Associated Press photographer who took the most famous pictures of the assassination from a position on the left side of the car somewhat ahead of it as it approached, wrote Doug Mizzer a rather extraordinary letter on November 21, 1994. He outlines the kind of mistake that crept into the official record through haste and inadvertence, and in the process, gives us new insight that has bearing on the subjects in this chapter we wish to illuminate.

I admire you for trying to put a square peg in a round hole—
a procedure that epitomizes what the Warren investigators faced

in reaching a conclusion with their investigation of the JFK assassination. Witness testimony, at variance from one another, created
a major challenge for the members in reaching a unified decision.

A great deal of reliance was placed on the Zapruder movie, yet
the experts had difficulty reaching a decision on feet per second
in order to plot critical timing sequence, a key to the number of
shots and intervals in between them. There were as many versions
of what took place, as there were witnesses that presented a very
confused scenario.

The feet per second issue refers to the speed the camera was set
at, an issue that must have been foremost in photographer Altgens's
mind as he wrote the above—realizing the crucial importance of
the time it took to fire, reload, and fire the alleged murder weapon.
If the camera had been running at twenty-four frames per second,
the shooting was too fast for one gun to have done what it was
supposed to have done. According to an FBI report, the FBI said
that the camera was running at twenty-four frames per second. Zapruder told the FBI that he had the camera fully wound and on
maximum zoom lens.[33] The camera was taken back from Bell &
Howell, which had requested it for its archives, and restudied by
the FBI for the Warren Commission and found to be running at
18.3 frames per second. Zapruder then testified to the Warren Commission that "they claimed they told me it was about two frames
fast—instead of sixteen, it was eighteen frames, and they told me it
was about two frames fast in the speed and they told me that the
time between the two rapid shots, as I understand, that was determined—the length of time it took to the second one and that they
were very fast and they claim it has proven it could be done by one
man. You know there was indication there were two?"[34] This discussion with Wesley Liebeler was terminated about one minute later.
Shortly before, Zapruder fearlessly told them that one of the shooters was standing behind him.[35]

Josiah Thompson found that *the camera did not have a speed setting
for twenty-four frames*, but only for eighteen frames per second and
forty-eight frames per second, which is slow motion.[36] This assumes
that Zapruder did not originally have a sound movie camera, which
takes pictures at 24 frames per second. I find it very strange that
Zapruder, who knew very little about cameras and had not had one
before, would state, as the FBI implies, that he had the camera set
for 24 frames when it was later found that a setting for 24 frames
did not exist on his camera. Although the following may not flow
from this discrepancy, the government's scenario needed to speed
things up, so they decided that Zapruder was mistaken and his

camera was running at 18 frames per second, which accelerates the limousine by some 30%, since it might have stopped or slowed to next to nothing at a key moment in the murder.

It is also possible that there were simply different versions of the camera, but that would have surfaced by now. Question: It seems awfully convenient for the government to change Zapruder's testimony. If they know so much, let the government explain where Zapruder could have even gotten the idea that the camera ran at 24 frames per second—if it was not written on the camera or in his instructions.

Shackelford suggests an explanation: "The statement that the film at 18 fps was 'two frames fast' derives from the fact that movie silent speed was originally 16 fps. That's the speed at which Chaplin's films, for example, were filmed and projected originally— one reason they seem to go a bit too fast on a Super 8 silent projector, which runs at 18 fps, and definitely too fast at sound speed of 24 fps."

James Altgens wrote:

> I am guilty of making an error in my deposition because I said that I was thirty feet from the President's limo when I made the picture showing the President after he received the first shot. I had turned my lens to infinity (my 105mm) which would be sixty feet. The other two lenses that I had in my pocket (a 50mm, and 28mm) have infinity at thirty feet. I called Mr. Liebeler's office the next day to correct that part of my deposition, but he had already departed for Washington. While Trask indicates in his report that I made an error, and the distance was sixty feet as opposed to thirty feet, he indicated this was his assumption, but I had already informed him that the distance should have been sixty, not thirty, as stated in my testimony.
>
> As for my position of being alongside the limo at the time the fatal shot was fired, I believe we are dealing in inches. Realizing that the limo was constantly moving, with airborne fragments coming my way, I still maintain that those fragments landed at my feet. And, the reflex of JFK's head—back then forward—as claimed in the Zapruder film, I did not see the backward movement. When first told about it, I figured that it was an optical illusion; yet, in talking with some wild-game hunters, they have convinced me that upon first impact, the body moves opposite of the impact, then moves in the direction of the bullet. At the time JFK got the fatal blow to the back of his head, I was officially fifteen feet from the car—the scale on my camera showed that footage—a distance for which I had already prefocused.[37]

DOUG MIZZER

"The frustrating part is that most of my previous work is meaning-less now, because I've been analyzing what amounts to a cartoon."[38]

Extensive study by Doug Mizzer, a researcher in Baltimore, of the various films in the case indicate that there was a second shot to the head at frame 324 of the Zapruder film, a half second after the first head shot from behind. The conspirators evidently did not detect evidence in the materials that might contradict their official story, or care about possible mistakes in their hasty and sometimes sloppy forgeries, since they controlled the main levers of power in the nation as a result of their coup.

Mizzer has shown us clear indication in the film that there was a shot at that frame from in front, and in the next frame, 325, appar-ent head matter falls to the trunk of the car just behind the seat where Jackie is sitting. The film appears to show considerably more damage to the head after frame 324 than after frame 313, when the first shot hits. Not exactly simultaneous, but close to it.

Interestingly, he spotted the head matter on the trunk of the car in the basic *Life* magazine copy of the Zapruder film that has been out there for nearly twenty years. No one ever noticed it before. These frames, so far, have not been shown in the popularized Bill Kurtis (Arts & Entertainment cable TV) version of the film, which ends a few frames after the first head shot, at frame 316.

Mizzer writes: "The shot originates from in front of the limousine and is the shot responsible for producing the hole in the rear of JFK's head."[39] Martin Shackelford and I saw this in the National Archives version, putting the lie to the autopsy photographs. One good photograph from those frames will expose the forgery of the official back-of-the-head autopsy photographs, which show intact scalp in the back.

Frame 326 shows a large blob of head matter on the trunk in the same position, and the material seen in the preceding frame has moved toward the rear. Frame 327 shows the blob and other head material moving farther toward the rear, and still farther in the following frame, 328.

Mizzer has correlated what he sees happening in frame 324 with the Nix film, which shows substantial new damage to the head about that time, following the first head shot, as seen by the camera on the opposite side (the left side) of the street.

"The impact of the second shot comes approximately a half second after the impact of the first shot. This means that they were almost simultaneous and is consistent with most of the earwitness testimony, especially that of the Secret Service agents riding directly behind JFK's limo. The majority of the agents testified that the last two shots were back to back or on top of one another."

Mizzer points out that "the first shot at frame 313 causes a shower of blood and brain effusion to be propelled forward from the right side of JFK's head toward Governor Connally. The physical evidence is that motorcycle officer Bobbie Hargis, who is riding behind and to the left of the limo, is struck with blood and brain effusion with such force that he thinks he was hit by the bullet." Billy Harper, a student, found a piece of skull bone on the grass to the left and behind where the car was during the head shot, and Mrs. Kennedy crawls out on the trunk to retrieve a piece of skull or brain. "The problem is," Mizzer writes, *the head shot at Z 313 could not have caused all of these conflicting actions!"* He believes that a whitish-pink area seen in precisely the same spot described as missing both at the autopsy and in Dallas can be seen on the frames surrounding 367 of the film, and that the hole is clearly there. Unfortunately, it's not as clear as we would hope.

Mizzer's examination of the trunk area concludes that it is clean of any blood and brain effusion from Z 313 to Z 324. "In frame 324, Mrs. Kennedy has her right hand on the top left side of JFK's head. It is barely noticeable in the Z frame, but is easily confirmed by examining the same frame from the Nix film. In frame 325, her hand has started to rapidly move upward and back. In the following several frames her hand continues its backward movement until it is well behind JFK's head. This rapid hand movement is an involuntary reaction to the impact of the second head shot. The impact of the shot throws her hand up in the air and propels it backward." And then we see brain effusion on the trunk. The first piece falls off the trunk, and the second "is the piece Mrs. Kennedy crawls out on the trunk to retrieve."

"After the rapid backward movement of Jackie's hand, she regains control and places her right hand on the lower right rear of her husband's head. This is just below where the hole in the head should be. Her hand is in this position for several frames and blood and brain effusion can be seen on top of her white glove. This effusion is also on JFK's right shoulder, next to Jackie's hand, and in the following frames can be seen on his right arm. The placement of her hand on the back of JFK's head is also consistent with her Warren Commission testimony that she tried to hold his hair on."

Mizzer feels that none of the brain effusion is visible prior to frame 324 and "therefore could not have been caused by the head shot at 313.

"JFK's movements after frame 324 are also indicative of being struck by a second shot. In the frames following 324, his back moves away from the back of the seat and he starts falling toward Jackie. His body goes limp and as soon as Jackie takes her hand away from the back of his head, he falls over onto her lap, as she crawls onto the trunk. . . . After 324, he goes limp, which would be consistent with the second shot removing the right rear of his brain."

Mizzer captions this as follows: "Notice the plotted point at Z 324, you'll see that it has veered off to the right of the line drawn through the rest of the frames. To me, this is an indication that something out of the ordinary has just happened. The movement that takes place from 323 forward to 329 is actually more rapid than the backward movement that starts after 313. From 313 to 321 when the President's shoulders strike the seat, his head has moved a distance of eight and a half inches in eight frames. From 323 to 329, the sideways head movement travels a distance of eight inches in only six frames."

MIZZER POINTS OUT THAT THERE APPEARS to be a major discrepancy between the Zapruder and Nix films with regard to Clint Hill's actions. Hill testified that he grabbed Mrs. Kennedy and "put her back in the back seat . . ."[40] This is what our study group saw in the Nix film, which was taken from the opposite side of the street from the Zapruder film. Nix was across Elm and more to the rear of the car than Zapruder. Hill is between Nix's camera and Jackie. He gets both feet on the step on the back of the limousine and moves forward so that he puts one hand on each of Mrs. Kennedy's shoulders. At one point he appears actually to be hugging her head and shoulders as he pushes her back into the seat. What I and a number of my colleagues see is not foreshortening from that angle that might make Hill and Jackie appear closer together than they are.

But the Zapruder film, taken from nearly a side angle, shows that Hill didn't reach her until she was back in the seat. I think this is good evidence of alteration because in the other film, Hill clearly does put his arms around Jackie's shoulders, just as he testified.

In the Zapruder film, he barely touches Mrs. Kennedy, with his right hand on hers, if at all. She backs up into the seat without his help. At this point a sprig from a bush obscures bits of the picture,

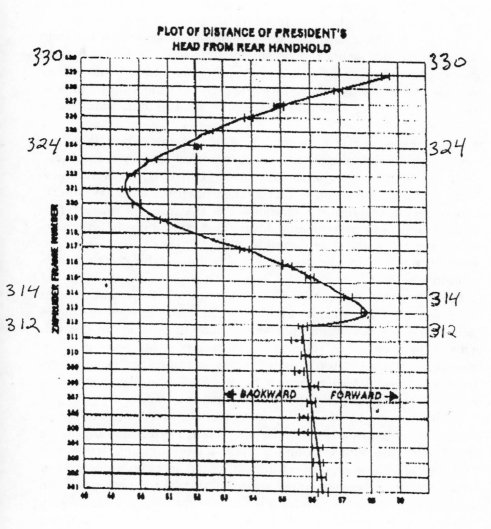

312—*First shot impacts the rear of the head at the bottom of the hairline. (Entrance wound reported by autopsy doctors)*

313—*Second shot impacts above and to the right of the ear. Bullet does not exit, but is probably responsible for opening flap behind ear.*

324—*Third shot impacts behind right ear and blows out the lower rear of the head. Notice that the point plotted at 324 does not follow the curve.*

and our attention has been directed away from the actions of Hill and Jacqueline by entrepreneurs (or propagandists) of the film to what was claimed to be a gunman in the bush.

Is it possible that Zapruder was a plant? I think the masterminds that planned this wanted to document the assassination on film so they could alter it, if need be, to support their story. It just seems too convenient, otherwise. If they could control the autopsy photos and X-rays, getting someone to film the assassination would be a piece of cake.[41]

Some researchers are puzzled by the fact that when the limo passes behind the lamppost, first the governor and then the President can be seen *through* the lamppost. (This is in the Kurtis A&E film.) "The reason we have that strange phenomenon," Weatherly says of seeing through the lamppost, "is that the film was stretch-framed by taking parts of one frame and combining it with parts of another to make a slow-motion film. We don't see this in the slides in the Archives because this is a technique for creating slow-motion film."

Put it this way. If you take a film that runs at 18 fps and transfer it to, say, film that runs at 24 fps, you have to show more frames per second. Six new frames per second have to be made or created. This is done either by repeating a frame once, or creating a new picture from parts of two frames. The extra frames are usually composites of several frames, which helps "fool" the eye into seeing continuous motion when the film is run.

In the frames 313–316 in the Kurtis version, there is an additional frame in between each frame. Again, this is stretch framing. If we try to study this film on our television set by stopping action and moving the film forward one frame at a time, just about every other frame will have been invented in order to make the original film slow enough to be compatible with the 30 fps format of television.

It is reasonable that the FBI would have possession of primary evidence in the crime (or any crime they investigate), and in this case, the original film. They had possession of the film as indicated in an internal FBI memo dated November 23, 1963. The memo said that Gordon Shanklin, the agent in charge of the Dallas field office, "stated he did not believe that the film would be of any evidentiary value; however, he first had to take a look at the film to determine this factor." Cartha DeLoach said in the same memo that "this matter would have to be treated strictly as evidence and later on a determination would be made as to whether the film would be given back to Zapruder or not."[42]

*　　*　　*

Some of us, like Mizzer, want to know "why the film has to be fine-tuned in the first place?" and "why does the limousine jump around so much from frame to frame in the so-called original? Why are the frames themselves so uneven in continuity? Why did the forgers make the splice for the missing frames so noticeable? Why did they enhance the head explosion at 313? Why, because it makes it that much harder to prove another splice was done or that another head shot took place. Unless you find another obvious splice point or head explosion, nobody's going to believe you! We all know that there wasn't any massive damage to the right forehead, but sure enough when the Zapruder film became public, it shows exactly what Zapruder stated on Dallas TV. The fix is in from the beginning!"[43] Shackelford thinks that the film jumps around due to film movement within the camera's transport mechanism, not unusual in 8mm cameras. The effect is increased by holding the camera in one's hands, rather than mounting it on a tripod.

Mizzer discovered that in one version of the Nix film there is a large piece of blood-tinged skull or brain leaving the rear of the President's head. "In another color enlargement of this same frame from the A&E documentary, *The Men Who Killed Kennedy*, this piece of skull is not present!"[44] It would appear that the A&E copy of the film was altered. "In Z frame 326," Mizzer wrote me, "and the identical frame from the Nix film, this large piece of brain and skull can now clearly be seen on the trunk of the limousine behind Jackie. The large piece only stays on the trunk for one frame in each film, but take note that it's the same frame in each film. Also remember that the motorcycle officer is struck by this debris and that AP photographer Ike Altgens commented that debris fell at his feet."[45] This means that there was a shot from in front, and it hit Kennedy quite a bit farther down the street.

Orville Nix's original film disappeared in 1978 after it was returned to UPI by the HSCA. Excellent copies of it were shown ever since Wolper's 1964 *Four Days in November*, the 1973 *Executive Action*, and the 1978 Anthony Summers documentary.

OTHER INDICATIONS OF ALTERATION

There are repeated examples of good testimony describing things which are not now seen in the Zapruder film, giving further indication that the film has been substantially changed as time passed. For instance, Roy Kellerman described to the Warren Commission seeing Kennedy reach back with his left hand behind him for a point on the back of his right shoulder, where we are told he received a bullet.[46]

The first time Dan Rather saw the Zapruder film, he said that the head "went forward with considerable violence" when he was shot.[47] Later on he saw the film again and corrected himself, saying that he made an honest mistake and that the film barely showed Kennedy moving forward: "At the risk of sounding too defensive, I challenge anyone to watch for the first time a twenty-two-second film of devastating impact, run several blocks, then describe what they had seen in its entirety, without notes. Perhaps someone can do it better than I did that day. I only know that I did it as well and as honestly as I could under the conditions.... Regrettably, it was not without error, in terms of what was unsaid about the movement of the President's head.... It is gruesome even now, and always will be, to talk about this scene, but the single most dramatic piece of the film is the part where the President's head lurches slightly forward, then explodes backward. I described the forward motion of his head. I failed to mention the violent, backward reaction. This was, as some assassination buffs now argue, a major omission. But certainly not deliberate."[48]

I no longer think Rather made a mistake when he reported what he first observed. There was a violent movement of the head forward, lasting for a number of frames. We now see the forward movement only for the space of one frame in an eighteenth of a second, and the movement has been measured to be only two and a half inches. Nevertheless, it is worth noting the opinion of James W. Altgens: "According to KDWF-TV News director Eddie Barker (a CBS affiliate), he says that Rather (then a correspondent for CBS), gave out false information to the network about the assassination because in his haste to get reports from the station, he gave incorrect information to CBS. After being questioned by Walter Cronkite, he returned to the station for more correct news reports, then called in a correction to his earlier report. It seems Rather did not see the entire Zapruder film because he was anxious to make a report to the network. Barker was not pleased at all with the way Rather used and scavenged their KDFW-TV news office. Evidently, that episode did not deter him from becoming the CBS news anchor."[49]

Perhaps Rather simply made a mistake, as he said, but I'm not sure.

Why would the forgers remove the violent forward head movement? Because they had a film showing *two* major and separate shots to the head almost a second apart from different directions, and had to eliminate one of them. Later on, it was said that the action of a shot from the rear would create a "jet effect," the dynamics of which would draw the head back toward the shot. It would also be claimed that the acceleration of the car drew the head back, knowing that the driver would step on it. The fact is that a shot came from behind and drove the head violently forward, and either before or afterward another shot came from the left front and drove it violently backward. The forgers compressed the two shots into one.

The backward head motion is not as powerful a piece of evidence as many say for a shot from in front. David Mantik suggests the following: Suppose that the film showed much more powerful evidence of a head shot from in front, such as blood, bone, and brain matter flying out of the back of the head and that the head goes backward in the direction of this effusion. If the forgers removed the worst frames from that sequence, then the backward motion would be much faster. They could not remove the whole thing, so they just took out the worst, and left us with a fast backward motion.

The forgers eliminated most of the evidence of the first head shot except for the two-and-one-half-inch forward movement which they evidently did not notice in their haste, and compressed the action, aligning the bottom half of each frame with new and stretched frames showing the car moving along the street and grass and people going by in the background.

Dan Rather said a lot more. The issue that is avoided in his "mistaken interpretation" of the film above is that he is either a far worse reporter than we want to think, or he saw an entirely different film. Taken together with the extensive eyewitness information that the car stopped during the shooting, as well as many other events that are no longer with us in the film, this nation has to start looking at this film in new ways.

After the President was first shot, Dan Rather narrated what he saw on the film the next day: "Governor Connally, whose coat button was open, turned in such a way to extend his right hand out towards the President, and the Governor seemed to have a look on his face that might say, 'what is it? What happened?' And as he turned he exposed his entire shirt front and chest because his coat was unbuttoned—at that moment a shot very clearly hit that part of the Governor."[50] We only see Connally's head during this time, as the rest of him is obscured by the highway sign.[51]

Newcomb and Adams wrote, "More evidence of tampering is indicated with the framing of the pictures, especially between frames

280–300. There, the heads of both the President and Connally scarcely appear, and almost disappear from view. This means that the original film was probably refilmed, and reframed, in such a manner as to remove certain material just below their heads.

"The possibility exists that the original Zapruder film was re-filmed on an optical printer. Modern cinematography laboratories are equipped with optical printing machines that can generate a new negative without the 'errors' of the original. Optical printers can insert new frames, skip frames, resize the images, along with other creative illusions. One hour on the optical printer could elimi-nate the Connally hit."[52] In consideration of the rather gross ques-tions with regard to the present Bronson film's authenticity,[53] as well as those proofs of forgery of the autopsy photographs and X-rays, one can presume, at this point, that the Zapruder film must be fake.

Connally is turned around looking at Kennedy when the car is behind the lamppost to Zapruder's left. It is quite possible then that Connally was hit with a shot from in front of the car to its left, from the storm drain on the bridge facing the car, and this bullet hit him in the back and came out his chest.

Motorcycle policeman Douglas L. Jackson, riding on the right side behind the limousine, saw Connally get hit: "Mr. Connally was looking back toward me. And about that time then the second shot went off. That's the point when I knew that somebody was shooting at them because that was the time he [Connally] got hit—because he jerked. I was looking directly at him . . . he was looking . . . kind of back toward me and . . . he just kind of flinched."[54]

So much of the description of the film that we have heard all these years has been a massive organized propaganda effort to cover up for the mistakes in the film, directing attention at other things. It is easy for critics to say that Connally was hit ten frames after Kennedy was, or a split second later, and so there must be a conspiracy, when there is no way in hell to prove that he was hit either with the same bullet that hit Kennedy or one just after-ward, as above.

THE EARLY TEAM OF RESEARCHERS, Fred Newcomb and Perry Adams, nearly decoded the entire forgery of the film. Their research and insight into the faking of the film was extensive—and detailed in a book that was never published: *Murder From Within.* It appears that they were taken over and their landmark research into the film distorted with entirely outlandish ideas. Newcomb and Adams were basically hurled aside—bitterly, it would seem—and forgotten. I resurrect some of their ideas in this chapter, in hopes that it will give leads to those now working on the fakery of the film.

Newcomb and Adams continued in the unpublished manuscript with a description of the film. "Most available copies, when viewed on a screen as a movie, are slightly jerky, especially in the movement of the limousine. Perhaps the maximum number of cuts was made, the greatest number of frames removed, without making it obvious to the casual viewer.

"Certain items could not be altered, such as the President's head and body snapping backward, without elaborate artwork. But, of those who have seen the film, the cuts are overcome by the way in which people see the movie. The viewer's focus is usually on the President, not on the other people in the limousine."[55] Here, note that many researchers have expressed the wish that the so-called "enhancements" of the film should not focus on the President's head for just this reason.

"Some of the action depicted on the film that was difficult to explain had to be eliminated. First, the limousine initially appears on available copies some forty feet down from the top of the street: it literally leaps into view. Yet, Zapruder stated that he filmed the limousine as it turned onto Elm Street from Houston Street.[56] The copy that CBS reporter Dan Rather saw two days after the assassination apparently had the turn on it because Rather described it.[57] The first frames deleted (155–56) probably showed the decoy shot being fired. . . . Cuts between frames 207–12 likely relate to two areas: reaction to the decoy (first) shot, and the second (throat) shot.

"Between frames 207–12, the President seems to swing his head very quickly to his left as if in reaction to the decoy shot. His action sharply contrasts with the lack of reaction by those agents in the front seat of the President's limousine. The President's reaction to the second shot, which hit him in the throat, is missing. Zapruder testified, '. . . I heard the first shot and I saw the President lean over and grab himself like this [holding his left chest area].'[58] We no longer see this. Dan Rather said that 'the President lurched forward just a bit, it was obvious he had been hit in the movie.' " Interestingly, the Commission failed to print the frames missing from *Life*'s version of the film, which had lost the frames 208–11, covered by a splice of 207 to 212.

Newcomb and Adams end their chapter on the Zapruder film with a discussion of "altering time."[61]

* * *

IT IS NOT CLEAR JUST WHERE Zapruder started filming, or if he stopped the camera after the lead motorcycles passed by, as we see in the present film. Many think that frames have been removed between the first sequence of the lead motorcycles and frame 133 when we first see the limousine. It is possible that Kennedy was shot first once or twice with a poison dart or missile just after the car turned the corner onto Elm Street, and this had to be removed. Zapruder does not speak of stopping the camera.

What he told the Commission about the camera's speed is of vast importance to the whole issue of the film's authenticity. The FBI came to retrieve his movie camera, a Bell & Howell.[62]

The Bell & Howell camera did not run at a uniform speed, simply because it was wound up with a spring and unwound at a variable speed. This alone shoots holes in the notion of the film as a "time clock of the assassination." Associated Press photographer James Altgens, who photographed the assassination as it was happening, wrote Doug Mizzer the following: "I believe that in order for you to plot events as they happened, you must know the feet per second that Zapruder's film was taken. The speed of that camera is variable depending on its winding. This is a camera designed mainly for personal use, yet it recorded the only full sequence of the assassination, becoming a very valuable instrument. Since the speed is questionable, you can readily see many questions about when the sequence of events took place."[63]

NEWCOMB AND ADAMS are convinced that some Secret Service agents shot at Kennedy from two directions or more. Their analysis is seriously impaired by the fantastic assertion that the driver William Greer shot both Kennedy and Governor Connally. This distracts attention from their massive research into whether someone near the limousine (not necessarily in it) fired a gun, and whether, at any point, the limousine stopped. One gets the idea that if agents really were involved in the shooting, their immediate control over the Zapruder film (through Forrest Sorrels), Marina Oswald, and other matters in this case tells us a lot. But more important is the possibility that Howard Donahue's theory of a Secret Service man accidentally shooting Kennedy, unsupported by any eyewitness testimony or visual evidence, was one more straw issue raised for the purpose of knocking down the real facts.

"The alterations after the fatal shot probably were concerned with eliminating the limousine stop and the rush by Secret Service agents upon it. Indeed, the Secret Service made an effort '. . . to

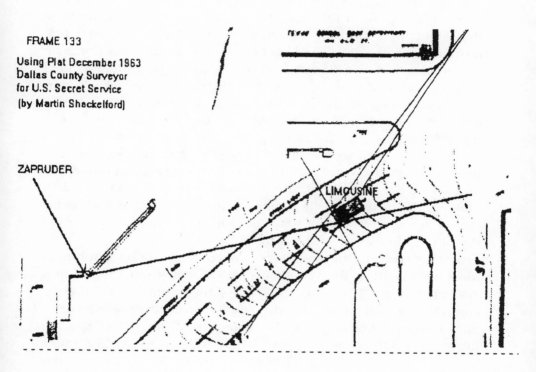

FRAME 133

Using Plat December 1963
Dallas County Surveyor
for U.S. Secret Service
(by Martin Shackelford)

ZAPRUDER

LIMOUSINE

*Where the limousine first appears in the Zapruder film,
at frame 133.*

ascertain whether any [movie news] film could be found showing special agents on the ground alongside the presidential automobile at any point along the parade route,' "[64]

There was extensive testimony that the shots came from either close to the car or in the car. At the time, some said the shots came from Secret Service men either in the car or close to it.[65] Photographer Hugh Betzner said that he "saw what looked like a firecracker going off in the President's car."[66]

Could anything like this have happened? Is there such a massive cover-up going on in this case that no one can even conceive of as thinkable the whole story of the great force that was used that terrible day in the ambush? That men shot Kennedy from alongside the street with poison fléchettes to freeze him in place, that a timed grenade was used under the car, that the car actually stopped during the shooting so that the long range snipers even two blocks away would not miss? Before dismissing such ideas as absurd, read the testimony in the following pages, and keep in mind that it comes mostly from sources that have been public for decades. The point is, researchers and critics for all of these years had us focused on *some* of the evidence in the case, distracting us from so much other evidence that the limousine stopped and that the shots occurred not at all where we were told they happened. And who has the time to find it all in the record?

Betzner said that he saw what "looked like a nickel revolver in someone's hand in the President's car or somewhere immediately around his car."[67] (This was probably sunlight glinting off the microphone in Kellerman's hand.) Even Associated Press photographer James Altgens said that shot came from "the left side of the car . . . if it were a pistol, it would have to be fired at close range for any degree of accuracy."[68] Some of the Secret Service men did describe it as a pistol shot. A man (George A. Davis) looking down from the overpass into the car before it passed beneath, said, "he saw guns in the hands of the Secret Service agents with President Kennedy, saw President Kennedy slumped forward . . ."[69] This was probably agent George W. Hickey of the follow-up car. The Zapruder film shows very clearly that the two agents in the front seat of the limo did not have guns in their hands. We see Kellerman talking on the radio, and that is about it. But what of Greer's early statement that it was *he* who talked on the radio—a statement he retracted.

"Well, the way it sounded like, it came from the, I would say from right there in the car," Austin L. Miller told the Warren Commission.[70] Ralph Yarborough, the former Marine and the United

States senator from Texas, was three cars back from the limousine and insisted that there was gun smoke in the street. He said it clung to the car all the way to Parkland Hospital.[71] This would seem terribly unlikely were it not for all the other witnesses who smelled gunpowder in the street. The street is not on the Knoll, nor could it come from the sixth-floor window, where no one smelled any smoke two minutes later when they got up there (Deputy Sheriff Luke Mooney was among them.[72]). They would have had to smell gun smoke had a rifle been fired. Billy Martin, another motorcycle policeman with the car, said that "you could smell the gunpowder. . . . you knew he wasn't far away. When you're that close you can smell the powder burning why you—you've got to be pretty close to them. . . . you could smell the gunpowder . . . right there in the street."[73]

Some of the other witnesses to the strong smell of gunpowder included the mayor's wife, Mrs. Elizabeth Cabell, who said that she was "acutely aware of the odor of gunpowder."[74] Congressman Ray Roberts, sitting next to her, had smelled it also.[75] Photographer Tom Dillard had smelled it. He "very definitely smelled gunpowder when the cars moved up at the corner [of Elm and Houston streets]."[76] Virginia Rackley,[77] Dallas police officer Joe M. Smith,[78] and police officer Earle Brown smelled it.[79] The *Chicago Tribune* put it this way that afternoon: "Seconds later the cavalcade was gone. The area still reeked with the smell of gunpowder." It's highly unlikely the smell came down from the window.

THE FILM MUST HAVE BEEN CHANGED because there were two strong head movements in opposite directions from two head shots a second or so apart, one from in back and one from in front. The two sequences were combined into one deadly visualization on the film in composite frames, and they decided to stick with the backward movement because of both its existence on other films out of the control of the conspirators and the difficulty of faking so many frames so quickly. The forward movement which Rather saw was simply excised.

Abraham Zapruder described it in his Warren Commission testimony to Wesley Liebeler: "Tell us what happened as you took these pictures."

"Well, as the car came in line almost, I believe it was almost in line, I was standing up here and I was shooting through a telephoto lens, which is a zoom lens, and as it reached about—I imagined it was around here—I heard the first shot and I saw the President lean over and grab himself like this [holds his left chest area]."[80] Zapruder cried when he testified to this. There is no background in the film other than green grass at the time of the fatal head shot. Presumably, the zoom lens removed the rest of the city close by.

Chester Breneman, one of the surveyors of Dealey Plaza working from *Life*'s slides made from the Zapruder film frames, said that the numbers of the frames were changed, and he described things in the frames that are no longer there. He told reporters that on November 25, 1963, he had still photos made from all frames of the Zapruder film by *Life* magazine and they showed "large blobs of blood and brain matter flying from Kennedy's head to the rear of the car."[81] We don't see this anymore.

Dr. Pierre Finck described what the film showed in his report to General Blumberg: "I saw the movie several times, at eighteen frames per second and at slow motion. I also saw the 35 millimeter color lantern slides made from this movie, frame by frame. The movie and the slides show the President slumping forward after being hit in the back. Then it seems that Governor Connally has a spastic expression on his face, as he has been hit. His thigh is not visible and there is no evidence that blood appeared on his injured right wrist. Then came the shot through Kennedy's head."[82] This is confirmed by Daryll Weatherly's examination of frames 242–78 in the National Archives, that there is no definitive evidence of blood on the wrist.

The film suggests that it was reframed after the sign, around frames 285–90, when we only see Connally's head, and not his chest during a time when he is turned halfway around and looking directly at Kennedy, long after he was supposed to have been shot at frame 235, at the latest. Again, Dan Rather saw a version of this film that showed Connally getting hit in the chest, perhaps at just that point.

Other versions of the film switch to blown-up frames showing only JFK and Jackie just after the car emerges from behind the sign, so that most background data is eliminated. The continual mixing of the different versions of the film on national television and in other presentations ultimately makes it impossible to know just what it is that we are seeing. In time, many more versions of the film can be expected to proliferate. In some of the same obviously modified (enhanced?) versions of the film, the Stemmons Freeway sign jumps around wildly and changes shape from frame to frame.

After the car passes the last lamppost before the head shot, during the key frames leading up to the head shot, the film starts changing and is reframed. The whole film is blown up at that point.

The blurs in the film are very pronounced, and they seem to be superimposed frames to make double images. This creates the illusion of movement, and fills in for missing frames.

For years, so much of the research on the film was limited to one or another of these wildly conflicting versions, and so misled countless people and produced very deficient or incompetent interpretations of what the film showed.

THE STOPPED LIMOUSINE

"For a chaotic moment, the motorcade ground to an uncertain halt." But the *Newsweek*[83] writer was not a witness.

Some events described that day in Dealey Plaza during the shooting are no longer seen in the film. Quite a few witnesses insisted that the limousine stopped altogether during the shooting. Chuck Marler, a researcher in Riverside, California, studied the issue of the film independently of our team, and his publication of an article in *The Fourth Decade*[84] seemed to be the first real notice in thirty years by someone in print in a research journal—outside of the assault I launched on the film in two of my previous books—that the question of the Zapruder film's authenticity was fair game.

But is there a confusion of the motorcade itself, versus the limousine stopping? Only a close analysis of each statement in the evidence might clarify it. Martin Shackelford writes, "The motorcade came to a halt in the confusion as the limousine sped off, then proceeded rather raggedly, as the films and photos show."[85] But there is evidence that the limousine slowed nearly to a stop during the shooting. The films don't show this.

Penn Jones was the first to try to make an issue of the stopping of the limousine, and Marler gives this listing of witnesses: Dallas police officer Earle Brown on the railroad bridge over Stemmons freeway: "After it made the turn and when the shots were fired, it stopped."[86] Officer James Chaney and others told Officer Marion Baker that "after the first shot rang out, the car stopped completely, pulled to the left and stopped . . . Mr. Truly was standing out there, he said it stopped. Several officers said it stopped completely."[87]

Corroborating this was the supervisor of the Texas School Book Depository. Roy Truly said: "I saw the President's car swerve to the left and stop somewhere down this area."[88]

Chaney was recorded saying more to a radio reporter at Parkland Hospital shortly after the assassination: "The first shot we thought was a motorcycle back-fire and then I looked to my left and saw President Kennedy looking back over his shoulder and when the *second* struck him in the *face*, then we knew that someone was shooting at the President."

"When you saw the bullet hit him, what did you do?"

"He slumped *forward* in the car, he fell *forward* in the seat."

"And Mrs. Kennedy did what?"

"I don't know, when I'd seen it, he was hit, well *I went ahead* to tell Chief Curry's group there that he had been hit and we took him on to the hospital."[89]

Senator Ralph Yarborough told the Warren Commission in an affidavit that "when the noise of the shot was heard, the motorcade slowed to what seemed to me a complete stop ... after the third shot was fired, but only after the third shot, the cavalcade speeded up."[90]

Mrs. Earle Cabell, the wife of the mayor of Dallas, told the Warren Commission that "she was aware the motorcade stopped dead still. There was no question about that."[91]

James Simmons, standing on the bridge overlooking the car, said the limousine "stopped, or almost stopped," prior to the fatal shot. Simmons worked for the railroad and was standing on the bridge in a perfect place to see what was happening over on Elm Street as the limousine approached him directly. He testified at the trial of Clay Shaw in New Orleans, February 15, 1969, and was asked "Then did the car speed up?"

"Yes, after they got the motorcycle policemen out of the way."[92]

One of the motorcycle policemen nearest the car, Bobby Hargis, said, "I felt blood hit me in the face and the presidential car stopped almost immediately after that."[93]

Governor John Connally said: "... then, after the third shot, the next thing that occurred, I was conscious the Secret Service man, of course, the chauffeur, had, ah, had pulled out of line ..."[94]

Officer Billy Martin said the car stopped "just for a moment."[95] Martin was on the motorcycle next to Hargis. Officer Douglas L. Jackson said "that car just all but stopped ... just a moment ..."[96] Officer Marrion L. Baker said that the other police told him the limousine stopped completely.[97] Joe H. Rich, a Texas highway patrolman driving Vice President Lyndon Johnson's follow-up car, said that "the motorcade came to a stop momentarily."[98] Robert Baskin, one of the reporters in the motorcade, said "the motorcade ground to a halt."[99] UPI's book *Four Days* said in a caption to a photograph made from a film: "The driver slams on the brakes ..."[100]

Newcomb and Adams wrote in their unpublished 1974 manuscript that "some twenty other witnesses at various locations in the plaza confirmed the presidential limousine coming to a stop," and listed them.[101]

Even Gerald Posner, who is not a witness, said the driver of the car "slowed the vehicle almost to a standstill." It is a mystery how he arrived at this conclusion, since it isn't what is shown on the film—and that is the issue here.[102]

There was evidence that the motorcade stopped for a moment after having passed under the railroad overpass at the entrance ramp to the freeway, apparently to confer on directions and what had just happened. It would be easy to confuse this stoppage of the cars with a stoppage or hesitation on Elm Street in the Plaza itself during the shooting.

Time put it this way: "There was a shocking momentary stillness, a frozen tableau."[103] This was the terrible moment when we are led to believe that Kennedy was first shot, but of what are they speaking with this literary flourish? Certainly, there is little movement if any in the backseats of the fatal car for many frames before the fatal head shot. The whole scene seems to be a set piece moved from frame to frame.

We cannot see the first strike on Kennedy because it is conveniently hidden behind the Stemmons Freeway sign.

CERTAINLY, FRAMES SHOWING THE CAR STOPPED had to be removed. One might suppose that the car was actually stopped when it was hidden from Zapruder's camera by the sign. Stretch-framing the film with composite frames was a good way to get the car moving again. "What is clear," Newcomb and Adams postulated, "is that frames have been removed. Time has been deleted from the film. With time removed, the film is useless as a clock for the assassination."[104] Keep in mind how many times this nation has been told on television and radio and college lecture audiences that the film was a clock of the assassination. That is what they wanted us to think and believe.

"Some of the altered frames are indicative of the car having been moving far more slowly than the admitted average speed of 11 mph," Daryll Weatherly says. If the car was moving slowly, the picture and background should be clear, with no blurring, but if there are conflicting vectors, then it is evidence of alteration to cover up a drastically slowed or stopped car. Other material may have had to be disrupted or removed, such as the actions of a bystander.

There is quite a blur of the film at frame 290, which might be

Zapruder's reaction to the shot that I think hit Connally at 286. Nobel laureate physicist Luis Alvarez said that this is the point where the Zapruder film showed that the President's car suddenly decelerated for about half a second from 12 to 8 mph. Greer probably took his foot off the accelerator. Alvarez speculated that Greer was reacting to the siren being turned on in the follow-up car behind him, but the important thing is his calculation based solely on the film that the car did in fact slow drastically just before the head shot one second later.[105] The car may not stop in the film that we now have, but it comes perilously close. It may very well have stopped for an instant, and this frame or frames were removed.

My tendency is to think the driver was part of the conspiracy, and he stopped or slowed greatly until Kennedy had been struck in the head. Greer, driving slowly at about ten miles an hour, then turned around and looked at Kennedy and waited for it to happen. That could get his foot off the accelerator.

I have been told that it is irresponsible to accuse Greer of doing this, but the terrible fact remains that he failed to get the car out of there for long seconds after the shots began to fly.

The stopped or radically slowed car had to be removed from the film. Some people give the explanation that the car stopped because Jackie crawled out on the trunk, but this did not happen until well after the head shot, and both agents in the front seat are faced forward and could not know she was out there. The car is clearly racing after that, as soon as Clint Hill got a foot on the step at the rear of the car and had a firm grip. If the car did stop while she was on the trunk, after the fatal head shot, then why does it not show in the film? What reason would there to be to remove that sequence? The car had to be stopped before she left her seat.

If the car was radically slowed or stopped, the other films would have to be rolling to capture it. The Nix and Muchmore cameras did not start again until just before the head shot. If the car was stopped or radically slowed in front of the Stemmons highway sign, closer to the corner of Houston and Elm, those films would not capture it.

Another belief is that Secret Service men tried to get in the car. It is not clear whether this merely refers to Clint Hill running after the car from the follow-up vehicle, or to others actually trying to get in, but once again there are several examples of testimony indicating that more than one agent tried to reach the car.[106] Yet, the film does not show this. We only see Clint Hill running after the car, after the fatal shot.

I think the driver of the limousine, Greer, in the Altgens photograph has been completely painted over so as to show nothing more than his silhouette, and no flesh tones or detail (we see him in left profile turned all the way around to his right) in the windshield of the head-on photograph of the car—where we see Kennedy clutching at his throat. Similarly, according to Newcomb and Adams, the movie shows that "retouching is evident on the front of the limousine windshield on the driver's side to obscure his movements."[107]

THE STEMMONS FREEWAY SIGN

There were three large highway signs on the right side of the last block of Elm Street, where the assassination took place. The first, nearest the corner, was that of the R. L. Thornton Freeway sign. The Stemmons Freeway sign was in the middle of the block and is the one hiding the motorcade from Zapruder during key seconds of the assassination. The third sign was near the underpass and directed drivers onto the Forth Worth Turnpike.

The Thornton Freeway sign was taken down just after the shooting, and replaced with a Stemmons Freeway sign, according to the testimony of the groundskeeper, Emmett Hudson.[108] There is much evidence that the Stemmons sign was immediately moved after the assassination, but perhaps not by much. One good reason for its removal was to scramble its position for the reenactment. The sign appears to have been replaced for the reenactments, but did they put it in the same place it had been before? Was the Stemmons Freeway sign seen in the Willis photograph and moved in Zapruder's film?

A study of the limousine indicated that it moved one foot per frame until it reached frames 197 and 218, when it was behind the freeway sign.[109] Then the car crawled forward just ten feet within twenty-one frames. Doug Mizzer detected an oddity of the film during that period, with the sign lengthened side to side in successive frames. Mizzer demonstrated the changing configuration of the sign to us at a conference held in the mountains in California on June 4, 1994. Mizzer saw this without knowing that Newcomb and Adams had noted it twenty years before. There were different versions of the film, showing different things. The sign seemed to widen when one edge was in the area between the sprocket holes. Perhaps this is an effect of the camera operation.

ENHANCEMENT

One of the more disquieting aspects of all this is the grave possibility that crucial photographic evidence has been tampered with by researchers under the guise of so-called "enhancement," ostensibly to improve our understanding of it, but really to obtain a supposed copyright or to sidetrack us from real understanding.

Enhancing the film removes crucial data and makes forgery harder to detect. Marler comments, "When one views the Zapruder film without the close-up enhancements, the limousine reduces its speed significantly between frames 255 and 313—substantially more than the 1.2 miles per hour. This obvious reduction of speed prior to frame 313 also occurs as the limousine is becoming more perpendicular to the location of Abraham Zapruder—which should visually appear to be going *faster*, even if there wasn't a reduction in speed. When tracking a moving object with a movie camera, the closer the object approaches the photographer, the faster the camera has to be moved to keep the object within the frame."[110]

The present film has the car moving at the very slow speed of ten to eleven miles per hour,[111] and our mathematical studies of the film along with my measurements of the distances between objects in the Plaza show that the car slowed down to seven or eight miles per hour at the moment of the fatal head shot.[112]

THE JIGGLES AND THE SHOTS

In 1967, CBS claimed that Zapruder's Bell & Howell camera may have been running a bit slower than the Warren Commission thought. CBS also believed that the first shot was fired at frame 186 (and missed), which was more than two seconds before Connally was hit but too late for the bullet to have been fired from Oswald's gun, and then fired again at Kennedy and Connally when they were both claimed to be hit.

It is interesting that the House committee found that a shot had been fired at frame 160, a very difficult if not impossible shot at a steep angle from the sixth-floor window looking down on the car. But the House had a second shot striking both victims at 188–191.[113] Kennedy is clearly reacting by frame 200. If we count back forty-two frames from 190, we get a shot at frame 148 at the earliest for the Oswald rifle's capability. The HSCA never thought through the conflicts in what they presented. Connally is not hit before 225, or perhaps 236—if he was hit at all then, which is what the Zapruder film now shows, according to many. Obviously, this gives us a few more shots than was possible for one man. Connally thought he was hit around frame 236. But then, he was looking at a fake film. Try frame 285.

What happened to the shot at 186? The House said it hit. Many years before, CBS said it missed, basing their analysis on the fact that the camera jiggled at that point. They ignore numerous other jiggles which could just as easily have been caused by rifle shots as well. At frame 318, a split second after the fatal head shot at 313, the camera moves violently.

CBS found two additional jiggles: at frame 190 and at 227. It seems to me that any of these might in fact be reactions to shots, but not all from Oswald, if he fired any at all. Since CBS did not mention other jiggles, do they know something we don't—that these were in fact shots? Are they speaking to us with a forked tongue, like those Russian writers who could not mention the Tsar's name in their writing, but spoke of a "Certain Person"? Perhaps the media *cannot* come right out and say what they think, in the face of the awesome power they must know was behind all of this. It's all very convoluted. As long as they say Oswald did it and did it alone, they can give other evidence adding up to conspiracy.

For the record, Josiah Thompson points out that there are much greater jiggles, at Z 197, Z 210, and Z 331.[114] "If each of the jiggles in the Zapruder film is to be correlated with a shot, then at least six shots were fired in the Z 170–334 interval alone."** This is not counting the jiggles (shots?) that appear both earlier and later. *Life* magazine supposed that the other blurs are most probably caused by imperfections in the camera mechanism that permit the film to move a short distance either toward or away from the lens.[115]

CBS claimed that the camera was running slower than the Commission thought. The Warren Commission printed the manner in which the speed of the camera was determined[116] both by Bell & Howell and the FBI, which came up with the same answer: 18.3 frames per second. How did CBS find that they were wrong? CBS did not have Zapruder's camera, so they used five other similar

---

**There are two important appendices at the end of Josiah Thompson's *Six Seconds in Dallas* dealing with the Zapruder film: Appendix B: Calculations From Zapruder Frames 301–330, and Appendix C: Calculation of Velocity of Presidential Vehicle From Zapruder Frames 301–330. Unfortunately, his book is very hard to find these days, and ought to be reprinted.

cameras for their tests, all of which ran at different speeds. Three
of them ran faster than Zapruder's camera. The average speed for
the five was within an infinitesimal .044 frames per second of that
which the FBI and the manufacturer found. Thompson says, "Once
again a so-called scientific test was used by CBS to throw dust in
the eyes of its viewers."[117]

THE MAN WHO HELPED CONDUCT the surveys of Dealey Plaza for both
Life magazine and the Warren Commission, Chester Breneman, said
that the Warren Commission falsified their figures from the survey.
"They [the figures in the survey] were at odds with our figures.
After checking a few figures, I said 'that's enough for me,' and I
stopped reading. For instance, on our map, we marked the spot
corresponding to Zapruder film frame 171. The Warren Commission changed this to 166 before they used it in the report. The
Warren Commission shows a 210 where we show a 208."[118]

Breneman saw some of the frames from the Zapruder film.
Within days of the shooting, *Life* had a team of investigators in
Dallas, one of whom wore a bulletproof vest. They used the frames
from the film to study where the shots occurred. Breneman saw
things on the photos of all the frames that no longer exist on the
film, such as large amounts of blood and brain matter flying from
Kennedy's head behind the car. Breneman was convinced that the
shots came from two different directions.

Breneman described examining a bullet mark on the curb on
the south side of the street. He talked about the highway sign being
removed just after the assassination which he was told had a stress
mark from a bullet. Nobody knows where the sign is. "It's my understanding that this particular sign was quickly taken down and no
one has been able to locate it."[119]

The *Life* investigator with the bulletproof vest told him, "My life
isn't worth a plug nickel on this investigation."

Surveyor Breneman said, "The only thing I know for sure is that
shots came from two different directions."

HOW TO FORGE A FILM

Richard Burgess, writing in *The Fourth Decade*, describes how a film may
be fabricated. My advisors say that this is accurate. Unfortunately, all
that Burgess discusses in his short article is what one would have to

do to add artwork to an existing film frame. His example is what I call the "blob" on Kennedy's face, which I'm sure has been clearly added onto the film, though I did not imagine that someone would take the last statement literally. A retouch artist does not paint on the film itself, which was Burgess's interpretation of what I wrote in *High Treason 2* about the "blob." See pages 363–68 of that book.

"Any attempted modification would necessitate the enlargement of the film to 35mm (to maintain clarity, and reduce changes in color saturation and balance, contrast, and grain), various types of optical printing with travelling mattes, and then reduction back to 8mm. The conspirators would have to begin by rear-projecting each frame onto the back of an animator's drawing table and tracing each successsive frame of Kennedy onto a piece of paper. This is known as rotoscoping. (Robert Groden uses this term completely incorrectly when he refers to his image stabilization of the Zapruder film.)[120] Then an animator would have to animate the 'blob' by drawing it into the successive rotoscoped images of Kennedy's head. These drawings would then be transferred to animation cels and painted. The area around the painted wound on each cel would then be painted black. Another set of cels would then be copied, but with the wound painted black and the rest of the cel clear. These images would then be filmed with an animation camera onto two sets of film, one with the wound surrounded by black (film 1) and the other with a black blob floating in mid-air on clear film (film 2). This is a travelling matte."

Burgess continues, "Next the Zapruder film enlargement would be run through an optical printer with film 2 on top in correct frame register producing film 3. This film would show a black hole where the wound should be. Film 3 would then be rewound and film 1 (the wound surrounded by black) would be run through the printer exposing film 3 again. Since black does not expose the film, the surrounding black of film 1 wouldn't expose the already ex-posed Zapruder film and, if the copying of the cels was done exactly and the job was done properly on a high quality optical printer, the painted wound would fit right into the unexposed hole in film 3 like a moving jigsaw puzzle piece. Film 3 is reduced back to 8mm and there you have it: faked Zapruder film."[121]

Daryll Weatherly, a mathematician with a background in physics, responds: "This is an accurate description of the basic technique that would be used, although a few things should be added. In the first step, enlargement to 35mm (or larger) film, the image area plus the sprocket hole area at the extreme left would have to be reproduced in the image area of the larger film, since the type of film magazine used by Zapruder had an aperture that allowed light to reach this area. In the final step of reduction back to 8mm film, it would be necessary to use this same type of magazine to ensure that the sprocket hole area is exposed."

Mark Crouch describes this method of forging a film: "To alter a film at this level doesn't even require much equipment. The film is projected frame-by-frame onto the rear of a glass screen. The corrupted copy is then recorded frame by frame. When they reach the head-shot frame, they just add a little paint to the glass, shoot that frame, then clean the glass. They then project the next frame, redo their little touch-ups to match perspective, then go on. They really only have to do about fifty frames and the alterations are very nondescript, like enlarging the 'blob' and blacking in the back of the head and the limousine."[122] This is called "aerial imaging" photography.

THE ARGUMENT FOR AND AGAINST FORGERY

Crouch then presents a very good argument for why and how the forgery would have happened.

The truth about the Z-film is that it was never meant to be micro analyzed the way it has. . . . The real 'evidence' of Z-film alteration is more subjective than objective. If you believe, as I do, that a trained and directed team of assassins were in the Plaza, then you must assume they observed Zapruder standing up there with his camera. The assassins would have had no way of knowing if he'd innocently panned his camera toward them just before or during the assassination. Therefore, if there was a trained and directed team in the Plaza, they would have been very concerned with what Zapruder's camera may have recorded. This is essential if you believe they were not only there to kill Kennedy but to frame LHO. The whole frame-up around Oswald would have melted like a snowball in July if there was clear photographic evidence of another shooter.

"Logic would therefore dictate that (and I'm assuming that Zapruder was not an accessory before the fact) the plotters *or their agents* would have to: (A) examine the Zapruder film closely before it was released for any incriminating evidence and (B) if it were incriminating they would have to either alter, destroy or sequester it.

"What would the plotters be most worried about (aside from the film actually showing an assassin)? The obvious answer is evidence of frontal head entry. To conceal this they would need to do three things which would have required only minor touch-ups on certain frames: They needed to conceal evidence of a bullet striking the forehead at the hairline. The flap/blob does this quite nicely. They would also need to darken in the hole in the back of the head that all the witnesses saw. This, too, required only a little touch-up of a few frames. The last thing they had to do was to obscure the white-pink matter that splattered the rear of the limo. This, too, is nothing more than a little blackout touch-up work.

"Take a look at some of the raw NBC footage from the ER entrance at Parkland. Kellerman and Greer have spread a tarp over the back deck of the limo! It must have been and should have been a mess, but I don't see a damn thing in the Zapruder film.[123]

But Doug Mizzer has found brain and head matter passing along the edge of the trunk for four frames of the film.

THIS IS IN RESPONSE TO Richard Burgess's article "On the Authenticity of the Zapruder Film" (September, 1994, *Fourth Decade*) in which he attacks any notion of forgery, while admitting that half of the forward part of Kennedy's head is missing in a series of frames sometime after the head shot.[124]

Burgess says that "since the Zapruder film does not match the eyewitness testimony, it is claimed that someone has darkened the back of Kennedy's head, thus obliterating the damage of the occipital-parietal area, and painted on what Livingstone calls 'the blob,' a red area that covers Kennedy's face and seems to reproduce the wounds of the autopsy photographs."*

Burgess starts with a logical fallacy: "Arguments of fakery should arise from peculiarities within the film itself, not from comparison with other evidence." This is a simplistic and preposterous distortion of criminal investigation. Yes, the intrinsic clues of forgery *are* contained within the film itself, but that is only one method of proof. The principal means of covering up this case has been just that sort of false argument: that the observations of the witnesses to gunmen in front of or to the side of the car is mistaken because there was no medical evidence of frontal shots; that the observations of a large hole in the back right rear of the head is false because the photographs and X-rays do not show it; that the observations

---

*See color photos in *High Treason 2*, and the chapter on the film in that book, as well as the chapter in *Killing the Truth*. See pp. 155–56 of the former book, and pp. 77, 89, 306–7, 339, 540–41 of the latter.

of a very small hole indicative of an entry hole in the throat are inaccurate because there was no gunman in front.

You can't easily dismiss the testimony of thirty people that the limousine stopped completely during the shooting. We don't see this in the film, if they mean the car stopped completely, except for the scene in the car. There are a lot of things we no longer see in the film. Shots were removed, and those that the film makes us aware of, are moved farther up the street. The film removed time and space.

Daryll Weatherly, a lecturer in mathematics at the State University of New York, utilizes vector analysis—one of the tools of physics—for identifying altered frames, and this is explained in his article in the Appendix.

Burgess attempts to technically debunk the possibility of forgery, but is way off base. I suppose it is hard for the average person to imagine how it could be done. They give up quickly, forgetting that there are plenty of master forgers around who know how to do these things.

It does not help for Burgess to state that "Livingstone believes that all one needs to do is draw or paint on the surface of the film." I did not express myself quite correctly in the statement he refers to in *High Treason 2* (p. 155). I did not mean that the paint was actually put on the film. An entirely different means is used to animate an actual film from real life. Color transparencies or mattes are used. Faking film is nearly as old as the art of photography itself. I meant that paint is used both to create the image one wishes to add, and to retouch a picture or frame. Paint is used to cover over and make opaque that which is to be removed, and to create an image. It is used on a clear celluloid acetate (same as film strip, but thicker) or other material and then photographed on an animation stand to make a new picture. Even paper can be used.

Burgess says that faking the "blob" would be a job for "masters." It was, and they did it. But it was relatively easy to create. Burgess's caveat to the problems in faking all of this is not substantial. It was easy to misstate my belief as to how the forgery was done. Burgess wrote that I "believed" that it was simply painted on the surface of the film. It is a painting that was composed with the film. In some frames, the whole scene in the limo is clearly a painting, especially Jackie's face.

The "blob" I wrote about in *High Treason 2* is clearly a fabrication. This year, Dr. David Mantik, Daryll Weatherly, Doug Mizzer, and I spent many hours in the National Archives studying the frames of the film. Mantik said that its location appeared to change from frame to frame. The "blob" on the front of the face does not correspond to any anatomic structure whatsoever. Close study clearly shows that it is not a flap of skin, brain, or scalp.

At one point after the fatal shot, President Kennedy's head becomes a mere stub, or stump as some call it, missing the entire front quarter of the skull from just in front of the ears to the top of the head, with the face gone. The most major mistake of the forgers was to leave only the rear stub of a head for several frames. Through the missing area we can see Jackie's dress perfectly where her husband's head ought to be. See p. 366 of *High Treason 2* for my earlier discussion of the stump.

For the preceding frames before "the stump," we have "the blob" to mystify medical people and any of us who thought about it. The "stump" and the "blob" will be the ultimate undoing of the film and the cover-up.

It is impossible, knowing what we know now, for the Zapruder film not to be fake, and it is anything but a completely true image of the wounds Kennedy received that day in Dallas.

The film once showed the second head shot, which was not simultaneous with the rear head shot. It came from the front—but farther down the street than frame 312. The film still has the evidence of the second head shot from in front.

Concerning the grain structure on the film, Burgess says, "The film into which this animated wound was to be set is very grainy; yet the animated wound would not be. It would show up instantly, since it would share none of the surrounding original grain (which it obviously does in the existing film). There is no way this could be faked. Even if the animated wound were filmed on 8mm film first and then enlarged to 35mm, the shifting grain structures would be different enough to reveal the joint, especially when blown up (as all images of the head by necessity are)."

Weatherly replies: "His argument has a basic weakness. The contention that composite images would have to show an irregularity in grain structure ignores the final step, reduction to 8mm film to simulate a camera original. The graininess of 8mm film would be an asset there, imposing a new grain structure on the entire scene."

Burgess tells us that any addition of an image to the film that had not been there during the original photography would not be as sharp as the rest and easily detectible. "This lack of sharpness would create a 'matte bleed,' that is, there would be an obvious 'line' around the matted wound where the image of film 1 did not fit exactly into the hole in film 2."

We are familiar with many movies, advertisements, and photo-

323 appearance of head wound

328 head wound

326 headwound

(327 similar)

329

(330 similar)

333

(334 blurred,)
otherwise similar

335

357

graphs that composite different images in one scene with no detectible evidence of it. Burgess betrays a flaw in his understanding of industry techniques able to do this for generations. They wouldn't do it if their work was not professional, and they do it all the time, though prior to 1977, composite movie frames were detectable, if one knew what to look for.

The basic thrust of Burgess's argument seems to be that the film cannot have any animated material, because an attempt at fakery would cause it to have the very features that lead us to suspect animation.

His argument seems to be that animation would make the "blob" look animated. That is a major reason why we think it is animated, not just the fact that no such wound was later seen by anyone: It looks patently fake, bobbing around on the head as it does in the moving film. The still slides of the film at the National Archives, in addition, show the "blob" to be unreal. It is rather obvious.

Burgess says that another "problem would be one of paints. How could the animator achieve a realistic-looking wound that didn't look like paint? The flap in the Zapruder film is obviously glistening flesh; reproducing that to match the colors, tonalities, and light source of the Zapruder film would be a job for a master."

There are many realistic artists throughout history who could paint things so realistically that they cannot be distinguished from a photograph. There are plenty of masters around. Burgess also makes a fallacious assumption here, that the wound is realistic. It isn't. It is *un*real, since it does not and cannot correspond to any anatomic structure of Kennedy or known wound of his. *It does not look real at all.* The slides in the Archives clearly show that it is not a flap, but in fact a "blob" as I have said. Burgess says that "reproducing" (he means *producing*) a wound would be a job for a master. He seems to be saying that a master could do it, but there are no masters. This is untrue.

As for the realism of the "blob," a photograph of a brain taken in the bright sun could have been used for the compositing, but it is little more than a *bright spot* on the film. This is no problem for an artist. In addition, no one has been able to determine just what the "blob" is, beyond theorizing that it is a flap of skin. It could not have come from Kennedy's known head wounds.

Another problem with the "flap" theory to explain the "blob" hasn't been addressed by Burgess and other critics: How could the flap hang down on the *front* of the face when the only possible position of a laceration along the right side of the head could not allow a flap to fall anywhere but down and certainly not reach around to the front of the face. What we apparently see is almost an entire brain hanging out of his right forehead.

Burgess says that the animation cannot work because the final version of an altered film would be three generations removed from the original. He then makes a patently false statement to bolster his argument: that the film is of "generally poor quality of the image to start with." Weatherly replies that, "Regarding the number of generations removed from the original that a fake would be, who is ever going to see the original? What we actually see are various 'enhanced' copies and slide sets, which we *expect* to be multiple generations removed."

Good copies of the film, such as the original *Life* slides in the National Archives and copies of it there, are crystal clear. Burgess has been looking at cheap bootleg copies and videos. "The final version [of the animation] would be so murky as to be almost useless, even with fine grain, low contrast 35mm masters and specialized color duping film." Wrong again. Working from a good original, the loss of definition would be little more than a copy of that original, though it went to 35mm and back again. Certainly, with good copy equipment, it is very hard to distinguish between an original and a first copy, especially when no one will ever see the original. The slides in the Archives are copies of copies and they are crystal clear. It is an amazing experience to see them.

"No matter how good the equipment, the wound is so small on the original film [as I noted above, probably no bigger than half or quarter the size of the head of a pin] that any image would lack sharpness, a problem exacerbated by the grain and the low quality optics of Zapruder's camera." Burgess again makes several inaccurate statements off the top of his head without citing any source material to back them up. Zapruder's Bell & Howell camera was their top-of-the-line commercial offering. The optics were very good, and that is easily seen in good copies of the film, where the clarity is quite startling.

In addition, the "blob" is clearer, in fact, than the head it is attached to. This counters Burgess above, but we don't know why it is so clear except to offer the possibility that the equipment and techniques used were superior to the camera and film that was being altered.

Burgess (and other critics of the film alteration evidence) fail to explain why in the frames following the head shot around frames 335-37, there is only the rear stub of Kennedy's head, and we see Jackie's shoulder and arm very clearly where his face and forehead should be.[125] *This*

clearly demonstrates that something else happened in that car during
those terrible moments that had to be so drastically changed, and
changed so fast, that they pasted in an incomplete image of John Kenne-
dy's head with an apparently whole brain hanging out of the right eye
over Jackie's torso.

Burgess agrees that part of the head is missing: "As Kennedy's
head bounces forward from its backward thrust, it is obvious that a
chunk of the top and side of his head is missing. As it moves forward
one can see Jacqueline's face and shoulder right through what
ought to be Kennedy's head. If the film were fiddled, this portion
must have originally been covered by Kennedy's intact head."[126]

It is at this point that we *know* that the famous film is fake. It was
done to trick the Warren Commission, the FBI, the Secret Service,
and *Life* into believing that Kennedy was shot in the head from
behind with a bullet that blew out the forward part of his head. He
may have been shot from behind, but the bullet did not damage
the forward part of his head, and only exited the right temple,
at most.

Burgess puts forward another argument: "The greatest problems,
however, are of blurring, registration, and adding missing background. Since Abraham Zapruder had his camera set on maximum
telephoto and had no tripod, the images jump around quite a bit
even when Zapruder is relatively steady; hence the importance of
image stabilization. . . . It would have been impossible in 1963 to
add anything to the film or alter any successive images and duplicate a realistic blur."[128] The latter statement is just bullshit.

The rotoscope process has as its primary intent the accurate registration of the mattes which causes the composite images to go
where they are supposed to go. Again, Burgess has not done his
homework and makes an illogical statement. The machine does not
exist to leave a trail of shoddy work and clues of compositing. As
for the blurs, assuming that a photograph of a brain was not used
to composite the blob with the head, and that it is simply artwork,
any blurs become that much easier to paint. Remember, artwork
and animated cartoons are drawn on large boards and then reduced
down, in this case to 35mm film or even larger. Burgess finally
mentions that it might be necessary to add missing background.
Again, that is no problem. That is what photo retouch artists are
all about.

Burgess, a classicist at the University of Ottawa, says that adding
the blob or any other change would never work. He flies in the
face of countless similar commercial and artistic alterations of

film, such as popular movies of real people and scenes which have cartoon characters added to the film. Originally, this effect was not done with computers, and the same matte technique described above was used. Two or more images were combined with one.

"If one accepts the theory [as I do]," Timothy Cwiek writes, "that President Kennedy's killer never wanted the lone-assassin theory accepted by everybody, then the taking of the Z-film makes all the sense in the world. The film was not shown to just anybody. . . . It was released to certain people, at different times, so that the new rulers could safely reveal their bloody work and gain therefrom the deference they felt entitled to. By the time it finally was shown to the public a dozen years later, no one was in a position to do anything about it. The important thing to remember is the film was released slowly and carefully—always on the killer's terms.

"For years, we researchers have viewed the Abraham Zapruder home movie as a great accident in history, a wonderful instance of the perpetrators being caught with their pants down. I would suggest, to the contrary, that the Z-film is just one more indication of the control of the situation that President Kennedy's killers had in Dealey Plaza that terrible day."[129]

IT IS A TRAGEDY that early suspicion of the film, such as the major analysis of forgery done by Newcomb and Adams, was suppressed or taken over or discredited with false leads and misinformation planted on them like poison.

Those who pandered the film all these years have suppressed dissent, and perpetrated a massive propaganda campaign which not only fooled all of us, but got us hooked on the importance of the film to prove evidence of frontal shots which in fact could not be proven by those methods. We were misdirected—as we were with so much else in this case: the trajectory, the wounds, the autopsy, and the rifle and the bullet. Our critic-leaders have been our own worst enemies.

In this case, if thirty witnesses stated that the limousine stopped during the shooting, and we don't see it in the film, then the presumption must be that the film is wrong and has been altered. If the original maps showing where the shots arrived were altered to move the shots up the street, there must be a reason for it, and we begin to get an idea of that reason when numerous people, including Dan Rather and Ike Altgens, described seeing things and being in certain places at the time of the shooting which no longer appear in the film.

KENNEDY'S MOTTLED JOWL

Kennedy's right cheek and jowl is very mottled or puffed up in the frames in the 280s. This seems unnatural, even if he had been shot in the throat or the back. This might be further evidence of composite frames that were not done perfectly.

THE "BLACK DOG MAN"

Martin Shackelford has exploded the myth of the "Black Dog Man," which was thrown out to the research community as someone perching with a gun behind the concrete retaining wall on the Grassy Knoll in Dealey Plaza. Shackelford credits Robert Cutler, Richard Trask, Bill O'Neill, and Matthew Smith for providing elements he pulled together in order to expose one more trick played on us by undisciplined and hasty "research." The problem with visual evidence is that it's like looking at a crystal ball through a fog. People can claim that almost anything is in a picture—and it may be difficult if not impossible to disprove it.

Abraham Zapruder's employee, Marilyn Sitzman, reported that she saw a young black couple having their lunch on a bench [no longer there] in front of and below the pedestal where she and Zapruder were standing while they filmed the motorcade.[130]

The bench was photographed at the time, and is located in a chart in Trask's book, *Pictures of the Pain*,[131] in a photo which shows the lunch bags and pop bottles,[132] and in a film frame.[133]

Shackelford writes: "When the shots began, the young woman was standing up, looking toward Elm Street. She appears as the image long identified as 'The Black Dog Man' in the Hugh Betzner and Phil Willis photos. An enlargement from the Betzner photo, published by Matthew Smith, definitely looks like a woman."[134] The HSCA noted flesh tones on the photo image[135] "and it is clear from good color copies of the fifth Willis photo that the flesh tones of the image are darker than those of most of the other people in the picture, including Zapruder and Sitzman. . . . When she stood up, she apparently set her orange pop bottle on the concrete wall, where it appears, orange tone visible in a good enlargement, in the third photograph by Jim Towner." Both Marilyn Sitzman recalled seeing the bottle,[136] and Barbara Rowland "mentioned police inspecting a pop bottle.[137] The young couple ran away after the last shot.[138] One of the pop bottles broke and left a pool of red pop, which photographer Malcolm Couch assumed was blood at the time, as he told the Warren Commission.[139]

Shackelford continues:

> An image often mistakenly cited to bolster the theory of an assassin in this location is frame 413 of the Zapruder film, which shows the back of a man's head and a straight image which somewhat resembles a rifle. The image of the 'rifle' passes between Zapruder and the leaves of the bush, indicating it [probably a branch] was closer to Zapruder than the leaves [similar images, though not as long, appear elsewhere in the frame, also crossing leaves]. On the other hand, leaves appear between Zapruder and the man's head, indicating the man was beyond the bush." Robert Cutler established that the man is probably one of the three men on the Knoll steps, visible in the Moorman photograph, the Muchmore film, and others.

> "The preponderance of the witness and photographic evidence," Shackelford writes, "indicates that the figure long referred to as 'The Black Dog Man' was in fact a young black woman, part of the couple having lunch on the Knoll that day. Logic tells us that an assassin is unlikely to have positioned himself in plain view of Zapruder and Sitzman. In addition, Sitzman clearly stated that no shots were fired from any location that close to her.[140]

'Black Dog Man,' rest in peace.

BILL GREER'S HEAD TURNS

One of the claims involved the second set of two head turns of the driver of the limousine, Bill Greer, when he looks at the wounded Kennedy behind him while driving. The first set of turns under discussion starts in frame numbers 280–84. At 284, Greer is turned all the way around, looking behind him at Kennedy. This sequence ends when he starts to turn his head forward at 290. At 295, his head is turned all the way forward again. It takes him four to five frames to turn his head each way. No one disputes that those head turns take several frames to execute. But at frame 302, Greer turns his head back to look at Kennedy again. Our observations on repeated occasions in the National Archives viewing the slides of the film together indicate that the second set of head turns again take several frames each time, but other observations first put forward by Noel Twyman and repeated at ASK 1993 in Dallas by David Lifton claim that there is a head turn of 150 degrees executed in one frame.

I need to correct a sentence about this in *Killing the Truth*, p. 334. That page deals with the hole in back of Kennedy's head, and just following, the incorrect text reads, "Greer turns back toward the front at frame 316. There is a very clear picture of Greer turned to his right at 317." This last sentence meant that he had turned enough that his head was now 90 degrees from forward, faced directly right. The first sentence should read, "Greer starts his turn back toward the front at frame 316." Greer continues to turn and completes his turn forward by 320.

Chuck Marler mentioned the rapid head turn in the May 1994 issue of the *Fourth Decade*, and published more information on this in the November 1994 issue, using this language: "Mr. Twyman [Noel] obtained excellent color prints made from the Zapruder film, and in studying the frames noticed that in frame 302 William Greer was looking straight forward and one frame later (frame 303) the driver's head had turned approximately 150 degrees and was looking over his right shoulder at Kennedy. Greer held this position through frame 316. Again, one frame later (frame 317) Greer is looking straight ahead. The obvious and inescapable conclusion is that at two separate occasions, William Greer had turned his head approximately 150 degrees within one frame. As Zapruder's camera was operating at 18.3 frames per second, Greer made this movement in .056 second."

Twyman has conducted extensive interviews with Erwin Schwartz, Zapruder's former partner.

Experiments with athletes and others conducted by Twyman and Marler with cameras moving at 18 fps show such a movement is impossible.[141] But is the head turn done in just one frame, or does it take more? Intense study of the slides made from *Life*'s copy of the film for the National Archives by Martin Shackelford, Daryll Weatherly, Doug Mizzer, David Mantik, M.D., and myself, indicate that there is no one-frame head turn. Some among us thought that it took three to four frames, and Weatherly and I felt that the head turns took four frames, as with the earlier turns. The same is true of Greer's head turn back to looking forward starting at 316. It is claimed that this is done in just one frame, but again, the *Life*/ National Archives version of the film shows it taking at least three frames and probably four.

Knowing the sources Twyman, Lifton, and Marler replied upon

(David Lifton's versions of the Zapruder film, including a 35mm reel, the Medio Multimedia CD-ROM version probably made from the film provided by the Zapruder family attorney, Jamie Silverberg, and a claimed observation seen in the reproduced frames in volume 18 of the Warren Report), one must ask if one film has been altered differently from the other. In other words, as the above researchers claim, is every other frame removed from the film in certain sequences during the shooting to speed up the car when it might have stopped, or is there some other explanation?

I would like nothing better than to be able to find evidence of alteration if we could prove that Greer turns his head completely around in an eighteenth of a second, and then back again in another second. Another possible explanation is that the source film for the above claim is different from the National Archives version.

So then we have to investigate just where researchers, the National Archives, *Life,* and the others got their films. That is the job of the presidentially appointed JFK Assassinations Records Review Board, which is in charge of collecting all such material. A clue to the films' origins might provide us with the answer as to who has been altering or tampering with such evidence. The reader might want to study the major chapter on the Zapruder film in my last book, *Killing the Truth.*

There was another development in the Twyman/Marler thesis of a rapid Greer head turn, as first put forward in the *Fourth Decade* article, "William Greer's Impossible Head Turn," in November 1994. On December 27, 1994, I received a letter from Chuck Marler revising his claims. The bottom line of what he is left with is a turn of somewhere between 100 and 130 degrees.

On January 20, 1995, a clarification came from Marler. He states that his estimate in *The Fourth Decade* of a head turn of approximately 150 degrees is described as being made in *four* frames, *not* in between two frames. "My December 27th letter to you clearly describes a 150-degree head turn in four frames which contains an impossible 120–130 degree turn in one frame. . . . the *absolute minimum* one frame movement was 100 degrees." This is very different from the originally published statement that "in frame 302 William Greer was looking straight forward and one frame later frame (303) the driver's head had turned approximately 150 degrees and [he] was looking over his right shoulder at Kennedy. Greer held this position through frame 316. Again, one frame later (frame 317), Greer is looking straight ahead."[142] Now we have the whole turn taking four frames instead of two. But what of the one big turn of one hundred degrees he says happens between two frames? It doesn't happen.

Our team studying the film is sure that (a) there is no significant change of head position discernible in the two sets of frames (302–03, 316–17), and (b) as they appear in volume 18. or in the Archives.

Daryll Weatherly then drove down from New York State and we went to the National Archives to observe the film close up. We were allowed to study carefully the original *Life* slides of the frames given to the National Archives. We think that Twyman has made two fundamental errors of observation.

The first error was to suppose that the head itself was turned 150 (or even 130) degrees backward on the body in order to look back at Kennedy. It is probably impossible for a human head to turn more than 100 degrees, and even with peripheral vision, the driver had to move his legs to the right as far as they would go, keeping his left hand on the wheel, and turn his body about 45 or 50 degrees maximum to the right. As he is doing this, his head is turning an additional 90 to 100 degrees. This gives us very close to the 150 degrees Marler and Twyman say Greer's body is turned.

The above researchers had not taken into account the body itself making one-third of the total turn, which puts it within the realm of possibility, and also dovetails with the angular movements we, as well as Shackelford, saw. At no time does Greer's head turn more than fifty degrees in a frame, excluding the body's additional turn.

Another possible mistake in observation is that Twyman and Marler may have been fooled by two badly blurred frames preceding Greer's final movement to face forward (which he reaches at frame 319). It is impossible to have any idea what Greer is doing in those frames. It is possible that those frames were removed from the film that Twyman and Marler studied. As for Greer's turn to the rear beginning at frame 300, Shackelford, Weatherly, and I agree that the National Archives film shows that the first part of the turn shows his head turning 40 degrees. By frame 302 the head has turned 30 more degrees. At frame 303 the head has turned 45 degrees, and at frame 304, the head has turned 25 degrees, for a total of 140 degrees in five frames.

Shackelford thinks the turn back starting at frame 315 is a total of 150 degrees, and his head has turned 45 degrees by frame 316; another 30 degrees by frame 317; 25 degrees by frame 318, and 50 degrees by frame 319.

*   *   *

I BELIEVE THAT Greer's head is turned around to look at Kennedy in the Altgens photograph, said to be taken at frame 255. Perhaps all three turns were *one* turn while the car was actually stopped, but when the film was re-created by the forgers, they made two separate ones—repeating one of them twice, to give more of an illusion.

Marler, a county official in California, strongly believes that the alteration of the Zapruder film concealed "what happened 'behind' the sign, the slow speed or stopping of the limousine—which means increased reaction time for the Secret Service to respond, the true wounds to Kennedy's head, and the double head shot to Kennedy."[143] I took Marler's measure in a meeting in California in December 1994, because I was concerned he was being used in some way and that his information was false. Before anyone jumps to engage in character assassination against those of us (now many) who believe this film to be fake, I'd like to say that Mr. Marler is a man of very fine character, a religious man. He provided the biblical quote at the beginning of this book, which I substituted for the one I already had.

Marler gave some additional reasons to suspect tampering: "The Zapruder film was at the CIA(NPIC)—the most sophisticated film lab in the world; the film was sealed away from public view for twelve years; the splices and damage at Z 155–56 and 208–11. After working for hundreds of hours editing 8mm film, it is difficult to believe two separate accidents occurred. I think the splices were used to conceal mistakes: The reproduced photographs made from the slides *Life* provided for the Warren Commission were dark and of extremely poor quality. It is suspicious that the Muchmore film has a split at (M 468) approximately the same location of Zapruder frame 313 (the head shot); the rear of Kennedy's head is blackened by dark shadows when corresponding locations of Governor Connally and Mrs. Kennedy are plainly visible; Kennedy's backward movement after being shot seems extremely fast."[144]

Catch that last observation? The famous backward head snap may be too rapid to be caused by a shot from the front, especially one that went through the head. How many exploiters of the film mentioned that? And how many eyewitnesses described the head snap before having seen the film? Probably none. Frames may have been taken out of the head-shot sequence and that would have speeded up the backward movement. This evidence of alteration is overlooked by those who must believe the film is authentic in order to prove their case that JFK was shot from in front.

I'd like to add to Marler's observations that the film was altered to remove shots—which perhaps primarily required the removal of a single frame for each shot erased (if more than one), and the addition of a massive wound (the "blob") on Kennedy's face and the right front of his head, which could be painted, rephotographed, and added to the picture. When examined closely, the blob is so out of register as to lack all credibility.

RED HERRINGS

Not only do we have to contend with different versions of the Zapruder film with little or no way to know their origin or authenticity—some with "enhancement," some with retouching, some with frames removed, some with frames added or repeated (stretch framed), some with image steadying (which removes parts of the original), some with different frame numbers than others, and some that apparently were deliberately altered for the purpose of giving people an idea to sell—but we have apparent "red herrings" planted in the films by the forgers to make decoding of the ultimate forgery more difficult.

There may be things seen or perceived in various versions of the film that are tricks played on us. Other claims (among many examples) involve everything from streaks seen on the film purported to be bullet tracks, to muzzle flashes. It would be nice if some of this holds up under scrutiny, but usually hard-nosed researchers put them down as "artifacts."

Some see the driver of the car in poor bootleg copies of the film turn around and shoot Kennedy, streaks on the film at the time of the head shot that show bullet tracks coming in, and microsurgery the detection of using very sophisticated splicing. Do copies of the film exist that really support these assertions? Or are we looking at altered films or videos which might give the impression that these things are happening?

THE PROBLEM WITH THE Stemmons Freeway sign, its actual removal and movement after the assassination, and its wild jumping around in some versions of the film (apparent stretching) have caused a problem for researchers. The sign appears to grow and stretch when it slips into the sprocket area as the camera pans to the right. This is probably an effect of the camera mechanism. All other objects entering the sprocket area do the same.

Another red herring may be the American flag on the right

fender of the limousine. Many note that the flag hangs relatively limp along part of the street, whereas the presidential flag on the other fender flutters merrily. The flag is limp in the Altgens photo as well. This is not evidence of alteration of the film, necessarily.

One of the early, widely distributed bootleg copies of the film seems to be shot from the photos of frames reproduced in volume 18 of the Warren Report, since both show the bottom of the preceding frame at the top, and the top of the following frame at the bottom. Is there any other technical explanation for this phenomenon?

SUMMARY

Ultimately, the background of the fatal car's driver, fifty-five-year-old William Greer, will go down in history as a key to the truth of the assassination. This man did not drive off when the shooting started. Instead, he turned around twice and stared at Kennedy after the shots began and did not get the car out of there until Kennedy's head was blown apart, a time span of at least six to ten seconds. And what of Kellerman, who sat beside him? Between the two Secret Service men, they should have got that car moving. Kennedy would have survived his first wound easily. Why did the Secret Service permit a man that old to drive the car in the first place?

Greer was a Protestant from Northern Ireland who lived on the estate of Henry Cabot Lodge and worked for him before he became JFK's driver. Greer must have felt some antagonism for Kennedy, at the very least, for his trip to Catholic Ireland and for his peccadilloes.

Kennedy's driver was linked to a man who benefited greatly from the assassination: Henry Cabot Lodge, a scion of an old, prominent, and very political New England blue blood establishment family. Lodge became the ambassador to Saigon in South Vietnam and literally ran the war from his embassy. The military didn't run it. The CIA didn't run it so much as Henry Cabot Lodge ran it. Lodge apparently wanted the war that Kennedy tried to stop, just as Robert McNamara, Kennedy's Republican Secretary of Defense in his bipartisan cabinet, evidently wanted it and worked for it for years after Kennedy was dead and Johnson prosecuted the war.

There was a fortune in that war for the Dallas-Fort Worth families and defense companies, such as Bell Helicopters and General Dynamics, with so much investment in the arms industry at stake.

*   *   *

ONE OF THE EXPERIMENTS that should be conducted is to film—using a 1963 Bell & Howell camera identical to Zapruder's—a car coming down the center of the street from Zapruder's pedestal with the full zoom lens on, to see if the developed film eliminates all the landmarks, such as lampposts and structures in the background. The famous film has not a single object during the fatal head-shot period that tells us *where* this is happening with reference to the Plaza. We are asked to assume that the zoom lens has brought us in so close that there is nothing else in the picture except the limousine and its occupants. Two women were standing beside the lamppost to Zapruder's left and they are entirely eliminated from the film, with the car appearing to be over their heads due to Zapruder's elevation.

In the appendix by Daryll Weatherly, we will learn that the film is in fact an animation, with parts cut out and moved from one section to another. Weatherly presents the physics of vector analysis to demonstrate his belief that the film is an animation. Those who took over this film and sold it to us were therefore doing the work of the cover-up. They never questioned the film's authenticity or allowed such questions, and viciously attacked those who asked. We were not even to *think* that the film was not authentic. Some people became targets for destruction because of this. No wonder. The film is a key to the case, and has been the principal means of covering up the real shots showing there were more than one gunman.

The Zapruder film was used to direct attention away from what really happened during the shooting. Although it seems to show evidence of a frontal shot, it does not prove it; the "jet effect" and "neuromuscular reaction" countered that, whether true or not. The film distracted researchers from asking significant questions, or they were prompted to ask questions about the action in the film that did not really matter. The idea was to sell the film as the most significant piece of evidence in the assassination.

The first third of the film was massively manipulated because that is where the first shots were fired. An entire sequence of the limousine turning the corner was taken out. A second head shot occurred farther down Elm Street and was combined with what we now see. The differences between CE 585 (the December 1963 Plaza survey map) showing where the shots fell, and the May maps (CE 882 and 883) are major. The December map shows the last shots happening farther down the street than the official story had it. The first survey has a chart showing where three shots hit the car, almost evenly spaced, but all three of these maps were printed in such small format that they cannot be very well read, if at all, and almost no one would notice this. More about this in the next chapter.

We were hypnotized with this film, and ultimately it was an exercise in mass mind control. It was never a "time clock of the assassination" as we were told, but the exact opposite. Time and action were removed. That is how we were tricked.

As Professor Philip Melanson has written, "It is possible that the film of the century is more intimately related to the crime of the century than we ever knew—not because it *recorded* the crime of the century, as we have assumed, but because it was itself an instrument of conspiracy."[145]

In the art of the film business, anything is possible. It is, after all, an art.

The next chapter deals with the major discrepancies between the findings of the criminal investigators (the FBI and the Secret Service) as to where the shots landed, and what the Warren Commission said and the film now shows.

6

From the Secret Documents: Conflicts in the Autopsy Evidence

The panel continued to be concerned about the persistent disparity between its findings and those of the autopsy pathologists and the rigid tenacity with which the prosecutors maintained that the entrance wound was at or near the external occipital protuberance.

—VII House Select Committee on Assassinations

NUMEROUS INTERVIEWS WERE CONDUCTED in 1977–78 by the House Select Committee on Assassinations with personnel from President Kennedy's autopsy. These were not available to the public or researchers until the winter of 1993–94. The interviews were highly specialized and sometimes contained such contradictory information that it is understandable why they were not thought to be for public consumption, *if* that is the reason for their nondisclosure.

Since the appendices to their Report contained many individual interviews and other highly specialized papers from various scientists and witnesses, one might well ask why was it not *all* printed, especially since these interviews dealt with many important issues in the case? The material that was printed in 1979 contained information that raises serious questions about the official story, such as the autopsy prosector's insistence that the entry hole in the back of the head was low, near the hairline, not four to five inches higher where it was claimed to be in the X-rays and photographs by the HSCA. The doctor's placement of the wound posed quite a problem for the Assassinations Committee, and the basic conflict in the evidence between the alleged photographs and X-rays and what the doctors say has become a central issue in the case. I have hammered away on this issue from a time when no one else dealt with it to the present when not only that but the authenticity of the photographs and X-rays and nearly everything else in the case is in question. Every effort has been made to silence this debate, which is not merely academic but involves the very soul of this nation and its history.

The most fundamental questions of where the wounds were has been so muddied from the beginning that after thirty years we still do not have definitive answers. We must weigh the evidence as a court would.

Another example of serious conflict: the statements made by the other doctors when Humes and Boswell were interviewed by a panel of physicians for the House Committee, with regard to where the large head wound shows on the alleged X-rays of Kennedy. Dr. Charles S. Petty said: "I think the question that we all have is whether this [the large hole in the head] is anterior to the coronal suture or posterior to it."

Dr. Angel: "Oh, there was damage that far forward?"

Dr. Petty: "I believe so. I think the damage is quite apparent here in the lateral view of the skull by X-ray."

Dr. Angel: "Yes, that's right."

Dr. Petty: "And also on X-ray no. 1, the anterior-posterior view, right side."[1] Later on the same page, Dr. Angel again refers to the massive missing frontal bone on the X-ray: "It's really hard to be sure, square this with the X-ray which shows so much bone lost in this right frontal area."

This chapter should be taken together with the Medical Encyclopedia found at the end of my last book, *Killing the Truth,* and other previous chapters on the medical evidence and conflicts therein as a reference to supporting documentation for each issue in this chapter. This is largely constructed from the new information contained in the interviews released in the winter of 1993–94. I have utilized *probably* every statement of any significance made by each medical witness in the heretofore secret documents and put them in categories in this chapter so that the reader may contrast them with each other. I have also inserted some information previously available on many of the issues, but this is not an exhaustive documentation, which would take an entire book. The Medical Encyclopedia in *Killing the Truth,* and chapters on conflicts in evidence in three of my last books, give much additional data. For instance, it would take a great deal of space to detail what each witness said in the past about the President's head wounds, but this can be found in my first book, *High Treason,* and in the Medical Encyclopedia in *Killing the Truth.* There is a major chapter (6) on "The Autopsy: Conflicts in the Evidence," in *High Treason 2,* study Chapter 5,

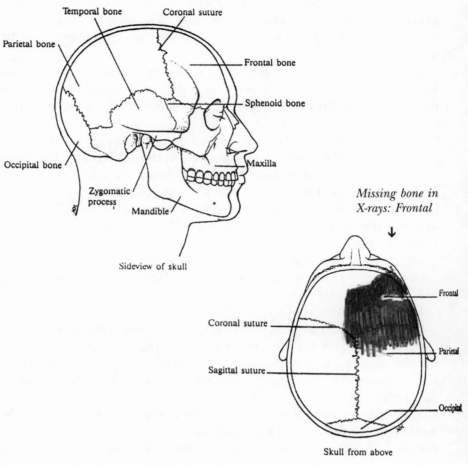

Temporal bone

Coronal suture

Parietal bone

Frontal bone

Sphenoid bone

Occipital bone

Maxilla

Zygomatic process

Mandible

Sideview of skull

Missing bone in X-rays: Frontal

↓

Coronal suture

Frontal

Sagittal suture

Parietal

Occipital

Skull from above

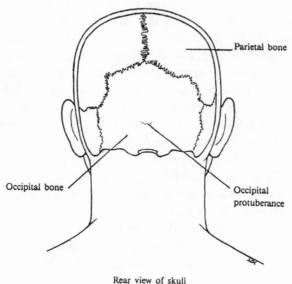

Parietal bone

Occipital bone

Occipital protuberance

Rear view of skull

"Bethesda Naval Hospital" (p. 125) and of course my own major interviews in that book with numerous autopsy witnesses.*

As for the primary conflict in the evidence discussed in this chapter—the two seriously opposing positions for the entry into the back of the head—one might bear in mind that the otherwise incompetent work done by the American Medical Association on the case in 1992–93 printed in a series of articles once more the autopsy doctor's insistence that the entry *was low* on the back of head.[2] Never once did the AMA's *Journal* answer any of the key points in the letters written to them questioning their work, nor did they grasp the significance of what the low entry meant. The placement of the wound is crucial, since a low wound could not have come from the sixth-floor window and blown off the back of Kennedy's head. The conspirators had to change both the placement of the entry and the place where the skull was missing. By creating a semantic problem for us—saying that bone was "missing" rather than "disrupted *or* missing," where there were hinged flaps of bone— we were given a much larger hole more forward on the head.

Dr. Mantik's findings in the National Archives (as expressed to me on June 16, 1995) are that the X-rays show that the large defect extended forward of the coronal suture into frontal bone as far as the hairline, where the bone appears to be broken off in a V-shaped notch above the right eye. The entire forehead is intact. Mantik believes that the apex of the slender triangular missing frontal bone is the site of a second bullet entry because it connects with the conelike trail of bullet fragments passing along the head's vertex and exiting at the rear well above the cowlick. If true, this is astonishing.

Was all of the bone missing on the top of the head? No. The large 9.5 cm piece of parietal bone which arrived at the autopsy at midnight was from the right side. This piece of bone broke off at the coronal suture across the top of the head from left to right, and more or less bordered the sagittal suture where a 10 cm piece of left parietal bone was broken off—but remained attached to the scalp in the form of a large flap. The large right parietal bone, two small fragments and one medium-sized piece (the Harper fragment) were blown off the back of the head by either the first or second head shot. Most of the torn scalp remained, leaving a missing area of scalp in the back about the size of an orange or a fist. There was no bone where the scalp was missing, as well.

*See also the chapter on the "New Evidence: The 1992 Dallas Conference," p. 283.

I believe the 10 cm piece was the skullcap, the piece that Clint Hill saw lying in the backseat, and that was later retrieved from the car.

After reading the many suppressed reports and interviews, it appears that there is some colossal secret being kept from us in this case beyond what we suspect, which can only dovetail with the obvious conclusions being drawn about the conspiracy by myself and some other researchers. Something else—a secret too dark, involving multiple gunmen and many shots—is being kept from us. Or the evidence of a shot hitting him in the forward part of his head. There are lies about where the back wound was. Or a staged autopsy.

The military barred civilians or reporters or any representative of the public from President Kennedy's autopsy. This, of course, leads to suspicion and certainly might have prevented a more independent perspective on what took place there. Some information makes it seem that the military or others may have lied and made it look as if the Kennedy family had limited the autopsy, when in fact someone else was limiting it to cover up the true nature of the wounds. To the contrary is a report that Admiral Calvin Galloway tried to get the family to take the body to an undertaker and not to a medical examiner.[3] This, of course, would have seen the body buried without an autopsy from a medical examiner in a murder case, which would controvert the law in every state in the nation. No autopsy means no medical-criminal evidence.

General Godfrey McHugh, the President's aide, engaged in a heated discussion with Admiral Galloway when they arrived at the hospital and the body was still in the ambulance. As reported by William Manchester, McHugh told Galloway that Jacqueline Kennedy wanted the preparations for burial and (presumably) an autopsy done by the Navy. Kenneth O'Donnell ordered Galloway to proceed with the autopsy, saying, "You heard the decision from the General [McHugh]." Galloway had told McHugh that the autopsy there "was not impossible . . . it's difficult, though. And it might be unsatisfactory."[4]

Why would Galloway say they didn't have the facilities when they had a morgue (and a new one at that, plus the old morgue) and did three to six autopsies there almost every day? Why was this dispute reported, and is it true? We know from much testimony that the hospital had been preparing all afternoon to receive the body, but at the last minute, they are trying to turn it away. Galloway would have known that the hospital pathologists might not have had enough ballistics experience. Dr. Karnei recalled that the other doctors wanted someone with ballistics experience.[5] Dr. Pierre Finck was called into the procedure late; and arrived at 8:30 P.M., almost an hour and a half after the body arrived, when the preliminary examinations, photography, removal of the brain, X-raying, and the large incision in the torso had already been done.

One purpose of this chapter is to demonstrate how all the investigations failed to deal with conflicts or always closely examine witnesses on their statements. Maybe deliberately.

BETHESDA NAVAL HOSPITAL

Was there a decoy ambulance used to get the body to Bethesda from Andrews Air Force Base? Richard Lipsey, aide to General Philip Wehle, the commander of the Military District of Washington, flew with Wehle by helicopter from Andrews to Bethesda and took JFK into the back of the hospital. A decoy hearse had been driven to the front, according to Lipsey. The key statement that he made to House investigators followed: "A decoy hearse had been driven to the front. *After* [author's emphasis] bringing the body into Bethesda," Lipsey said that "Jackie Kennedy and the family entered the front of Bethesda and traveled to the 'Presidential suite.' "[6]

Paul O'Connor told me that "there were decoy ambulances and caskets that night before we received the casket with the body."[7] I have the idea that a researcher had access to a great deal of information from the HSCA, including addresses and phone numbers of witnesses. He took the information that was being developed and created his own interpretation to all of it. Here we have a clear statement indicating that the body was dropped off first and then the ambulance drove around and let Jackie and the others out at the front. Certainly Francis X. O'Neill's statement in his interview contradicts this. He says that the ambulance stopped at the front entrance where Jackie and RFK disembarked.[8] James Sibert, the other FBI man present, also wrote that "When the motorcade from the airport arrived at the Naval Hospital, Bobby Kennedy and Mrs. Kennedy were let off at the Administration Building. Mr. O'Neill and I helped carry the damaged casket into the autopsy room with some Secret Service agents."[9]

Not much time might have elapsed, but it is probable that the body was taken in and removed from the coffin when some of the men saw Jackie enter from outside. Much was made of the fact that they thought they had the body before she got there, and a sinister twist was put on this. Although I can't prove that the body wasn't stolen at some point, I don't believe it, nor do the vast majority think it was possible.

I can imagine that the widow and some of the others stood outside for a time, as we know there was an argument between McHugh and Galloway in front as to whether the body should be autopsied there, had a cigarette, stretched their bodies and breathed fresh air after a terrible day, being cramped up in the ambulance sitting on each other's laps, and the preceding long flight from Dallas. Then they went in, and probably remained near the front door for a time, or in the anteroom near the front door.

When did the Bethesda people know they were going to perform the autopsy? Dr. Boswell stated that he was notified in the early afternoon of his forthcoming role in the autopsy by Bruce Smith, the Acting Director of the Armed Forces Institute of Pathology. Boswell was the first one contacted (Humes was off at the time.) Boswell then contracted the commanding officer of the medical school and hospital. "He [Boswell] was told that Dr. Burkley had insisted that the President be brought there."[10] After Boswell learned that he was to perform the autopsy, "he went to do some 'moonlighting' at Suburban Hospital and was called back approximately six o'clock."[11] It would seem that Burkley perhaps decided that the body would go to Bethesda *before* he had an agreement from Jackie. If Humes learned of this in the "early afternoon," which we would think means before 3:00 P.M., or midafternoon, then this is essentially *before* the plane took off in Dallas (3:47 EST), a time zone one hour earlier. The official record shows that the decision to go to Bethesda was not made until the plane had been flying for some time. Corroborating Boswell is the fact that he thought he had time to work at another hospital.

On the day of the assassination, James Curtis Jenkins, who assisted at autopsies and was a student lab technician, said that he learned of the death at approximately 3:30 P.M. while in class. He said classes were subsequently dismissed. He was told to prepare the morgue at approximately 4:15 to 4:30 P.M., his orders coming from the "Duty Section Chief."[12] If accurate, the time was 3:15 or 3:30 in Dallas, and the plane had been in the air with the body flying back to Bethesda only a short time, having taken off at 2:47 CST. They knew then that the body was coming to Bethesda.

He said he got there about thirty to forty minutes before the autopsy. The body arrived and Jenkins logged the autopsy number in the ledger book (which is missing) but did not enter a name.

Jenkins was told *not* to put the name in the log. He noticed that later that evening someone had written the initial "C" or "CNC" where the name normally would be. Subsequent to the President's autopsy, an Air Force colonel[13] and a child[14] were autopsied that night and would have been logged into that ledger book before it was "retired." Jenkins identified the body to the funeral home people, and it was he who put a tag on the big toe.

Why didn't the Warren Commission or the HSCA ask each witness when and how they found out the autopsy would be at Bethesda?

How was it that Dr. Finck was brought in to the autopsy? Dr. Boswell indicated that he and Dr. Humes decided during the autopsy that Dr. Pierre Finck should be brought in from the Armed Forces Institute of Pathology. Previously, the AFIP had offered the services of anyone on their staff. Humes and Boswell decided on Finck when they first examined the body and recognized that the main problem was bullet wounds.[15] Finck had little active experience in actual autopsies. His job was reviewing thousands of files of violent death. By Finck's testimony, the brain had been removed by the time he arrived at 8:30.[16]

Where should the autopsy have been performed? Dr. Boswell said it should not have been performed at Bethesda but at the Armed Forces Institute of Pathology (Walter Reed). Boswell told Bruce Smith that it was "ridiculous to do the post here." He said that he was told that Dr. Burkley had insisted that the President be brought there.[17]

Legally, it should have been performed in Texas.

Was the autopsy complete? Dr. Pierre Finck at first felt that they should not check off the autopsy as having been complete.[18] He said that in retrospect some things did not appear to have been completed, but the decision to call it "complete" was based on their having performed the main functions of determining the cause of death (gunshot) and deciding on the direction from which the shots came.[19] Finck said that "Humes declared that the block 'complete autopsy' should be checked."[20] This was done and the autopsy report was signed on November 24.

Finck wrote: "After the publication of the Warren Report, numerous physicians criticized the autopsy protocol that did not describe the adrenal glands of Kennedy, who suffered from adrenal insufficiency. The prosectors complied with the autopsy permit and its restrictions. I was told that the Kennedy family first authorized the autopsy of the head only and then extended the permission to the chest. Organs of the neck were not removed because of the same restrictions. I feel that the prosectors accomplished their MISSION that was to determine the direction of the shots and the cause of death. The head wound was definitely fatal. There were rumors—and even testimonies—that the President had been shot from behind and from the front. I established that Kennedy had two wounds of entrance in the back: one in the back of his head and one in his upper back at the base of the neck. After the completion of the postmortem examination, the Surgeon General of the Navy (Admiral Kinney) told us not to discuss the autopsy with anyone, even among the prosectors or with the investigators involved. . . .[21]

"I was denied the opportunity to examine the clothing of Kennedy. [The following passage was censored, but later typed in:] One officer who outranked me told me that my request was only of academic interest. The same officer did not agree to state in the autopsy report that the autopsy was incomplete, as I had suggested to indicate. . . . Despite the incomplete or the inaccurate information we had at the time of the autopsy (for example, we were told that a bullet had been found on Kennedy's stretcher whereas it was on Connally's), such as gross microscopic and spectrographic study of the clothing (FBI), and by independent experiments such as those conducted in Wound Ballistics at the US Army Arsenal, Edgewood, Maryland."[22] Finck also had not seen the photographs he had supervised at that point.

Dr. Boswell stated to House Committee investigators that Admiral George Burkley, the President's personal physician, supervised the autopsy as the liaison for the family and was not interested in a full autopsy. They were only looking for a bullet. Boswell and others present agreed that they should do a complete autopsy.[23] Nevertheless, the neck organs were not removed, the back wound was not dissected, the clothes not examined at the autopsy and so on. The HSCA printed an extensive critique of the autopsy.[24]

At the beginning, Dr. Burkley gave instructions and said very early on that the police had "captured the guy who did this, all we need is the bullet." Dr. Boswell said, "We argued with him at that point . . . saying the autopsy must be complete and thorough."[25]

"Dr. Burkley indicated he wanted just a limited autopsy to the thorax, and this was then extended to the head. Dr. Humes insisted there be a complete autopsy, saying, for example, the adrenals were extremely important. Dr. Burkley said it would be okay to examine the adrenals if they could reach them through the upper opening.

Dr. Boswell reached down and tried to reach the adrenals but could not and Dr. Burkley agreed that they could do a full autopsy.''[26] Perhaps the most important witness of all, Dr. George Burkley, was not interviewed by the Warren Commission—nor was there a serious interview with the HSCA.

The House panel of doctors discussed with Dr. Pierre Finck whether or not the autopsy was complete. Finck had been brought in because he was more expert in dealing with forensics, though he did not actually perform autopsies in criminal investigations. "Looking back, the autopsy accomplished its purpose. I think Dr. Humes made that point. He said the purpose of the autopsy was to establish the number of wounds, the direction of the projectiles, and establish a cause of death, and from that viewpoint it was complete.''[27] It was pointed out to Finck that his own memorandum to General Blumberg questioned the completeness of the autopsy, but he agreed with Humes that it accomplished its purpose.

Dr. John I. Coe then asked Finck if his statement that the autopsy was incomplete was based on a lack of examination during the autopsy or a lack of ability to write all the information which was garnered from the examination. They were not allowed to discuss the adrenal problem, which I feel was a red herring used to mask other things that could not be discussed. Finck answered: "Lack of examination at the time of autopsy, in that sense."

"In what sense?"

"Well, more dissection of the neck, in that sense."

"Abdominal?"

"Or an autopsy complete, all the cavities should be examined. But when the wounds involved the head and the neck, if the abdomen is not examined it is of secondary importance so I finally felt I could—"

"Is it your recollection that the abdominal organs were not examined?"

"I don't remember in detail whether it was examined or not because again as I said at the beginning, I was there for wounds.''[28] See the discussion of this question on pages 13–15 of vol. 7 of the House Committee books.

Francis X. O'Neill told the House investigators that Admiral Galloway resolved the issue of a full versus a partial autopsy by ordering a complete autopsy.[29]

Jan Gail Rudnicki, the Navy lab technologist who stood at the table throughout the evening, felt that the autopsy was not complete because the procedure seemed to be limited to finding only missiles or missile tracts. He felt the general atmosphere indicated that the pathologists were not performing a full or standard autopsy. For instance, Rudnicki stated that he could not recall tissue specimens being taken from the internal organs.[30]

Was the autopsy report changed? Dr. Pierre Finck testified that Admiral Galloway "personally ordered changes in the autopsy report after it was drafted."[31] *No one seems to have asked him what the changes were.* The report was, therefore, *altered.*

Were chest tubes inserted in Dallas to drain the chest? This is in some dispute. The evidence seems clear from the Dallas doctors that the tubes went all the way into the chest and fluid was being pumped out,[32] but the autopsy doctors and technicians dispute this and say that the incisions were merely started but did not penetrate into the chest.[33]

Was the President's face marked or damaged? I collected massive evidence that there was no damage to the face, other than the right eye being divergent and slightly popped from the orbit.[34] The photographs show no damage in the face other than a slight bruise above the right eye, which was described by some witnesses. Roy Kellerman commented on this when he told Andy Purdy and Jim Kelly that "the face was unmarked."[35] *All* witnesses said essentially the same thing. The "stare of death" photo cannot be real because the open right eye is normal.

This is corroborated by the Dallas doctors and is noted in the autopsy report: ". . . with abnormal mobility of the underyling bone."[36] But there were indications that the bone inside the skull behind the face was damaged. Jerrol Custer, who took X-rays of the skull, told me that the scalp and skin of the face was "mobile" and the skin drooped.[37]

The question of damage to the face is a major issue when one views the Zapruder film and the X-rays, which show apparent major damage to the face. Both are false. I could be wrong about what the Zapruder film apparently shows (most of the President's brain hanging out of his right eye and temple), as there is a strong opinion that what I call a "blob" appearing on the President's face is in fact a flap of scalp falling down. I do not believe that the necessary laceration of the scalp was present in Dallas but occurred as the body was moved onto the plane or later. The flap would have fallen down at Parkland during many movements of the head and been noticed. No one saw such a flap, and it could not account for the appearance of the blob in any case.

Dr. Mantik, myself, and two other researchers entered the National Archives to study the Zapruder slides, and it was clear that the large "blob" is not a flap and cannot be a flap, but is an alteration to the film to make it appear that a shot from behind damaged the right front of his skull. Furthermore, the area superior to the "blob" should not contain hair if the "blob" is an inverted flap. But this area above the "blob" seems to contain hair.

Tom Robinson, the mortician who did the cosmetics for what they thought was going to be an open coffin, told the House investigators that "I remember the tracheotomy; I remember the bones of the skull and face badly shattered." "Where on the face were they shattered, which of the bones?" "You cannot see that from the outside. This is looking through the opening that the physicians had made at the back of the skull."[38] Many others agreed and said the face was "perfect" and not damaged in any way. Perhaps this can account for the thinned-out or missing frontal bone just above the hairline of the right frontal face in the X-rays.

Yet, Lt. Richard Lipsey said that "one bullet entered the back of the head and exited resulting in part of the face and head being blown away—"[39] Taking this together with the X-rays and the Zapruder film, we begin to get a picture of two autopsies and two bodies, however untrue that may be. The confusion seems intentional.

When were the photographs and X-rays of the body taken? Dr. John Ebersole described the taking of the skull films prior to the commencement of the autopsy at 8:00 P.M.,[40] but X-rays continued to be taken at intervals during the night. And, obviously, photographs were taken after the brain was removed to capture the beveling on the inside of the skull and the interior of the chest after the organs were removed. It appears that more X-rays were taken at the midnight hour, and three X-rays were made of the pieces of bone that came in at midnight from Dallas.[41] There doesn't seem to be anything new here.

Ebersole repents that most of the X-rays were taken early. The issue came up when two abdominal X-rays were discussed. Both were apparently taken early, "because there does appear to be fecal in the large intestines on both," meaning the intestines had not been removed yet. Dr. Michael Baden says, "The second go-around was after the autopsy had been done." Ebersole corrects him, though Baden cannot be faulted for confusion in the face of so much conflict in the record, with no clock times registered on the X-rays themselves. Ebersole replies, "No, certainly the autopsy was not completed at the time of the second one. It would have possibly been started, but all X-rays with the exception of fragments were taken fairly early in the evening.''

"Do you recall independently whether the pelvic organs were looked at and examined in the course of the autopsy?"

"Yes, they were."[42] Ebersole then described seeing the pelvic organs removed and "I specifically remember seeing the kidneys being laid outside the body."[43] That is when they searched for the adrenals, one of the big mysteries of a generation. There must have been an incision *into* the pelvis in order to do this.

When were calls made to Parkland in Dallas? There is no credible evidence of the autopsy doctors' calls to Parkland Hospital from Bethesda before the body left the autopsy. Humes has repeatedly testified that he made the call on the following morning and ostensibly learned of the tracheostomy and the frontal bullet wound then. Audrey Bell's statements to me that calls came to Dr. Perry during the evening or night from the autopsy have not been corroborated by Perry or anyone else, though they may very well be true. She could have the day wrong, too. Nevertheless, it seems reasonable that others would have called Parkland during the autopsy, and don't want to admit it.

Dr. Ebersole stated to House Committee investigators that "Somewhere in the course of the evening Dr. Humes received information from Dallas re the procedures that had been carried out there, number one. . . . Somewhere in the course of the autopsy Dr. Humes was made aware of the surgical procedures at Dallas vis-a-vis the neck."

"And what was that information?"

"The information was that there had been a wound of exit there, a tracheotomy and a suturing done."[44] This latter, of course, is new and probably wrong. Yet, he told others he saw sutures. It's certain that none were done, we think. And, no one in Dallas ever called the throat wound one of entry.

Dr. Humes is quite strong on the time he made the call to Dallas, indicating that there was no phone in the autopsy room itself (He must have meant an outside phone. There was a phone on the wall, but it was probably a hospital phone) with which to call outside the hospital (see below) and that "Saturday morning we got together and we called Dallas."

Dr. Humes: "We called Dallas. . . ."

Dr. Michael Baden: "Now this is the day after?"

"The day after, within six to eight hours of having completed the examination, assisting Gawler's and so forth for the preparation of the President's remains. We got together and discussed our problem. We said we've got to talk to the people in Dallas. *We should have talked to them the night before* [emphasis author's], but there was no way we could get out of the room . . . so I called Dr. Perry. We had a very nice conversation on the phone in which he described a missile wound, what he interpreted as a missile wound, in the midline of the neck through which he had created a very quick emergency, as you can see from the photographs, tracheotomy incisions. In effect destroying its value to us and obscuring it very gorgeously for us. Well, of course, the minute he said that to me, lights went on, and we said ah, we have someplace for our missile to have gone."[45] This is about the most revealing statement in the medical evidence, since it shows how the whole idea of a bullet transiting from back to front—and that way could pass through Connally—was fabricated at least one day later. Humes had told the same thing to his friend Arlen Specter, when interviewed by him for the Warren Commission—that he called Perry the next day and found out about the throat bullet hole. Of course it was all a lie.

Dr. Robert Livingston, as reported in *Killing the Truth,* stated that he spoke with Humes before the autopsy began and told him that Dr. Perry had announced publicly that the President had an entry wound in his throat.[46]

Was there a "Y" cut or a smaller "U" cut used to open the body? The autopsy report states that a "Customary (Y)-shaped incision is used to examine the body cavities."[47] The bottom part of the "Y" cut is down the abdomen as far as the genitals, with the upper part having two cuts on both sides of the chest to the shoulders. But there is adequate testimony from those present that this was not done, that in fact they used a different incision, and removed the abdominal organs through the chest. An interview with Dr. Boswell flatly contradicted his own autopsy report. He told investigators for the House Committee that they did not make a "Y" incision; rather they did an incision from axilla down below from the chest.[48]

Dr. Finck was asked repeatedly by the House Forensic Panel what sort of incision was used, and he referred them to the autopsy report. He repeatedly said he did not remember what incision was used,[49] but he testified under oath at the Clay Shaw trial that "the usual Y-cut incision had been made."[50]

Custer told me that a "Y" incision had been made.[51] It is possible that after authority was extended to do a more or less full autopsy and it was found some organs could not be removed through the chest, the incision was extended from the solar plexus down to the genital area. But this is not clarified in evidence.

Were the organs weighed at the autopsy? Yes, or at least some of them. Dr. Ebersole describes the weighing of the kidneys and liver in his interview with the House. He said that Boswell actually weighed the organs.[52] Some try to explain the strange weights given some of the organs (a weight of 1,500 grams was given for the brain, and 650 grams for the liver) as "dry labing." I believe this to be part of the trail left by the doctors and federal agents to indicate they were coerced. According to this idea, the organs were not weighed, but different and contradictory weights were simply assigned later when the report was written. There is no autopsy in the world that would not weigh the organs, a standard procedure to compile statistics as well as to gauge the health of the deceased. The proof that dry labing was not done is in the fact that John Kennedy's liver was given a weight far too small to sustain adult human life. There would be no such mistake in fabricating weights, and instead, we have a clear indication that the doctors were trying to alert us that something was drastically wrong at the autopsy. They had a figurative gun to their head.

James Curtis Jenkins told House investigators that he recalls writing down the weights, but doesn't "believe he actually weighed them."[53] This apparently means that someone else put the organs on the scale. Jenkins repeated that the organs were weighed later in his interview, and told me the same thing.[54] (See the later section in this chapter under "Drawings.")

Jenkins told me that the brain was not weighed.[55] The interview was before three television cameras and in the presence of some of the Parkland witnesses and two others from the autopsy. The theory that the brain or some of the weights were fabricated therefore is credible.

Were there two or more examinations—on and off the record? The report or record of the autopsy seems to conflict on a number of points with the actual observations at the autopsy: There is adequate evidence showing that the bullet that struck the President in the back did not pass into the chest or through the body and come out the neck. Not only did the FBI and other observers report that the bullet did not pass into the body, but it is impossible for any bullet to have come out of the throat without doing major damage to the bony structures behind it and to the trachea, at the very least.

*   *   *

What did CBS know and when did they know it? Were the FBI men actually in the room? Did a bullet pass through the body? A secret CBS document dated January 10, 1967,[56] says that "Jim Snyder of the CBS bureau in D.C. told me today he is personally acquainted with Dr. Humes. They go to the same church and are personally friendly. Snyder also knows Humes's boss in Bethesda; he is a neighbor across the street from Snyder. Because of personal relationships Snyder said he would not want any of the following to be traced back to him; nor would he feel he could be a middleman in any CBS efforts to deal with Humes. Snyder said he has spoken with Humes about the assassination. In one conversation Humes said one X-ray of the Kennedy autopsy would answer many questions that have been raised about the path of the bullet going from Kennedy's back through his throat. Humes said FBI agents were not in the autopsy room during the autopsy; they were kept in an anteroom, and their report is simply wrong. Although initially in the autopsy procedure the back wound could only be penetrated to finger length, a probe later was made—when no FBI men were present—that traced the path of the bullet from the back going downward, then upward slightly, then downward again exiting at the throat.

"One X-ray photo taken, Humes said, clearly shows the above, as it was apparently taken with a metal probe that was left in the body to show the wound's path.

"Humes said that a wound from a high-power rifle, once it enters a body, causes muscle, etc., to separate and later contract; thus the difficulty in initially tracing the wound's path in the case of Kennedy. Also, once a bullet from a high-power rifle enters a body, its course can be completely erratic; a neck wound could result in a bullet emerging in a person's leg or anywhere else.

"Humes refused to discuss with Snyder the 'single-bullet' theory in which the Warren Commission contends the same bullet described above went thru both Kennedy and Connally.

"Humes also said he had orders from someone he refused to disclose—other than stating it was not Robert Kennedy—to not do a complete autopsy. Thus the autopsy did not go into JFK's kidney disease, etc.

"Humes's explanation for burning his autopsy notes was that they were essentially irrelevant details dealing with routine body measurements, and that he never thought any controversy would develop from his having done this."

This story has its questionable aspects. Attorney Roger Feinman, a longtime researcher into the assassination and former colleague of Sylvia Meagher, wrote Congressman John Conyers, who held hearings on the case in November 1993. He said that CBS, which presented a major four-part investigative report on the Warren Commission controversy, did not disclose the information about the probe passed through the body and photos and X-rays taken of it. Instead, Feinman says that they told former Warren Commissioner John J. McCloy, who was employed by President Lyndon Johnson, about it. McCloy's daughter, Ellen, worked for CBS News. Within a matter of days, the doctors were ordered to go to the National Archives on January 20, 1967, and look again at the photos and X-rays (they saw them on November 10, 1966. As you will read elsewhere in this book, Dr. Pierre Finck was suddenly ordered back from Vietnam and the Department of Justice made the doctors sign a statement about the photographs and X-rays, attesting that they did not change the findings of their autopsy report. Barefoot Sanders, a friend of Johnson and fellow Texan, wrote the statement which the doctors were asked to sign. Meanwhile, the case against Clay Shaw in New Orleans was getting under way for conspiracy in the assassination of President Kennedy. Finck ultimately testified in the trial in 1969.

Feinman tells us that he later talked to Jim Snyder, who confirmed most of the details but denied the part about the probe. "When it came to the probe story, however, he attempted to disclaim that he had ever said anything of the kind to Richter."[57] More doubt is cast on the story by the claim that they didn't investigate JFK's adrenal disease, when we now know they did, and the claim that the FBI men weren't in the room. The document seems spurious, or Humes was making smoke to cover himself. This memo appears clearly fake in light of the extensive testimony that the bullet did not pass through the body. Dr. Humes testified under oath to the Warren Commission that it was impossible to probe the back wound.[58]

Putting the lie to the memo is a heretofore secret report of an interview with Secret Service man James K. Fox in 1978, who developed black-and-white prints from the color autopsy pictures he'd taken to the Naval photo processing center. He commented on the probe issue long before Roger Feinman unveiled his CBS memoradum, saying that no metal probes were present in the photographs.[59]

Were the FBI men actually in the room? FBI agent Francis X. O'Neill told House Committee investigators that he helped Sibert, Greer, and Kellerman place the casket on a roller and transport it into the autopsy room. O'Neill stated that he was present when various persons placed the body on the autopsy table. Doctors then proceeded to remove the sheet covering JFK and to photograph the body. O'Neill remained "right next to the body," a distance of closer than two yards. O'Neill said that Sibert, Greer, and Kellerman were also present.[60]

FBI agent James Sibert stated that either he or Francis X. O'Neill were present at all times in the autopsy room.[61] He was not asked if that meant the anteroom. It is questionable whether the HSCA knew of the CBS memorandum on what Humes had to say privately to a fellow parishioner, but Roger Feinman, the source of the memo, might know. James W. Sibert mentioned that "he and O'Neill were close enough to get anything that the doctors said about measurements. He also said that if he 'couldn't understand the measurements spoken by Humes, he had him restate them.' "[62] They were in fact in the room, not talking back and forth through the closed door to the anteroom. Sibert wrote that "We were always close to the doctors, and as measurements were made by Dr. Humes or other doctors we would write them down. If I didn't understand the measurements, I requested Humes to repeat them."[63]

O'Neill said that both a Secret Service man and an FBI man were always present. He only left the room once with Kellerman and McHugh to get a sandwich. No presidential aides were present, but later on, Kellerman and O'Leary, both Secret Service agents, entered the room.[64] Sibert wrote that "either O'Neill or I was present in the autopsy room with the exception of when photographs and X-rays were taken, at which time everyone other than radiologists and photographers was asked to leave the room. Most of the time O'Neill and I were both present during the autopsy."[65]

Did the autopsists investigate Kennedy's adrenal disease? Yes, although it was never revealed until I published it in *High Treason 2*.[66] Dr. Robert Karnei described to me the search for the adrenals in great detail. They spent quite some time looking for his adrenal glands and found none,[67] but this was not reported. Boswell told the HSCA that he looked for the adrenals and that they were atrophied.[68] Boswell also said that Dr. Burkley made clear that he didn't want a report on the adrenal glands, wanting that information only to be reported informally.[69]

Ebersole lied outright about this matter to the House panelists when he was asked if there was some concern at the autopsy about the condition of the adrenal glands. "No, sir, I don't see any. . . . we all had heard that he may have had adrenal insufficiency but certainly this was not discussed or to my knowledge even mentioned the night of the autopsy."[70]

When was the bullet found at Parkland? Roy Kellerman told Andy
Purdy and Jim Kelly that when they were taking the casket out of
Parkland to go to the airport, FBI agent Richard Johnsen came up
to him and said ". . . a man gave me a bullet." Kellerman said that
apparently this was the only bullet which "didn't explode" during
the assassination. Therefore, Kellerman knew of the finding of the
bullet when he was present at the autopsy during the discussions
about where the bullet had gone in the body.[71]

The other doctors later learned of the bullet when the FBI agent
called the FBI lab and was told about it.

When did the doctors learn about the bullet found at Parkland?
James W. Sibert, the FBI agent present, said that he called Chuck
Killion at the FBI lab (to find out about "ice" bullets) and was told
about the bullet found in Parkland. Sibert said he didn't believe
anyone called Parkland Hospital that night to find out what had
happened there.[72] It would be logical for the doctors to conclude
that the bullet fell out of Kennedy's body, unless there was information given to Sibert that the bullet had been found on Connally's
stretcher, which it was not. If they had been told that, they could
still conclude that the bullet fell out of Kennedy's back. They did
not know how many shots were fired and the FBI assumed that
Connally was hit with a separate bullet, a position they may never
have retracted. The FBI itself never accepted the single-bullet theory easily.

Kellerman explained that he told Finck they had found a bullet
at Parkland while Finck was probing the back wound. The other
doctors may not have heard this, as Kellerman was standing next
to Finck and they were on the back side of the body a little away
from the others.[73]

Jan Rudnicki said that he recalled the doctors discussing the bullet found in Dallas.[74]

It seems logical that the official story was not entirely formulated
ad hoc, or after the fact, since it's clear that somebody would have
wanted the autopsy doctors to know right then that a bullet had
been found on Connally's stretcher. No one said the bullet had
been found on Connally's stretcher. Had they done so, there still
might not have been a conflict since they were not yet limited to
only two bullets striking both men. As things stood, there was evidence of two bullets striking Kennedy, if we ignore evidence of
other shots striking Kennedy, and one striking Connally. They also
could ignore the shot that kicked up cement and hit James Tague
down the street, because they didn't know about it. The trajectory

of that shot lined up with the car and comes from nowhere near the building where Oswald was (the Texas School Book Depository) but leads to the Dal-Tex Building.

It seems reasonable that the doctors in fact did not have the official story yet and so things were stalled until the conspirators knew what framework they had to fit the facts to and "suggested" to the doctors that one bullet passed through Kennedy back to front. The story had been preplanned for only three shots, but hitting Connally was unplanned and caused a big problem.

The place where a cover-up was needed was going to be on the President's Commission for which they had to have Johnson's cooperation. I'm sure they knew before the assassination that that was how it would be handled. It didn't matter much what the autopsy found, as long as the conflicts were kept secret.

What did the doctors think about the bullet found at Parkland? O'Neill wrote: "I know for a fact that when the autopsy was complete, there was no doubt in anyone's mind in attendance at the autopsy that the bullet found on the stretcher in Dallas came out of JFK's body."[75] They thus believed it came out of his back, since they knew the bullet that hit him in the back did not pass through the body. They believed that the bullet was pushed out during external cardiac massage.

Kellerman suggested to Finck: "Do you suppose that with the cardiac massage they gave him that the bullet came out?" Kellerman said this explanation "solved it for me . . . until I saw the films."[76] Finck evidently did not pass it on. He told pretty much the same thing about supposing that the bullet worked its way out of the back to Arlen Specter of the Warren Commission.[77] Kellerman denied to Specter that there was any conversation of any sort concerning the possibility of a point of entry from the front of the President's body.[78]

Was a bullet found in the autopsy room? There was a report by Captain Osborne, later retracted, that a bullet rolled out of the wrappings encasing Kennedy at the autopsy.[79] Captain Stover cannot recall ever seeing an intact missile in the autopsy's body room.[80] Paul O'Connor, one of the Navy Corpsmen who assisted the doctors, said no foreign objects, specifically a missile, or fragments of a missile, dropped onto the autopsy table, the morgue floor, or were otherwise detected while removing the sheet wrapping. He said that no missiles were discovered at any time during the autopsy.[81] Jerrol Custer reported what appeared to be a whole bullet which rolled out of the President's wrappings when they put the body on the table.[82]

Were the wounds "punctures" or "penetrating"? Dr. Finck carefully defines for us the distinction between "puncture" and "penetrating" in forensic examinations of gunshot wounds. Finck explains that a penetration does not pass all the way through, but a perforation or puncture is a through-and-through wound.[83] Dr. Humes in his handwritten draft of the autopsy report crossed out the word "puncture"[84] and wrote in "lacerated."[85] I am certain that he did so when the three doctors met the day after the autopsy to go over his preliminary draft and discuss the examination, and Finck pointed this out to Humes, a hospital pathologist almost completely unfamiliar with the medical investigation of violent death by gunshot, who might not be expected to note the fine distinction.

What was the purpose of the X-rays? To find bullets or fragments. Ebersole says "these X-rays were taken solely for the purpose of finding what at that time was thought to be a bullet that had entered the body and not exited. If we were looking for fine bone detail, the type of diagnostic detail we want in life, we would have taken the pictures in the X-ray department, made the films there, but we felt that the portable X-ray equipment was adequate for the purpose, locating a metallic fragment."[86] In other words, as Finck said to the House panel, they weren't looking for entries and exits through tissue with these X-rays. Ebersole was questioned closely as to why they did not take the body upstairs to good X-ray machines and he said that it was not part of his thinking.[87]

Ebersole said that there were no other X-rays with images other than the ones he put in the Archives.[88] In addition, the portable machine they used could not do the job that a permanent X-ray could do.

Were there or were there not high brass present at the autopsy? Numerous generals, admirals, and captains were listed on the FBI report as being present in the autopsy room, as well as being listed by others. This list included: Gen. Godfrey McHugh, AF, aide to John Kennedy; Admiral George C. Burkley, Kennedy's personal physician; General Philip C. Wehle, Commander in Chief of the Military District of Washington; Captain James H. Stover, Commanding Officer of the Naval Medical School; Captain Robert O. Canada, Commanding Officer of Bethesda Naval Hospital; Captain David Osborne, Chief of Surgery at Bethesda; Admiral Calvin B. Galloway,

Commanding Officer of the US National Naval Medical Center. Admiral Edward C. Kinney, the Surgeon General of the Navy, was present, according to Dr. Robert Karnei, who was in charge of who got in the room.[89] This list is part of that compiled by the House Committee.[90] Chester Boyers said that a General Curtis was also present, along with Commander Ewing.[91] Dr. Karnei thought that the Surgeon General of the Army might have been there also.[92]

John Thomas Stringer, the civilian Navy photographer present, said the operation was like a three-ring circus, with so many people present, including a number of flag rank military men.[93]

Who was Admiral Kinney? Surgeon General of the Navy, Edward Kinney is the officer who ordered those present at the autopsy not to discuss the case.[94] Admiral Galloway conveyed the written order threatening court-martial to those present, which each person signed.

Who gave the orders? Humes directed the autopsy, although Dr. Boswell was first asked to perform the autopsy and he asked Humes (who was on vacation) to participate.[95] Boswell said he told Bruce Smith it was "ridiculous to do the post here," (at Bethesda) and was told that Dr. Burkley had insisted that the President be brought there. Boswell felt the postmortem should have been done at DFIP (AFIP?).[96] Dr. Robert Karnei, a resident, assisted.[97] Karnei would normally have performed the autopsy.[98] Admiral Osborne also assisted. The regular radiologist, Captain Loy Thietje Brown, had been sent to Chicago, and Dr. John Ebersole took his place. Dr. Pierre Finck was brought in after the autopsy started and arrived about 8:30 P.M. Dr. Burkley conveyed the feelings of the family to Humes, with Robert McNamara standing in between Burkley and Robert and Jacqueline Kennedy. Finck's testimony at the Shaw trial is confusing as to whether or not someone outside of the above chain of command interfered or directed portions of the autopsy, but it appears he did not mean to say that someone other than the above did so.

But Francis X. O'Neill, one of the two FBI agents present, said that "Finck seemed to take over the autopsy when he arrived."[99] They all passed the buck. Others say the FBI or Secret Service men directed it.[100] Admiral Galloway is said to have ordered the full autopsy.[101] It was not entirely full.

Jerrol Custer felt that Ebersole was running it as far as the X-rays were concerned.[102] The photographer present, John Thomas Stringer, does not recall anyone giving orders to the autopsy doctors. Stringer said that while General McHugh kept coming in and out and manifested a great deal of emotional upset, he did not issue any such orders.[103]

Stringer qualified what he said by noting that he recalled something near the beginning of the autopsy which indicated discussion about them not doing the complete autopsy. He believed the President's physician (Admiral Burkley) was at the center of these discussions and seemed to be acting on the instructions of someone else, presumably the Kennedy family.[104]

Admiral Galloway said that no orders were being sent in from outside the autopsy room either by phone or in person. He said that Pierre Finck, the pathologist with the greatest expertise, seemed to be the person exercising authority. Galloway felt that occasionally some people, such as the senior staff members of the President, were entering and exiting the autopsy room.[105]

James Curtis Jenkins said that the whole attitude of the autopsy room changed when Dr. Humes came in. He had a sense that it was very restricted and that he had to watch what he said. He said the whole thing became a "guarded type of thing." Jenkins had the distinct impression that someone in the gallery was "telling them what to do." He recalls Humes discussing with someone the problem of finding the bullet. He said this discussion amounted to a "disturbance." Jenkins had the impression that everything "seemed like it was predesignated . . . seemed they had an answer and wanted to prove it . . . A lot of people were taking notes in the galleries . . . some in suits and some in uniforms."[106]

Did the Kennedys control the autopsy?* Dr. Boswell stated that Admiral Burkley supervised the autopsy, acting as liaison for the family.[107] The autopsy began without written formal permission, but this was obtained later. Boswell said *Robert McNamara seemed to have acted as liaison between the family and Dr. Burkley*. McNamara kept his head throughout, according to Boswell, and he implied that McNamara was never actually in the autopsy room but was working out of the room where the family was staying.[108] Dr. Finck stated that the Kennedy family first limited the autopsy to the head. He thought that Admiral Galloway "was the one as far as I can remember communicating those restrictions to us."[109]

---

*A very fine article has appeared in *The Fourth Decade* (May 1995, p. 5) "Blaming the Victims: Kennedy Family Control over the Bethesda Autopsy" by James Folliard, that extensively explores this question and Dr. Burkley's role.

FBI agent James Sibert had the impression that the doctors were getting clearances "step by step from the Kennedy family" before proceeding with the steps of the autopsy.[110] He wrote that "there was talk about consultation with Mrs. Kennedy before going ahead with contemplated X-rays and incisions. I believe that there were a couple of liaison people to Mrs. Kennedy present. I had the impression that the doctors were getting clearances for certain phases of the autopsy from the Kennedy family."[111]

Francis X. O'Neill wrote that "Mrs. Jackie Kennedy gave permission for a partial autopsy and Dr. George Burkley reiterated her remarks. There was no question that Burkley was conveying the wishes of the Kennedy family. Admiral Galloway resolved this by ordering a complete autopsy after checking with the FBI and Secret Service agents in attendance."[112]

One of these middlemen might have invented the whole business of control by the Kennedy family. Autopsies are mandated by law in violent death, and nobody could limit the investigation. Of course, one could argue that once outside of Texas jurisdiction, they were not subject to any law and did what they thought was right or required moment to moment by the circumstances. Many of those present were stricken with deep shock, and others were acutely sensitive to the family's grief.

The law of the State of Maryland would have ruled, nevertheless.

What restrictions if any were put on the autopsy? Dr. Finck stated to the House Forensic Panel that "there were restrictions coming from the family and we were told at the time of autopsy that the autopsy should be limited to certain parts of the body. For example, autopsy limited to the head and modest extension but there were restrictions. . . . For example, from what I remember we did not remove the organs of the neck because of the restrictions."

"Was an examination of the organs in the thoracic area permitted?"

"Yes, because there was an extension after those preliminary restrictions were mentioned. The lungs were removed."[113] Finck says on the same page that the restrictions were modified but he didn't know why. "It is hard for me to explain them except it came from the family."[114]

Ebersole, again casting doubt on whether he was actually present or not too alert, made the following comment: "To the best of my knowledge there were absolutely no restrictions and it was Dr. Humes's decision as to the extent of the autopsy."[115] He repeated this several times later in the interview when closely questioned about outside interference.[116] Of course, this might be a personal perception justified by the fact that they got what they wanted by way of an examination, basically, which wasn't everything.

Did anyone give orders that the back wound was not to be probed? Boswell said that no one gave orders that they not probe the back wound.[117] Yet Dr. Boswell told my investigator, Richard Waybright, that they were not permitted to track the wounds, but that they probed the back wound briefly and it led toward the throat.[118]

THE THROAT WOUND

Did the doctors examine the incision or wound in the throat? Yes, according to Finck. "I did not see a wound of exit along that tracheotomy incision and that was the puzzle, having a wound of entry with no corresponding wound of exit, and that was one of the reasons for asking for additional X-ray films which I requested. So that is for the wound of the upper back/lower neck on the right side."[119] Finck compulsively places the posterior wound in what he calls the upper back/lower neck area, when we are quite confident it wasn't, but lower. Admiral Burkley "verified" Dr. Boswell's face sheet drawing showing the wound *considerably lower*, and Admiral Burkley's placement of the wound in his death certificate was at the third thoracic vertebra. Ebersole told Mantik that it was at T4. There are numerous descriptions placing it on the border of the scapula.

We know that the doctors in fact knew about the statements made in Dallas that there was an entry hole in the throat from in front.[120] I speculate that they would pretend they didn't know it so as to avoid a major confrontation on the spot with the Dallas doctors, and results of the autopsy were not immediately made known.

Ebersole tells us that he did not see the wound in the neck and associate it with a bullet wound of exit after it had been pointed out that the tracheostomy had been through that area. "No, sir, I can't say that I did. After the dissection had started I saw the area that Dr. Humes was very interested in. He pointed out to us that this was a track running over the apex of the lung—I think he used the term bruising the apex of the lung and pointed to the middle line. . . ."[121] By track he meant an imaginary one: They connected up three points: throat, apex of lung, and back wound.

FBI agent James W. Sibert told House investigators that he didn't recall the neck opened up for examination.[122]

Was the neck wound probed with a finger? Dr. Boswell told House investigators that Humes probed the back wound with both a metal probe and his little finger.[123] This may be a confusion between the words "neck" and "back." There was previously considerable mention by numerous witnesses that the back wound had been probed with a finger.

Did the autopsists know there had been a tracheostomy? The FBI men present wrote that "it was also apparent that a tracheotomy had been performed"[124] when the body was unwrapped and they first observed it. It is never too clear if we get *their own first observations* with each of their statements, *or* if they wrote down *what they heard* from the doctors and this was not clarified for each of their statements when they were interviewed by the House Committee— or if they wrote down what came after the fact, when they *later* learned that there had been a tracheostomy performed. Nevertheless, it would seem that the FBI men heard that the surgery had been performed, either from their own sources, from those who were in Dallas and then at the autopsy, or perceived it from their own observation and knowledge of wounds.

Yet the affidavit Francis X. O'Neill executed for the House of Representatives states that he "understood that Humes did call Parkland on 11/23/63 and learned at that time that a tracheotomy had been performed over a wound in the President's throat." This statement casts some doubt on whether O'Neill knew that Humes knew of the tracheostomy prior to the 23rd.

Knowledge of the tracheostomy has become an issue since the documents were released, as the doctors were made to look as though they took the tracheostomy incision for a large and ragged wound of exit. Certainly there was an attempt to pass it off as such when drawings of the wound were later released.

Dr. Boswell told HSCA investigators that they were *not* aware the tracheostomy was performed on the wound before they spoke with Dallas[125] (which was the next day!). "Dr. Boswell indicated that regarding the tracheostomy, the doctors 'thought it was a wound.' He meant to convey the impression that the doctors thought it was a bullet wound. (This becomes potentially significant in later stages of the interview). [Author's note: the latter comment is not my note but that of Andy Purdy.]"[126] Independently corroborating this, Lt. Richard Lipsey, aide to General Wehle, conveys the impression that the doctors did not know that there was a tracheostomy there, and thought the slash in the throat was a bullet wound, possibly of exit.[127] The doctors later pretended that this never happened. An early (1966) interview with Dr. Boswell in the *Baltimore Sun* said that "The pathologists had already been told of the probable extent of the injuries and what had been done by physicians in Dallas."[128] This is not a quote from Boswell but leaves the impression that he said it, which I don't think he did. It is the kind of reporter's supposition that leads to much of the confusion on the part of the media in this case. The same interview also said: " 'The wound in the throat was not immediately evident at the autopsy,' Dr. Boswell said, 'because of the tracheotomy [sic] performed in Dallas. . . . We concluded that night that the bullet had, in fact, entered in the back of the neck, traversed the neck and exited anteriorly.' "[129]

Specifically, Boswell told the House investigators that the autopsy doctors assumed that the anterior neck wound was a wound of exit, saying the hole was not that big and that it was "far bigger than a wound of entry." He said the doctors didn't explicitly discuss the possibility of a tracheostomy having been performed, but said it was assumed that this was a possibility. Boswell said Parkland did not really do a tracheostomy in the sense that they never inserted a tube.[131] (See notes on interview with Dr. Perry.[130])

Yet, Boswell indicated to me in the course of a discussion about the issue in the FBI report of "surgery to the head area" that the FBI men were mistaken because the only surgery they heard discussed was the tracheostomy.[132] Boswell makes it sound very much as though they had been discussing the tracheostomy.

In addition, Chester Boyers, the chief petty officer in charge of the Pathology Department, present at the autopsy, "noted a tracheotomy incision in the neck."[133]

Dr. Boswell said he remembered seeing part of the perimeter of a bullet hole in the anterior neck.[134] This last statement drives a massive wedge in Dr. Boswell's credibility. Perhaps *after the autopsy* when he learned about the bullet hole in the throat, he then recalled seeing the semicircle on the edge of the large hole he has told us appeared to be a large exit wound, and at other times a tracheostomy.

House Committee investigators asked Boswell why the back wound was probed if the autopsy doctors knew the bullet had exited out the anterior neck. Dr. Boswell said that Dr. Burkley didn't mention that a tracheostomy had been performed. He said that Dr. Burkley was very upset and this might have explained his failure to mention this important fact. Dr. Boswell said (without indicating that he was being inconsistent with his previous statement) the doctors felt anterior neck damage was caused by a tracheostomy wound and in the later courses of the autopsy thought it may have included the exit wound of a bullet. Boswell is a little vague as to when the doctors felt that a bullet may have fallen out the back or neck wound, but seemed to indicate it occurred around the time they learned the bullet had been discovered in Parkland and prior to the time when they began to feel there was a very real possibility of an exit wound in the anterior neck.[135] Contradicting all this is the doctor's expressed belief that the bullet fell out of the back during "external cardiac massage" at Parkland.

Boswell, in the above statement, first clearly implies that he (they) did not know that a tracheostomy had been performed because Burkley didn't tell them. This could be why Ebersole embellished that wound after the fact with sutures, saying when the body arrived the throat wound had been sutured up. Nevertheless, Boswell adds strength to the supposition that they did not know, as is indicated by another witness. This is what they want us to think: They did not know. Dr. Robert Livingston called them before the body arrived and told them that there had been a bullet wound to the throat. Thus, pretending they did not know of the tracheostomy, they learned both secretly from Livingston before the autopsy, and officially the next morning from Dallas, that there was both a trach wound and a bullet hole in the throat, which they were told was an entry. No longer having the body and relieved of further necessity to prove anything they would write, they converted the throat wounds to an exit wound. They did not have to report a probe's later passage through the area, if that happened, and did not jibe with the official story as it was emerging.

Late in Finck's interview with the House doctors, Andrew Purdy repeats to Finck that he had said he did not know about the wound in the throat until Humes's call to Dallas the next day.[136] He asked, "Is it not correct that you did not know when the autopsy was finished that there was a wound of exit in the front of the throat?"

"Probably not. That sounds all right."

"When the autopsy was concluded, then what did you think could have happened to the bullet if it was not in the body and didn't exit the front of the body?"

"It is hard to say now, but I don't know. With no bullet shown on X-ray films, a wound of entry in the back, I don't know."[137]

Dr. John Ebersole is asked by Michael Baden: "And is it your impression that before the autopsy was finished at ten-thirty at night contact had been made between Dr. Humes and—"

Ebersole: "I must say these times are approximate, but I would say in the range of ten to eleven P.M. Dr. Humes had determined that a procedure had been carried out in the anterior neck covering the wound of exit. Subsequent to that the fragments arrived."[138]

James Curtis Jenkins, the student lab technician present, said that he noted the throat wound and that it looked like a tracheotomy, "because it looked like a surgically made incision."[139]

What did the autopsy doctors know about the neck wound? Ebersole says (and repeated more than once during his House interview), "The taking of the X-rays again were stopped to the best of my remembrance once we had communication with Dallas and Dr. Humes had determined that there was a wound of exit in the lower neck anterior at the time that the President arrived at the hospital in Dallas. I think once that fact had been established that my part in the proceedings were finished."[140] The communication, if it happened, was not direct, but through third parties that night.

Ebersole, or whoever told him about the Dallas call, also seems to be lying when he says that they heard from Dallas that the wound was a wound of exit in the throat, unless a middleman involved in the cover-up told them the entry was an exit. No medical witness in Dallas told them it was an exit, since they announced to the world that the throat wound was a wound of entrance.

Boswell told us that he and the other doctors did not know about the throat bullet wound until the next day when Humes called Dallas.[141] This is in conformity with their official story. So, Humes did not tell the others of Livingston's call.

FBI agent James W. Sibert said that he called Chuck Killion at the FBI lab because the doctors were at a loss as to where the bullet went that struck Kennedy in the back. He said nothing was ever mentioned about the anterior neck wound being a possible exit wound. They were wondering if it was a kind of bullet that "fragmentizes" completely. That is why Sibert left the room to call the lab, to find out about that type of bullet. He believed that the wound in the front neck was characterized as a tracheostomy incision by someone.[142] This tells us that the House investigators also were curious as to whether or not they knew the tracheostomy had been performed, or could recognize it as such on the body. The FBI report of the autopsy said that "following the removal of the wrapping . . . it was also apparent that a tracheostomy had been performed. . . ." Again, this could be after the fact.

O'Neill stated that he did not recall anything about the tracheostomy incision that indicated a bullet had damaged the area. When shown the tracing of the tracheostomy, he had no recollection or comment concerning the apparent bullet wound perimeter.[143]

Dr. Karnei said that the wound of the throat "looked like a tracheostomy ellipse," but said there was no discussion of that fact. He said he thought it was assumed. He said he recalled no talk about there being a wound of entrance in the front of the neck. He gathered from his conversation with Dr. Boswell that the doctors didn't come to a "full conclusion" that night.[144]

Richard Lipsey said that he could not recall the doctors specifically saying that the wound in the throat was caused by a bullet, but he does feel the doctors were convinced that a bullet exited from the front of the neck, though it was not the one that struck Kennedy high in the back.[145] The House Committee discussed what Lipsey had to say in a footnote: "He also concluded that the entrance in the rear of the head corresponded to an exit in the neck. This conclusion could not have originated with the doctors because during the autopsy they believed the neck defect only represented a tracheostomy incision."[146] This latter statement is also in great doubt. "Lipsey did properly relate the preliminary conclusion of the doctors during the autopsy that the entrance wound in the upper back had no exit. The doctors later determined that this missile had exited through the throat. Thus, although Lipsey's recollection of the number of defects to the body and the corresponding locations are correct, his conclusions are wrong and are not supported by any other evidence."[147] By "determined," they mean "theorized." Lipsey described *three* entries in the rear, so the last comment that he was correct is very telling.

Dr. Finck wrote that "he examined the tracheotomy skin wound and the trachea and did not find evidence of a bullet wound. Having a wound of entrance in the back and no corresponding exit, I requested a whole body radiographic survey, the results of which were negative."[148] The bullet hole had been obliterated by Dr. Malcolm Perry in Dallas, but there might have been some evidence. Others see the semicircular wound in the throat photographs. Finck wrote that he saw no damage to the trachea.

John J. McCloy asked Dr. Humes during his testimony to the Warren Commission, "I am not sure what induced you to come to that conclusion if you couldn't find the actual exit wound by reason of the tracheostomy."

"The report which we had submitted, sir, represents our thinking within the twenty-four to forty-eight hours of the death of the President, all facts taken into account of the situation. The wound in the anterior portion of the lower neck is physically lower than the point of entrance posteriorly, sir."

"That is what I wanted to bring out."

"Yes, sir."

"May I ask this: In spite of the incision made by the tracheostomy, was there any evidence left of the exit aperture?" McCloy asks.

"Unfortunately not that we could ascertain, sir,"[149] Humes says.

Dr. Humes told the House Committee's Forensic Panel that "the day after, within six or eight hours of having completed the examination, assisting Gawler's and so forth for the preparation of the President's remains, we got together and discussed our problem. We said we've got to talk to the people in Dallas. We should have talked to them the night before, but there was no way we could get out of the room. . . . So I called Dr. Perry. Took me a little while to reach him. We had a very nice conversation on the phone in which he described a missile wound, what he interpreted as a missile wound, in the midline of the neck through which he had created a very quick emergency, as you can see from the photographs, tracheostomy incision. In effect destroying its value to us and obscuring it very gorgeously for us. Well, of course, the minute he said that to me, lights went on, and we said, ah, we have someplace for our missile to have gone. . . . we were at a loss because we hadn't appreciated the exit wound in the neck."[150]

Roger Feinman points out that "the throat wound ignorance story" was planted early in the investigation.[151] He cites New York *Herald Tribune* and UPI stories of November 24, 1963.

Was the trachea removed? Boswell said it was not removed.[152] Tom Robinson, the mortician, may or may not indicate that some sort of massive removal of the organs of the neck occurred. Robinson told Purdy of the HSCA that "all that was removed" in referring to the throat. (Interview of January 12, 1977, p.11.)

"Yes, I mean looked at and cut."

"How big a cut? Where would the cut have gone from and to?"

"I don't remember if it went off in many angles. It was not a nice clean cut." Ebersole also told Dr. Mantik that he was "quite surprised at the trach. He'd never want one like that!"[153]

"So there was a cut open in the neck to look in there?"

"They had this all cut."[154]

Finck was asked the following by Andrew Purdy of the House Committee: "If you had known during the autopsy that there was a wound of exit in the front of the throat, would you have taken or exercised any different autopsy procedures than you did do? . . . Would you have done more extensive work in the area of the trachea?"

"From what I remember there were restrictions, and this was the reason for not working in that area."

"Did you ask that you should be permitted to examine the trachea more than you were permitted?"

"We were told to do certain things. I don't recall if someone asked for permission to. I don't recall that."[155]

Ebersole was asked if he had an independent recollection of whether the neck organs were examined during the autopsy, referring specifically to the trachea and blood vessels in that area and larynx. Ebersole replied, "No, my memory is very vivid for seeing a bruise in the right apex of the visceral pleura in the service sic of the right lung, but I was not close enough or was away on one of these X-ray runs when that area was examined or the trachea specifically." Ebersole notes that X-ray no. 10 of the chest doesn't show a tracheal air shadow, "Which I do not expect to see since I don't see lungs either."[156]

Did anyone have to suggest to the autopsy doctors that the bullet might have passed from back to front and exited Kennedy's throat? Are we dealing with the power of suggestion here, to enlist the autopsy doctors as unwitting perpetrators of the fraud? Or was there something far more sinister in the fact that Humes claimed that the day after the autopsy, he learned there had been a bullet hole in the neck? He promptly used this to explain the lack of a bullet in the body and an imaginary connection with the back wound.

A very telling and revelatory statement is made to Andy Purdy of the HSCA in 1977: "We had gotten ourselves in dutch with the neck and throat wounds with regard to the Secret Service." What this meant, we don't know. It sounds as though they did not say what they were supposed to say. If anything should have been followed up in the case, it is this, but it wasn't.[157]

Was there a wound in the back of the neck? We have several indications that the wound described by Humes and Boswell near the hairline on the back-of-the-head pictures is also thought of as a "neck wound" and not really the entry into the head that blew it apart, as the autopsy report said it did. Conceivably there is a semantic problem here. "I am quite sure that the EOP wound was never connected to the throat wound—except possibly by a fragment going down that way," David Mantik told me. The Dallas doctors thought that a fragment from the throat entry exited the back of the head. This would hole part of the skull and hit the spine, but there is no record of such damage.

None of this adds up, and there seems to be another massive lie. I find incredible that there are such conflicts as to where these wounds are.

Some of the drawings made by those present show an entry wound so low on the back of the head that it truly might be considered the neck by some, "but not by the pathologists," Mantik adds.

Lipsey describes an entrance in the lower head as being just inside the hairline.[158] At other times he calls this the top of the neck.[159] It is both, and he may be pointing out a semantic problem that is causing part of the trouble, but it is also as likely that he means that the bullet that struck near the hairline came out the neck, as is stated elsewhere by Lipsey,[160] and which seems to be backed up by the following statement by Secret Service agent Roy Kellerman to the Warren Commission: "The reason for the hole in the throat, the tracheostomy; I am thinking they were of the opinion that when the—when he was shot in the head, and they had found this piece remaining above the eye underneath; I am sure there was some concern as to where the outlet was, and whether they considered— this is all an assumption now; whether they considered this—that there was a hole here in the throat prior to the tracheostomy, I don't know. But to complete the examination, they lifted him up by the shoulders and there was this hole."[161]

Was the back or throat wound probed? The autopsy report states that "The missile path through the fascia and the musculature cannot be easily probed."[162] As to whether or not a probe passed into it, Dr. Humes testified to Arlen Specter: "Attempts to probe in the vicinity of this wound were unsuccessful without fear of making a false passage."

"What do you mean by that, Doctor?"

"Well, the defect in the fascia was quite similar, which is the first firm tissue over the muscle beneath the skin, was quite similar to this. We were unable, however, to take probes and have them satisfactorily fall through any definite path at this point."[163]

The original evidence available from the FBI report and testimony of Dr. Pierre Finck indicated that no probe could enter through the alleged bullet hole in the President's back, and that this wound did not penetrate the thorax. This was backed up by descriptions given to me by the men at the autopsy and was presented in my book *High Treason 2*.

The CBS memo indicates that a probe was passed through the

wound after midnight. When the FBI men had left, photographs were taken of the probe through the wound and then destroyed because the trajectory could not have come from the sniper's window. As previously stated, the memo appears fake because Dr. Humes would have no reason to lie in the above-quoted statements, which tend to disprove the government's theory of a bullet having to pass through Kennedy's body.

Thomas Robinson, one of the morticians present, described to House investigators extensive probing of the body, but not through any back wound, which he did not see. He said the probing was through the low and large hole in the back of the neck and implied that it came out the neck.[164]

Finck told the House panel that "the probing [i.e., of the back wound] was unsuccessful . . . you cannot go into a track when—you know, this is difficult to explain. You can make an artificial track if you push hard enough with an instrument so you go gently to see that there is a track, and the fact that you don't find a track with a probe may be because of contraction of muscles after death."[165]

Dr. Finck testified at the Clay Shaw trial that the back wound was not probed or dissected. He was asked about this by the House Forensic Panel: "You stated that all of you had been ordered and that your recollection was that it was an Army general whose name you did not recall." Finck responded, "I still don't remember his name. I read my notes and I found in my notes an Army general and I don't know who it was."

"Then you certainly remember that somebody did give you orders not to do certain things."

"I cannot say that it was this Army general. I don't recall that precisely. I remember the prosectors and Admiral Galloway. As far as saying now so and so told me that or didn't tell me that, it is extremely difficult. There was an Army general in that room and I cannot really pinpoint the origin of those instructions to comply with those family wishes."[166]

Ebersole said this: "I remember I was looking from the anterior aspect into the chest after the viscera had been removed and a probe had been passed from the wound of entrance and one could see the bruising of the poridal [sic—I think.] pleura."[167] "After the dissection had started I saw the area that Dr. Humes was very interested in. He pointed out to us that this was a track running over the apex of the lung—I think he used the term bruising the apex of the lung and pointed to the middle line. I remember the area was open and he was pointing this out to us."[168] Again and again, he (and the panel) fudged the issue they all knew was an issue: did the probe actually pass into the wall of the chest? Ebersole seemed to answer this above when he implied that the probe didn't get very far: "... and *appeared* to go toward or near the midline of the lower neck." Internal organs are bruised or torn when the body is struck violently, and this may account for the damage to Kennedy's lung when he was shot.

Ebersole did not actually say that the probe went through. The weight of the evidence is by far that the probe did not break through the musculature of the back's wall into the chest cavity. So there was no way to see which way that bullet might have gone had it broken though. They somehow had to get a bruise on the apex of the lung to establish a track going the way they wanted it.

Dr. Robert Frederick Karnei, who assisted at the autopsy, told me that the back wound didn't go anywhere. "He couldn't get it to go anywhere—the one in the back of the neck—he couldn't get it to go anywhere because his probe would not go anywhere."

"Did you watch this probing?"

"I didn't watch all of it. I know that he was having a hard time."

"Well, they did. They tried every which way to go ahead, and try to move it around, but the rigor mortis was getting to be a problem. . . . They were working all night long with probes trying to make out where that bullet was going on the back there."

"They spent some hours in it?"

"It was a long time. I don't know how long it was."

"Just on that?"

"Just on that, trying to figure out where in the dickens that went."[169] Karnei told the House investigators that Dr. Finck was "working with a probe and arranging photographs."[170]

Boswell told us that they were not permitted to track the wounds(!), but they probed the back wound briefly and "it led toward the throat."[171]

Roy Kellerman recalled Dr. Finck probing the wound about four to five inches (this doesn't make much sense, as it would be to the trachea!) as he was trying to "get the probe to come out ..." Kellerman said the doctor didn't probe the wound with his finger first, saying it was "not that big."[172]

Jan Gail Rudnicki recalls them probing the back wound but could not discern its track. During this time, the doctors took measurements of the wounds, he said.[173]

James Jenkins told House investigators that he didn't believe the doctor found that the probe "penetrated into the chest."[174] Jenkins described to me in great detail watching the probing from the other side as he looked into the opened-up chest. The probe could not penetrate into the chest. There was no passage for it.[175] Jenkins further described this to House investigators in recalling the attempt to probe the back wound. He said the probe they used was a metal one, about eight inches long. He said that "most of the probe went in . . . between the skin . . .'' and not into the chest cavity. He said Humes could probe the bottom of the wound with his little finger and said that the metal probe went in two to four inches. He said it was quite a "fact of controversy" that the doctors "couldn't prove the bullet came into the cavity."[176]

Jenkins said he didn't remember anyone looking to see if the trachea was torn. He said that the probing of the back wound was attempted toward the center as indicated in the drawing, but said that in actuality the only way the probe was able to go in was at a "fairly drastic angle downward so as not to enter the cavity." He thought the entry wound in the back was lower than that shown in the drawing. He said he didn't notice any bruising at the tip of the lung. He said that according to his recollection of the location of the back wound the bullet would have been going upward through the body to have exited in the front of the neck. He said he is basing his impression of the direction of the bullet on the fact that the probe did not enter the body cavity.[177]

Was the Dallas throat surgery sutured before the body reached Bethesda? Other than Ebersole's statement to House investigators,[178] and to reporters,[179] there is no other testimony or record that the neck had been sewn up. Dr. David Mantik asked Ebersole (now deceased) if he actually saw this, and Ebersole denied it to Mantik. There were "no sutures," Ebersole said.[180] There has never been any indication that the wound was sutured in Dallas. Ebersole must have thrown this in as his own means of alerting us to interference with the autopsy.

Someone tampering with the body and suturing the throat would alert others that the body had been tampered with—if it was not sutured in Dallas. We are fairly certain of the latter. If the throat was sutured, then, once again, someone is leaving a trail. Does anyone have a better way of explaining it? Ebersole may simply have confused the time when the morticians sutured the throat wound for the open coffin viewing they thought was going to happen, and some late night X-rays he may have taken, when he saw the throat already sutured for burial.

Ebersole's next statement on the neck wound is more than a little mysterious. He says, "I believe by ten or ten-thirty approximately a communication had been established with Dallas and it was learned that there had been a wound of exit in the lower neck that had been surgically repaired. I don't know if this was premortem or postmortem but at that point the confusion as far as we were concerned stopped."[181] The confusion was over what happened to the bullet that hit Kennedy in the back. This is about the only indication that there had been a call to Dallas that night, and is contradicted by Humes's testimony saying he didn't call until the next morning when the body was gone. Since we know from Dr. Robert Livingston that the doctors did know about the throat wound in the tracheostomy area, Ebersole is clearly mixed up on what story he has to tell, or maybe he is just telling the truth. There was a call at the beginning of the evening conveying the above information, but it came from Livingston. What does this tell us about Ebersole's claim of suturing which did not happen in Dallas? He says he saw it. "There was a sutured wound, a transverse wound at the base of the neck."[182] Of course, the Secret Service and the FBI were obtaining information from Dallas—such as the discovery of the bullet at Parkland—and a certain amount was passed on to the doctors.

Both Jan Gail Rudnicki[183] and Jerrol Custer[184] told me that there were no sutures on the throat wound when the body was unwrapped.[185]

Was there much trauma to the neck? Dr. Boswell stated that there was not much trauma to the neck area.[186]

What evidence was there that a bullet had passed through the body from back to front? The autopsy report gives a certain amount of data that indicates the wound had to have been probed or that there was evidence of a track through the body, in spite of hard evidence to the contrary. Dr. Boswell said that in the area of the neck wound there was a "contusion along the inner margin of the apex of his lung" which was "the only way we could trace the entire path of the track of the bullet." He said the bullet passed through the upper thorax (this is merely a supposition); he said he thought they photographed "the exposed thoracic cavity and lung . . ." but doesn't remember ever seeing those photographs. He indicated that he is certain that there was no major blood vessel damaged by the path of the missile.[187] If the photos showed none of this, that's a good reason for them to have been missing!

Dr. Ebersole, the radiologist, observed the probing and said: "Dr. Humes in probing the wound of entrance found it to extend perhaps over the apex of the right lung bruising the pleura and appeared to go toward or near the midline of the lower neck."[188] This does not mean that the probe entered the chest through the wall of the back. Ebersole did not say this, though one would think it might be implied. I believe that this is what Ebersole was expected to say, so he did as he was told or as it was suggested to him. The fact that the statement is not clear indicates that he did not intend to say that the probe passed through part of the body beyond the wall of the back.

James Sibert told the House that his impression was that Finck and Humes agreed (after the probing) that there was no exit wound of the bullet in the back, and said he had no recollection of how far in the probe went.[189] He wrote in his affidavit for the House that "As for the anterior neck wound which was described as a tracheotomy incision, I don't recall the neck wound being opened up for examination and nothing was mentioned about it being a possible bullet exit wound."[190]

The FBI report he and Francis X. O'Neill wrote also stated that the bullet did not pass through the body. O'Neill wrote: "I do not see how the bullet that entered below the shoulder in the back could have come out the front of the throat."[191] "It was and is my opinion that the bullet entered the back came out the back," O'Neill repeated a page later.[192] He meant that whatever hit him in the back went no farther, and fell out. Or melted, as he thought it might be an ice or glycerine bullet of some kind.

Admiral Galloway said he recalled a discussion that attempted to determine where the missile that entered the back could have exited. Galloway said this problem remained ambiguous until Dr. Humes called Parkland Hospital on Saturday morning and ascertained that a doctor had performed a tracheostomy directly through the missile track, thus obliterating it. Galloway said the doctors actually suspected this during the autopsy, but couldn't prove it.[193]

There is precious little if any evidence that the bullet passed through the body or even entered the chest. James Curtis Jenkins said that the back wound was "very shallow . . . it didn't enter the peritoneal (chest) cavity."[194]

Dr. Finck wrote that a "Western (the manufacturer) 6.5mm Mannlicher-Carcano bullet . . . produced an entrance wound seven-by-four in diameter in the skin of the posterior upper chest and an exit wound approximately 5mm in diameter in the skin of the anterior neck. The bullet did not disintegrate. An X-ray survey revealed that it obviously had not struck bones."[195] Finck is attempting to demonstrate that certain types of bullets under certain conditions can make a larger entrance hole than exit. It seems very strange that he would say this. Is he contradicting his other statements, tending to indicate that he did not believe the bullet passed through the body?

One might put this generalization in a class with the doctor's generalization about beveling through skull, which has been questioned by some. Or, is Finck again trying to tell us something is not right in Denmark and that they had to invent it by stating that the hole at exit was a lot smaller than the entrance?

Jerrol Custer remembers seeing damage to the cervical spine,[196] although this flies in the face of the reading of the X-rays by the Clark Panel that there was no damage in the bones of the neck, of numerous statements by many doctors that no bullet could pass from back to front and out the front of the throat without massive damage to the spine. This latter fact is proven by CAT scans of the neck. No damage to the neck was seen or noted by any other witness at the autopsy.

Was the body moved to determine the angle or trajectory of the bullet through the body? Boswell says not.[197] Dr. Robert Karnei told me that they moved the body and turned it around and "they tried every which way to go ahead, and try to move it around, but the rigor mortis was getting to be a problem."[198] Karnei told House investigators that he recalled them putting the probe in and taking pictures (the body was on the side at the time). He said they felt the hole in the back was a wound of entrance and they were "trying to figure out where the bullet came out."[199] If they were taking pictures of the body with a probe sticking in it, as Karnei seems to say, this corroborates the CBS memorandum quoting Dr. Humes at the beginning of this chapter. Of course we have not officially heard of this photograph. It's not on any inventory of the photographs.

If they didn't know that there was a wound in the throat, then they couldn't have supposed that the bullet passed through that way. If they tried to probe the back wound, they had to sit the body up or move it on its side, and we have plenty of descriptions of fingers and probes inserted in the back wound. How can Boswell resolve the conflict?

Were there any metal fragments in the neck? Boswell does not recall any fragments in the neck path. He said the radiologists concurred there was no damage to the cervical spine.[200] We again note that it would be impossible for any bullet to pass through the neck and come out the center of the throat without doing *massive* damage to the bony structures in the neck, or causing a pneumothorax.

According to both Dr. Humes's testifying to the Warren Commission,[201] and the later Clark Panel review of the X-rays and other materials,[202] there was no X-ray evidence at the time of fragments in the neck, nor was there any damage at all to the bones themselves.

Jerrol Custer said that he remembered seeing metal fragments in the neck and that Ebersole had commented on them.[203] *They aren't on the X-rays we have now.*

What kind of bullets were thought to have been used? O'Neill stated that some discussion did occur concerning the disintegration of the bullet. A "general feeling" existed that a soft-nosed bullet struck JFK's head. In reference to the back wound, there was a discussion that the bullet could have been a "plastic" type or an "ice" bullet—one that dissolves after contact. *"There was also no real sense either way that the wounds were caused by the same kind of bullet,"* O'Neill wrote in his affidavit.[204] I revealed that O'Neill told me that they called the FBI lab about "ice" bullets,[205] and a lot of people thought I was nuts. He had already said this to House investigators, but it took fifteen years for the documents to appear and corroborate me.

Sibert also discusses this in his affidavit for the HSCA: They could not determine what happened to the bullet that hit the President in the back. "The doctors also discussed a possible deflection of the bullet in the body caused by striking bone. Consideration was also given to a type of bullet which fragments completely. In connection with a possible deflection of the bullet entering the back, some discussion ensued regarding X-rays of the lower body and the femur areas. Following discussion among doctors relating to the back injury, I left the autopsy room to call the FBI laboratory and spoke with Agent Chuck Killion. I asked if he could furnish any information regarding a type of bullet that would almost certainly fragmentize."[206] And Sibert was then told about the bullet found at Parkland.

THE BACK WOUND

When was the back wound found? The FBI report says that the back wound was located "during the later stages of this autopsy"[207] but Dr. Ebersole responds to having this statement read to him by saying, "Does it seem reasonable to you that a pathologist would carry out an autopsy of this nature without looking at the front and

back of the body? My remembrance is that we were aware of the
wound of entrance relatively early in the game."[208]

Ebersole is questioned further. Dr. Weston says to him that "you
gave the impression that everybody had the impression that there
was a bullet hole in the back of the neck. You gave me the impression that they rolled the body over almost immediately. Is that a
correct impression?"

"I don't know whether we looked at the anterior or posterior
aspect first. I would suspect it was posterior."

"You looked at the posterior first?"

"A head wound and a wound of entrance."

"They saw the wound of entrance on the back of the neck almost immediately?"

"Yes. At least immediately, yes." Then he garbles it, after moving
the wound to the back of the neck from the back. This again is a
question of recollection of whether it was the posterior or anterior surface.

"But you said they didn't recognize this as being an exit wound
until after the conversation with Dallas which was ten or ten-thirty,"
Weston asks.

"Or later."

"By that time you had already taken two sets." (Of X-rays.)

"No, no, no," Ebersole says. It must have been tough on Ebersole
in there.

"Oh," Weston responds, astonished.

"When both aspects of the body had been viewed, and I do not
know in what order they were reviewed, we were faced with the
problem of a wound of entrance and not a known wound of exit,
so at that point we perhaps would never have taken any X-rays had
we had a wound of entrance and a wound of exit. . . . We had
certainly not to my knowledge planned to take any X-rays at this
autopsy, but when it became apparent we had a wound of entrance
and no known wound of exit, this is when I was brought into the
action."[209] Remember, they thought the bullet fell out during external cardiac massage. He speaks as if he was in on the planning and
was there when he had not been called to be there because they
hadn't planned to take X-rays.

Dr. Baden asks, "if there were an obvious wound of exit that
perhaps an autopsy would not be necessary?"

"No, sir, that was not my impression."

"What was your impression?"

"My impression was we have no wound of exit, we have to proceed
with the autopsy, and I would have stayed in my corner all night."[210]

Dr. Humes said the bullet wound in the back was found right away and not discovered in the "later stages of the autopsy." This was discovered during the complete examination that was made of the body before the autopsy work began.[211]

Roy Kellerman told the Warren Commission that "While the President is in the morgue, he is lying flat. And with the part of the skull removed, and the hole in the throat, nobody was aware until they lifted him up that there was a hole in his shoulder. That was the first concrete evidence that they knew that the man was hit in the back first. . . . They had been working on him for quite some time, Mr. Specter—through the photos and other things they do through an autopsy. And I believe it was this Colonel Finck who raised him and there was a clean hole."[212] Finck came in, remember, a half hour after the incision, or a good hour and a half after the first examination of the body. The pictures of the back had to have been made before then.

Dr. Finck said that he saw the back wound when he arrived,[213] as Kellerman describes. Roger Feinman notes that Finck "is careful not to impute knowledge of the back wound to others when asked if they had already discovered it. Nevertheless, he says emphatically that the wound was discovered early in the autopsy."[214]

Lt. Richard Lipsey said that the doctors first examined the body and he thought they had found all of the wounds at that time.[215]

Was there a back wound? The autopsy report stated that there was a wound of entry in the back. One of the more harebrained "critics" of the Warren Report claimed that there was none, and that it was manufactured.

Diana Bowron and the other nurses who helped prepare the body for the coffin saw the hole in the back at Parkland.[216] Perry would have told the doctors if he knew about it. Dr. Marion Jenkins stated that he felt the hole while palpating the back, the back of the neck, and the back of the head as Kennedy lay dying at Parkland.[217]

Tom Robinson, one of the morticians, did not see any wound in the back at all. "I saw the body turned over, it was turned over and examined on its side, rolled from each side. I saw nothing down below where the doctors had been working on the head."

"Did you see anything between the head wounds and the . . . on the back that could have been a wound?"

"No."[218]

"Specifically, when you saw the body, you saw the back, I want to know specifically if either you know there was not a wound from the head down to the waist anywhere on the back, neck or whatever, or that the autopsy work may have either obliterated it or made it not evident to you that there was such a wound?''

"It might have done that, there was . . . but the back itself, there was no wound there, no.''

"Were there any wounds in the neck, the back?''

"Now, this is where I'm hazy. I can remember the probe. The probe of all this whole area. It was about an eighteen-inch piece of metal that we used.'' Note the use of the term "we.''

"Do you feel they probed the head or they probed the neck?''

"It was at the base of the head where most of the damage was done, the things that we had to worry about. So it all runs together in my mind.''[219]

At the end of his interview, Robinson is asked, "Do you remember any discussion of the possibility that there was a wound in that area? Is it your impression now that there was a wound in that area, or was the only wound present on the back of the President in the back of his head?''

"No, I wouldn't say that.''

"What is your sense of that? Is it your impression now that there was a wound in the back of the neck or in the upper back?''

"I don't remember. Vaguely in my mind that there is. . . .''[220]

Then he said, "The press was not kind. Undertakers are Texans at the time.'' This was his final, cryptic line of the interview.

Dr. Pierre Finck described it as a wound in the "upper back of the President, to the right of the midline, was oval and had a regular, soiled inverted margin. I stated that this was an entrance. My attempt to probe the path of the bullet was unsuccessful.''[221]

Adding to the confusion is the statement of Edward F. Reed, one of the X-ray technicians present at one of the autopsies of the bodies that night: "I found right between the scapula and thoracic column a large, inch-and-a-half wound that looked like an exit wound.''[222]

Francis X. O'Neill personally described to me the back wound and its probing.[223]

Paul O'Connor also was a witness to the probing of the back wound "to a depth of about two inches, but found no exit wound.''[224]

Of course, the doctors said and wrote there was a back wound there.

Was it incised? Francis X. O'Neill says that the doctors "did not cut through into the back of the neck.''[225] Humes choked on this question when the House Forensic Panel's Dr. Michael Baden asked him: "Now, for example, not exploring the wound from the back to the neck, that was not done. I mean, cutting it open completely, that wasn't done specifically. Was that because somebody said, don't do it?''

"Now wait a minute, that wound was excised.''

"The back wound?''

"Yes, sir. The back of the neck, and there are microscopic slides of that wound.'' Then Baden begins to take Humes through it, in front of the other doctors: "I see. The skin was taken out. And then was it—''

"It was probed.''

"Was it opened up?''

"It was not laid open.''

"Now, that was your decision as opposed to somebody else's decision?''

"Yes, it was mine.''

"With everything else going on at the time?''

"Yes. Our collective decisions, I suppose.'' Boswell chimes in, "We had exhibited the midportion of the track and the chest by that time, and demonstrated the contusion on the apex of the lung and subpleurally, and we had at that point two points of the wound and then subsequently the wound of exit.''

"Pretty good course,'' Humes says. We still only have a passage of a bullet from back to front by inference that the throat wound was an exit, and that there was some minor damage to the top of the right lung, which they could imagine was caused by the shock wave of a bullet, or something.

"The track definitely did not go through the pulmonary tissue?''

"There was a contusion of the dome of the right side of the thorax and a contusion, as Dr. Boswell said, a retropleural contusion, and it was a contusion of the upper lobe of the lung.''[226] The problem remains: They had no idea there was a bullet hole in the throat until the body was long gone. They never saw that wound.

Where was the back wound? It is possible that we are being lied to on such a grand scale that lies are the only way to explain the great confusion between one witness and another and their combined statements. Finck places the rear body wound as being in the juncture of the upper back with the lower neck, and writes that the back wound is "in the region of the right trapezius muscle, at 140mm from the right acromion process and at 140mm from [Author's note: the autopsy report clarifies this more by placing the wound *below* and not *from* . . .] the tip of the right mastoid process

(I took these measurements). The wound is OVAL, 7 × 4 mm, and shows well demarcated edges."[227]

This is in great conflict with other evidence. Finck repeats the position almost obsessively, as though it is what he was told to say, or what he knows is needed to get the right trajectory down from that window and through Connally. The coat and shirt show the hole about six inches down from the shoulder.

The autopsy report placed the back wound as follows: "Situated on the upper right posterior thorax just above the upper border of the scapula there is a seven-by-four millimeter oval wound. This wound is measured to be 14 cm from the tip of the right acromion process and 14 cm below the tip of the right mastoid process."[228]

Dr. John Ebersole gave the technical language for the placement of the back wound as "a textbook classical wound of entrance upper right back to the right of the midline three or four centimeters to the right of the midline just perhaps inside the medial board to the upper scapula. Again, I would like to emphasize this was a textbook wound—round, smooth, pure pellish, no raised margins."[229] Ebersole told Dr. David Mantik in a recorded conversation that the back wound entered to the right of the fourth thoracic vertebra. "He was consistent in his placement of the wound there."[230]

Dr. Boswell drew this wound on the back at the level of the third or fourth thoracic vertebra, or about six inches down on the back, on his autopsy face-sheet drawing. Dr. George Burkley, the President's physician, wrote in his death certificate that the wound was to the right of the third thoracic vertebra.[231] That is about four inches down from the shoulder. Burkley also "verified" the drawings Boswell made at the autopsy, which show the wound four to six inches down on the back. Dr. Finck said that he "saw a wound in the upper back/lower neck on the right side which I identified as a wound of entry. It had soiled, inverted edges which in nontechnical language means turned inward. I interpreted that wound as a wound of entry."[232]

Floyd Riebe told me that the lower hole in the photograph showing the back is the actual wound.[233] Chester Boyers "also saw an entrance wound in the right shoulder blade, specifically just under the scapula and next to it."[234] Jan Gail Rudnicki saw the wound in the shoulder blade region of the back.[235] Was it above or below the scapula? Big difference!

James Curtis Jenkins, the student lab technician assisting the doctors, stated that the back wound was "just below the collar to the right of the midline."[236] Paul O'Connor is adamant that the higher wound in the photograph was the wound,[237] but British nurse Diana

Bowron, a very credible witness who washed the President's back in Dallas, say that none of the wounds are correct and that the photograph is not of Kennedy's back.[238]

James W. Sibert wrote that it was "in the upper back."[239]

Clint Hill testified to the Warren Commission that the wound was "about six inches below the neckline to the right-hand side of the spinal column."[240]

The Warren Commission chose not to publish either Dr. Boswell's drawings of the wounds, nor Dr. Burkley's death certificate, both of which place the wound too low for a bullet to have come out of the neck. No matter how you cut it, the wound was nearly six inches down on the back, where Boswell's autopsy drawing places it. This conflicts greatly with the autopsy photographs, which have it much higher, near the neck.

At what angle did the bullet strike Kennedy in the back? O'Neill wrote that he "heard Humes say that the bullets entered from a forty-five-to-sixty degree angle. Pierre Finck seemed to be more attuned to the angle of the bullets that entered JFK's body."[241] This is the generally accepted angle.

Was the back wound probed with a finger? (Ebersole pp. 57–8) The FBI report states that "this opening was probed by Dr. HUMES with the finger. . . . Further probing determined that the distance traveled by this missile was a short distance inasmuch as the end of the opening could be felt with the finger."[242] They didn't make this up.

FBI agent James W. Sibert told the House Committee that the doctors probed the wound with a finger and that Dr. Finck used a metal probe.[243] Sibert said the doctors "concluded it only went so far and they couldn't find it."[244]

What happened to the bullet that struck Kennedy in the back? Although the Warren Commission and the autopsy report ended up stating that the bullet passed through the body and came out Kennedy's neck (and according to the Commission, struck John Connally), there is little or no evidence that this ever happened. Fifteen years after the murder, FBI agent Francis X. O'Neill, present at the autopsy, told the House Committee investigators that he is "positive" that the bullet that entered the back came out of the back.[245] That is how he ended the interview. O'Neill also said that when the autopsy was complete there was no doubt in anyone's mind that the bullet in Dallas was the one that fell out of JFK's body.[246]

This raises vast conflicts because the theory that the Warren Commission then perpetrated upon the world and history had no basis whatsoever either scientifically or rationally. There was no evidence for a bullet passing through the body.

Richard Lipsey said that he thought the bullet that hit high in the back or at the bottom of the neck did not exit. "Lipsey says that he recalls the doctors discussing the third bullet which he believes entered low in the neck and was deflected down into the chest cavity."[247]

Chester Boyers said that the path of the bullet that entered the upper back, seemed to indicate that the bullet exited through the tracheotomy.[248]

James Curtis Jenkins said that according to his recollection of the location of the back wound, the bullet would have been going upward through the body to have exited in the front of the neck. He based his impression of the direction of the bullet on the fact that the probe did not enter the body cavity.[249]

Did Humes state that the pattern was clear that the one bullet had entered the President's back and had worked its way out of the body during external cardiac massage? This is what the FBI reported Humes as saying. He also told the Warren Commission that that is what they first thought. Notice the severe conflict in his story. Dr. Ebersole was asked, "Do you remember some tentative discussion as to whether the bullet entered and then dropped out?"

"Yes, a great deal of discussion of that type."

"Is your impression at that time during when the X-rays were taken and after the X-rays were taken that this was considered as a possibility?"

"Yes."[250]

Ebersole quickly began to backpedal with Dr. Baden's *next* question, as it must have dawned on him that that conclusion conflicted with the need to do any further X-rays. It seems reasonable that the military doctors did not want to commit themselves in the autopsy report to much of anything at all, and so had decided to say that the bullet had fallen out. They came under pressure to have a bullet pass through the body, and changed their conclusions after the fact. There is no evidence they had any *proof* of a transiting bullet. "Is it your impression perhaps . . . if we assume that the information about the tracheotomy through a bullet hole was not available to the doctors that evening but came later on, could there have been a tentative conclusion reached that evening that in fact the bullet entering the back region had dropped out and that is why it was not present and that explain the autopsy and X-ray findings?"

"I don't remember such conclusions being reached, but assuming it, I suppose it could have."[251] If no such conclusion had been reached, then the entire autopsy was a failure because they could not explain the bullet wound in the back, and they technically didn't know of the bullet wound in the throat. Since there has been a tentative admission that they might not even have known that the throat wound was a tracheostomy, there was at the end of the autopsy no explanation at all for what happened to the bullet that hit President Kennedy in the back. It was decided the next day when they were told what the official story demanded, though it might not have been put to them that way.

Ebersole then retracted this without acknowledging the contradiction, when he was asked: "Your X-ray taking may have been related to an initial concern that had been expressed and that you remember being expressed of the back bullet entering and then dropping out in Dallas, correct?"

Dr. Ebersole: "No."

Dr. Baden: "I am sorry."

Dr. Ebersole: "My initial impression is that we have a wound of entrance and we do not have a wound of exit and I don't remember any conversation about a bullet dropping out."

Dr. Baden: "I am sorry."

Dr. Ebersole: "I don't remember any conversation about a bullet coming out."

Dr. Baden: "Do you remember a conversation when this back wound was probed that it appeared to end in the back?"

Dr. Ebersole: "No, I don't remember any conversation of that kind."[252] Ebersole either misspoke himself when he told them that he had heard the discussion of the bullet falling out, or he got caught up in the knots that came with this story.

The FBI report had something to say about this. For weeks or months after the autopsy, the FBI blissfully maintained that separate bullets struck Kennedy and Connally, evidently not seeing the problem that would be raised by a shot having hit the curb of Main Street. Their report of the autopsy says that because they learned during the autopsy that a bullet (they didn't know on whose stretcher!) had been found at Parkland and that external cardiac message had been performed, "it was entirely possible that through such movement the bullet had worked its way back out of the point of entry and had fallen on the stretcher. . . . On the basis of the latter two developments, Dr. Humes stated that the pattern was clear that the one bullet had entered the President's back and had worked its way out of the body during external cardiac massage. . . ."[253]

*   *   *

Was there bruising of the pleura at the dome? Finck said that yes, on the right side, "I would say [it] is explained by a high velocity bullet creating what has caused a temporary cavity with a lot of contusion and disturbance of tissue."

"You actually saw it?"

"I think so."[254] Martin Shackelford comments: "This is not a very strong confirmation by Finck of a key element of the neck-wound path, the bruising of the pleura! How firm are Humes and Boswell on this? Finck is supposed to be the wound ballistics specialist, and he seems to hesitate in endorsing this evidence."[255] Again, the bruise could happen as a result of a bullet striking the body with great force somewhere else.

How many bullet wounds did Kennedy have? Richard Lipsey, charged by his commanding general never to take his eyes off the body during the autopsy, believes that there is no question in his mind that the doctors felt there were three separate rear entry wounds and three separate bullets from behind.[256] Not two.

This is reasonable, especially if you postulate that one of the shots to the head was actually from the front, and what they saw was half of a small exit wound on the edge of the crater in the skull, but on the posterior side of the skull. The orientation of the photograph which we have from Paul O'Connor (published in *High Treason 2*) would indicate that the outwardly beveled edge is in fact on the back of the head.

One of Lipsey's wounds, the tangential head shot, may have been from in front. We are quite certain that the Dallas doctors observed an entry wound in the throat. It is possible that the President was struck twice in the head. Could everybody lie about any of the rearward shots? It seems certain that they saw a back wound, and it is at least half as strong that there had been an entry hole in the back of the head. The autopsy doctors would have to be lying if this was not so. Of course, that entry hole is subject to the interpretation of "beveling" on its inner aspect, inside the skull, and the head would have to be reexamined to prove it. But were there minute metal fragments on the intact part of the skull? "No, definitely not," Dr. Mantik, who examined the fake official X-rays, comments. We have nothing about that in the record, but it is said that there are metal traces on one of the "Midnight" pieces of bone that helped complete the bullet's entry hole.

The reason why this tragedy has got us tied in knots is because there were several gunmen and quite a few wounds. This is a big thing to cover up, and nobody can keep their story straight. If therewere wounds on the front of the body, I'm sure everyone was ordered not to see them, and that certainly has tied things up forever.

DRAWINGS

Was Dr. Boswell's autopsy descriptive sheet drawing accurate, or was it altered? James Sibert stated that "the drawing was pretty accurate as to what we described." He said the general location of the wounds "looked accurate." Sibert also said that CE 385 and CE 386 looked accurate as well.[257] O'Neill, on the other hand, said he disagreed with Dr. Boswell's depiction of the location of the back (thorax) wound which Dr. Boswell had drawn on a diagram during an interview with the HSCA in the fall of 1977.[258]

It was the job of James Curtis Jenkins to do such drawings, and he is acutely uneasy about the autopsy descriptive sheet. He recalls that he "put in the chest incisions and tracheotomy." He doesn't think he drew the back wound. He said it was possible that Dr. Humes added to the sheet. Mr. Jenkins said that five or six years later he saw a publication (perhaps *Time* or *Newsweek*) that included an autopsy descriptive sheet which he "didn't feel was the same one he wrote on." He said this made him very uneasy. Specifically, he "didn't believe it was my handwriting." He is sure he "wrote at least some of the information on the sheet." He said his recollection was "very striking." He said it was a situation where he looked at something and "knew" it was wrong. Jenkins believes that he wrote on the sheet in pencil. It was a "requirement that it had to be done in pencil," and the sheet was on a clipboard that had a string with a pencil attached. He recalls that the back side of the figure was on the back of the sheet and said he has no recollection of a drawing of a head on the sheet anywhere. He believes the writing on the sheet would have had to have been Paul O'Connor's, one of the doctor's, or his own.[259]

Jenkins, whom I know to be a highly intelligent and educated gentleman, told House investigators why he expressed doubts. He was a very acute observer at the autopsy, standing next to the table, and he told House investigators, ". . . with the Warren Commission findings, you can understand why I'm skeptical."[260] He also said he was "surprised at the conclusions the doctors reached" with regard to the head wound.[261]

The House investigators, highly suspicious of the official evidence and endeavoring to cover all the bases, went to visit James Jenkins in Mississippi, where he was in a doctoral program, and showed him the Warren Commission's version of the autopsy descriptive sheet (CE 397).† Jenkins pointed out that the front page should have a Navy number on the top left. This exhibit has a lot of blank spaces on the lines to have been filled in, and Jenkins notes: "all the top would have had to be filled in." He said that the numbers looked like his handwriting. He noted that the number on the top left of the page was stamped or typed in and he said "it would be written in." He said he believes he handwrote in that number on the original autopsy descriptive sheet. He said the writing concerning the head wound on the diagram itself was not his, and he said that the slit he drew at the autopsy to represent the throat wound was "not crescent-like . . ." like the one in the Warren Commission volumes. He said it was normal for the pathologists to sign the descriptive sheet which was not done on the version in the report. Jenkins said all the heights and weights "would be filled in . . ." but said he could not remember specifically writing them in. He said the notations regarding the lung, spleen, and kidney look like his handwriting. He said that it was "possible the rest is Paul's [O'Connor]."

He said that he would write in the starting time. The starting-time blank was not filled in. Regarding the diagram, Jenkins said, "None of that handwriting looks like mine." He said that the autopsy descriptive sheet in the Warren volumes does not look like the one he saw in the publication five to six years after the autopsy. *Jenkins does not recall a small hole in the head as drawn on the descriptive sheet; he said that the big hole would have covered the area where the little hole was drawn on the sheet. Regarding the back wound he said that he "thought it was a little higher up, underneath the collar."*[262] (Author's emphasis.) He said the wound itself was "below the collar at an angle, in a downward trajectory."[263] A bit later in his interview, he said that the wound at the top part of the head in CE 386 (CE 388),‡ the drawing of the back and back of the head made for the public and published by the Warren Commission, looked familiar but said he had no recollection of the little bullet hole in the head. He said that the neck wound he recalled was lower and more to the midline than that in the drawing. He reiterated his belief that the wound in the back was "below the collar line which is what the picture shows." Regarding CE 385 (the profile view showing a bullet

† 17 H 45–46.
‡ CE 386: 16 H 977, CE 388: 16 H 984, drawings by Harold Rydberg, a Navy artist, for the Warren Commission under Dr. Humes's direction.

passing through the neck from back to front), Jenkins said he didn't
see the possibility that it was accurate . . . Jenkins said he believed
the autopsy face sheet was essentially accurate regarding the location of the wound in the back.[264] As with Jerrol Custer, the essential
contradictions in the recollections of the enlisted men nearly thirty
years later, after their attendance at the autopsy at very young ages,
cannot be easily resolved.

Jenkins also said he found strange that he possibly drew the back
scar, but didn't think so, and said that he is "positive" he didn't
draw the head wound. He said the number of the patient on the
log and on the descriptive sheet would be the same. He said he
thought they may have had a stamp for putting the number of the
log, but didn't for the descriptive sheet. Jenkins believes he would
have filled in the physical description where the descriptive sheet
is blank regarding the color of the eyes, the race, the hair color
and the height. Jenkins said the chest measurements or the location
of the chest incisions were not made by him, and were possibly
made by Paul O'Connor.[265]

Normally, erasures on the autopsy sheets must be initialed.[266]

Dr. Boswell said that he did not write the weights of the organs
on the sheet, but he wrote "everything else." "All of the notes on
the diagrams are mine, and this diagram on the back is mine, this
and this."[267]

We have the possibility that there was a certain amount of alteration to the drawings and figures or other diagrams made on the
autopsy descriptive sheet. The other serious conflicts, such as in the
brain and liver weights, indicate that there is something drastically
wrong with this autopsy.

Why was there no description of the body? Was it a different body?

**Were the Warren Commission drawings made by a Navy artist
with the guidance of the autopsy doctors accurate?** Francis X.
O'Neill stated that the Navy medical illustrator, the Commission
employed Harold Rydberg, did not accurately depict the President's wounds.[268] Others, as reported above, say the drawings
are accurate.

FRAGMENTS

Was there any other metal in the body? Boswell said there was a
small fleck in the spinal canal.[269] Dr. John Ebersole, the radiologist,

dropped a bomb on Committee investigators when he told them that there was one "buckshot" in the President's pelvis,[270] but this was kept quiet. I wonder if Boswell is not speaking of the same missile, though he reduces it to a "fleck." The investigators talking with Ebersole reduced the buckshot to "bird shot,"[271] which is quite a bit smaller, and then reduced it altogether so that it was never spoken or written about again. It seems to be possible that whatever hit Kennedy high up on his body could have traveled down his body, as bullets will do (they sometimes follow arteries or veins) and lodged in his pelvic region.

Boswell said that the X-rays showed a unique object in the lower back which he described as a "radio-opaque piece of material" and characterized as a "milagram [sic—*myelogram* is correct] die [sic— dye] residual."[272] This is probably the "buckshot" again. Ebersole describes "myelographic media present in the spinal canal. This caused one of the Secret Service men to question if that might not be a—here we are. . . ." and the subject is changed.[273] They are speaking of dye that is used to inspect the spinal canal. But the very next comment by Ebersole is the following: "At the time of the autopsy, I felt that this metallic fragment to the right of the midline represented myelographic media. I think what this really represents is a buckshot, since it is well to the right of the canal. This is the other possibility. It represents a buckshot or a myelo- graphic media. This can be very positively identified as taken that night. This was the rounded material. The myelographic media would be in or near the midline of the spinal canal where this appears to be near the right. It could represent either thing al- though I expect from its density and its rounded appearance it means buckshot." Is Ebersole *trying* to discredit himself?

"What do you mean by buckshot there?"

"A pellet from the shell fired by a shotgun," Ebersole replies.

"Are you implying that this would have been a pellet fired into the body at some previous time?"

"I am saying at some previous time he ate a duck or a rabbit and this is either in the appendix or the—I expect out in the street we would find something like 15 or 20 percent of the population to have that."[274] (!) This discussion was halted and not resumed after the tape was changed.

One cannot put it past the secret Confederate societies and Socie- ties for the Protection of Texas to have employed snipers using 1860s-vintage Kentucky sharpshooting rifles, which—firing Minié balls—were among the finest long-distance target rifles ever manufactured. Modern versions of these long rifles are being made and sold today.

Dr. Finck describes ballistics tests carried out by firing steel spheres, which "always reveal a wound of entrance larger than the wound of exit, because of the constant presented area of the missile and the lack of tumbling or fragmentation of the steel spheres used. Light [Author's note: Dr. F. W. Light, Jr.] observed that both the entrance and the exit wounds have the same gross appearance."[275] I wonder if Finck is also trying to tell us something with this. He had only a very obscure publication to suggest that round missiles might have been used, since in the very next comment he tells us that there was a smaller wound of exit in the assassination of Kennedy than the alleged wound of entrance.

What bullets, therefore, correspond to the above spheroid types? Certainly, a missile that leaves evidence which appears to entirely reverse the direction from which a bullet has been fired would be a rather brilliant stroke in an assassination. Some of the murkier aspects of the shooting in Dealey Plaza could be explained by sharpshooters posted one and a half to three blocks away with long rifles in undetectable positions where their shots could not be heard in the Plaza. Deadly shots are made by sharpshooters at half a mile, and even one mile with a .50 caliber rifle.

Robinson, one of the morticians, said that he believed a metal fragment had been removed from the thorax. "Somehow I feel like there was something found in the thorax.... I think that they found a piece of metal, a piece of bullet."[276] Certainly something must have hit the chest in order for there to have been fluid that the doctors in Dallas wanted to drain off. But this could have been from the throat hit.

Then we have what I think was a veiled reference to a metal track through the body which resulted in some disorder in the panel meeting and what might have been anger on Dr. Ebersole's part. Dr. Weston says, "I would like to call your attention to one particular pattern, Dr. Ebersole, which is—well, for the record appears to be located over the second rib. You will note here that there is a triangular thing and then there seems to be trailing off of three little things in that direction as it—do you see that commonly as an artifact?"

Dr. Baden: "Let the record reflect Dr. Ebersole and Dr. Weston are discussing film No. 9, chest X-ray."

Dr. Ebersole: "I feel this is really no different from this type of thing seen here."

Dr. Weston: "The only difference is that they seem to be lined up as if there were something there and then something—" (Weston seems to want to say that he sees a bullet track!) Ebersole shoots Weston down:

Dr. Ebersole: These also appear to be lined up but this is seen, yes, with artifacts. It is if it is due to dirt."

Dr. Weston: "You feel more comfortable talking about artifactual material in an X-ray than you do about some of the other things. I mean, certainly you have seen many, many X-rays."

Dr. Ebersole: "I feel these are really too bright. Here is a very typical dirt mark."

Dr. Weston: "What about these?"

Dr. Ebersole: "These are the same."

Dr. Weston: "Thank you, sir."

Dr. Ebersole: "I think it might be well for you as you look at these to put up a film that we have of a known metallic density such as that birdshot."

Dr. Baden: "Can we have some decorum, please."[277] They then went off the record—and the discussion was completely changed when they got back on. They never returned to the possible metal track through the chest, which would have certainly answered many questions. Unless the next issue that came up referred to a bullet in the chest, or some strange thing, like a nylon bullet. That bullet had to hit the back of John Connally's seat or the floor of the car. But the car was reconstructed and the bottom replaced, according to my investigation.

They were discussing X-ray no. 8 of the right upper chest and right upper extremity: "There is a prominent radio lucency on the right side." Ebersole interprets the X-ray as having been taken after the viscera were removed.[278] But then we are directed to the neck and something metallic, if we can figure out what they are referring to in these unillustrated interviews. Ebersole points it out as metal. "Almost immediately lateral to the right lateral mass of C-7 is an opacity that might represent metal." (Mantik says that it's just "dirt on the X-ray. It's not seen on the X-ray at the beginning of the autopsy."[279]) And a little later he says, "I suspect that may be a fracture of the lateral prospect there. I am not being sure on the basis of these X-rays."[280] Ebersole says it would be C7-T1. "Here is the first rib."

Others suggest that it might be a bone fragment.[281] As the discussion progresses, Weston tries to corner Ebersole on the metal issue. In discussing one of the other "things" on the X-ray, he asks Ebersole, "Would they help you to reach a conclusion whether that was a metallic or a bone fragment?"

Dr. Ebersole: "No. . . . Those I feel strongly and still feel are artifacts."[282] Mantik agrees.

What did the receipt for a "missile" found at the autopsy mean? Sibert said the receipt certainly was not for a "whole missile." He said it was for "some fragments." He said that if he had written it himself, he would have listed the items as metal fragments, and that the term "missile" to him means quite a bit of substance, more of a whole bullet.[283] O'Neill emphatically stated that the doctors removed only two fragments and not a "missile."[284]

The receipt was typed by Chester Boyers, a Navy Chief Petty Officer in charge of the Pathology Department, who was interviewed by the House investigators. "Boyers said he typed out a receipt to give to the FBI present at the autopsy for the missile fragments recovered from the body during the autopsy. Boyers said he had a Xerox copy of this receipt. Boyers said several fragments were given to the FBI, with the largest being 2mm. He said that even though the receipt states that a 'missle' [sic] was recovered, this is in error; only fragments were recovered. Boyers never saw a fully intact missile."[285]

The autopsy report lists these fragments as being removed from the "surface of the disrupted right cerebral cortex" and the same measurements which follow in the FBI report. The FBI report lists them at 7 × 2 mm and 1 × 3 mm, both removed from the "right side of the brain." This was actually from above the right frontal sinus. It is not possible for either of these fragments of that size to have come from the back of the head. The back of the head fragment now seen on the altered X-rays is 6.5mm across. It did not exist on the night of November 22, 1963.

Who ended up with the bullet fragments and the photographs and the X-rays from the autopsy? Francis X. O'Neill said that the FBI did not keep the photographs since the case was somewhat outside of their jurisdiction. He said that the FBI obtained the bullet fragments because Hoover wanted them.[286]

The Secret Service kept the photographs and X-rays.

Was there a discussion of two bullets striking the head, possibly including one from in front? Jan Rudnicki, the lab tech who stood close by the table all evening, said that there was a discussion by the doctors about the possibility that two bullets struck the head in

the same general area, causing a massive defect.[287] James Curtis
Jenkins also described to me that such a discussion had occurred,
and this seemed to involve either an entry or an exit in the right
temple.[288]

REAR HEAD ENTRY

Was there a rear head entry? To ask this question casts doubt on
the entire autopsy report and implies that several of the doctors
are lying. We would have to suppose that things were described in
the autopsy report and in the testimony which were totally false and
never happened. This is not beyond the impossible. We have the
doctors insisting on a small wound of entry some inches lower than
where it is claimed to be in the photos and X-rays, and other clearly
unexplainable conflicts. Although a couple of others at the autopsy
mark a small wound of entry near the hairline in their drawings, it
is possible that it was never there, and that what we in fact have is
only the larger "orange"-size hole, either of exit or entry.

It is highly probable that there was an entry wound, and that it
was where the doctors say it was, since it was against their interests
to insist—as they do—that the entry is not where it shows on the
photos and X-rays. The only other possibility is that they were forced
to invent it and are all lying. After they invented it, their placement
for the wound was moved four inches higher because of bad planning, leaving them high and dry, appearing to be mistaken, incompetent, and discredited. Dr. Mantik comments on the manuscript
here: "The 7 × 2 mm fragment location above the right frontal
sinus is very consistent with an EOP entry. Also, there are several
tiny bullet fragments consistent with this, EOP and right forehead."

The other explanation is that Tom Robinson simply missed the
small wound of entry. I find this rather difficult to believe, since he
reconstructed the rubber coffer dam on the back of the head and
closed up the head. But Mantik says it was easy to miss, since it was
only a part of what would have been a hole had there been complete bone there perforated through and through.

Robinson, the mortician, *did not see any small wound of entry in the
back of the head, but not being so formally trained in forensics, might have
missed it.*[289] But it was his job to close up the head using the dam
to prevent leaks. He prepared the body for burial in what they
thought would be an open coffin. Robinson describes the large
defect as an orange-sized hole low in the center of the back of the

head near the hairline (see his drawing). The interview with House investigators discuss this large hole as though it were an entry hole, since it is in the area where the autopsy doctors placed an entry hole, but the size of an orange. Bullets are known to make a much larger hole of entry in bone if they are of a different velocity or configuration than a military jacketed bullet.

"Do you think it was possible that there was some other wound under the hair? [Author's note: Purdy is looking for the small wound of entry described in the autopsy report.] Did you look for other wounds?" "Oh, yes, we would have found that."[290] Normally, morticians actually do their own examination of a body, drawing on autopsy face sheets, making notes (in this case none of that was done).[291]

"Where do you feel the bullet entered and in that back major wound. What would have caused a three-inch hole?"

"I think when that bullet hit that bone, it just shattered."[292] Robinson thought that the bullet that hit that low in the head might have come out the throat,[293] which is what Lt. Richard Lipsey thought: "Another bullet entered at the top of the neck (rear) which exited in the front portion of the neck," to quote the House report.[294] Lipsey also said that it was another bullet that hit him in the head and came out the right side of his head.[295] I'm strongly inclined to think that Lipsey observed that there had been a bullet entry near the hairline, perhaps the same one that the doctors stated was the fatal head shot, since they place it about the same place that Lipsey does. But *that bullet could not have* come out of the side or top of his head and come from the sixth-floor window.§ Lipsey does not have a clear entry for the portion of the head that he has drawn as being blown away. He therefore must be describing the same sort of tangential head shot that others talked about, which of course would leave only a partial semicircle of a bullet entry and perhaps the same for an exit, taking off all the connecting bone. Or is he merging missing scalp with missing bone in his mind? One story is that they put plaster in the head and placed the three "midnight fragments" back on the head. Then why worry about leaks, putting a rubber dam over the hole, if plaster was used?

Robinson said the shot was "either coming from the head down and out or from the back." The possible entry of a bullet low on the skull with a fragment exiting the throat was mentioned in *Six*

§"But a bullet *fragment* could!" Mantik comments. "Furthermore, the 9.5 cm bone fragment extended to the coronal suture—where tiny metal fragments were seen on the bone fragments. It very likely did exit here! Where else did it go?"

Seconds in Dallas by Josiah Thompson.[296] This is controverted by the Zapruder film, which shows the President bringing his hands up in front of his chin sometime before the head shot. To me and many others it looks as though he is trying to clutch at his throat, but it could have been a reaction to having a specific nerve struck, as Dr. David Mantik tells me. It is conceivable that such a low-down head shot exiting the throat was not visible on the film and would not remotely appear like what we see on the film. Some of the Dallas doctors thought the opposite—that the bullet that hit him in the throat took off the back of his head.[297]

Robinson describes a "nasty-looking" tracheostomy[298] (this is consistent with Ebersole's description), and indicates that there either had been a lot of the neck organs removed or something else was drastically torn up.

Lieutenant Richard Lipsey, the aide to General Wehle charged with watching the body throughout the autopsy, stated that he felt there was no real entrance in the rear of the head: "He feels that one bullet blasted away an entire portion (entrance and exit)."[299] I think he means there was a tangential shot, which is the feeling of numerous other witnesses who saw the body. But was it possible from those angles? Lipsey's observation does not necessarily conflict with the notion that there was a semicircular entry on the intact skull, and the rest of the bone was carried away by the shot. The doctors claim the circle was completed by a late-arriving piece of bone. Just what bone it was is in dispute. Boswell said it was a small one.

James Curtis Jenkins said that the wound to the head entered the top rear quadrant from the front side.[300] He is saying that a tangential shot took off the right rear quadrant of the head from the front. He is not speaking of an entry hole in the back of the head as described by others. He says that he thinks the bullet entered the right temple area and cites metal smears there. Jenkins told me that he did not see the entrance wound described in the autopsy report and by the Bethesda doctors in their testimony. He didn't completely believe that it was there.[301] "And the opening and the way the bone was damaged behind the head would have definitely been a type of exit wound. The reason I have said this is I saw this before any other wounds and it was very striking."[302]

There is a rather devastating statement by James W. Sibert in his affidavit. He wrote: "I have no recollection of hearing or writing down measurements relating to the entrance wound in the President's head."[303]

Was he asleep? Did it never happen? Is he saying he saw no entrance wound, or was he only referring to the measurements of it?

How did they find the rear head entry? Finck tells us that they first located it by the hole through the scalp, which lined up with what remained of the hole in the skull.[304] The autopsy report says the same thing, making it clear that the hole in the scalp corresponded to the hole in the skull.[305] Therefore, they have that wound coming and going. They have it two ways and it would appear to be very solid that it cannot be some four inches above, as it is claimed in the photos. Dr. Petty asked Finck, "In order to expose that area where the wound was present in the bone, did you have to or did someone have to dissect the scalp off of the bone in order to show this?"

"Yes."

"Was this a difficult dissection and did it go very low into the head so as to expose the external aspect of the posterior cranial fascia?"

"I don't remember the difficulty involved in separating the scalp from the skull, but this was done in order to have a clear view of the outside and inside to show the crater from the inside."[306]

Where was the rear head entry? The placement of the entry wound in the head is one of the most major disputes in the case, and there are many. Andy Purdy talked on the phone with Dr. Humes before Humes, Boswell, and Finck appeared before the Medical Panel, and Purdy brought up the whole issue of whether the entry was high or low on the back of the head. "I asked him whether the wound was in the upper or lower part of the head. Dr. Humes said that it was in the 'lower head' area. I asked Dr. Humes about his knowledge of the Clark Panel Report. He said he knows some of the people who served on it and he thought they confirmed the essential findings of the autopsy doctors. *I cited to him the Clark Panel's recitation of their determination that the autopsy doctors had miscalculated the location of the head wound by a vertical distance of approximately 100 millimeters (they said the autopsy doctors place the wound that much lower than it really was). Dr. Humes stated categorically that his physical measurements are correct and emphasized that he had access to the body itself and made the measurements of the actual head region.* **In addition, he said that photographs and X-rays have inherent limitations which are not present when one is examining the subject** [author's emphasis]."[307] My own interviews with Dr. Humes over the phone in Detroit in 1980 showed that he had not budged on this issue and that he would never retreat from the low-entry position on the head. Although he talked to me for as long as an hour at a time and I learned precious little, he was very strong on this issue.

The autopsy doctors insisted that the wound was a through-and-through wound in the intact skull down near the hairline on the back of the head. They told the panel of forensic experts examining them in 1978 that the wound was not in the cowlick area. But one said the rear head wound was assembled from an attached fragment hinged to the intact skull. Dr. Boswell: "It tore right down to that point. And then we just folded that back and this back and an interior flap forward and that exposed almost the entire—I guess we did have to dissect a little bit to get to—"

Dr. Humes: "To get to this entrance, right?"

Dr. Boswell: "But not much, because this bone was all gone and actually the smaller fragment fit this piece down here—there was a hole here, only half of which was present in the bone that was intact, and this small piece then fit right on there and the beveling on those was on the interior surface."

Dr. Petty: "Then was this below the tentorium or above the tentorium on the inside? Do you recall?"

Dr. Humes: "Everything was so disrupted, I'm not sure."[308] I don't think Humes wanted to answer that question because the tentorium is the tentlike structure of tough tissue fiber that is stretched over the cerebellum in the very back of the head, and we are quite certain that that area was ruined and "on the cart" in Dallas. The autopsy would have had to examine that area and determine what happened there.

Chester Boyers saw the entry hole in the back of the head "to the right of the external occipital protuberance."[309]

Boswell repeatedly described the finding of the rear head *entry* wound, to me in *High Treason 2,* to the HSCA forensic panel of doctors as above, and in his HSCA interview with Andy Purdy, Colleen Boland, and Jim Kelly, in which they wrote, "Regarding the head wound, Dr. Boswell said the wound was fairly low in the back of the head and that the bone was completely gone above the entry wound. He said that during the autopsy, a piece of skull fragment was brought in which included a portion which corresponded to the missing half of the entry wound in the head."[310] The term "entry" is repeated often enough here so that we can be fairly sure they don't mean "exit," but it is confusing because we have the idea from others that there was a through-and-through or circumferential small bullet wound of the intact skull in that area. We are told that an *exit* wound is seen on one-half of the intact skull more forward on the head, and on one-half of a piece of the alleged bone that came into the autopsy room at midnight.[311]

Dr. Boswell again repeated during his 1977 House interview that the entry hole was only approximately half in evidence, the other half being part of the skull fragment which was brought in.[312] So, both entry and exit holes in the skull were only half present on the intact skull.

At another point in their interview in 1977, the autopsy doctors are asked, "I know how difficult it is, but is there any way that you could show us where the entrance was in that wound?" (They are looking at the autopsy photographs, specifically no. 45.) Boswell responds: "I don't believe it's depicted in that picture."

Humes: "How about here, Jay?"

Boswell: "Well, I don't believe so, because, as I recall, the bone was *intact* [author's emphasis]. I am sure that Humes was pointing to the area above the hairline in the back of the head, which appears intact in the photograph, where we believe there was no scalp at all] at that point. There was a shelf and then a little hole, came up on the side and then one of the smaller of the two fragments in that X-ray, when that arrived we were able to fit that down there and complete the circumference of that bone wound."

Humes responds with an important comment: *"I don't remember that in that detail* [author's emphasis]."[313] It's important because Humes and Finck describe the entry hole's position differently—as a circumferential through-and-through hole—from that of Boswell, who did the work. Was it a circumferential through-and-through wound of otherwise intact bone, or was it part on the intact skull and part on another piece attached to tissue, but fractured away? Was it half on intact skull and half on a missing piece brought in hours later? We have three different descriptions.

Dr. Finck said he "saw in the back of the head on the right side a wound corresponding to that wound of the scalp. I observed a hole in the skull. That hole in the skull in the back of the head showed no crater when examined from the outside of the skull, but when I examined the inside of the skull at the level of that hole in the bone, I saw a crater and to me that was a positive unquestionable finding identifying a wound of entry in the back of the head."[314] This seems to be a through-and-through hole, but was not clarified in the questioning. Was the hole merely part on the intact skull and part on some other piece of bone?

Finck was asked where the hole was. He was interviewed six months after the other doctors. "Was that above or below the level of the tops of the ears?"

"It was above the external occipital protuberance which is not— I am showing now with my finger."

"It was above it?"

"Yes."

"A long distance above it or just a short distance above it or just about at?"

"Slightly above it as I remember. . . . It was 2.5 centimeters to the right of the midline."[315] He repeats "slightly above" one more time on that page. This is the exact language and position of the autopsy report, which he has memorized, since he says that he took the measurements.[316] But Dr. Humes said that the wound was *below* the EOP, and both he and Boswell insisted on this when the same forensic panel of doctors interviewed them the previous year.[317]

In trying to place the entry, Finck says, "I think we have photographs to go by for that." Dr. Petty responds, "We sure do."[318] It would certainly help if we could see these pictures, which are apparently nowhere in evidence, because later Finck tells us that the photographs showing the entry are missing.

Finck then locates the entry hole on photograph no. 42, pointing to a mass "right at the junction of the hair with the neck."[319] Photo no. 42 shows the back of the head with intact scalp and what has been called a piece of brain matter near the hairline. The autopsy pathologists have insisted that that "brain matter" is where the bullet entered the skull and that there was a wound corresponding directly to it that penetrated the skull. The Panel again and again tries to shake him and move the entry hole to the cowlick, but Finck doesn't buy it: "This is the one by the hairline?" Dr. Petty asks him. "By the hairline," Finck responds, unmovable. These same doctors struck out with the other two autopsy doctors before, yet the Committee led by our elected Representatives betrayed the public and perpetrated one more cover-up on the nation and said that all three autopsy doctors and the radiologist were mistaken. According to the official story, four out of four doctors were wrong. Thus, the Committee went with the fake photographs and X-rays, and the conclusion that they were fake is the only conclusion that can be drawn when they don't show what the doctors saw.

Finck goes on, fighting his lonely battle in a room full of doctors. "We have here a black-and-white blowup of that same spot. [Author's note: Stringer said that no black-and-white photographs were taken at the autopsy. So what are the doctors being shown? Yet, the autopsy report says that black-and-white photos were made. Stringer was the photographer.] You previously mentioned that your attempt here was to photograph the crater—I think was the word that you used."

Dr. Finck: "In the bone, not in the scalp, because to determine the direction of the projectile the bone is a very good source of information so I emphasize the photographs of the crater seen from inside the skull. What you are showing me is soft tissue wound in the scalp."[320] The photos he took of the crater in the bone were missing.

But a low entry wound meant that no bullet struck the head from that window and blew off part of the back of the head, exiting high on the skull.

Was it necessary for the forgers, for the conspirators, to fake the photos at all? Is this some sort of vast red herring? The real issue is, *did a bullet strike the President from in front and blow off the back of his head? Was there really a bullet entry hole on the back of the head at all?* The doctors simply stuck with what they originally saw, and that turned out to be a mistake, because the forgers put the hole much higher in the photos and X-rays. "We would not be expected to see only half of a circumference of a wound on the back of the skull on the lateral X-ray. On the AP, it is obscured by dense bone at the front of the skull," Dr. Mantik says.[321]

Ebersole was asked by Dr. Baden for the House Committee, "Do you on examination of these films have an opinion as to where the gunshot wound of entrance was in the head radiologically?"

"In my opinion, it would have come from the side on the basis of the films. I guess that is all that can be said about the films at this time."[322]

Dr. Boswell told my investigator, Richard Waybright, that the rear head entry was right where we see a small piece of brain tissue near the hairline on the back of the head.[323] Very low down. He says this to everybody.

Roy Kellerman told the HSCA he recalled seeing one large hole in the head and no small hole. There wasn't, of course, a through-and-through entry hole until more bone arrived at midnight, which Kellerman saw and described to the Warren Commission as being in the hairline.[324] ·

Boswell said the Clark Panel explicitly agreed with the autopsy doctors' essential findings with regard to the entry and exit wounds of the head![325] They, of course, are grossly mistaken.

Do the X-rays in fact show the entry hole on the back of the head? Dr. Ebersole, not a diagnostic radiologist by trade, though he practiced radiation therapy, was of the opinion that the X-rays did not show the entry. He was asked that on the basis of the X-rays, if he "felt like there had been a bullet wound on the right side of the head, is that correct?"

"No, I would say on the basis of those X-rays and X-rays only one might say one would have to estimate there that the wound of entrance was somewhere to the side or to the posterior quadrant."[326]

In fact, the placement of the wound in the cowlick area by the Clark Panel and these same panelists for the House Committee seems to be by inference *only* because they think there is a large metal fragment on the outer table of the skull half an inch from the perimeter of a small wound which is in no way visible and which they seem to infer from photographs which show a "red spot" in the area, but no large bullet fragment. It is half an inch from a large piece of displaced bone on the top rear of the head.

And, *was there an entry hole in the X-rays at all?* Dr. David Mantik, the radiologist who has seen them[327] says, "There is too much overlying bone on the anterior view to see into that area. On the lateral view, you're looking tangentially through this area. I don't think the human eye can discriminate the area where there is no hole to the area where there is a hole. At posterior skull sites where the AP skull X-ray clearly shows absent bone, it is not apparent on the lateral X-ray. The human eye is simply not capable of making such fine distinctions."[328]

What was actually in the cowlick, where the photos and X-rays were said to place the entry? This is another great conflict in the case. Dr. Finck, when shown the photographs with the "red spot" in the cowlick, the alleged entry, was asked if that was the entry: "I don't know what it is."[329] These are the almost the identical words used by Drs. Humes and Boswell to this same panel six months before, and which led to the comment by the Committee which is at the head of this chapter.[330]

Dr. Boswell told Richard Waybright that the "red spot" is not the entrance wound but possibly may be blood or a mixture of blood and water.[331]

More on the "red spot" in color photograph number 43. Andy Purdy asks Finck: "If you were shown a photograph containing—as does no. 43—showing the back of a person's head and showing that red spotted area, if that doctor—well, first of all what inference would you draw if you saw just that?"

"On the basis of the photograph alone, nothing."[332](!)

Again and again Purdy assails Finck on this issue and Finck stead-fastly maintains that "No, I don't know what answer I would give really. See, I am influenced by something I have seen, described, and when shown something outside I cannot say that there was an additional wound really."[333] After another try by Purdy, Dr. Davis says, "Let's presume that these photographs have nothing to do with the assassination of President John F. Kennedy and we look at the transparency through the magnifying lens at that red dot that is close to the ruler up here in line with the upper portion of the ear. Would you say just looking at this, disregarding who this picture is, but does that suggest to you to have some characteristics—I am not saying it is a wound or not, but does the photographic appear-ance have some consistency with the wound or some exactness of a wound? Just take a look at it with the magnifying glass."

Dr. Finck replies: "That is terribly embarrassing. To commit your-self on the basis of this is a hazardous thing just looking at a photo-graph."[334] Dr. Joseph H. Davis tries and fails one last time to get him to agree that the "red spot" might be a wound.

The most important fact to consider is the repeated and vehe-ment insistence by the autopsy doctors during their interview with a large panel of forensic specialists in 1977 that there was no entry in the cowlick area anywhere near where we now find a fragment on the outer table of the skull. Dr. Humes: "I submit to you that, despite the fact that this upper point that has been the source of some discussion here this afternoon is excessively obvious in the color photograph, I almost defy you to find it in that magnification in the black and white."[335] Both Humes and Boswell continued to insist that there was no entry wound at all in that position but that it was down near the hairline, *below* the EOP, some four to five inches away. Their insistence on this implies that they were almost certainly *not* faking the EOP site.

Was there a clean shot through the skull on entry (a "through-and-through" shot)? This would mean that the bullet struck one part of the head, passed through, and then struck it again on the other side, blowing out pieces of bone with it. We seem to have a primary description of a tangential shot which left us with a semicir-cle fitting half the circumference of the bullet on part of the intact skull in the back, and another semicircle exit of the bullet more toward the right side and higher. Part of the bone between the two semicircle, according to this description, was blown off, and part remained on hinged flaps of tissue.

The autopsy report does not clarify if the entry wound was a circumferential wound or on separate pieces of bone. Humes testified to the Warren Commission that "this wound in the right posterior region was in a portion of scalp which had remained intact. . . . When one reflected the scalp away from the skull in this region, there was a corresponding defect through both tables of the skull in this area . . . there was a through-and-through defect corresponding with the wound in the scalp."[336]

Dr. Finck wrote (1965) that he "examined the wounds. The scalp of the back of the head showed a small laceration, 15 × 6 mm. Corresponding to this lesion, I found a through-and-through wound of the occipital bone, with a crater visible from the inside of the cranial cavity. This bone wound showed no crater when viewed from outside the skull. On the basis of this pattern of the occipital bone perforation, I stated that the wound in the back of the head was an entrance."[337] Finck presents a conflicting description in his report to his commanding general, when he wrote in the same report, ". . . the skull shows a *portion* [author's emphasis] of a crater . . . this occipital wound is a wound of ENTRANCE."[338]

Nobody got this clarified with Finck. Just think of all the great questions the AMA could have asked Finck instead of using him for their own political purposes and throwing him away. Understandably the doctors are skittish, if the whole thing was fabricated and they were left holding the bag.

Boswell describes this the same way, saying that half of the entry was on intact skull and the rest on a broken-off piece of bone. On the other hand, it could represent one more serious conflict that has some other meaning we cannot easily fathom, except insofar as the doctors themselves may have deliberately muddied up each issue in order to leave a trail and point out serious problems with the photos and X-rays used to trick Earl Warren. As Humes responded to Boswell's description of the entry, he said: "I don't remember that in that detail. . . ."[339]

Was part of the skull wound of entry on a separate piece of bone? This is another way of asking the previous question. All three doctors commented on this. Finck was asked, "Did you see the wound of entry in a separate piece of bone that was handed to you or was that still hooked on the body?"

"It was definitely attached to the body, the wound of entry."[340]

This still doesn't answer the question: Was half the entry hole on the body (skull) itself, and the other half on a separated piece of bone, either on a hinged flap of scalp or on one of the "midnight fragments" that came in late.

Dr. Boswell stated to me that part of the small entry wound was on a separate piece of bone. "I vaguely remembered that. The small piece, three or four centimeters across, and when we reconstructed that, that was part of the wound of entry. There was one circular area on one side that we determined to be a wound of entry. Or a portion of the bone was a wound of entry. . . . It was a semicircular piece of bone, and on one side of that piece of bone there was another hole right in the edge, and there was beveling on one side which showed us which was on the inner surface. So the wound of entry was on the outside, with fragments of bone on the inside."[341] Was he speaking of the exit?

What was the trajectory of the bullet through the skull? Francis X. O'Neill said that the autopsy doctors felt that the bullet that entered the head struck the center, low portion of the head and exited from the top, right side, toward the front.[342] There is a consensus on this by most. It's an impossible trajectory, though, so all the fools who insist the bullet came from the sixth-floor window will say it isn't so.

Was there a large fragment on the outer table of the skull at the time of the autopsy? The existence of a large fragment on the back of the head on the X-rays is used to claim that there is an entry hole through the cowlick a half inch away. No large fragment was either noted in the autopsy report, on the X-rays, or in testimony of any of the participants. The only evidence for any other fragment, later seen on the X-rays that turned up years later, was in the FBI report of the autopsy, which stated: "The next largest fragment appeared to be at the rear of the skull at the juncture of the skull bone."[343] Neither FBI man was asked by the Committee if they saw this large fragment or where the "juncture of the skull bone" was.

The main point of the autopsy was to search for such fragments for police examination. The hair of a victim is supposed to be combed, looking for such fragments and penetrations in the skull.

One must question the competence of the FBI agents at the autopsy, considering that they misspelled nearly every name and wrote other statements that seemed wild or unsubstantiated. But the answer may lie in the fact that when James W. Sibert was interviewed by the House investigators, he said that he took possession of the little bottle containing the metal fragments that had been removed from the body. He believed that there were "probably two fragments." Sibert believed that both fragments came from the head, possibly from the frontal sinus region.[344] Certainly, if there had been a large fragment on the back of the head, it would have been removed and put in the same bottle with the other fragments. It is not even mentioned here by Sibert.

The FBI report of the autopsy says that "the two metal fragments removed from the brain area were hand carried by special agents Sibert and O'Neill to the FBI Laboratory immediately following the autopsy and were turned over to special agent Kurt Frazier." If there had been more, they would have said so. The autopsy report speaks of the two fragments removed from the "disrupted right cerebral cortex [part of the brain directly behind the right eye]" and given to the FBI agents. Dr. Humes also described this in his Warren Commission testimony: "I will refer back to the X-rays which we had previously prepared. These had disclosed to us multiple minute fragments of radiopaque material traversing a line from the wound in the occiput to just above the right eye, with a rather sizable fragment visible by X-ray just above the right eye."[345] That fragment was seven-by-two and the other was three-by-one. Certainly the large 6.5mm fragment at the rear of the present skull X-ray would have been spotted and commented upon by now. Unless it had been removed and found to be of a different composition than the Mannlicher bullets. But Dr. Mantik thinks that whatever 6.5mm fragment is on the X-rays, what is on the AP view is inconsistent with what is on the lateral view. "They are spatially consistent," David Mantik told me.[346] "It is consistent in *space,* but the *visible* size on the AP is totally opposite the size which is implied by the optical density measurements," Mantik wrote on this manuscript.

We still have not answered the conflict in the evidence. So far, the only way to respond is to see that the bullet portion has been added to the X-ray after the autopsy. Since J. Edgar Hoover, a probable party to the conspiracy, controlled the FBI, they slightly doctored their report on the autopsy proceedings and added a fragment in at the juncture of the skull bone. They could simply tell the men that there had been a later examination of the X-rays. Nobody dared make too many changes in the documents for fear their authors would become greatly suspicious and find a way to blow the whistle.

Roy Kellerman told House investigators that when they were examining the X-rays of the head at the autopsy, they showed a "whole mass of stars, the only large piece being behind the eye which was given to the FBI agents when it was removed."[347] This certainly indicates no such very large fragment existed on the back of the head.

Some feel that if such a piece of metal was there, it was shrapnel, or that it was a ricochet from a bullet that struck the street behind the car.

Dr. David Mantik proposed that it was originally not the same size that we see on the AP view, which he thinks was altered to make it look like a 6.5mm fragment, to link it with Oswald's alleged murder rifle.[348] Of course, the Clark Panel's examination of the X-rays in 1967 was the first news that such a large fragment was on the head. The fragment is one cm above the depressed fracture.

This large fragment was missed by three pathologists and one radiologist, as well as all the other personnel who were at the autopsy. The 6.5mm size was not mentioned in the FBI report.

HEAD EXIT

Did the autopsy doctors spot any part of the exit of the bullet on either the intact skull or on bone fragments in the autopsy photographs and X-rays? Finck could not answer this question: "The part of the skull that was still attached, you see any evidence in that of an exit wound at the margin of the large defect?"

"I don't recall."

"I give you no. 44 [photo] and ask if this in any way refreshes your memory?"

"No."

"Do you see anything on that photograph which would represent the exit hole of a bullet?"

"I don't know what this is."

"His answer is no," Andrew Purdy states. "I will point out at this time at the margin of the skull there is not a straight edge, there is a variation there. Could that audible [sic] semicircle be an exit wound?"

"No. Hazy, blurred."[349]

Finck could not even identify the bones in the X-rays as those he handled the night of the autopsy.[350] There does appear to be an exit half circle made by a bullet in the photo (no. 44) showing the large defect. This is what the HSCA pathology panel called the exit. But the autopsy pathologists disagreed.

An *exit* wound of a bullet had half of its semicircle on the edge of a fracture of the intact skull, with external beveling, and the other half of the circle was on one of the three midnight bone fragments, which they assembled when it came in, completing a circular hole through the skull—according to the autopsy doctors speaking to the HSCA forensic panel.[351] We see external beveling in the photograph showing a large hole in a skull, but it would seem that the hole is in the back of the head and shows an exiting shot from in front. Orienting the picture is unsolved.

The partial exit hole on a late-arriving piece of bone is mentioned in the autopsy report: "At one angle of the largest of these fragments is a portion of the perimeter of a roughly circular wound presumably of exit which exhibits beveling of the outer aspect of the bone and is estimated to measure approximately 2.5 to 3.0 cm in diameter," meaning the diameter of the circle. They mention minute particles of metal on the perimeter of this bone in X-rays. Dr. Finck also mentioned it in his letter to General Blumberg, after saying that they had no exit wound identifiable when he came into the autopsy a half an hour after it started. "But close to midnight, portions of cranial vault are received from Dallas, Texas. X-ray films of these bone specimens reveal numerous metallic fragments. Two of the bone specimens are 50mm in diameter, reveal beveling when viewed from the external aspect, thus indicating a wound of exit. Most probably, these bone specimens are part of the very large right skull wound, 130mm in diameter . . ."[352] He does not describe part of the exit wound as being on the intact skull as does the autopsy report which he signed.

Yet, Dr. Humes told the Warren Commission that there was no point of impact by the *exiting* fragment: "A careful examination of the margins of the large bone defect at that point, however, failed to disclose a portion of the skull bearing again a wound of—a point of impact on the skull of this fragment of the missile, remembering, of course, that this area was devoid of any scalp or skull at this present time. We did not have the bone."[353]

At the time of the autopsy, Boswell drew on the face sheet the skull with some of the fractures and missing area. To one side of the drawing he has a crescent-shaped piece of bone which has a small semicircle along one edge as though from a bullet passing through. The large piece of bone seems to correspond to a 10 cm crescent or fracture line on the left side of the head in his drawing, causing some confusion (as per the drawing by Fred Newcomb and Perry Adams in Dr. Charles Wilber's book on page 210§ and after

§Wilber, Charles, *Medicolegal Investigation of the President John F. Kennedy Murder,* (Springfield, Ill.: Charles C Thomas). Out of print.

page 24 of my first book, *High Treason*) as to whether they are the same or separate pieces. But Boswell told us that the crescent-shaped piece of bone he had drawn to the side of his depiction of the head was one of the pieces of bone brought into the room later.[354]

Finck describes two of the three pieces of bone fragments as showing beveling "on the external aspect, thus indicating a wound of EXIT. Most probably, these bone specimens are part of the very large right skull wound, 130mm in diameter and mentioned above."[355]

Did Finck help take photographs of the occipital entry wound? He is very strong that he did this, supervising photos of the entry from both the inside and the outside.[356] We have no such photos today, and Finck told *JAMA* the same thing.

THE LARGE HEAD DEFECT

One of the tragedies of this case was that the witnesses were not asked if their perception of the large defect was with or without the remains of scalp reflected (rolled back.) There are *four* conflicting locations and descriptions of the large defect.

What was the size and location of the large defect in the head? This is where the problems get even stickier, and the location of the large head wound represents one more vast conflict in the evidence. The autopsy report states that it was 13 cm in largest diameter. Boswell's drawing made at the autopsy indicates that it was seventeen centimeters, and he notes this without comment while looking at his drawing with the House forensic panel.[357] But this may be a matter of semantics, as he says, "this was an attempt to illustrate the magnitude of the *wound* [author's emphasis]. . . ." By wound he means the total area that was entirely missing bone and which had flaps of tissue with bone attached but which was broken off from the skull. Boswell told Dr. Gary Aguilar that the large defect was 13 cm across (as Humes and Boswell have stated) after the bone fragment completing the entry hole was inserted at the EOP, along with two other fragments. It was 17 cm without it, and two (small triangular-shaped pieces) of the three that came in from Parkland at midnight added up to 4 cm in size.[358] These two small pieces, plus the Harper fragment (which they did not see that

night), may account for the fist-sized hole in the back of the head
seen in Dallas. At the autopsy, they said it was the size of an orange.
The large 10 cm piece of parietal bone made up the rest (this also
came in that night). But this area of missing bone was covered with
scalp or hair and not seen.

There were three major flaps on the skull and bone was attached
to each.[359] Boswell said, "Some of the bone fragments, though, are
partially extruded, as we see in X-ray no. 1." Humes then says:
"Some of them were adhered to partially torn scalp." Boswell:
"Which accounts for some of the missing bone."[360] The point of
this is the word "missing" in what we just heard did not mean that
all of that bone was *literally* missing. Some of it was on flaps and
some were the pieces that came in to the autopsy after it was almost over.

Boswell tells us in the same exchange with the doctors that a
second ten centimeter piece was fractured off.[361] Nobody saw much
bone missing at all anywhere but the back of the head. "With Boswell's statements—the wound extended to the EOP—the confusion
is *over*. This part of the case is closed!" Mantik says. Where Boswell's
drawing says "missing," it wasn't all gone.

There seemed to be different positions for the large head wound.
The fact that no one could agree shows how well the muddying of
the evidence succeeded.

Dr. John Ebersole, the radiologist present at the autopsy, simply
said that "the back of the head was missing."[362] This is identical to
testimony of *all* of the Dallas witnesses, including Clint Hill and Roy
Kellerman, who saw the body at Bethesda as well. Not the side of
the head. Not the top of the head. Not the front of the head. Those
are the other positions for the large wound. The visible large wound
in the back of the head was ten centimeters maybe, but not thirteen
or seventeen centimeters.

A number of drawings made by some of those present at the
autopsy, reproduced in this book, surfaced in 1994 and indicate
that the large hole in the back of the head was precisely there,
either limited to the back of the head only, or coming around to
the right side only a little. There is no drawing that shows the hole
coming either over the top, into the frontal bone area, or running
along the side of the head to the ear and possibly forward of the
ear. The other drawings are impressions made before the scalp was
reflected showing no other bone missing on the top of the head.
Boswell's drawing may be perfectly accurate after all, once it is
understood.

It would seem clear that *when the hole was first seen at Bethesda, it had not enlarged from the time it left Dallas.* The one sure thing is that the Dallas doctors were entirely correct in their description of the size and placement of the wound. Until we get to the later autopsy description and that of the doctors. Clearly, either the hole greatly enlarges magically, or it is a semantic problem: large pieces of bone are on flaps on top of the head and to the right side. Or they made it up and are lying.

The wound seemed to grow. The autopsy report, written after the body was gone, indicates that it was centered more on the right side and extended as far as the temporal bone, with nothing about the frontal bone. When the X-rays were seen again years later, obviously not entirely the same X-rays that were seen the night of the autopsy, the wound had moved into the frontal area and was not in the back of the head at all.

Dr. Boswell's drawing made at the autopsy seems to show the top of the head "missing," and as just explained, this has caused a great deal of confusion. Only part was actually missing. The rest was on flaps still attached to the head.

James Curtis Jenkins, an enlisted man assisting at the autopsy, may have actually written in the figures on Boswell's drawing representing the size of the wound, and probably drew in the arrows, as he wrote in the organ weights. (There is certainly a question about those figures!) Boswell said that "everything else on here is mine. All of the notes on the diagrams are mine, and this diagram on the back is mine, this and this."[363]

Dr. Boswell explained: "This was an attempt to illustrate the magnitude of the wound again. And as you can see it's ten centimeters from right to left, seventeen centimeters from posterior to anterior. This was a piece of ten-centimeter bone that was fractured off of the skull *and was attached to the under surface of the skull* [I think he meant *scalp* here, or this was a typo]. There were *fragments attached to the skull* or to the scalp and *all the three major flaps.* I guess the— I'm not sure in retrospect what I meant by that [author's emphasis]."[364] It sounds like Boswell just noticed the word "missing" written there and its implications, because he just described bone that was there, hinged on flaps of scalp that could be pulled back to expose the interior of the skull. The bone was not actually "missing." With reference to the scalp on the back of the head, or lack of it, we've heard a lot about "flaps" before!

Another possibility is that pieces of bone fell in as the evening progressed, or were removed to take the brain out, and the drawing depicts that and not how the head looked when the body first arrived. Even though it might have been possible to squeeze what

remained of the brain through the existing hole, this would not
have allowed an examination of the interior of the skull to look for
entry and exit missile holes. Bone had to be removed, but the existing fractures and flaps provided sufficient egress with very little
sawing, one would imagine, since they sawed very little (if at all) to
remove the brain.

There is no photo that shows for sure where the large hole is. There is a
photograph that shows a large hole in somebody's head but *the adjoin-
ing flaps of scalp and bone are nowhere visible.* On the edge of the bone
in this picture is a semicircle with the beveling on the outside of the
bone, which indicates an exiting bullet or fragment. The HSCA forensic panel of physicians attempted to orient this large hole in the front
of the head with the scalp pulled down over the face. It is far more
likely that the large hole is in the back of the head, just where all the
testimony placed it. The following exchange took place at the above
meeting of doctors: Dr. Angel: "Well, this must be well forward then
on the frontal bone, I was interpreting it as being—this itself as being
near the pterion." (Finck told *JAMA* that he helped direct the photographing of the President's wounds.[365])

Dr. Baden: "Yet here is the gap." (Photos nos. 8, 13, and 44,
and X-rays 1, 3, and 6 were being studied.)

Dr. Humes: "That is not frontal bone where that semicircle is—
it's either temporal or parietal bone, Dr. Angel."

Dr. Angel: "I don't see how it can be. That's what it looks like
to me."

Dr. Humes: That's exactly what it is."[366]

Could so many people who drew the same wound (with the possible exception of Boswell) at Bethesda be mistaken? It would seem
impossible, since they independently drew the same wound seen in
Dallas, corroborating them.

GENERAL PHILIP WEHLE, commander of the Military District of Washington, "did not see any significant damage to any other part of the
head. He noted that the wound was in the back of the head so he
would not see it because the President was lying face up; he also said
he did not see any damage to the top of the head."[367] Wehle said he
noticed a slight bruise over the President's right temple.[368] Wehle was
only present during the later stages of the autopsy. This and what follows repeats the exact experience Dr. Jackie Hunt and others had in
Dallas—they could not see the wound until the head was lifted up.

Tom Robinson, the mortician, received the body after everyone
else was done with it. This is what he saw. Asked by House investiga-

tor Andy Purdy with regard to the large hole in the head, "Could you tell how large the opening had been caused by the bullets?", Robinson answered, "A good bit of the bone had been blown away. There was nothing there to piece together, so I would say probably about [the size of] a small orange." "Could you give us an estimate of inches and the nature of the shape?" "Three." "And the shape?" "Circular." "Was it fairly smooth or fairly ragged?" "Ragged." "Approximately where was this wound located?" "Directly behind the back of his head." "Approximately between the ears or higher up?" "No, I would say pretty much between them."[369] His drawing, made for the House, is startling in its similarity to what was seen in Dallas, and in how low he has the wound. Robinson told them what he told me in 1991: "Putting the head into the pillow of the casket would have hidden everything."[370] Robinson described precisely the same position for me when I interviewed him years later, in 1991,[371] not knowing about the above interview in 1977.

A basically unanimous placement of the large defect in the back of the head on the right is detailed in my first book, *High Treason,* in the head wounds chapter, and in the Medical Encyclopedia in my last book, *Killing the Truth.* Additional corroboration as detailed above has come from those interviewed by the House Committee but was suppressed all of these years. FBI agent James W. Sibert told the Committee investigators that the wound was in the "upper back of the head." He drew this for the investigators, in addition.[372] So did his partner at the autopsy, Francis X. O'Neill, who drew the wound in the right rear portion of the head.[373] Sibert wrote that there was a "large head wound in the upper back of the head with a section of the skull bone missing . . ."[374]

Dr. Finck refers several times in the report to General Blumberg that the large defect in the "right *fronto*-parietal-occipital region, is 130 millimeters in diameter" thus including part of the right frontal bone, which is not stated in the autopsy report or anywhere else. The autopsy report places the wound in the *temporal* [emphasis author's], parietal, occipital region.[375] Finck told the generals what they wanted to hear and then seriously contradicts this when he *published* his own version of what happened: "The bullet, striking the back of the head at a range of approximately 265 feet (81 m), perforated the occipital bone, disintegrated into numerous small fragments, and produced a very large and irregular right *temporal-*parietal-occipital [emphasis author's] wound of exit, approximately 130 mm in diameter."[376]

He told one thing to Blumberg in 1965, and another a few

months later to the military's medical community. Is this just one
more innocent mistake that has little meaning or impact on the
case, or is it part of a pattern?

Jan Gail Rudnicki, a third-class petty officer and lab technologist
present in the autopsy room when the body arrived and who helped
do the work all night, told House investigators that "the back-right
quadrant of the head was missing."[377] He stood at the autopsy table
and ensured that containers in which to place specimens were
ready. See the chapter on Mr. Rudnicki in *High Treason 2*.

James Curtis Jenkins, who assisted at the autopsy, stated that when
the body was unwrapped he saw a head wound in the "middle
temporal region back to the occipital."[378]

**How can the different appearance and location of the missing
skull and missing scalp be reconciled?** This question has caused all
of us a considerable amount of grief. Dr. Boswell clarified the matter in one of my talks with him. Think of the scalp as a sack holding
a broken globe or head, with a small hole roughly the size of an
orange through the scalp. That much of the scalp is missing in the
very back of the head where it would be obscured if the head was
lying on a pillow or a stretcher, as Dr. Jackie Hunt described to me
in Dallas.

First there was a shot from the rear that severely fractured the
skull in the back and made an exit on the right side of the head.
A second shot struck in front. Large parts of the skull in four separate pieces covering about 13 centimeters, were blasted out of the
torn scalp. Still more of the remaining bone was broken off from
the intact skull, but that bone was hinged on flaps of dura or scalp
and fell in or fell to the table at various stages of the autopsy.[379]
The scalp was lacerated from the margins of the missing portion.[380]

Boswell describes a badly lacerated (torn or mangled) scalp. Then
he told me, "A pretty good-size piece of the frontal and right occipital portion of the skull had separated and was stuck to the undersur-
face of the scalp [author's note: what he describes are *flaps*, two of
three on the head that, with the exception of the area where at
least four pieces of bone were blown out, pretty much closed the
head up. This flap is not a large flap of scalp that some say existed
on the *back* of the head which could cover up the area of missing
bone]. So when that (the flap) was reflected, then it was true, there
was a big bony defect in the *right side* of the skull. The brain was
removed through that defect. But the scalp was somewhat intact
overlying that, so that superficially, externally, you couldn't tell that
there was a big hole in the skull [he means in the area of the flap

when it was in its natural position, and he means that no hole could be seen on the right side when the flap was closed].''[381] Several bones were missing from the back of the head, and only shredded, macerated, and incomplete scalp was left there, with some missing about the size of a small orange, as Robinson, McClelland, and others described it. The larger 9.5 cm piece of bone came from the top of the head.

Boswell's use of the term "big hole in the skull" is how we get confused. Most of the hole was only there if the flaps were open ("reflected"). This is not the same hole that was seen by everyone in Dallas, but was quite a bit larger with the flaps open, and which is otherwise described identically at the autopsy as being in the right rear of the head. I explained it more or less in these terms in my last two books, with the second hole above the ear that Dr. Grossman described and which I believe Jackie closed, and a piece in between on the right near the ear (it's still there on the X-ray. It might have fallen in after the X-ray, Mantik says), and the missing bone in the back. I described to Boswell the fact that the men from the funeral home told me that they did not have to fix up the scalp or use patches. With the head on the pillow, the area of missing scalp could not be seen. "Right," Boswell told me.[382] Did the laceration from the hairline above the right eye extending to the rear of the head constitute a flap? Yes, Mantik says.

It became clear in my talk with Boswell that there was a semantic problem with the manner in which we all used the term "defect." To him, a defect meant the area defined by the fractures, which then could become "missing" in his mind, but did not mean that the bone was actually blown out, which was there in the form of flaps.

"And that was basically the area where the large defect was?" I asked him.

"Well that defect was a lot larger—do you mean in the skull?"

"Yes. That area of missing scalp was in the center of a larger defect?"

Boswell responded: "Well, no, it was more posterior than the defect in the scalp. Most of the scalp could be reattached. It was a laceration. It wasn't an avulsion of scalp, really. I don't even remember a defect once the morticians repaired the skull and everything."[383]

Humes corroborated the fact that there was much more bone missing or fallen in than scalp was missing with his Warren Commission testimony: "There was a defect in the scalp and some scalp tissue was not available. However, the scalp was intact completely past this defect."[384] There was a lot more bone missing or fallen in than missing scalp.

Are the three late-arriving skull fragments the ones that were lost from the head? Ebersole recognized them from the X-rays he was shown by the House panel: 'Do you recall seeing those three fragments and X-raying the bones?" "Yes. This was maybe midnight to one o'clock when these fragments arrived from Dallas."[385] Ebersole said that he X-rayed the fragments himself.

A fourth fragment, the "Harper fragment," did not show up until the following week.

One of these was the large (10 × 6.5 cm) crescent-shaped skull fragment which, according to Gerald A. Behn, SAC of the White House Secret Service detail, was found on the floor of the car between the front and rear seats, after the wounded had been removed.[386] (It is also described as 9.5 cm long.) This has to be the back of the President's head which Clint Hill said had been lying on the backseat on the trip to the hospital. I think this is the skullcap, and Mantik agrees. It would be easy to confuse this late-arriving piece with the 10 cm flap of scalp and bone still attached to the head at the autopsy.

The autopsy report states that "At one angle of the largest of these fragments is a portion of the perimeter of a roughly circular wound presumably of exit which exhibits beveling of the outer aspect." The FBI report said the piece "was brought to Dr. Humes who was instructed that this had been removed from the President's skull. Immediately this section of skull was X-rayed, at which time it was determined by Dr. Humes that one corner of this section revealed minute metal particles, and inspection of this same area disclosed a chipping of the top portion of this piece, both of which indicated that this had been the point of exit of the bullet entering the skull region."[387]

THERE IS A PROBLEM WITH THE CHAIN OF EVIDENCE. We are told these bone pieces filled most or three-quarters of the area of missing bone on the head (the autopsy report says, "Received as separate specimens from Dallas, Texas, are three fragments of skull bone which in aggregate roughly approximate the dimensions of the large defect described above."[388] The Harper fragment never got there that night, but there does not appear to be enough room for both it and the 10 cm fragment at the top of the skull. Ebersole recalled a large occipital defect that he thought would fit it.

*   *   *

What part of the head were the late-arriving skull fragments from?
Dr. Ebersole stated: "Perhaps about twelve-thirty a large fragment
of the occipital bone was received from Dallas and at Dr. Finck's
request I X-rayed these."[389] This had to be the skullcap, which Clint
Hill described as lying in the backseat, which he could see as he
lay on the trunk of the speeding limousine. "The back of his head
was lying on the back seat."[390] Mantik noted here that, "even if
Ebersole misidentified this bone as occipital, he is clearly implying
that there was a large occipital defect where this bone might fit!"

Ebersole further described the large bone fragment. "Later on
in the evening, between midnight and one A.M., a large portion of
the skull was sent up from Dallas . . . that represented the back
portion of the skull."[391] This must be the 10×6.5 centimeter piece
which Boswell described as largely filling the area of "missing
bone." They testified that the three pieces filled three-quarters of
the actual missing area. There is a massive conflict in the evidence
raised by this, unless we accept that there was a similar piece of the
same length already on the head on a flap of scalp as already explained. The HSCA made an effort to add all these pieces up with
paper cutouts to see how they fit together.[392]

Dr. Humes told the Warren Commission: "Some time later on
that evening or very early the next morning while we were all still
engaged in continuing our examination, I was presented with three
portions of bone which had been brought to Washington from Dallas by the agents of the Federal Bureau of Investigation. . . . We
were most interested in these fragments of bone, and found that
the three pieces could be roughly put together to account for a
portion of this defect."

"How much remained unaccounted for, Dr. Humes?"

"I would estimate that approximately one-quarter of that defect
was unaccounted for by adding these three fragments together and
seeing what was left."[393]

The dimension of the large defect was 13 cms in its largest diameter, according to the autopsy report. One can see that if one of the
pieces was 10 cm long, that takes up most of the "missing area."
The remaining one-quarter would probably take up the size of the
Harper fragment, which was from the occipital bone, and which
did not get to the autopsy.

Some think the head was reconstructed for the X-ray as we now
see it: the skullcap may have been placed back on the rear of the
head and a new X-ray taken, in my amateur interpretation of the
existing lateral X-rays. But Ebersole denies this: "The skull films
were definitely taken before the autopsy."

"Did you repeat the skull films?"

"To my knowledge."[394] Whatever that is supposed to mean. If Ebersole faked some other aspects of the evidence, then it seems possible that he might not have this correct, and/or was lying. The head may have been reconstructed by placing on top of it the missing 10 cm × 6.5 cm piece of bone and the three flaps closed around that and perhaps the two other pieces of bone which had come back after midnight. My theory may be faulty if we accept (another conflict!) that the 10 cm piece was occipital bone, as Ebersole[395] said, which is lower than the place where the skullcap—the large piece of bone—is displaced posteriorly as seen on the X-ray.

Dr. David Mantik feels that visual inspection of the X-rays is inadequate to determine if there is significant bone missing anywhere in the back of the head. He also thinks it was hardly possible to reconstruct the head as in the above comment, "unless it was precisely positioned *and the correct piece*. If not, it would stick out like a sore thumb."[396]

As to whether one could see that bone was missing from the X-rays in the back of the head, Mantik wrote me: "On the left lateral X-ray, looking tangentially at the back of the skull, it would be hard to see this. The bones at the left and right rear *overlap*. On the AP X-ray, there *is* missing bone on the posterior skull, both visibly and by optical density measurements—but the HSCA refused to face these issues." As for Mantik's "great white patch" (see X-ray chapter) covering the right rear skull, clearly, if a bullet entry showed there, it had to be covered up. If the X-ray showed the large defect primarily in that position (indicating a frontal shot) it had to be covered over, as well.

Ebersole was asked, "Was any attempt made that you recall to reconstruct the defect in the skull utilizing these three bones?" "Not to my knowledge."[397] Ebersole seems not to have been present too often. He said that he accompanied or himself carried the X-ray films to be developed upstairs, so was out of the room during those periods, and the midnight reconstruction when three of the missing bones arrived.

Ebersole felt there were metallic fragments from the bullet on one of the pieces of bone, but he could not recall discussing this with any of the other doctors in the room.[398] Ebersole is asked about "that serrated margin on that fragment," but he has nothing to say.[399] He also did not see beveling on the margin of the largest fragment.[400]

Yet, Finck did not seem to recognize the photos and X-rays we have of the late-arriving fragments.

Dr. Finck said that the three late-arriving bone fragments when assembled "corresponding to the large head wound" accounted for 130mm (13 centimeters) in diameter of missing bone "in the right side of the cranial vault. After identifying their anatomic external and internal surfaces, I noticed that the beveling of the fragments was apparent when viewed from outside. I stated then that these portions of bone were part of a wound of exit. Therefore, the large irregular wound in the right side of the cranial vault was a wound of exit."[401] The autopsy report also says that the three fragments of skull bone in aggregate "roughly approximate the dimensions of the large defect described above."[402] Or 13 cm "in greatest diameter."

What happened to these skull fragments? "Both Dr. Humes and Dr. Burkley informed the Committee that these fragments were placed back in the skull of the President."[403] Dr. George C. Burkley said the one that was found in the street (the Harper fragment) had been given to the FBI. He said he'd received a letter from the uncle (presumably Dr. Harper) and that the fragment came to him at the White House and he then gave it to the FBI. Regarding the three skull fragments that were used to reconstruct the defect in the skull at the autopsy, they were not saved. He believes they were put back in with the body.[404]

Where did the "Harper fragment" come from? Harper, a pre-medical student, found a piece of bone on the grass after the assassination, and two days later showed it to his uncle, Dr. Jack C. Harper, who took it to Methodist Hospital in Dallas and showed it to other doctors. "Dr. Harper said the consensus of the doctors who viewed the skull fragment was that it was part of the occipital region.... the skull fragment had relatively fresh blood on it. Dr. A. B. Cairns (Chief of Pathology at Methodist Hospital examined the skull fragment) ... said the piece of skull fragment came from an area approximately two and a half to three inches above the spine area. He said it had the markings of a piece of skull fragment from the lower occipital area, specifically: suture and inner markings where blood vessels run around the base of the skull.

"Dr. Cairns remembered a small area of the skull fragment showing grayish discoloration suggesting metal had stained the bone. He said he had experience with lead-caused damage in the past which looked similar to this discoloration. [Author's note: If true, we have evidence of a bullet passing out of the back of the head.]

"Dr. Cairns said he could see blood markings which indicated the skull fragment had been dislodged recently . . . he did believe it was part of the assassination . . . said the skull fragment had no indication of being an entry or an exit wound. He said (in other words) the edges of a wound did not show. However, he said he believed the skull fragment came from an area close to the entry wound by virtue of the way the 'tables' were broken."[405]

Occipital bone may be distinguished from the other bones of the head by its thickness, perhaps the suture line, and the meningeal grooves (blood vessels).

The Harper fragment was roughly two and a half inches on a side and more or less triangular, with two of the corners broken off. It is also called trapezoidal and measured 7 cm by 5.5 cm.[406] The House claimed it came from the upper middle third of the parietal area.[407] We can take that with the same grain of salt with which their cover-up artists made the following comment: "The defect in the skull and the inward beveling thereof provide definitive evidence of an entrance wound of the head at a point corresponding to that noted by the panel in the upper back of the scalp, rather than 'slightly above' the external occipital protuberance as indicated in the autopsy report, or in the lower part of the head near the hairline, as stated by the autopsy pathologists in their interview with the panel."[408] Or: "All members of the panel except Dr. Wecht concur that there is one and only one wound of entrance in the head and that it is located in the 'cowlick' area of the back of the head, and that the white substance referred to by the original prosectors is a fragment of brain tissue. Dr. Wecht agrees that there is an entrance wound in the 'cowlick' area and that the white substance is brain issue, but he cannot exclude the possibility that it might overlie a very small skin and bone performation [sic?] of either entrance or exit."[409]

Was there surgery to the head area? Dr. Boswell told me that the FBI men made a mistake when they reported this in their report of the autopsy. "That whole question is related to: (1) had he had a tracheostomy, and (2) they had started to put tubes in his chest to evacuate blood from his chest. The only thing that we, the autopsy surgeons, were talking about was the tracheostomy. That was related to the wound in the body. He hadn't had any surgery to his head. He hadn't had the wound on his neck which was the wound of exit from the back wound that came out through his larynx and that had been extended in efforts to do a tracheostomy, which they never did." (Author's note: Does he mean that there had been no tracheostomy performed, or does he mean that they never performed surgery to the head area, which we are quite certain was not done in Dallas by any of those involved in trying to resuscitate him.)

"I know that those FBI men misspelled some names and—" I said.

"Well, they also misinterpreted a lot of things that they heard. They didn't know what they were listening to or talking about."

"They wrote that there was 'surgery to the head area, namely to the top of the head.' That is the quote from their report."

"That was never discussed. There was never any question about that."[410]

James W. Sibert, one of the two FBI men present at the autopsy, was asked about this. He wrote the following answer in his affidavit: "When the body was first observed on the autopsy table, it was thought by the doctors that surgery had possibly been performed in the head area and such was reflected in my notes made at the time. However, this was determined not to be correct following detailed inspection and when the piece of bone found in the limousine was brought to the autopsy room during the latter stages of the autopsy."[411] Why did the idea of surgery to the head area survive in his official report, then, or is that what he calls his "notes"?

Was any or much of the frontal bone missing? Contrary to the weight of the evidence, there is massive documentation in the work of the House that a major amount of frontal bone is missing in the X-rays. I give a compendium of this in the Medical Encyclopedia at the end of *Killing the Truth* (p. 697), and a discussion and references in the X-ray chapter,[412] and in a Summary of the Evidence in that same book. But the first outside radiologists who have seen the actual films are inclined to think that most of it is there. Some people, such as Linda Newman, suggest that perhaps osteoporosis induced by the steroids Kennedy was taking thinned out the bone, but the problem with that is that it is only on the right side and to the front of the head, behind the forehead.

"The frontal bone is gone above the hairline," Mantik wrote me. Over the lateral portion of the orbit there is a notch where even more bone is missing—just below the hairline. Lattimer's drawings of the X-rays clearly show the frontal bone to be missing and none in back missing.§ Interestingly, Boswell described one of the three flaps of bone and scalp as being in this same frontal bone area.

Showmen for the fake Zapruder film could talk until they were blue in the face about a shot from in front, but that really isn't the

§After page 384 of *Killing the Truth,* by the author.

main message of the film, which is a shot from behind blowing off the face. This backs up the phony X-rays.

But David Mantik, a radiologist (which I'm not), disagrees, and told me that it is not a necessary hypothesis to assume that the X-rays are composites. The white patch that he discovered with his tests in the National Archives was all that was needed to cover up the missing bone and make it appear present. This still doesn't account for the apparently missing frontal bone in the X-rays.

Was there another entry into the head? The bullet fragment trail tells us a lot about that. There are plenty of indications of another entry, and if the radiological research of Randy Robertson is correct, another shot hit the head from in front. James Jenkins described metal smears at the autopsy that indicated a bullet had struck the head in the right temple, and there was eyewitness testimony to the same thing. There are other reports of perforations of the skull on either the right or left front. Joseph Riley, a brain anatomist, proposes a shot from in front by analysis of the brain evidence.§

Thomas Robinson, one of the morticians from Gawlers in Washington, described a perforation of the right temple either going in or going out. He said it could have been filled with wax and no one would have noticed it in an open coffin. I first revealed this in my interview with Robinson in *High Treason 2*,[413] but he had already told this to the House Committee[414] though no one outside the Committee was aware of the interview. Mantik told me that "it is striking that there is a notch in the right frontal bone (over the lateral orbit). Such missing bone fits very well with a frontal entry at exactly this site."

I strongly feel that there could not have been any fragment or entry on the head in the cowlick area where it is now claimed, simply because there was no bone there.

Is there a conflict between the X-rays and the autopsy report? There are several conflicts, all of them major, which indicate that the images we see on the X-rays are partially altered. A major conflict regards the line of metal fragments seen across the very top of the head in the X-rays. The autopsy report says this: "Roentgenograms of the skull reveal multiple minute metallic fragments along a line corresponding with a line joining the above described small occipital wound and the right supra-orbital ridge."[415] The small occipital wound is the entry, and it is certainly more than four inches

§See pp. 308–9 of *Killing the Truth* by the author; *Third Decade,* March 1993.

below the place where the line of fragments meets the skull in the back of the head, well above the place where a large fragment is stuck onto the back of the head near the cowlick, where they say the entry was in the X-rays. Some say the high trail of fragments is evidence of a second head shot.

If Ebersole took the X-rays, why did he not say that the ones now in evidence could not be the ones he took?

Other conflicts: the X-rays don't show all of the large rear head wound described in the autopsy report, and the X-rays appear to show much bone missing where it could not have been.

THE BRAIN

Was the cerebellum "on the table" or on the cart as it was claimed in Dallas? It had to be *on the cart*, if the part of the head in the back was blown out from a frontal shot, as all described that part of the head missing in Dallas and as we now know from the drawings made by some of those at Bethesda for House investigators. The government's official story is that the brain is not damaged in the area of the cerebellum, and that the only damage to the skull in the back is that claimed on photographs and X-rays now known to be fake, which show only a small entry in the cowlick area of the head, five inches above where the cerebellum would be.

The forensic panel of doctors noted that the cerebellum was intact.[416] But this was the brain that they had at the supplemental examination later, evidently not Kennedy's.

A proof that the case was faked is the gross conflict between the cerebellum everyone in Dallas saw "on the cart," and the government's denial it ever happened. This helped cover up a shot from in front, and in fact helps prove it happened.

When Dr. Finck was asked, "Was there any injury to the cerebellar hemisphere?", he couldn't remember.[417] I think that he could remember something like that very well, but it was easy to get caught between the official story and a hard place.

How was the brain removed? "How had the skullcap been taken off to remove the brain?" Andy Purdy asked Dr. Finck. Actually, we know that the skullcap had been lying in the backseat of the limousine, so it was already off. Dr. Finck did not see the removal of the brain because he had not arrived yet, but he said that "Dr. Humes told me that the fractures of the top and right side of the head were so extensive—that wound was about thirteen centimeters in diameter, it was a very large one. The fractures were so extensive, there was so much fragmentation of the skull that Dr. Humes did not have much sawing to do or he may not even have had any sawing to do."[418]

"You mean he did not have to extend around to the left side of the head to remove the brain intact?"

"He may have had a little sawing to do, but as compared to an intact skull where you have to do complete sawing to remove the calvaria, the skullcap. That was not the case because of the extent of the fractures and damage to the skull."[419]

Roy Kellerman does not recall the brain being removed, though he stood next to the table and the doctors.[420] Neither does Paul O'Connor, whose job it normally was to remove the brain.[421] James Curtis Jenkins, whose job it was to infuse the brain, said that he assisted with the removal of the brain, and that it was not necessary to cut the brain loose from the head, but it just slipped out.[422] Dr. Boswell strongly denied to me that the brain was either not in the head or loose when it arrived and slipped out, when I presented to him what Jenkins had told me.[423] I might speculate that if this in fact happened, the brain may have slipped out while O'Connor and even Kellerman were out of the room for a moment. The brain was then put into a bucket out of the way for the time being. But it is hard to get around Boswell's statement to me that the brain was not loose in the head.

It's recommended to the reader interested in pursuing this that the material in the chapters dealing with the above witnesses be studied carefully in *High Treason 2* by the author. The conflicts in what they all say is quite extensive. Maybe there is a sinister reason. Note what follows.

Jenkins, who normally removed brains, is supposed to have told the House investigators (Andy Purdy and Jim Kelly) that *he couldn't recall whether or not the brain was removed.*[424] I have a lot of trouble with that. Jenkins described in great detail to me seeing the brain come out of the head.[425] Yet, here Jenkins is saying he can't recall it. One might get the idea that this is a good way to discredit what he really had to say, since it conflicts with the official story. Or, Jenkins lied to me, but I don't think so.

How much did the brain weigh, and was it possible? The Supplemental Autopsy Report stated that the brain weighed 1,500 grams, much too heavy and more than an average adult male brain, let alone one that had lost much of its mass. The fixative formalin solution could not add any significant amount to the brain weight.[426] The trouble is, James Jenkins, who infused it, would know if the brain had been weighed, and he stated to me that it was not weighed at the autopsy.[427] Jenkins describes handling a small brain at the autopsy.

Was the brain switched? It would seem so. Switching is a more reasonable explanation than giving the brain a somewhat average weight minus a portion for that which was missing. It is more likely that it was switched, because here the doctors were leaving us a clue, and it seems deliberate.

The brain must have been substituted when it was kept unguarded in the closet of the commander of Bethesda Naval Hospital in order to permanently destroy evidence of other shots. The new brain had no damage to the cerebellum. Since there was no examination of the brain at the autopsy itself, the doctors said that the cerebellum was intact, since that is what they saw a few days later.

Other dead drops seemed to have been used in this case as well, such as the safe in Robert Bouck's Secret Service office, and the Dallas Post Office.

The brain examination. This was conducted on December 6, 1963, two weeks after the autopsy, although we have two other dates before that. Interestingly (I say this with tongue in cheek, since the following statement is astounding), Dr. Cyril Wecht, who evidently knows something we don't, asks Dr. Finck the following: "Pierre, you will recall that you along with Dr. Humes and Dr. Boswell conducted a supplemental examination of a normal and fixed brain, on December 6, 1963. . . ."[428] Is this just a slip of the tongue? Or did they just play a huge game on all of us, and sat there with somebody else's brain which weighed more than an average normal brain: 1,500 grams.

"Normal" might also be a transcriber's mistake, when the term "formalin" was used in the phrase "formalin fixed brain" instead of "normal and fixed brain," as Weatherly suggests.

As some told me that the autopsy doctors treated Kennedy's remains kindly, Stringer reported to the House that they did not section the brain serially, and he also said he believes the doctors "cut some pieces from the brain . . . while normally they would cut it right in half."[429] It sounds as though he was there during the examination, which then would have been a lot sooner than two weeks. Two or three days. It doesn't sound like the brain in evidence, some doctors comment.

Dr. Boswell told investigators that the brain was so torn up it would not have shown a bullet track.[430] The significance of this statement is that it indicates that the brain examination may have in fact been fabricated.* That is, they had so little viable brain to work with, they faked the exam either with another brain or no brain at all. The 1,500 gram weight is another example of this.

But in the same interview, Boswell said that the brain was "sufficiently exposed" so that the doctors didn't feel they had to cut into it. In other words, they thought that they could sufficiently see the injury without doing serial sections. He said he didn't remember whether or not they took serial sections or any other sections, saying "the records" should show if the doctors had cut into it. He indicated that Dr. Humes and he worked on this procedure with possibly two lab technicians, including Dr. Karnei (who served as chief assistant) and the chief hospital corpsman, who he believes was a man named Mason (status—HMC). Dr. Boswell said following the examination, the brain was taken by the doctors in a chrome bucket up to Captain Stover's office along with the slides, paraffin blocks (from which the slides, prepared by Chester Boyers,[431] were made), and tissue blocks from each organ in a mason jar.

He said these materials were later hand-carried to Admiral Burkley, presumably by a Secret Service man. During the chain of custody of this material, Dr. Boswell said he believed "Smokey" Stover undoubtedly had a receipt for "everything which transpired."[432] With this kind of inattention to the chain of custody, anybody could have taken that stuff and substituted materials.

Dr. Karnei, a resident who served as chief assistant during the autopsy, was also present during the brain examination, according to Boswell.[433] Dr. Karnei, interestingly, seems to deny this. He said he personally was not present for the sectioning of the brain, but said it normally occurs about two weeks after the autopsy. He added that he has no information regarding a subsequent brain examination. Dr. Karnei said that normally a neuropathologist is present for the examination of abnormal brains. He said this brain would be "considered such because of the extensive damage." He said the brain in such a case would "normally be taken over" to AFIP. He repeated that the disposition of such materials is governed by the tri-service agreement.[434]

Dr. Burkley, the President's physician, said the doctors didn't sec-

*Mantik comments: The 7 photos of the brain do not match this description at all. There is an obvious parasaggital laceration. Is Boswell describing different brains on these two occasions?

tion the brain, and that if it had been done, it might be possible to prove whether or not there were two bullets. Dr. Burkley thinks there was one bullet, but conceded the possibility of there having been two. He said he was responsible for saving the brain after it was fixed in formalin. Dr. Burkley said he thought they could do serial sections of the brain of both the damaged and undamaged portions. He was particularly interested in examining the normal portions because he thought the President was of exceptional intelligence and that this might be reflected in the extra development of the brain. Dr. Burkley then indicated that he had all of this material in the Executive Office Building.[435] Andy Purdy, who talked to Burkley, did not clarify here if he was inserting his own thoughts about two bullets—and Burkley merely conceded the possibility, or if Burkley was actually expressing doubts about one bullet.

When was the brain examined? I detect another conflict. Stringer repeats twice that he took his pictures two or three days after the autopsy.[436] They may have photographed the brain at that time, but did they also examine it then? The supplemental examination of the brain is dated the sixth of December, two weeks later, but reports were often written, signed, and dated after the fact.

On December 2, Chester Boyers prepared eight sections and six paraffin blocks of tissue from the brain. Boyers said that these sections showed the bullet path through the tissue of the brain. He described this as what you would expect from punching a pencil through a piece of paper. Boyers said all of these materials were filed under Bethesda Naval Hospital number A63-272. He speculated that they could still be there or are possibly at the AFIP.[437]

Dr. Finck wrote his commanding general that Humes called him on November 29, a few days after the autopsy, and told him that they would examine the brain. There is no indication that the brain was then examined on some other date. Finck also says that he asked if a representative of the Neuropathology Branch of the AFIP would be invited to the gross examination of the brain. "Humes told me that no additional persons would be admitted."[438] Finck's next statement in this report to Blumberg is that the "brain weighs 1,500 grams," undoubtedly alerting him in the official record that it wasn't JFK's brain.

Clearly, there is something drastically wrong with what we are seeing here. Humes has refused to allow a brain scientist to observe the proceedings and then they produce a brain that cannot possibly be Kennedy's! Is Finck trying to alert us to the truth by his juxtapositioning of the facts? Is this why we knew so little about Finck for thirty years, and he was basically inaccessible in Europe?

Were black-and-white photographs taken of the brain? Stringer was unsure.[439] The autopsy report says none were taken, and they are now on the inventory.

What happened to the brain? The brain was placed in a stainless-steel bucket, said to be seven-by-eight inches, which Captain Stover said was placed in the closet of Admiral Galloway.[440] It disappeared after the autopsy. Investigation at Arlington National Cemetery by the HSCA indicated that the brain *was not* reinterred with the body,[441] but the story that Robert Kennedy obtained the brain and interred it with the reburial of the body persists. At one point the brain was kept unguarded in the office of Captain Stover after the autopsy, and at that time it could have been substituted for the brain that later was examined.[442] The lack of security seems to be deliberate, as the brain then disappeared altogether in this shell game.

Dr. Humes wanted to put the brain back in the body, but Admiral George Burkley decided to keep it.[443] Had the brain been put back in the body, we could perform a DNA study today and determine if it was JFK's brain, unless the grave was robbed. Burkley took it to Robert Bouck of the Secret Service and it stayed in his office until it was taken to Evelyn Lincoln's office (Kennedy's secretary) where it resided in a locked trunk, and was found to be missing in 1965.[444]

Dr. Burkley indicated to Andy Purdy of the House that he had all of this material in the Executive Office Building. He said that he took the brain and tissue sections (presumably the paraffin blocks) to the National Archives and personally gave them to Evelyn Lincoln. She mentioned without explanation that Giordano, a door-keeper at the Capitol, was working under Mrs. Lincoln's direction at the Archives. When asked about this unsolicited comment, he said that he did *not* give the material to Giordano; rather he gave it personally to Mrs. Lincoln.[445]

Admiral Galloway could not remember what happened to the tissue specimens and the brain. He also did not know exactly where these materials were stored between the autopsy and microscopic examination.[446] I find this fact—if it means he didn't know where the brain was after the autopsy—highly suspicious. Everyone claims that the brain was stored in Galloway's closet, and either they are setting him up, or he doesn't want to admit custody of the brain which disappeared and was probably switched before the brain examination.

Dr. Robert Karnei, present at the autopsy and possibly during the brain examination, told the House Committee that he thought the brain transfer was handled by Dr. Humes and Dr. Boswell. He said ". . . he has a feeling Dr. Humes locked it in his office."[447]

As to whether the brain actually went into a steel bucket . . . there is one more of the countless problems with this evidence. James Curtis Jenkins, whose normal job was to remove the brain and infiltrate it with formalin, said the brain was possibly put into a glass jar. He then said the brain is usually first put in a fusion bucket (crock or porcelain) before it is put in the glass, usually about twenty-four hours later.[448]

What telephones were used during the autopsy? Dr. Boswell stated that the FBI or Secret Service agent was on the wall phone at the head of the autopsy table during the entire autopsy.[449] "He seemed to be implying they were on the phone that was in the main autopsy room," a Committee investigator wrote.[450] Photographs of the body in the morgue show a phone on the wall next to the center of the table. Some of the men deny there was any phone in that spot.[451]

Dr. Robert Karnei said that there was a phone on the wall about three and a half to four feet away from the table but doesn't remember anyone using it. He also said there was a phone in the anteroom.[452] The phone in the autopsy room itself might have been only an interhospital phone.

Jan Rudnicki and several witnesses indicated that "many phone calls were made during the autopsy, possibly by the Secret Service and FBI agents."[453]

John Stringer said that someone was directed to telephone Parkland Hospital during the autopsy, and he thought it was Humes who asked that the call be made.[454]

Was the body embalmed? This question may seem prima facie preposterous, but there is a statement in the record that the body was not embalmed. If it wasn't, that is a good way to destroy the evidence in the event of a future exhumation, which is bound to happen some years hence. One of the morticians, Thomas Robinson, states that the body was embalmed.[455] Dr. Pierre Finck, in his interview by House investigators, implies that the body was embalmed. "From what I remember the body had been embalmed, reconstructed and closed."[456]

Was the body reconstructed? Yes, in the sense that the morticians and Navy Corpsmen put it back together to prepare for an open coffin (the coffin was not open for viewing). Dr. Finck was asked: "The reconstruction of what portion of the body required the most time?" "I would assume the head."[457]

Who was responsible for closing up the rear head wound and the body? Paul O'Connor told me that he assisted the morticians with this task.[458] Thomas Robinson, one of the morticians, was asked by House investigators: "Were you the one that was responsible for closing these wounds in the head?"

"Well, we all worked on it. . . . we all tried to help one another"[459] "Did you close up the head, did you help close up other parts of the body as well?" "Yes, I did." "The back and the front?" "I did the front, yes."[460] Edwin Stroble and John Van Haeson also helped, all from Gawler's.

James Curtis Jenkins said that he recalls that they used some type of plaster molding to close up the head, and that there was a problem with the right eye because it wouldn't remain closed. He recalls the mortician trying to arrange the small skull fragments in the head and believes some of them were put in a small jar during the autopsy.[461]

Could there have been an open coffin? The opinion seems to have been unanimous that the coffin could have been open. Evidently the family decided not to do this. In my own mind, I think large numbers of the population would have felt such grief that there might have been widespread collapse. The shock of his death was so vast in the world that the massive funeral cortege was only a glimmering of what the majority of the world's population felt.

Francis X. O'Neill said that in his opinion JFK could have had an open casket.[462] This of course was the intent and the opinion of the morticians.

James Jenkins said that the fact that they could not get the right eye to stay closed was one of the reasons the body was not viewed with an open casket.[463]

Was the body in a "body bag" when it arrived at the autopsy? Paul O'Connor was quoted by the HSCA as saying that the body was *wrapped* in a "body bag,"[464] and volume 7 referred us to outside contact report 013613. The trouble is, that contact report says that O'Connor said "the body was *in* a rubber 'body' bag."[465] The way this is phrased indicates that it is not what is generally called a crash bag of the type emergency workers and the military use. Some reports said the body was wrapped in broad rubber straps or a rubber sheet when it left Parkland,[466] and the whole issue remains murky, since the sheet was also called clear plastic. The body was also wrapped in a sheet.**

Was the body altered prior to the autopsy so that the camera was fooled? No. There was no hair in the area we see as perfect scalp in the photographs showing the back of the head. Secret Service agents Kellerman and Greer were asked this question and both said that no one had the chance to alter or did alter the body in transit from Dallas.[467]

The wounds, except for a laceration on the scalp, were identical to those seen in Dallas. The so-called growth of the large hole in the head was a misunderstanding due to the flaps of scalp and bone which Boswell marked as "missing" on his drawing. Nobody denied that there were bones left on the street, in the car, and on the grass in Dallas that came from the back of the head. The country was exposed to a massive hoax because of this.

What is wrong, though, is that the X-rays don't show anything like this, and the position of the small wound of entry is four inches away from where it was at the autopsy. That's the real hoax, and it was perpetrated by the government, or the conspirators using the government as a cover.

Were any of the HSCA interview transcripts altered? It would certainly seem that this happened, and there are a number of examples. We find the following exchange in Tom Robinson's interview seconds after he described a piece of metal found in the President's chest: "You said later, when you read some things about the assassination or the autopsy, you heard or read something which struck you as incorrect. What would those things be?"

"The time the people moved [autopsy]. The body was taken . . . and the body never came . . . lots of little things like that."[468] Can you make sense of that? This is the only point in his discussion where it is broken up. There is no note of it being unintelligible. Robinson speaks clearly and distinctly in my experience. What could he have said?

The portion of the HSCA's Forensic Panel discussion on September 16, 1977, with Drs. Humes and Boswell where Dr. George L. Loquvam says: "This shouldn't be in the damn record!" appears to be well doctored.[469] We have no idea what they were talking about.

On page 10 of Dr. John Ebersole's interview, Dr. Michael Baden

**See the Medical Encyclopedia in *Killing the Truth*, pp. 673–77.

starts to ask a question which is cut off and not pursued: "Sutured incisions that might have been—"

Dr. Ebersole: "No."[470] The next question changes the subject entirely and asks him how Dr. Finck came to the autopsy room.

Dr. Petty's question appears to be severely garbled during a key line of questioning at the end of page 59 of Ebersole's interview on March 11, 1978. Petty says: "There is an inconsistency in this because they state right off that everybody was requested at the time the photographs and the X-rays were taken and yet the photographs that we have show very clearly a wound in the upper right back, if that is the way you refer to it, and if that was not discovered until very late in the autopsy procedure there must have been a second exposure of film somewhere so as to illustrate that. . . ." You figure it out.

Dr. Finck's entire March 12, 1978 interview ends in mid-sentence. Fascinating is the issue being discussed: ". . . that measurement relative to the occipital protuberance that's contained within the—"

The beginning of Finck's interview must have been severely edited because he had to be screaming about the fake pictures of the back of the head. See my chapter on the autopsy pictures (chapter 2) for what he says.

Missing is the drawing made by Dr. Boswell of the wounds for the HSCA. I think it's no accident!

Daryll Weatherly performed a laborious word-for-word comparison of the transcript found in the National Archives for the September 16, 1977, meeting of Humes and Boswell with the HSCA forensic panel, and found that many words were changed—generally in favor of the official story.

In line with my comments above is a note written by Andy Purdy about a phone call from Dr. Michael Baden, the chairman of the HSCA medical panel. Baden told Purdy that he was almost finished with the Humes and Boswell transcript, and that he believed that it "can be cleaned up enough to be in evidence."

The next paragraph says that a staffer spoke with Dr. Weston, also on the medical panel. "Weston said he'll have changes made and get the report out soon."[471] I find both of these comments deeply disturbing. Certainly, this is clear evidence that the transcript of the Humes and Boswell interview mentioned above, where Dr. Loquvam made his demonstration against certain things being in "the damn record," was in fact edited ("cleaned up"). Someone left us a clue when they retained Loquvam's expostulation in the damn record.

What of the fact that the killer was facing prosecution and the

autopsy was vital to the state's case? The military and federal agents had taken the body and were not subject to the laws of the State of Texas in the sense that a coroner had to conform to the needs of law enforcement in his investigation of violent death. Finck was asked some very good questions about this by Dr. Weston: "At the time this examination was done there was going to be a criminal prosecution. What is your practice as a forensic pathologist to stop short of doing a short medical legal autopsy in face of criminal prosecution notwithstanding the wishes of anybody else?"

"What you are saying, we should not have listened to the recommendations—" Finck said.

"No, I am not saying anything. I am asking you if it is not accepted medical legal practice when you anticipate a criminal prosecution to do a complete examination?"

"Yes," Finck replies.

"Okay. Then the reason that you did not do a complete examination was that you were ordered not to, is that correct?"

"Yes, restrictions from the family as the reason for limiting our actions."

"But do you really believe that the family has—is this not physical evidence which belongs to the state notwithstanding the wishes of the family when there is a suspected criminal prosecution?"

"Of course it is ideal. In those circumstances you are told to do certain things. There are people telling you to do certain things. It is unfortunate." (!)

"What do you consider would be the personal consequences of you or any of the other members of the team had you chosen to withdraw from the examination and not complete the examination or sign your name to it in view of the restrictions placed upon you? Did you consider that at the time?"

"No. It is a delicate situation to say the least."

Dr. Weston: "I understand that, but it is still a delicate situation." (!)

"We were handicapped by those restrictions."[472] Were the high-ranking Navy officers relaying the "wishes" of the family actually doing that, or were they themselves placing restrictions on the investigation, which in spite of a more complete autopsy being performed, did not actually investigate the wounds. Robert McNamara should be questioned closely about this.

Did the autopsy doctors lie? Of course. Their first lie is in saying that they did not know about a bullet hole in the throat that was identified by the Dallas doctors as an entry wound. We now know that Dr. Robert Livingston, head of two institutes at the National Institutes of Health, spoke to Humes prior to the start of the autopsy and told him that Dr. Perry was saying that there was an entry hole in the throat.[473] It is also improbable that the Secret Service men who had been in the emergency room along with Dr. George Burkley and who were all then present at the autopsy, did not tell the autopsy doctors of the throat entry wound.

The big lie comes after some choking statements in the autopsy report which make it easier to lie at the end. First we begin with a wound "presumably" of exit, and by the end of the autopsy report, a bullet has "made its exit through the anterior surface of the neck."[474] Not that any bullet could pass through the neck to the center of the throat from anywhere behind and not shatter a lot of bone. No damaged bone was on the X-rays, and no metal fragments.

Another lie was the weight given for the liver and brain. One weighs more than an average male brain, and the liver is too small for an adult.[475]

Finck seems to be lying when he says that the back wound was "in [Kennedy's] upper back at the base of the neck."[476] This would seem to be something he was told to say, *or else,* because he certainly throws a monkey wrench into some of the other key evidence needed to establish a clean official story.

Then there is the major clue to the true nature of the assassination of John Kennedy. In January 1967, Dr. Pierre Finck was suddenly ordered back to Washington from Vietnam and shown the autopsy photographs and X-rays. The Department of Justice prepared a statement for the doctors to sign, which said: "The photographs and X-rays corroborate our visual observations during the autopsy and conclusively support our medical opinion as set forth in the summary of our autopsy report.

"It was then and is now our opinion that the two missiles which struck the President causing the neck wound and the head wound were fired from a point behind and somewhat above the level of the deceased.

"Our examination of the photographs and X-rays lasted approximately five hours, and at its conclusion the photographs and X-rays were returned to the Archivist of the United States."[477]

Dr. Finck made some notes on this dated February 10, 1967, in which he says: "My conclusion is that the photos and X-rays of the autopsy of President Kennedy do not modify our conclusions stated in the autopsy report." Of course, the photos and X-rays contradict the autopsy report, so Finck's note above rejects the photos and X-rays as an authority, and implies that they were forced to sign a statement they did not believe.

Interestingly, the person who made them sign the January 1967 document was Barefoot Sanders, a close friend of President Lyndon Baynes Johnson. Both men are from Texas. The false statement also contains the following: "Our finding, as stated in the autopsy report, that the wound low in the back of the neck was an entrance wound is supported by photographs nos. 11, 12, 38, and 39. They show the edges of the wound to be inverted, regular, and smooth. At such a location and in such tissue these are the principal characteristics of an entrance wound." But, "*low in the back of the neck?*" No way. That wound has moved one more time! Yet, this is what Lt. Richard Lipsey, the aide to the commanding general of the Military District of Washington,[478] observed. There are simply more wounds than the public could be told about.

The whole issue of the placement of the entry hole in the back of the head is seriously fudged in the statement prepared for the autopsy doctors to sign by President Johnson's Department of Justice: "Due to the fractures of the underlying bone and the elevation of the scalp by manual lifting (done to permit the wound to be photographed), the photographs show the wound to be slightly higher than its actually measured site. The scalp wound shown in the photographs appears to be a laceration and tunnel, with the actual penetration of the skin obscured by the top of the tunnel. From the photographs this is not recognizable as a penetrating wound because of the slanting direction of entry. However, as we pointed out in the autopsy report, there was in the underlying bone a corresponding wound through the skull which exhibited beveling of the margins of the bone when viewed from the inner aspect of the skull. This is characteristic of a wound of entry in the skull."[479]

DR. PETTY: "PIERRE, we want to thank you so very much for coming by. You are among lots of good friends. It is good to see you again."[480] So, they all knew each other and had been visiting right along. Surely, they had asked many questions before, and the formal interview, heavily doctored as it appears to be in places, was just for show.

Dr. Humes is a good friend of Arlen Specter, and went to medical school in Philadelphia. When did they meet?

Senator Arlen Specter is running for president.

SUMMARY

The newly released documents from the House Select Committee on Assassinations were fifteen years coming. There is not much that is startling, and no smoking guns, except one.

It is also clear that at times the autopsy doctors were screaming about the photographs of the head and saying that they did not show the wounds. The doctors were more than "persistent" (as the House Committee called them) in their typification of the bullet entry into the back of President Kennedy's head near the hairline—rather than four or more inches above in the cowlick area. They fought a bitter and lonely fight about it, apparently, not realizing they were dealing with a stacked deck at our elected House of Representatives.

In these documents we learn that there was apparently a slug or metal ball in Kennedy's pelvic area, and it was the belief of the radiologist at the autopsy that it was not dye, not anything but "buckshot." But it might have struck him on November 22, 1963.

The documents contained drawings made by numerous autopsy witnesses showing that the large hole they saw on the back of the head was precisely the same as that seen in Dallas and no larger. It was in the same place behind the right ear and it was about three to four inches across. Missing from the documents is the drawing made by Dr. Boswell for the HSCA and shown to Francis X. O'Neill.[481]

We find some differences in what the young enlisted men observed, not trained in medicine as doctors are, but they generally corroborate what the doctors saw.

We learn that there was no evidence at all that the bullet that hit Kennedy in the back actually passed through the body. In fact, quite the contrary. Yet, we are told that there was a bruise near the top of the lung, for whatever reason. There was no damage to the bones of the neck, which would make it impossible for any bullet to have passed through. The heretofore secret interviews tell us many times over, from everyone who was at the autopsy, that the bullet that struck him in the back did not perforate the wall of the chest, no matter how much they probed it. They did not force an opening or track. It is therefore a rather devastating truth that the statement of fact at the end of the autopsy that the bullet exited the throat was only made upon a mere supposition. Worse, it was undoubtedly forced upon the doctors.

Dr. Humes told Finck not to bring along an expert on brains to the supplemental examination of the brain. We find some severe conflicts as to the dates when the brain examination actually occurred—on one of three different dates. And the brain weighed too much to have been Kennedy's after it was blown apart.

The conflict between the size of the large hole on the head and its position has been resolved:

The doctors state that a piece almost ten centimeters was missing from about the cowlick area forward to the coronal suture, a distance of four inches (ten centimeters). The piece came in at midnight. Taken together with the two other quite small pieces and the Harper fragment missing from the back of the head, this pretty much fills up the hole they claimed was there at the time of the autopsy. But a hole extending to the coronal suture seems to conflict with what was seen in Dallas, and is larger. Their testimony has to be taken together with what Boswell told me about the scalp having a smaller hole in the back, just as in Dallas, but clearly, the larger pieces of bone were blown out through it. A significant amount of scalp three to four inches across was missing in the back of the head, and it would seem that there was no possibility of a large flap of scalp in that position, as the photos seem to show. Some of the remaining scalp was in the form of three flaps with bone on them, but the scalp was not all there in one piece as in the false pictures.

The evidence of how complete the autopsy was is difficult to sort through, but it was not entirely complete, though basically they performed the job. The claim runs through these interviews that the autopsy was limited, and yet it is called more or less complete by the doctors. Again, we have to look at the House critique of the autopsy in volume 7 of their work,[482] and that of Dr. Charles Wilber. Clearly, the neck was not dissected and the organs not removed, which might be lucky for history if the body is ever exhumed and there is anything left. It is still not clear if the spinal cord was removed.

A long list of high military brass, including generals and admirals, emerges in the testimony of the participants at the autopsy. Finck's sworn testimony before the court in New Orleans in the late sixties was accurate. Someone among them was giving orders and making suggestions, and it's also clear that Admiral Burkley, and perhaps Robert McNamara, were deeply involved in the decision-making process. Some of the men told me that Burkley gave the orders,[483] although Jerrol Custer felt at times that Dr. Ebersole was in charge of more than X-rays.[484] What remains to be resolved is the question of whether the family upstairs at the Naval Hospital actually was involved in the decision-making process. I don't think they were. They were used, without their knowledge, as a means of covering up the military's control.

There were games about the tracheostomy, because it was convenient to say the wound (tracheostomy incision) in the throat looked like an exit wound. In fact, the latter happened after the House released a drawing made of it, and many thought it was an exit wound.

No one seems to have asked Admiral Galloway what changes he had made in the autopsy report, as Pierre Finck testified in New Orleans, or questioned Finck about it.

There are major conflicts in the autopsy X-rays and photographs, and that is taken up in this book in their separate chapters.

No evidence of any damage to the face turned up in the documents, and none has been heard from any medical witness, except for Lipsey.

Although there is evidence of phone contact with Dallas during the autopsy, there is no credible evidence of any phone conversations by any of the doctors. Messages were carried back and forth, as the Secret Service and FBI men present were in communication with Dallas and their offices, and evidently some things were told to Dr. Humes, and they were told about a bullet being found in Dallas. That gave the doctors the idea that it fell out of Kennedy during heart massage, and this was what they figured explained the fact that no bullet was found in his body or perforated the wall of his chest in the back.

There were no questions asked about the strange weights of the brain and liver. Surely someone should have noticed this. The adrenal issue was not dealt with.

The issue of the FBI receipt for a "missle" (sic) was resolved with affidavits from both the FBI men and the Navy corpsman who typed it, all of whom said it meant fragments and not a whole bullet. We are expected to believe this—but it has the ring of truth to me.

Corroborating my own interviews with Francis X. O'Neill in *High Treason 2*, he describes calling the FBI lab to find out about plastic and ice bullets.[485]

They saw no fragments in the neck, and the issue of surgery to the head area was explained as merely a misunderstanding by the FBI men of what was being said by the doctors. I'll accept that, because I don't feel that any alteration to the head was necessary to cover up this case. It was also impossible.

We find major conflicts between the X-rays and the autopsy report on several scores, but little or nothing is offered to deal with this.

It seems clear from the tone of the doctors' discussion of the brain examination sometime after the autopsy that it was not Kennedy's brain, and they knew it. We know it was never buried with or reinterred with the body when the grave was prepared.

We get an idea that major statements were edited out. A close word-for-word comparison of the transcript which was found at the National Archives by Anna Marie Kuhns-Walko of the September 16, 1977, meeting among Drs. Humes, Boswell, and the Committee's forensic panel shows that many words were changed to favor the official story. Daryll Weatherly performed this laborious study, and it is worth the effort to know that we are not getting a government work product with integrity.

After a massive effort to obtain information about the autopsy by the House Committee staffers, we aren't much closer to what really happened that terrible day and night. We have more pieces of the puzzle, but what we end up with are colossal and unresolvable conflicts.

That is the way our society works, and that is basically what we have running through much of this case.

It is clear that the autopsy doctors did not take an entirely safe route. I think they tried to leave a trail of clues, as did some FBI and police, and let us know something else was going on. Between the lines, the interviews tell us that the doctors had a gun to their head and were forced to lie.

When they come up with a 1,500 gram brain from a man who lost half of it on the street, they are trying to tell us something.

The doctors were also trying to tell the House and JAMA something when they insisted many times that the photographs of the back of the head don't have the entry hole in the right place.

AFTER MORE THAN THIRTY YEARS and so much effort, there are no clear answers to many of these questions. That can only be because there are so many lies.

The case only comes together and can be understood when we see that there were several shooters, an overthrow of the government, and a faked case for the public to swallow.

7

Gerald Posner's *CASE CLOSED*

In Case Closed *some of the weakest sections of the Warren Commission argument have been strengthened by suspect methodologies and even falsehoods, so systematic they call into question the good faith of the entire project.*
—Peter Dale Scott
The San Francisco Review of Books

An increasing amount of published work is a dangerous mixture of good information with a liberal dose of falsehoods. Sifting out the truth is increasingly difficult for those not well versed in the facts.
—Gerald Posner

GERALD POSNER, sometime attorney and writer and a newcomer to the Kennedy case, joined the list of Warren Commission loyalists covering up the true nature of the evidence in John Kennedy's murder. Part of a massive propaganda attack that began with *The Journal of the American Medical Association* in 1992, he tried to controvert or ignore the fast-developing evidence of forgery of the medical evidence. As my last book, *Killing the Truth*, went to press, Posner issued his *Case Closed* in 1993, a book largely cooked from misstatement and inaccurate research. It is a biased lawyer's brief and not a balanced work of historical research—part of a well-orchestrated program by major elements of the media to "close the case." Our adversarial system of justice, with its commendable qualities, comes with a built-in flaw: bias, rather than neutrality and objectivity in our legal and criminal affairs.

Posner's book is highly praised on the dust jacket by Tom Wicker, who in 1979 wrote an introduction to the House Select Committee on Assassinations report (*New York Times* edition) praising the Committee's vindication of the Warren Commission, then later confessed he hadn't read the Committee's report which found a conspiracy in the case; by novelist William Styron; by intelligence analyst David Wise, whose five books have been published by Posner's publisher; and by historian Stephen Ambrose, biographer of Presidents Eisenhower and Nixon, whose only work on the JFK case appears to be a survey piece in the *New York Times Book Review*.[1]

It would seem no coincidence that a major news magazine, *U.S. News and World Report,* would devote almost half an issue to Posner's book in a huge and coordinated propaganda effort which required extensive preplanning and the cooperation of the media. Why would the media go to such lengths on the thirtieth anniversary of Kennedy's death? As we began to break the case in the medical evidence, JAMA counterattacked with a press conference announcing a series of articles in their tabloid. *JAMA*'s press conference was an attempt to discredit a new book, *Conspiracy of Silence,* by Parkland eyewitness Dr. Charles Crenshaw, as well as my own *High Treason 2,* which made a frontal attack on the official story of the case.*

The same media controlled information so that the real news did not come out in the United States in the fall of 1993: it came out all over the world, but not here in America. The British documentary, *The Men Who Killed Kennedy,* was shown in over ninety countries before U.S. viewers were given the opportunity to see it. The new evidence in the Kennedy case has received similar treatment, and remains unreported in the American press. This is another consequence of the growing concentration of American media ownership into fewer hands, as documented by Ben Bagdikian and other media critics.

Random House, the publisher of *Case Closed,* refused to publish Walt Brown's masterful mock trial, *The People* v. *Lee Harvey Oswald,* and my own first book on the case, the best-selling *High Treason.* Fox Broadcasting killed an investigative Kennedy special.[2] The Associated Press killed a November 18, 1993, wire story (reprinted in

*Mark Crouch wrote the following about *High Treason 2* to the author: "You never realized how important *High Treason 2* was! You had made the case for cover-up with your in-depth questioning of the witnesses. Their observations and comments on the autopsy pictures was the crucial element of your research.... In *High Treason 2* you reported in depth the numerous discrepancies between what the witnesses saw and remembered and what the "official record" said. What you and many of the critics failed to realize was that you were standing at the threshold of proving that the medical evidence in this case had been corrupted by the United States Government, thusly proving a cover-up. *I mean really proved it!* Proved it in such a simple and irrefutable way that even the press could understand it. The cover-up operatives had to do something. They couldn't retract Humes, Boswell, Fink, and Lattimer, so they had to discredit me, discredit you, and discredit *High Treason 2.*" (Letter of November 12, 1994.)

I apologize to Dr. Crouch for the nightmare that befell us when our enemies played us off against each other and I attacked him. I'm sorry.

the appendix to this book) outlining the new medical evidence presented by a team of doctors at a major New York press conference which I organized. Readers in Europe read all about it, but not a single newspaper in the United States that I know of covered it. Serious books critical of the official story are not reviewed at all, or are dismissed in a sentence or two in *The New York Times*.

As the JFK Assassination Records Act began to be implemented—after Posner's book was finished—and massive numbers of newly released documents became available, some of them casting important new light, Posner's "closing" of the case distracted attention from this authentic new evidence. Like the *JAMA* articles, he offered "enlightenment" by selectively rehashing old stuff, with various distortions passed off as "new research."

Case Closed is a narration of how Lee Harvey Oswald supposedly killed Kennedy. The conclusion and reasoning is nearly the same as that of the Warren Commission but with some new twists. Posner found, he says, information about Oswald that the critics missed. Posner relies heavily on his idea of the psychobiography of Lee Harvey Oswald, and thinks it is proof that Oswald shot President Kennedy. He simply ignores important evidence in the attempt to indict the critics of the Warren Report, Oswald, and conspiracy theories. As James Folliard has pointed out, Oswald's personal history only becomes relevant "when and if Oswald is conclusively linked to the crime."[3] Novelist, Norman Mailer has followed the same process while completely ignoring the physical evidence in the tragedy, thus producing a nearly worthless book, and co-opting the case in the process.

Professor of law Robert Blakey, the former chief counsel of the Assassinations Committee, said that Posner's book would end up being a mere "footnote" in a bibliography of assassination literature.[4] "What's troublesome for me in Posner's book is that he's a lawyer writing the brief for one side, and there's no reason for a person who's seen or heard all the evidence to credit his book as opposed to someone else's."[5]

U.S. News and World Report wrote about Posner's book that "Posner achieves the unprecedented. He sweeps away decades of polemical smoke, layer by layer, and builds an unshakable case against JFK's killer.... Posner now performs the historic office of correcting the mistakes and laying the questions to rest with impressive finality, bringing the total weight of evidence into focus more sharply than anyone has done before.... The high quotients of common sense, logic and scrupulous documentation found in *Case*

Closed are niceties not often found in the field of assassination research."[6]

We shall see.

Posner, mentally challenged, has restated the Warren Commission's Report on the assassination of President Kennedy in perhaps the best recent example of twisted "scholarship" in American history. He writes, "But the troubling issues and questions about the assassination can be settled, the issue of who killed JFK resolved, and Oswald's motivation revealed. Presenting those answers is the goal of this book."[7] Possibly true, but Posner failed—in spite of devoting almost half his book to his new biography of Oswald.

Have critics engaged in sloppy scholarship? No one denies this. Yet every valid criticism made of a critic by Mr. Posner has been made previously by other critics, upon whose work he feeds. And he is clearly a careful student of the flaws of others, for he adopts them in his own work.

A detailed analysis of his entire book would require at least another volume in itself, but the examples provided below expose the techniques used to dissemble and deceive.

In April 1995, Gerald Posner and I had our first public encounter. Posner crystallized the differences in approach in this fashion: He said that his case against Oswald and for the Warren Commission was entirely dependent upon the evidence being authentic. My case depends upon proving that the evidence in the case is fake, forged, planted, or missing and that the pattern of same shows a conspiracy prior to the assassination.

There can be no doubt of this. The current spate of books which rely heavily on making out some sort of case against Oswald are of little or no value. It does not matter for most purposes of analysis of the evidence if Oswald committed the crime or if he did not. It doesn't even matter if he was part of a conspiracy. Oswald is immaterial to the case I make that the faked autopsy evidence and clearly coerced medical and autopsy reports prove beyond a shadow of a doubt a conspiracy to overthrow the Kennedy administration.

Whether or not Oswald was a part of it is a non sequitur. If one can prove that Oswald was framed, or if he did it and had help, then that is proof of conspiracy. But this is secondary to the fact that the autopsy evidence was faked, and much other evidence fabricated or gone missing.

1. SELECTIVE REPORTING:
THE CASE OF FAILURE ANALYSIS

A keystone of Mr. Posner's "new evidence" is the scientific analysis of Dr. Robert Piziali. Presented as if it was the result of many years of careful study and an objective breakthrough in the case, Piziali's work was completely ripped out of its context.

In the summer of 1992, the American Bar Association asked Failure Analysis, a Menlo Park, California, firm that investigates disasters and tragedies of various kinds, to study and present at their San Francisco convention both the government's one gunman case against Oswald, and evidence showing that more than one gunman was possible.

An example of Posner's selectivity of material and evidence is his use of only that part of the company's work that fit his needs.

Three executives from Failure Analysis participated, including Dr. Roger McCarthy—its president[8]—Dr. Robert Piziali,[9] and Dr. Martin Fackler.[10] I traveled to Menlo Park and met with the people at Failure Analysis who described to me how the decision was arrived at as to who would take which side of the issue. They flipped a coin. I conveyed this information to Martin Shackelford, who passed it on to the research community. I then printed in *Killing the Truth* the entire presentation of all three participants from Failure Analysis, with the best wishes of the American Bar Association. Gerald Posner was about to print only *two* of the three experts: Robert Piziali—and Martin Fackler who presented the government's official story as a result of a coin toss.

Posner laid out Piziali's arguments as though they had resulted from many years of study (not the two weeks in which they were prepared from scratch) and as though Piziali's words and arguments constituted a decisive breakthrough in the case. Posner completely ignored the refutation of Roger McCarthy, president of Failure Analysis, and in fact gave the impression that no contrary presentation ever existed.

This is just one of countless examples in Posner's tawdry propaganda exercise (which shows how little Random House thinks of the public). Jeffrey Frank wrote in the *Washington Post Book World* that "McCarthy, the firm's CEO, has since expressed outrage over what he calls a 'fundamental misrepresentation' of the data—including an implication that the work was commissioned by Posner."[11]

Patricia Holt wrote that "according to Angela Meyer of Failure Analysis, 'our job for the ABA was to provide evidence and expert witnesses for *both* the defense and the prosecution.' Posner appears to draw from testimony for the prosecution's case, not the defense case."[12]

In fact, Dr. Roger McCarthy, the CEO of Failure Analysis, offered a "startling conclusion" on a TV program. He said his company made a "compelling argument that Lee Harvey Oswald did not act alone."[13] McCarthy said the gunman "gave up some awfully good shots to take some awfully bad shots" to "[drive] the quarry into a second shooting" by other assassins. McCarthy, a good shot himself, said that he could not equal what the assassin was supposed to have done.

Posner writes that "an FBI agent . . . using only a dime as a tool" put together the disassembled rifle in six minutes.[14] Dr. Roger McCarthy found that a dime would not fit the screws in the rifle, and said that the rifle was hard to put together.[15] This was another Failure Analysis finding that Posner chose to ignore.

I printed what all three Failure Analysis scientists had to say about the firearms issue in my chapter on Firearms and Ballistics in *Killing the Truth*. I had no idea what Posner was putting in his book and this was just lucky happenstance. Misguided selectivity is something Posner should have avoided.

Posner caught such hell over his unethical scholarship with the Failure Analysis material that he added a few lines to his footnote on pages 317–18 (316–17 of his paperback version), which incorporated only the slightest handful of changes and corrections. His feeble attempt to explain is really beyond my desire to comment. I will quote one statement: "The Failure Analysis presentation did not take into account that ballistics experts conclude that a target coming toward and below a shooter is a more difficult shot with a telescopic sight, and that Oswald was better hidden from the view of neighboring buildings by choosing a line of fire along Elm Street." The trouble with that is that the Dorman film was taken from a floor (fourth) well below Oswald's alleged perch, and it shows JFK clearly available as a target to shots past John Connally, sitting in front of him. As for being in a window clearly visible from neighboring buildings, Oswald was not better hidden by simply turning his body and weapon 90°. This kind of reasoning is far more than lame.

Throughout the above footnote, there are no sources cited for the "experts" or for his discussion of glycerine bullets. He admits for the first time that the Failure Analysis study was done for the

American Bar Association and not for him, and claims that the defense mounted by them for Oswald achieved no new "technical breakthroughs." At the same time he says that (p. 318) "the only technical breakthroughs were on the prosecution work, and they are presented in this chapter." He implies that the defense at the ABA convention presented "no new evidence" but completely ignores the fact that they had presented a great deal, so much so that the president of the company believed there was a conspiracy. Posner singles out two points made by the defense at the mock ABA trial: the computer animation, which he says was not accurate (then why should we trust the animation done for the prosecution? Shackelford asks) and the fact that they contradicted his "ballistics experts," whom he does not name or cite.

He ignores the computer animation demonstration of the problem of losing the target each time the rifle's bolt is operated, yet his book relies on what have to be the craziest computer-generated solutions to the trajectories in history!

2. INTELLIGENCE SOURCES, UNINTELLIGENT METHODS

With the collapse of the Soviet Union, former KGB officers hastened to sell their stories to the highest bidders. Their extensive training in disinformation should lead us to treat their accounts with caution, but Posner seems willing to rely on their veracity.

Posner accepts on what the KGB told him, which seems very curious. The KGB was a mortal enemy of the United States for a long time, and upon the collapse of the Soviet Union, individual agents and executives of the KGB, scrambling to stay alive, sold their services to any country that came along, often saying whatever they had to say to survive. Unquestioning use of the KGB as a source completely discredits Posner. Norman Mailer made the same dumb mistake. After all, the Russians need to curry favor with the U.S. Government these days, as well.

Peter Dale Scott notes that "Posner more than once acknowledges help from 'confidential intelligence sources.' " This gained him access to Yuri Nosenko, the Soviet KGB defector unavailable to most researchers (an exception being Edward J. Epstein, who also had assistance from the CIA). Posner relied heavily and uncritically on Nosenko. This is folly, as all students of the Nosenko case would agree, since the man was not very credible. There were "significant inconsistencies" in much that he said, as the House noted.[16]

In a footnote on page 41, Posner lists ten Soviet defectors who he says backed Nosenko's credibility. We have to take Posner's acceptance of their own credibility on faith since there is no citation. One of the names on the list is Vitaliy Yurchenko, who made headlines in 1985 when he redefected to the Soviet Union.

Other witnesses who have declined interviews by critics made themselves available to Mr. Posner, including former Dallas Assistant District Attorney Bill Alexander. According to Posner, ". . . Alexander and two local reporters concocted a story that Oswald had been FBI informer S179 and had been paid two hundred dollars a month. Lonnie Hudkins, one of the reporters, printed the story, attributing it to an unidentified source." Posner quotes Alexander as having said: "I never much liked the federals. I figured it was as good a way as any to keep them out of my way by having to run down that phony story.' "[17]

This is Posner's idea of a credible source, a man who would willfully mislead other official investigators. Long ago, Sylvia Meagher and George O'Toole discussed Alexander's probable role in planting the story.[18]

Witnesses such as the Sheriff of Dallas County, Jim Bowles, have told researchers that Posner misinterpreted what they told him. In some cases witnesses such as Carlos Bringuier and autopsy doctor J. Thornton Boswell have denied talking with Posner at all.[19]

Evidence linking Oswald to the intelligence community finds no place in Posner's work. Former House Assassinations Committee staffer Gaeton Fonzi comments that "that conclusion flies in the face of an enormous amount of evidence (including the notation of 'microdots' in Oswald's notebook and the Minox spy camera and negatives of foreign military installations found among Oswald's possessions after the assassination) and contradicts the firm opinion of many previous investigators of the assassination."[20] Dr. Philip Melanson devoted an entire book, *Spy Saga*, to this evidence.†

Former Senator Richard Schweiker of the Senate Intelligence Committee had said that "Oswald had intelligence connections" and the "fingerprints of intelligence" were all over him. "I think that by playing a pro-Castro role on the one hand and associating with anti-Castro Cubans on the other, Oswald was playing out an intelligence role. This gets back to him being an agent or double agent. . . . I personally believe that he had a special relationship with one of the intelligence agencies, which one I'm not certain.

---

†Dr. Philip H. Melanson, *Spy Saga: Lee Harvey Oswald and U.S. Intelligence*. Praeger, 1990. See also *Oswald and the CIA* by John Newman, Carroll & Graf, New York 1995.

But all the fingerprints I found during my eighteen months on the
Senate Select Committee on Intelligence Activities point to Oswald
as being a product of, and interacting with the intelligence community.[21] As an operative, Oswald may have been available to the FBI,
the CIA, the Office of Naval Intelligence (ONI), and others.

Posner disposed of the allegations that George de Mohrenschildt
had a CIA relationship by reverting to the Warren Commission
method of letting the CIA answer the question: "CIA officials have
provided sworn testimony that there was no de Mohrenschildt-U.S.
intelligence relationship." He deleted this sentence from his paperback edition (p. 85), perhaps after learning of the documents discussed by Edward Epstein in *The Assassination Chronicles*, which
conclusively establish such a relationship. And there is massive evidence developed by the U.S. House of Representatives of such intelligence ties.‡

Professor Peter Dale Scott writes that "there is no excuse for
Posner's repeating, uncritically and without footnotes, another old
CIA claim, that at the time of the assassination, 'Oswald's CIA file
did not contain any photos' of Oswald. The CIA used this excuse
to justify the false description of Oswald it sent to other agencies
on October 10, 1963, six weeks before the assassination. But as
Anthony Summers pointed out thirteen years ago in his book *Conspiracy*, the CIA preassassination file on Oswald contained four newspaper clippings of his defection to the Soviet Union in 1959, two
of which had photographs of him. The recently declassified Lopez
Report to the House Committee called explanations offered by CIA
employees on the matter of the false Oswald description 'hard to
accept' and 'implausible.' It is also hard to think of an innocent
defense for Posner's repetition of the CIA falsehood in a chapter
where he is specifically rebutting Summers. In short, this book is
not 'a model of historical research,' as the historian Stephen Ambrose has claimed. It is a lawyer's brief."[22]

Gaeton Fonzi,§ a former leading staff member of the HSCA, had
this to say about him: "Mr. Posner apparently failed to conduct
enough original research to evaluate the validity of the evidence
produced by the Warren Commission, the Senate JFK Subcommittee, and the House Assassinations Committee. In addition, it's obvious that he did not have access to numerous documents which
contradict his conclusions."[23]

‡See this section in my first book, *High Treason*, under Clemard Joseph
Charles, p. 260 in the Conservatory Press edition, and pp. 302–3 in the Berk-
ley edition.
§Author of *The Last Investigation*, Thunder's Mouth Press, 1993.

In his original volume, Posner denied that the CIA debriefed Oswald (p. 79). In the paperback edition, he is forced to acknowledge a debriefing by Andy Anderson (p. 78), but assures the reader that "those familiar with its contents" (his intelligence sources) describe it as "innocuous," and its concealment "misinterpreted by critics as the cover-up of a murder conspiracy."

One of the red herrings in the case is the attempt to link Oswald specifically to the CIA. Posner, having set up this tired old straw man, then dismisses the links Oswald might have had to other intelligence agencies.

He was also led down the garden path by the most famous disinformation specialist of all, a person known for right-wing sympathies who for a long time had the confidence not only of most greenhorns and researchers needing help, but that of the like-minded leadership of the critical community. It is unfortunate that most of the information was either wrong, or misdirected researchers from the central evidence that should have been pursued. This person was full of more horse shit than anyone else, and Posner bought it because they had the same sympathies.

The operative concept here is that Oswald probably worked for several agencies. He was a sort of free agent, not a free-lance, but available to the FBI, CIA, ONI, and so on.

3. FRIENDLY EXPERTS, UNRELIABLE EVIDENCE

Posner has a close relationship with Dr. Lowell Levine who identified the alleged body of Dr. Joseph Mengele, the Nazi concentration camp monster. Levine authenticated the so-called official X-rays of John Kennedy (for the HSCA) and examined the jaw bone of Mengele, and worked with Posner on his book about Mengele. The X-rays in the JFK case are altered and are composites. This has been a keystone of my research since 1979, and Posner tries to go around this with sophist arguments.

Scott tells us that Posner has reversed the verdict on Jack Ruby.[24] A massive amount of information was developed over the last thirty years showing that Jack Ruby had many Mob associations. The House Committee concluded that Ruby had a "significant number of associations" with organized crime.[25] Scott writes that "The Warren Commission's portrait of Ruby as a loner, based on misleading reports and suppression of evidence by the FBI, was clearly false."[26] Remember, J. Edgar Hoover had his own close Mob associations and was a gambler. He told this nation time and again that there was no organized crime, until the New York State Police raided a meeting of the national syndicate at Apalachin and arrested many bosses. Hoover had an interest in making sure that Ruby was pictured as a lone wolf. Posner quotes Tony Zoppi as saying that "only conspiracy theorists" would "believe that Ruby was part of the Mob."[27] Posner relies on Zoppi as a witness to make his case that Ruby was a "real low-level loser."[28]

Both Zoppi and Ruby were close to Lewis McWillie who worked for Meyer Lansky in one of his casinos in Havana, where Ruby regularly visited.[29] Were these visits innocent, as Zoppi claims? Not at all. Scott asks, "Why would Posner choose a discredited casino employee to claim that Ruby was not connected to the mob? The answer, surely, is that he is a lawyer out—like the Warren Commission—to 'close' a case. Posner opposes the thousand pages of House Committee documentation, not with new rebuttal documentation, but by extended oral interviews with just four witnesses, each of them dubious."[30] Scott tells us that "the Chicago FBI office covered up Ruby's organized crime links in the first place."[31] The Assassinations Committee found that the FBI was delinquent in investigating the Ruby underworld connections.[32] Naturally, with so many people on the take from Ruby and the Mob in Dallas, even their bosses are going to lie to cover it up.

A LOT OF PEOPLE GO THROUGH LIFE with blinders on. It is unfortunate that all governments and politicians lie. Accepting the official story about anything in these assassinations is to be blind. Ruby had a long and violent history with the Mob.

Jim Folliard, in his landmark demolition of Gerald Posner, deals with "Posner as Psychiatrist: The Hartogs Testimony," and "Posner as Psychologist" and more things that don't add up in his writing.

"Posner's main thesis hinges on a Lee Harvey Oswald who was none-too-tightly wrapped. No one has ever argued that Oswald was 'just an average guy.' However, about 80 percent of this 'Oswald persona' material is based on Marina Oswald's testimony—often as mediated through Priscilla Johnson-McMillan (whose book Norman Mailer later bought out for his mental gymnastic on Oswald). . . . Marina's story is a controversial subject, one that an honest and thorough author would be bound to comment on. Posner does not want us to know that the Warren Commission itself had heavy reservations about Marina's changing stories: one Commission lawyer was moved to write that she 'has lied to the Secret Service, the

FBI, and this Commission repeatedly on matters which are of vital concern.'[33] Yet this is the material Posner relies on to build his own case against Oswald—with no reference whatsoever to challenges to it. Marina's story deserves as much critical scrutiny as those of, say, Jean Hill, or Sylvia Odio. Lest we forget, she is the only primary source for things like the Walker attempt, and the Nixon threat, key 'incidents' in making a case for a violence-prone assassin.'[34]

Posner wraps much of his argument for Oswald having killed President Kennedy in a psychological assessment of Oswald—made by Dr. Renatus Hartogs, the psychiatrist who saw Oswald—when he was thirteen and in school in the Bronx. We might conclude from this, since it is part of Posner's pattern of upgrading anything he thinks supports his theory, that this is not just sloppy workmanship, but deliberate distortion.

Hartogs found that Oswald had "definite traits of dangerousness" (sic) and a "potential for explosive, aggressive, assaultive acting out ...."[35] Folliard tells us that Posner then says that Hartogs's 1953 evaluation did not explicitly mention Oswald's potential for violence: to have done so would have mandated the boy's institutionalization. (Posner offers no citation or documentation for this "casual" and innocent-appearing remark.) "Hartogs—out of kindness, we are to presume—lets someone he found with 'traits of dangerousness' and capable of 'explosive, assaultive acting out' in effect 'go free'! .... If we recall the diagnostic treatment attitude in psychology forty years ago, which was much more 'institutionalization-oriented' than today's. It looks like one of those situations that just 'don't add up.' "[36]

"But sure enough, investigation reveals that once again Posner has resorted to selective sound-bites of evidence to make his case for Oswald as psychopath. The Warren Commission concluded that "contrary to reports that appeared after the assassination, the psychiatric examination did not indicate that Lee Oswald was a potential assassin, *potentially dangerous*, that 'his outlook on life had strongly paranoid overtones,' or that he should be institutionalized."[37] Commission counsel Wesley Liebeler asked Hartogs about the discrepancy between his 1953 assessment and what he told the Commission. Hartogs reread his own report and he said that it failed to mention potential violence or assaultive or homicidal potential. He testified that *if he had found such traits he would have mentioned them in his report*.[38] "Not a word about leaving them out so Oswald could escape institutionalization," as Folliard points out. "Nor does he mention that the Warren Commission was quite obviously unpersuaded by Hartogs's 1964 version of Oswald's psyche.

This is not to defend or endorse the Commission's assessment of Oswald but to call attention to Posner's highly selective, distorted, and incomplete rendering of the record. On this score, at least, the Warren Commission acted far more responsibly."[39]

"After placing such stress on the importance of Hartogs's evaluation, Posner's handling of the issue looks all the more suspicious. Neither his reporting nor citing of evidence can be trusted, it seems."[40] Posner jumps on the critics for ignoring Hartogs's testimony, as the Warren Commission pretty much did. Unless Oswald is actually connected to the crime of assassinating Kennedy, his psychiatric background is irrelevant. And the critics by and large do not connect Oswald to the crime. But to say this deals a death blow to Posner's main argument, which is circumstantial: that Oswald had the propensity to commit such a crime. As James Folliard points out, Posner attempts a psychobiography of Oswald, for which he has no qualifications, and employs "neo-Freudian jargon" in attempts to discredit witnesses like Sylvia Odio. Martin Shackelford adds that "when he is describing people's states of mind, Posner has a tendency to use 'apparently' and 'must have' quite a bit."[41]

If Dr. Hartogs is such an important source, then why doesn't Posner say anything about his book, *The Two Assassins*?[42] Did the title scare him off (it refers to Oswald and Ruby), or was he just unaware of it?

As Folliard says, the "pathological" theory of assassination sees all American assassins as acutely disturbed, isolated, bitter persons, delusional, deranged, and schizophrenic. "Most disturbing is the fact that this circular and pyramiding body of questionable literature provides the basis for the conclusions of important official documents . . . and defines the operational understanding of assassins for the Federal Bureau of Investigation and the Secret Service.‖ They reduce the complexities of the act to the presumed pathology of unconscious motives as defined by the social and political values of the examine. . . . The contaminating effect of social value judgments is a very serious problem in psychiatric diagnosis."[43]

"One would think that Posner used these statements as instructions for compiling his 'authoritative' psychobiography! As well as for the neo-Freudian jargon he brings to the task of discrediting

‖James Clarke remarks in his book *American Assassins* that this psychological literature exhibits "scant evidence of any primary research. Rather, the references reveal a heavy reliance on secondary sources as well as a kind of incestuous process of citing each other's work to 'document' the same questionable conclusions." Folliard adds: "This of course never happens in assassination research!"

unwelcome witnesses, like Sylvia Odio (pp. 175–80), and the man in the Dallas jail, dismissed by the FBI because he had been arrested for 'lunacy' (pp. 229–30). Thus, psychology—Posner style—gets allied with ideology."[44]

I recommend the pages in the Warren Report dealing with Oswald and Hartogs.¶ It's a good story.

4. ATTACKING THE CRITICS: AIMING FOR THE WHITE SPACE

Large publishing houses and the media are responsible for the increasingly low level of intelligent criticism in America. Wave after wave of fabricated books hit the stores, far too often with no devotion to the truth, valid research, or historical reality.

Those who doubt the possibility of such an orchestrated plan by people who know each other well in the interlocking directorates of this nation and its media giants with their banks and Texas owners should take notice that there is considerable proof that such is the case. There is a concerted attempt to cover up JFK's death, though not entirely monolithic. Nobody wants to rock the public's boat, so lull everyone to sleep and let the critics think what they want to think. Just don't seriously do anything about it. Don't set history straight. This is how to preside over the decline of a briefly great nation. No nation suvives this kind of intellectual and historical corruption.

Posner saves the lowest blows in his book for some of the Dallas doctors, using one against the other at times. He quotes one doctor as saying that Dr. Charles Crenshaw, who published *Conspiracy of Silence* in 1992, causing a furor among those trying to cover up the case, is "over the hill."[45] This "close Crenshaw friend" is obviously no friend. Crenshaw's book spoke for all of the other Dallas doctors, corroborating what they themselves had previously said and written about the wounds, though it added a bit (as they all have) of information unknown to some of the others. Posner thinks such character assassination helps his case, which could not be further from the truth. It may work with the gullible media, but it isn't going to work with history. Tactics like this damage people's lives. Posner's attack on Dr. Robert McClelland is low, wrongheaded, and unfair. Unfortunately such character assassination is the name of the game

¶WR GPO edition, pp. 379–81, 677; WR *NY Times* edition, pp. 355–56.

in this as in our politics. Character assassination is a political tactic that has become a tool of history telling.

Posner saves some of his cleverest sleight of hand for Dr. Charles Baxter. He has Baxter telling him that he doesn't remember that Dr. Charles Crenshaw was present when Kennedy was dying.[46] Posner lost all credibility because Baxter swore to Arlen Specter and the Warren Commission that Crenshaw was present.[47] In fact, Crenshaw was the first one Baxter named. *The Journal of the American Medical Association* made the same mistake the year before and claimed Crenshaw was not present and was lying, which became one of several counts in Crenshaw's libel suit against *JAMA*. That cost *JAMA* a hell of a lot of money.

The attack on Crenshaw cited above substituted for evidence. In the paperback edition, issued a year later, much of this material is deleted (p. 312), but the terrible damage to a respected doctor's reputation and integrity had been done.

Posner ignored research which refuted various of the premises he needed to construct his lone-assassin theory. We can judge the level of his scholarship by those statements about me and my work which are untrue (see below), part of a widespread attempt to build in the public eye a false image of me—the principal proponent of forgery and falsification of the evidence—at the moment when the third volume of my work tried to reach the country. Posner ignores fine points in the evidence and buries appropriate questions with simplistic generalizations. He fails utterly to prove his points in the medical evidence or for a lone assassin. Not an experienced investigator, he questions witnesses so that he gets the answers he wants, and ignores the truth.

In writing about the medical evidence, Posner claims that I "devote more than thirty pages to highlighting this conflict between the Parkland and Bethesda descriptions of the head wound." There is no such thirty pages. I simply pointed out the vast discrepancy as part of the requirement for journalistic balance. Posner, not a historian (though he claimed that he is), systematically avoids the academic requirement of *total evidence*. It is true that I was in error in an Afterword at the end of my first book, which presented apparently conflicting testimony and to some extent the conclusions of another writer that the body may not have been the same at Bethesda as it had been at Parkland (many of us made this mistake), before I had interviewed his witnesses myself. I had been unable to find them for years. After finding the witnesses, I saw that I was wrong, and this stimulated my second book, *High Treason 2*. Posner fails to note that my primary findings are that there was *no change* in the wounds between Dallas and Bethesda (and therefore the idea that the body was altered is in error) and that the autopsy pictures have to be fake. This is proven by the heretofore secret interviews conducted by the HSCA with the autopsy witnesses and presented in this book.

If a researcher devotes a book to the details of Dealey Plaza, or to Jack Ruby, or to organized crime, or to the photographic evidence, or to the medical evidence, Posner will emphasize that the researcher ignores Oswald's childhood. That's pretty tough.

Not up to speed on the case, Posner fights fifteen-year-old battles.

5. DOCTORS WITH A SUDDEN CHANGE OF HEART

Repeatedly, Posner reports interviews in which medical witnesses contradict every one of their earlier statements on the same topic. He also distorts what the doctors told the PBS *NOVA* program in 1988 (p. 310 footnote), when each placed his hand on the backs of their heads to indicate the location of the large exit wound in the President's head. Posner would have us believe the autopsy photo showing the back of the head intact accurately represents what the doctors reported.

A photograph of each of them showing the placement of the large defect in the President's head is printed in *Killing the Truth*. All his attempts to explain the undamaged scalp and head in the false autopsy photographs of the back of the head fail.

On the same page, Posner claims that the Zapruder film shows the large defect over the right ear: "It's very clear on the enhanced frames that there is a wound, but the back of the head is clean. That film is incontrovertible evidence that there was no defect on the rear of the head."[48] The large hole is exactly where it is in the autopsy report and in the Dallas descriptions, but extending into the back of the head, which part is blacked out on the altered film before the public. Posner's claim that there is no wound showing on the back of the head is not entirely true. Some of the slides in the National Archives do show the margins of the hole in the right rear quadrant of the head, where it was described in the autopsy report.

Why Posner wants to negate the autopsy report itself—and therefore the autopsy doctors—is not clear. Like so many others he's got to have that evidence authentic. To suggest otherwise is to tamper with the man's stability. It's conceivable that some of these creatures could go completely mad if disabused of their illusions.

The Case of Doctor Jenkins

We can easily demonstrate Posner's method when in his own words, he writes that Dr. Jenkins "returned to the head of the table and said to the others, 'I think you better look at this first,' pointing toward the President's head. 'We have no way of resuscitating him. I think it's time to declare him dead.' "[48] Posner writes: "Dr. Kemp Clark, the only neurosurgeon in the room, put on a pair of gloves and quickly inspected the head wound. 'That was the first time anyone looked at it,' says Jenkins."[49] This last statement clearly implies that there was another inspection or two of the head wound which followed.

"*High Treason* asserts that Jenkins originally said JFK was shot in the chest. Jenkins laughed when the author read him the charge" (p. 312). I wrote nothing like this distortion. I asked Jenkins (*High Treason*, p. 76 of the Conservatory Press edition): "Have you ever changed any of your original opinions in connection with the wounds received by President Kennedy?" Jenkins responded: "I guess so. The first day I had thought because of his pneumothorax, that his wound must have gone—that the one bullet must have traversed his pleura, must have gotten into his lung cavity, I mean, and from what you say now, I know it did not go that way. I thought it did." Jenkins had written at the time of the assassination that "there was also obvious . . . chest damage" and I speculated that Kennedy might have been shot in the chest, meaning thorax. Being shot in the back is being shot in the chest, in my book. It's all the thorax, and we know that the bullet from behind hit him well down on the back. Apparently the bullet never entered the chest.

After all, Kennedy had a "bruise" on his lung at the autopsy, and drainage tubes had to be inserted at Parkland. Yet, intense effort at the autopsy could find no passage for a bullet into the chest.

Gerald Posner claims that he interviewed Dr. Jenkins in 1992. He quotes Jenkins as saying, "The description of the cerebellum was my fault. When I read my report over I realized there could not be any cerebellum. The autopsy photo, with the rear of the head intact and a protrusion in the parietal region, is the way I remember it. I never did say occipital."[50] Jenkins could not have forgotten his own memorandum written the day of the murder, when he noted that there was "a great laceration on the right side of the head (temporal and occipital)."[51] And he could not have forgotten or been mistaken when he told staff members of the House of Representatives that "occipital or temporal bone" was missing. Jenkins told Andy Purdy of the HSCA that he, Jenkins, an anesthesiologist, "was positioned at the head of the table so he had one of the closest views of the head wound . . . believes he was 'the only one who knew the extent of the head wound.' [sic]. . . . Regarding the head wound, Dr. Jenkins said that only one segment of bone was blown out—it was a segment of occipital or temporal bone. He noted that a portion of the cerebellum (lower rear brain) [sic] was hanging out from a hole in the right—rear of the head."[52] Jenkins also told the *American Medical News* that "Kennedy had part of his head blown away and part of his cerebellum was hanging out."[53]

But Jenkins was dying when Posner interviewed him, so it seems he thought it was safe to twist the words of the soon to be dead.

I cannot believe that the two or three doctors Posner employs to discredit the others would have criticized colleagues with whom they were close friends—working in either the same hospital, town, or metro-complex—on such an issue. Using the same approach, the tabloid *Journal of the American Medical Association* also slandered some of the doctors with whom the magazine disagreed.

For example, Posner uses Jenkins to try to discredit Dr. Robert McClelland, a deeply religious, gentle, and honest man. Posner has Jenkins saying that McClelland had been mistaken about an entry hole in the left temple (where undertaker Robinson first told me there had been a small hole). "I was trying to take the President's temporal pulse, and I had my finger on his left temple. Bob thought I pointed to the left temple as the wound."[54] Posner was too stupid to know how he was being set up by Jenkins, for it was Jenkins who had testified to the Warren Commission that "I thought there was a wound on the left temporal area, right in the hairline and right above the zygomatic process. . . . I was feeling for—I was palpating here for a pulse to see whether the closed chest cardiac message was effective or not and this probably was some blood that had come from the other point and so I thought there was a wound there also."[55]

I think it's a matter of the integrity of the writer or reporter.**

**James R. Folliard comments on an underlying problem with Posner's criticism of my work and that of others. Approached from a philosophical angle, "common sense should place more credence on such testimony than that derived from layer after layer of 'reinterviews' over thirty years. Memories

Gary Aguilar writes that "Jenkins's earliest 'unenhanced' recollections must be given greatest weight and considered the most likely
to be reliable, as in any police investigation. Fortunately, they also
agree with the earliest recollections of other Parkland witnesses, an
important corroborative factor."[56] Of the greatest importance is Dr.
Aguilar's interview with Dr. Boswell* and Boswell's flat denial that
Posner had ever spoken with him.[57] In other words, Posner made
this up—along with so much else.

On page 310 Posner writes that *"High Treason* asserts that some
doctors examined the wound with a flashlight and that Dr. Jenkins
picked the head up from the stretcher to show other doctors the
extent of the rear wound." This statement implies that Jenkins
shined the flashlight in, but I never wrote that, and anyone familiar
with my book knows that it was Giesecke and Baxter. The doctor
who used the flashlight did so when only a couple of people were
present. Although some doctors may not recall every detail of my
recorded conversations many years ago when I went to see them,
Posner's implication that I fabricated this is wrong, and for him to
say so implies that every one of the Dallas doctors was lying when
they said the back of the head was missing.

And, interestingly, Posner, like so many other authors, cites as a
source an authority who has seriously discredited himself through
inconsistencies in the past, as had Jenkins. The problem in the JFK
case is that nearly *every* witness is discredited by twisting and dis-
torting what they said since their original observations were recorded—leaving only the autopsy photographs and X-rays as the
supposed "best evidence." The most serious problem then con-

---

and stories do change—not always for the better. Additionally, we must largely
take the writer's word for it that they are quoting the witnesses they interview
accurately. But we have Posner ascribing statements, to the Parkland staff
especially, that are flatly at variance with their quoted remarks to others. I'm
inclined to think that Posner is providing 'selective sound bites' from his own
interviews here—*à la* his handling of Frazier-Randle. But who can tell? One
would like to see complete transcripts of these interviews. See, for example,
p. 310, where Posner cites the Parkland physicians, 'in their discussions with
the author,' as flatly contradicting how they were reported in *High Treason*;
and as 'almost unanimous' 'in supporting the autopsy findings . . . and that
there was no sign of damaged cerebellum.' The statement about the cerebellum is particularly amazing! Given the thirty-year record, there is no way
anyone even casually familiar with the sources and issues can accept 'discussions with the author' as adequate or authoritative documentation on such a
point!" (Author's note: My interviews with the Dallas doctors and that of the
Boston Globe were taped and the tapes placed in JFK Library. The interviews
were corroborated by others.)
*See Appendix.

fronts us on the merry-go-round of witnesses, when book after book and investigation after investigation rely on the testimony of many medical witnesses, all of whom, at one time or another, has gone on record saying something they do not believe or which contradicts what the actual evidence was in 1963. Jenkins, one of the best observers in the best position to study the head, was rapidly ruined in this manner, and I'm sure it was no accident. It is more than passing strange that Posner would then use him to castigate and destroy with character assassination the character of another good man: Robert McClelland.

More Surprises From Parkland

We have a major operation under way—directed by people well trained in political warfare—who know very well how to wreck testimony that is unfavorable to their cause.

I myself placed a list of those medical witnesses in Dallas, who had testified that Crenshaw was present, in the hands of Dr. Lawrence Altman, the medical reporter for *The New York Times*, whom I met at *JAMA*'s 1992 press conference. Altman came to my own press conference the following week. He shortly published an article establishing that Crenshaw was in fact there and helped out.[58] This is one more damning example of how bad was the research of both the AMA's journal and Gerald Posner.

He completely ignores all that I discovered in many medical interviews to back that up. Both the X-ray technician and the photographer present at the autopsy insist the X-rays and films in the official evidence are not what they took, nor do they represent anything they saw. Posner perhaps means that there is a massive difference in what the autopsy *photographs* and *X-rays* show, what they show that was *not* seen at the autopsy, and what was described at the autopsy and not seen on the photos and X-rays—rather than the essentially identical *descriptions* of the back of the head which he mentions from both hospitals and the autopsy report. The autopsy pathologists indicate that something is seriously wrong with the photos and X-rays, disputed major aspects of the photographs, and indirectly, the X-rays. This is at the crux of the medical issues.

The X-rays certainly fooled many doctors. I was suckered by televised interviews and at first failed to grasp that the missing scalp in the back of the head constituted only part of the area of missing bone which mislead some to think that the hole had moved.

Posner misuses or fabricates quotes from Dr. Charles Carrico. He quotes Carrico as saying, "We saw a large hole on the right side of his head. I don't believe we saw any occipital bone. It was not there. It was parietal bone. . . ."[59] Eliminating the distortion in this by Posner, Carrico is saying that they didn't see occipital bone because it was not there. It was blown out. The only bone they saw was some of the parietal bone in that region. Carrico told the Warren Commission that there was a large hole in the back of the head at least 5 cm around, and said that the "defect was in the posterior skull, the occipital region."[60] Is he going to tell Posner something different?

Posner tells us that Dr. Malcolm Perry, the surgeon who performed the tracheostomy, said, "I did not see any cerebellum."[61] How can we believe this when Perry testified under oath to the United States House of Representatives that: "I looked at the head wound briefly by leaning over the table and noticed that the parietal occipital head wound was largely avulsive and there was visible brain tissue in the macard and some cerebellum present."[62]

Dr. Gary Aguilar writes (of a Posner interview) that it must be "taken with great caution as there was clearly a bias on the part of the questioner, Posner, seeking elicitation. As noted, earliest, uninfluenced witnesses' recollections are most reliable."[63]

Posner seems to have elicited from Dr. Paul Peters what no one else could over thirty years: an apparent change in his story which tends to discredit him. Nothing is changed, but what we have a clarification. Peters originally described to the Warren Report (and to me, and everyone else) a large hole in the back of the head. Posner quotes him as saying, "I now believe the head wound is more forward than I first placed it. More to the side than the rear."[64]*

This would be correct. I have contended that Jacqueline Kennedy closed up that part of the wound that was seen on the side of the head extending from the back, but that she was unable to entirely fit the bones together and the open flap we see in the back-of-the-head photographs above the ear was closed by her—but ajar, as it would not fit completely back in its space. Dr. Robert Grossman at Parkland saw and noted this second hole, as I reported in my first book.[65] A small piece of bone separating the two holes fell in during the transportation of the body to Bethesda, Maryland.

The entire hole, including the flap, the large hole in the posterior part of the head, and the small piece of bone between, therefore, is correctly described in the autopsy report as extending to the temporal area of the head on the right side. This is all Peters is

*See Appendix for Dr. Peters's clarification to the author, April 17, 1995.

saying, but he is merely expressing an opinion, not what he actually saw, because the side of the head portion of the large defect described in the autopsy report was still closed when he observed it. When Peters said, "more forward that I first placed it," this is strictly because of what he has been told and because the autopsy photographs show an intact head in the back. Extending the hole in the skull (though scalp was present) in the rear more to the right side does not change the fact that a large amount of bone and scalp was missing in the rear of the head.

Unfortunately, Posner makes Peters sound like a witness to the enlarged hole at Bethesda, which he was not. Posner repeats speculation and presents it as though it is eyewitness observation. This is how fake pictures fool even the witnesses.

Posner has attempted in his book to obfuscate the existence of a large wound in the area where it is placed in the autopsy report and by the Dallas witnesses, though the latter did not all see the missing bone along the right side and top of the head from the back. One of the enormous lies in this case is the desperate claim that the Dallas witnesses did not have the opportunity to see the back of the head. Another crime is *to discredit even that which the autopsy doctors honestly reported*: the placement of the wound on the right rear side of the head in their autopsy report, as well as the placement of the entry wound on the back of the head four inches below where it is now supposed to be.

It would seem that Posner's real mission is to discredit the autopsy doctors themselves.

The cover-up artists are attempting to discredit this evidence because it doesn't show in the autopsy photographs and X-rays and they have no other way to prove their case. They can't face the fact that the photographs and X-rays are fake. Posner and the other cover-up specialists' mission is to support the findings of the Warren Commission whatever the cost. The autopsy report no longer mattered, once the doctors were forced to stretch a few points. We are spectators and victims of a smoke-and-mirror show where someone can refer obscurely to the "autopsy findings" or the "documents" and then ignore what they say when convenient. Now you see it, now you don't.

Many of the Dallas witnesses at one time or another described looking at the back of the head: Dr. Richard Dulaney told Ben Bradlee, Jr., of the *Boston Globe*: "Somebody lifted up his head and showed me the back of his head. We couldn't see much until they picked up his head. I was standing beside him. The wound was on the back of his head. On the back side." They lifted up his head and "the whole back-side of his head was gone."[66] Dr. Clark picked up the head to show it to Dr. Robert Grossman.[67] Baxter said that he could not see the large hole because it was in the very back of the head and it could not be seen without picking up the head. Baxter said that he saw the wound in the right parietal area. "It was such a benign wound that we thought it was an entry wound."[68] And of course Dr. Giesecke reported to me in 1979 that the head had been picked up. "In fact we shined a light in the cranial vault there, and noticed a large amount of brain missing."[69] And add to this list my finding of Nurse Diana Bowron, who describes in great detail the missing scalp and bone on the back of the head, which she washed and wrapped. Yet one Gerald Posner claims no one in Dallas examined the back of the head. This was worth a lot of money. That is, if he got the publicity and sold the books.

In making your judgment for history, keep in mind what seems to have the most corroboration, or as Dr. Aguilar says, "Eighteen of twenty Parkland witnesses who gave early unrehearsed, and specific descriptions of the head wound, either in writing, verbally, or both, place a major skull defect unambiguously posteriorly on the right. . . . The conclusion that there was a major skull and scalp defect in the rear of JFK's skull based on the descriptions of very qualified and experienced Parkland witnesses cannot be easily or satisfactorily dismissed. The later, contradictory conclusions of those who, despite good credentials, arrived at vastly different conclusions based upon only photographs and X-rays can only be viewed with profound puzzlement."[70] Aguilar goes on to tell us that *all* of the Bethesda witnesses' testimony, including that of the radiologist, the photographer, three Secret Service agents, five technicians, a hospital corpsman, a presidential aide, a physician, and a mortician corroborate the Parkland descriptions of the head wounds.

The conclusion of this is that fourteen Bethesda witnesses, the autopsy doctors, and at least eighteen Parkland Hospital witnesses are wrong in locating the major skull defect in the rear of the skull, according to Posner.[71]

ONE WONDERS AT POSNER'S INCREDIBLE PRESUMPTIVENESS and arrogance when he distorts the evidence—thereby killing the truth. An experienced and nationally respected brain surgeon in Dallas, Dr. Kemp Clark, picked up Kennedy's head and examined the wound. He pronounced Kennedy dead and examined the head more closely. Dr. Clark wrote out a summary the next day and sent it to the President's personal physician, Admiral George Burkley. That summary said that there was "a large wound in the right occipitoparietal region. . . . Both cerebral and cerebellar tissue were extruding from the wound."[72] How could Clark have seen this if he had *not* examined the wound?

Did Admiral Burkley ask for this? Was he trying to find out what the Dallas doctors already knew about this?

6. MISREPRESENTING THE PHOTOGRAPHS AND FILMS

Longtime researcher Martin Shackelford, a state social worker from Saginaw, Michigan, specialized in studying the photographic evidence of the case. He devoted twenty-one pages to Posner's errors in an issue of the research journal, *The Investigator*. He notes Posner's claim that in response to a shot, "the President's arms jerked up," though it is clear in the film that the President's right arm was coming down from a wave. Also, Posner "implies that driver Greer turned back once to look at Kennedy, though the film shows him turning back twice."

Shackelford repeatedly points out incidences of Posner citing photographs to prove some point, but then doesn't include the photo, such as saying that Ruby had a gun in the police station at a press conference on Friday evening, November 22 (p. 379). We don't have any way of knowing what photo he refers to.[73]

Posner "clearly misrepresents the contents of the [Zapruder] film," Shackelford says. Posner wrote that the "The Zapruder home movie shows (Jean) Hill never moved or said a word as the President passed, and she was not even looking at him when he was first shot."[74] Martin says that "At the time of the first shot, (argued at from Z-frame 161 to 210) Jean Hill isn't visible in the Zapruder film (she doesn't appear until frame 287) so the film provides no evidence as to whether she said anything or stepped out and back prior to frame 287."

Posner calls the Zapruder film "incontrovertible evidence that there was no defect on the rear of the head." In fact, the rear of the head is blacked out in currently available copies of the film, with a deeper black than comparable shadows elsewhere in the same film frames. Despite the blacking out, some frames may still show portions of the margins of the rear wound. For further discussion of these issues, see the chapter on the Zapruder film in this book.

He claims to have based his conclusions on "computer enhanced" versions of the Zapruder film, but never says what edition of the film, bootleg or LMH version, how many generations from the original, or what exactly he is calling enhancement. We never see any actual pictures, and the one description given of an "enhancement" technique sounds a lot like computer animation.[75] He cites unenhanced videotape versions of the film that may have no validity whatsoever.

In his attempt to discredit another witness, Ed Hoffman (p. 258), who claimed he saw the assassination, Posner writes: "Even if he was there, his view, 750 to 900 feet away, was blocked. Photographs and independent testimony reveal there were four large railway cars over the Elm Street tunnel that day, effectively obstructing any view from Stemmons into the rear of the Grassy Knoll."[76] If that is the case, and one police officer testified that it was, the railroad cars should show up in Phil Willis photo no. 5, James Altgens photo no. 7, the Patsy Paschall and Mark Bell films, and the Mel McIntire photos, but all show an empty roadbed on the overpass, and no train near enough to have been there at or shortly after the time of the shots. As elsewhere, Posner had here cited "photographs" without providing a clue (or a footnote) as to which photographs he means.

Posner states that "no Secret Service men rode on the running boards," but Shackelford notes that photos taken at the time of the turn on Main Street and after, show agent Clint Hill on the rear running board.

Posner states that Ron Reiland's film footage of Oswald's arrest inside the Texas theater was so underexposed that "nothing developed."[77] The film of the arrest, although underexposed, is good enough to be a part of the videotape, "Films From the Sixth Floor."

Posner also claims that Reiland was the only reporter inside the theater, ignoring reporter Jim MacCammon's photo, published by the Warren Commission (Hill Exhibit A) on the same page as a second MacCammon photo Posner includes in his book (photo section p. 13).

The photo allegedly taken by Oswald of the home of General Edwin Walker has a hole in it where the license plate of a car would be visible. Posner makes a misleading statement (p. 117, footnote 2) about this: "A photo of evidence taken from Oswald's flat after the assassination shows the hole was in the print at that time."

As described in my first book and by other authors, Chief Jesse Curry's book has a photograph of the evidence found at Ruth Paine's house in Irving, and we see the photograph of General Walker's house with a Chevrolet parked in the driveway and a rear license plate clearly visible. The license plate has been cut out of the photograph in later versions of the print. Therefore, Posner's statement is in error. We can see the photograph completely intact on page 113 of Curry's book.§§ The layout of evidence is also known as Exhibit No. 55.

Posner states that he relied on "computer enhancements" of the Zapruder film, including "one done by Dr. Michael West . . . with Johann Rush," though what West and Rush did was a videotape using the film, not a computer enhancement of the film.[78]

7. THERE ARE NO WITNESSES, BUT IT'S THE TRUTH

Posner agrees with the Warren Commission that Jack Ruby entered the basement of the police headquarters via a police ramp to shoot Oswald. But the police officer guarding the ramp, Roy Vaughan, passed more than one lie detector test question that Ruby never got by him that way and must have come in by some other route.[79] Vaughan sued Mark Lane for repeating the same story in a movie made from his work.[80] No witnesses saw Ruby enter down the ramp. Eight witnesses said Ruby did not enter by that route, but the Warren Commission claimed that he came in that way, and Posner buys this. Nobody dared admit what really happened.

Police sergeant Patrick Dean, who was close to the city's Mob boss, Joe Civello, failed a lie detector test with regard to his reassignment of police guards away from the elevators and a door to a stairway next to them just before Ruby shot Oswald. Dean admitted that the door was not locked. The House Committee found that Ruby may have had help from Dallas policemen in entering the basement. I had gone to Donovan Gay, an early aide to the Committee, with information obtained from high-level Dallas sources that Ruby had in fact come down the elevator with assistant chief of police Charles Batchelor. Batchelor later replaced Jesse Curry as chief, after losing both his security charges, President Kennedy and Lee Harvey Oswald, to bullets. Batchelor was far more cooperative with the FBI than Curry had been.

Forrest Sorrels of the Secret Service in Dallas told the Warren Commission under oath that he did not recall hearing Ruby comment on how he got into the basement area. Many years later it was claimed that he heard Ruby say he came into the basement on the ramp. Posner rebuked the Committee, as Scott writes, for ignor-

§§*JFK Assassination File,* Jesse Curry, Limited Collectors Edition, 1969, no longer in circulation. It can also be seen in the third photo section of my book, *High Treason.*

ing " 'the fact that Secret Service agent Forrest Sorrels also said he heard Ruby tell [the Dallas Police] that he had come down the ramp.' He thus rebukes the Committee for ignoring a 'fact' that emerged after its report was published [in 1979].

"Here again Posner downplays an important Committee finding" Scott writes, "by turning again to questionable witnesses and totally ignoring the evidence of official cover-up, in this case by the Dallas police." *Some* of the Dallas police! Not all. Not as an organization. "The lawyerly habit of preferring convenient but discredited witnesses is widespread throughout the book."

Posner tries to do what even the police could not do. The most difficult problem the Warren Commission and the FBI had was to place Oswald in the alleged sniper's window. The Chief of Police of Dallas, Jesse Curry, could not put Oswald there. "Posner's worst abuse of testimony occurs with respect to Oswald's location before the fatal shots," Scott writes. Too many people saw Oswald on the first and second floor (where he was interviewed by a policeman and the Depository supervisor ninety seconds after the last shots were fired) minutes before the shooting began, in fact at the very moment that the motorcade was due by, though it was five minutes late. Five other witnesses who later claimed they saw Oswald on an upper floor before the assassination also saw Oswald on the second floor when the officer did. If Oswald had intended to kill Kennedy, he would be in the alleged sniper's window, and not on the first or second floor at the time the motorcade was due.

Scott writes that Posner "reports such alleged sighting as fact: 'At 11:40 one of the workers, Bonnie Ray Williams, spotted Oswald on the east side of the floor, near the windows overlooking Dealey Plaza.' "[81] This is more than three-quarters of an hour before the shooting, and "the problem with this convenient story is that Williams, as if to satisfy his exigent examiners, changed his story not once but twice. An earlier FBI interview on November 23, 1963, reported Williams as saying that he had seen Oswald on the fifth floor about 11:30 A.M.; and that Williams had returned to the sixth floor about noon and seen no one. On November 22, only a few hours after the assassination, Williams had signed and sworn to a Dallas police affidavit saying categorically: 'I didn't see Oswald anymore, that I remember, after I saw him at 8:00 A.M.' " In a Southern city where a number of the police were members of the Ku Klux Klan, here were some terrified black people who would say and do what they were told which would vary from hour to hour or day to day according to who was making them do what.

Scott points out that the Warren Commission knew the problem with Williams and did not use this testimony which Posner relies heavily upon. But the Commission did use his safer story that he heard shots fired from the floor above him and plaster or cement falling on his head. Of course the floors and their beams were wooden!

Williams's story was corroborated by Harold Norman and "Junior" Jarman, his two coworkers with whom he watched the motorcade on the fifth floor. Scott comments that

indeed, the corroboration is so precise that one's suspicions are raised, especially since none of the three had reported their important earwitness accounts to the Dallas police.

The Warren Commission needed an eyewitness to Oswald on the sixth floor in order to combat three eyewitness stories that Oswald had spent this period on the first or second floor of the building. . . . Posner reports the elevator-encounter story [with Oswald] as if it were incontestable fact. Posner also names Jack Dougherty as a witness to an 11:45 A.M. elevator-encounter citing, without page reference, an 'affidavit of Jack E. Dougherty, November 22, 1963.' *When Posner omits page references one's suspicions are rightly aroused* [author's emphasis]. The affidavit says nothing about an elevator encounter at all. The big problem here is that the witness score of five (for upstairs) versus three (for downstairs) had originally been one, or later two (for upstairs) versus four (for downstairs). The problematic nature of this evidence had been noted in an early Warren Commission internal memo of February 25, 1964. By March, all five who had declared for upstairs had changed their stories so. None had done so more suspiciously than the one witness, Charles Givens, whom Posner chooses (without any hint of this problem) as his main source."[82] Sylvia Meagher pointed out in 'The Curious Testimony of Mr. Givens,' that Givens altered his story four times in less than half a year.[83] He started as a downstairs witness and ended up as an upstairs witness!

According to an FBI memo of November 22, 1963, Givens had told the FBI that at 11:00 A.M. he had seen Oswald reading a paper in the 'domino room' on the first floor. In his Warren commission testimony of April 8, 1964, Givens told counsel Belin that he had never made the earlier statement, and claimed (for the first time in the official record) that he had seen Oswald on the sixth floor just before noon. Meagher reported that police intelligence chief Jack Revill told the FBI in February 1964 that he believed that 'Givens would change his story for money.'[84] Revill testified to the Warren Commission in May 1964, that Givens told him on the day of the assassination that he had seen Oswald on the sixth floor.

Finally there is the lawyerly approach: to tell less, not more, to suppress the difficulties with the testimony that is preferred, and to invent nonexistent problems with the testimony of witnesses one wishes to discredit. This is the approach of Posner in *Case Closed*. Instead of admitting, and discussing, the problems with the sixth-floor witnesses who recanted their own testimony, Posner completely ignores these problems, and creates the false impression that it is a key first-floor witness who has contradicted herself.[85]

That witness is Carolyn Arnold, who told Anthony Summers that she saw Oswald in the second-floor lunchroom at 12:15, ten minutes before the motorcade was due. Posner and other apologists have got to knock her out of the case at all costs. Not only Arnold but two other witnesses saw Oswald there: William Shelley and Eddie Piper. Posner says that Shelley saw Oswald on the sixth floor at 11:45 A.M. and Posner supplies no citation for this statement.[86] Even if true, this is sufficient time for Oswald to go downstairs. Shelley told the Warren Commission that he saw Oswald on the first floor at "about ten to twelve." Scott writes: "The difference of five minutes, trivial in practice, is devastating to Posner's logic, for 11:50 is the Commission's time for the first encounter at the elevator on the fifth floor. In other words, Shelley's testimony cannot be written off as compatible with the highly dubious elevator story."

Scott then accuses Posner in the most polite way possible of hallucinating:

> The apparent problem with Arnold's testimony is an artifact of Posner's own lawyerly imagination. Arnold never told the FBI she 'did not see (Oswald) at all.' She said that she 'did not see Lee Harvey Oswald at the time President Kennedy was shot.' [Neither did anyone else in the building, and they were all later asked this.]
>
> It is highly misleading to say that 'Arnold told Summers the FBI misquoted her, though she had signed her statement as correct.[87] Here Posner conflates two different FBI statements, one of November 26, 1963, about seeing Oswald on the first floor (where she later claimed to have been misquoted), and one of March 28, 1964, about not seeing Oswald at the time of the assassination (which she had signed as correct.) Thus there is no evidence that Arnold ever contradicted herself. One might normally suspect witnesses who deny making statements attributed to them by the FBI. But Posner has no grounds for doing so in this case. As he is quite aware, three of his upper-floor witnesses (Givens, Williams, and Norman, whose final stories are reported as gospel)

had denied under oath making earlier statements attributed to them by the FBI and/or Secret Service. Arnold's different memory after fourteen years is hardly comparable to the dramatic differences in reported stories from Givens after a few weeks, or even hours.

Scott begins to close his review of Posner's book with a very strong statement: "I call Posner's treatment lawyerly, because he is trying both to make some very problematic sixth-floor witnesses seem cleaner than they were, and to make a first-floor witness seem more problematic than she really was. But at times his abuse of evidence goes beyond legal propriety. . . ." and then after giving an example of Posner's with regard to the testimony of Danny Arce, Jack Dougherty, and Charles Givens (all three of them upper-floor witnesses who had changed their stories and claimed that they were eating in the lunch room at 12:15 and saw no sign of Oswald there) Scott notes that Posner gives a footnoted citation in 6 H 351 of the Warren Commission Hearings. "But on that page we find the exact opposite testimony." David Belin asks Givens if he ate in the building, and he replies that he did not. "Givens's testimony is consistent with his original affidavit to the Dallas Police that at twelve noon he took his lunch break and left the building. After this discovery, one can raise questions about the other alleged witnesses as well.

"Not every page of Posner's book is as full of distortions as this one. I have no trouble admitting that the evidence is confusing and the Depository witness testimony problematic. It is Posner, in his desire to find the *Case Closed*, who must introduce a false simplicity that in fact is not to be found. There will be those who argue that Posner is after all a lawyer, and we should expect no better of him."[88]

8. THERE IS NO EVIDENCE, BUT IT'S THE TRUTH

Delving into the mind of Lee Harvey Oswald, Posner says that guns were "things he had wanted for some time," but presents no supporting documentation of any kind.[89]

Posner attempts to dispose of a number of other questions that would take exhaustive exposition here to expose, beyond the scope of this chapter and which are adequately dealt with elsewhere. Among those points are the fact that witnesses, including a police officer, were met by men on the Grassy Knoll after the last shot who showed police or Secret Service credentials. Posner dismisses this as mistaken identity.* He writes that "no evidence of a shooter" was found on the Grassy Knoll[90] to mean that there was none, when the other evidence taken together (the Zapruder film, medical observations, footprints in the mud, mud on a fender, the sound of shots placed by witnesses there, and so on) indicates that there were shooters in the area. The indications are far too strong to ever be dismissed as long as the history of this case will be read in the future. Posner cannot reverse that fact.

Posner says that Kennedy's throat wound was "obliterated" by the tracheostomy,[91] though the wound's margins are seen clearly in the frontal autopsy photo (unless the semicircle on the edge of the center of the lower lip of the wound is the impression of a tracheal tube), enough so for Shackelford to reconstruct the wound from the photo for the March 1994 *Fourth Decade*, p. 24.

Posner sets up straw men to make himself look good when he knocks them down. Here is another example: He writes that "There is an oft-repeated story of an FBI photographer without any prior autopsy experience, who allegedly took the (autopsy) photographs,"[92] but gives no source for this. No news like this ever surfaced before Posner came along, and there is nothing at all in the testimony or evidence about any FBI photographer. Posner's purpose becomes clear when he then burdens Dr. Humes with the issue. The doctor vehemently denounces the notion in the next sentence. Making Humes angry is a good way to get his cooperation and tire him out at the same time. The book is a continuing exercise in faulty logic. Posner's game gives him something to ask Dr. Humes, which Humes can vehemently denounce as "more nonsense from the critics."

The FBI photographer story comes not from a Commission critic but from Dr. Michael Baden, upon whom Posner relies heavily. In his book, *Unnatural Death*, Baden fantasizes that this FBI man "had never taken autopsy pictures before and was untrained in photographing gunshot wounds. His pictures showed it. . . . None of his pictures clearly defined the entrance or exit wounds."[93]

Was Humes told that Dr. Baden was the source of this "incredible lie"? That would get a rise out of him, certainly. But Posner's readers don't need to know.

_____

*An important analysis of the question by Chris Mills, "The Man Who Wasn't There," was recently published in England in *Dallas 63* (June 1995) which showed that Secret Service agent Lem Johns had left the motorcade just after the shooting and run up on the Knoll where he encountered NBC photographer Dave Wiegman and Dallas police officer J.M. Smith. This is one explanation, if the man with the credentials is real.

Posner claims that the man who found the "magic bullet" (CE 399), Darrell Tomlinson, "was not certain from which (stretcher) the bullet had dropped,"[94] but, as Shackelford points out (as did Josiah Thompson long ago, in *Six Seconds in Dallas*) Tomlinson's "description of the stretcher from which the bullet came didn't match Connally's stretcher; Posner also accepts that the bullet was CE 399, though Tomlinson's and O. P. Wright's descriptions of it don't match CE 399."[95]

Shackelford comments that "Posner greatly exaggerates the number of people who would have had to be party to 'a plot' for Ruby to have been planning to kill Oswald."[96] But, like guerilla armies, conspirators coalesce like streams finding rivers after a storm.

9. SINS OF OMISSION

The evidence is well established that Oswald thought highly of Kennedy and bore no grudge against him. It is not rational, therefore, that he would have participated in a plot to kill him, or killed him on his own. Had Oswald shot Kennedy, he would have been glad to see him dead, and this would have been immediately apparent. It wasn't. Posner's failure to deal with the subject of Oswald's admiration for Kennedy is one of many serious flaws in his book.

Again and again Posner misuses Failure Analysis, stating that he relied on a computer study they did "proving" Oswald did it alone, and ignores their other study demonstrating more than one gunman. In addition, Posner ignores the presentation by Failure Analysis president Dr. Roger McCarthy showing that holes in a skull, with "beveling," can be caused *without* a bullet entry *or* exit in that location, as the result of explosive damage to the skull blowing *out* weak spots.[97] Posner notes that Failure Analysis' "cone" projection centers on the sixth-floor Depository window[98] but fails to add that the cone includes windows of the Dal-Tex Building across the street, a more likely place for some of the shots to have come from. Posner's and Random House's illustration fails to place the Dal-Tex Building, well within the cone, in the picture of that city corner at all. "This version deals with the problem by simply omitting the Dal-Tex Building, lest the reader become 'confused' by all the facts," Shackelford writes. "Also, the smaller cone only works if the reader accepts the 'single bullet' and Posner's choice of Zapruder frames for the moment when it impacted."[99] Posner misleadingly refers to computer analysis of the Zapruder film as "enhancements" and not what they are: analysis.[100] Garbage in, garbage out!

"It sounds impressive that they 'fixed the position of the limousine and the postures of Kennedy and Connally at the precise moments of impact,' except they fixed the positions at the 'precise moments' they were *told* were the frames of impact. If that information was inaccurate, so is the analysis. Of course, Posner states this is based on 'careful analysis', but fails to note this analysis was *not* done with a computer,"[101] Shackelford tells us.[102]

Posner's drawing also inaccurately depicts all of the windows in the building as being closed. At least twelve were open, and the sniper's window was not all the way open, as Posner has it, but open only about one-third of the way.[103]

"He avoids a detailed a description of the Mannlicher-Carcano rifle ordered by Oswald," Shackelford writes, "thus avoiding having to explain why it didn't match the one found in the Book Depository in November."[104]

"He regards the issue of the three tramps resolved by the identifications in February 1992,[105] but eleven arrest reports were found for the railroad yards," Martin writes, "and it is not clear the three publicized were the 'famous' three photographed by newsmen."[106] Then Posner makes some demonstrably false statements: He attributes the Chauncey Holt-Charles Harrelson tramp story to the *Globe* tabloid,[107] instead of other researchers who long ago believed that Harrelson was the tall tramp. Police trained in photo identification have since confirmed this to me. Posner wrote that "the conspiracy press suddenly and quietly abandoned the issue,"[108] which is untrue since several articles were published after that.[109] This is another example of Posner's sloppy research.

Posner fails to mention, as Martin notes, "that the palm print on the rifle was an old one, definitely not put there on November 22,[110] and that the print is not where a print would result from assembling the rifle."[111]

"Posner repeats the myth that Guy Banister was mistaken for Clay Shaw in the Clinton, Louisiana, incident.[112] What he fails to mention is that one of the witnesses, Henry Palmer, had served in the Navy with Banister, and was quite firm the man was not Banister."[113] Also, Sheriff John Manchester, who identified Clay Shaw from his driver's license, said: "He gave Clay Shaw, which corresponded to his driver's license."[114]

The same methods are used when Posner states: "There simply is no credible evidence that Oswald ever had an office at 544 Camp Street or, much less, that he knew Guy Banister." This requires him to dismiss the testimony of two witnesses, and ignore at least nine more. Oswald didn't rent an office, but he used Banister's address. Banister was a government operative running Oswald in New Orleans.

Posner claims that there was no tape of an Oswald phone call to the Soviet embassy in Mexico City.[115] How could there not be a tape of whoever it was claiming to be Oswald? Can anyone imagine that we did not have that embassy bugged? And certainly, the CIA has always put forth or claimed all sorts of evidence that Oswald called there. W. David Slawson of the Warren Commission heard the recording of the alleged Oswald.[116] Shackelford comments that "Posner goes on to say: 'Since there was no—tape recording proving he was there,' as though he had proven the tape was nonexistent.[117] A few pages later, he notes Oleg Nechiporenko's mention of a call from Oswald."[118]* Someone *posed* as Lee Harvey Oswald, and it wasn't really him. That's why no one can hear those tapes.

Posner uncritically accepts Humes's statement that "Nobody made any decisions in the morgue except me. Nobody distracted or influenced me in any way, shape, or form."[119] He ignores extensive evidence of numerous flag officers present and the statements of several of the doctors and others that there was in fact interference. The House Committee found that Humes himself was responsible for certain things not being done, such as tracking the alleged bullet through the neck, sectioning the brain, and so on,[120] but he nevertheless checked off that the autopsy was "complete,"[121] a conclusion that Lt. Col. Pierre Finck disagreed with.[122] Nevertheless, the critique of the House Select Committee of the autopsy itself,[123] which among other things stated that "proper photographs" were not taken[124] and much more, must be taken into account.

We have every indication, including that of the FBI report, that the bullet that struck the back did not penetrate, and Posner ignores massive evidence that the back wound did not penetrate the back, including statements of the men present,[125] the FBI report (Sibert and O'Neill) of the autopsy, and so on. Something *else* got into the chest which caused the need in Dallas for drainage tubes to be inserted.

Posner states that the autopsists "'did not know there was an exit hole in the front of his neck." True, they did not know that. The next day, officially, they were told that there was an entry hole in the neck, but that it was obliterated by the tracheostomy. Dr. Humes

*See articles by Gary Rowell on Oswald and Mexico City in the first and second issues of *The Investigator*, printed by him, in November 1992 and February 1993.

converted the entry hole by supposition into an exit hole, neither of which he had seen. Dr. Burkley was in Dallas and had to have known and told the Bethesda doctors about it. Dr. Robert Livingston wrote me to say that he told Dr. Humes before the autopsy began that there was a bullet entry hole in the throat,[126] and there are other mentions of it in the interviews the House Committee held back from the public. Audrey Bell reported calls to Dr. Perry "in the middle of the night,"[127] and Dr. Robert Karnei said, "I was convinced they talked to somebody that night ... Pierre Finck, I think, talked to somebody."[128] An entry hole is not an exit.

10. BLENDING THE EYEWITNESS TESTIMONY

Jim Folliard is an accountant in Newport, Rhode Island, with an usually fine sense of language and a philosophical turn of mind. He has published many well-written articles and has intensely studied the Kennedy assassination.

"Posner's methodology," Folliard writes of *Case Closed*, "persists in confusing rather than clarifying the key issues in the case; one that rarely engages in analytical dialogue with the basic sources and with previous accounts and interpretations. More often than not, it misrepresents, distorts, or ignores them, and instead pursues a never-ending spiral of new witnesses, new documents and new 'sources.' This 'methodology' virtually guarantees that the case will *never* be closed."[129]

Nowhere does Posner prove Oswald did it. He makes his case with what he calls "common sense, logic, and scrupulous documentation." Folliard then picks to pieces that so-called documentation and scholarship beginning with the Frazier-Randle testimony about how Lee Harvey Oswald supposedly got the rifle into the School Book Depository.

In his analysis of Posner, Folliard takes the approach of spotlighting one small detail in order to point out just how Posner's methods work. Posner writes that when Oswald was supposed to have taken a package of curtain rods (later alleged to be the rifle) to the Book Depository the morning of the assassination, "He held one end of the brown-paper-wrapped object tucked under his armpit, and the other end did not quite touch the ground."[130]

"To build 'an unshakable case' for Lee Harvey Oswald as JFK's killer, it must be established that: (1) Oswald owned or had access to the alleged murder weapon, and (2) that he got the weapon from its storage place (allegedly Ruth Paine's garage in Irving) to the Texas School Book Depository where he worked, and where he presumably fired the fatal shots."[131] A homemade paper bag was found in the Depository which was thirty-eight inches long. The disassembled rifle was thirty-five inches long, and put together with its stock was about forty inches in length. It is claimed that Oswald put the bag together, took it home with him and returned with the rifle, driven by Wesley Buell Frazier. Frazier lived with his sister, Linnie Mae Randle.

It is in this bag that Oswald allegedly brought the rifle to the Depository, and both Frazier and Randle saw it but said Oswald told them that it contained curtain rods. The key in this story is the size of the bag and how Oswald carried it. If there was a rifle in the bag, it would have been impossible for Oswald, whose arm was not that long, to have one end of the bag under his armpit and the other cupped in the palm of his hand, yet this is how the witnesses described his carrying of the bag.

Mrs. Randle told Joseph Ball of the Warren Commission that Oswald "carried it in his right hand, had the top sort of folded down and had a grip like this, and the bottom, he carried it this way, you know, and it almost touched the ground as he carried it."

Ball: "And where was his hand gripping, the middle of the package?"

Mrs. Randle: "No, sir, the top, with just a little bit sticking up."[132]

Then, in a separate incident, Wesley Buell Frazier testifies to how the bag was carried.

Ball: "When you saw him get out of the car, when you first saw him when he was out of the car before he started to walk, you noticed he had the package under the arm?"

Frazier: "Yes, sir."

Ball: "One end of it was under the armpit and the other he had to hold it in his right hand. Did the package extend beyond the right hand?"

Frazier: "No, sir. Like I say if you put it under your armpit and put it down normal to the side."

Ball: "But the right hand on, was it on the end or the side of the package?"

Frazier: "No; he had it cupped in his hand."[133]

"Posner has taken two separate incidents involving Oswald's use of two separate methods for carrying the bag, and conflated them into one," Folliard writes. "This of course conveniently conveys the impression that the bag was long enough to reach from armpit to just above the ground—long enough to hold the disassembled rifle. And long enough to match, in size, the paper wrapper found at the sniper's nest and entered into evidence as a Warren Commission exhibit."[134]

Posner has repeatedly melded parts of testimony from two or more different areas into one impression and then proceeds to make it say what he wants it to say. He did it with Dr. Marion Jenkins and others. Both he and *The Journal of the American Medical Association* are guilty of the same sort of academic crime. In fact, he often seems to have switched the question he has asked a witness to another, which he attaches to the answer his question got, if he didn't get the right answer.

I measure twenty-five inches from the inside of my armpit to the tip of my fingers on my right arm, holding a yardstick. If I cup my hand, it is twenty-two inches long.

Frazier had described the bag as follows: "It is right as you get out of the grocery store, just more or less out of a package, you have seen some of these brown paper sacks you can obtain from any, most of the stores, some varieties, but it was a package just roughly about two feet long." Twenty-four inches! That's one foot too short for his disassembled rifle.

Posner says that "Both Randle and Frazier said [the Warren Commission exhibit] looked like the same one Oswald carried that morning."[135] Yet, Ball asks Frazier, "Now we have over here this exhibit for identification which is 364 which is a paper sack made out of tape, sort of a homemade affair . . . Does it appear to be the same length?"

"No, sir."

Ball: "When you were shown this bag, do you recall whether or not you told the officers who showed you the bag—did you tell them whether you thought it was or was not about the same length as the bag you saw on the backseat?"

Frazier: "I told them that as far as the length there, I told them that it was entirely too long."

Ball continues to question young Frazier: ". . . put it [the bag] under your armpit. . . . Are you sure his hand was at the end of the package or at the side of the package?"

Frazier: "Like I said, I remember I didn't look at the package very much, paying much attention, but when I did look at it he did have his hands on the package like that."

Ball: "But you said a moment ago you weren't sure whether the package was longer or shorter."

Frazier: "What I was talking about, I said I didn't know where it extended. It could have or couldn't have, out this way, widthwise, not lengthwise."

Ball: "In other words, you say it could have been wider than your original estimate?"

Frazier: "Right."

Ball: "But you didn't think it was longer than his hands?"

Frazier: "Right." He did not observe the bag's width very well, but he never wavered in his observations about its length, as Folliard points out.

Linnie Mae Randle talked about how the bag looked, too. Ball asked her, "We have got a package here. . . . You have seen this before, I guess, haven't you, I think the FBI showed it to you. . . . Now, was the length of it similar, anywhere near similar?"

"Well, it wasn't that long, I mean it was folded down at the top as I told you. It definitely wasn't that long."

"This looks too long?"

"Yes, sir."

"You figure about two feet long, is that right?"

"A little bit more." Randle folds the bag to the size she remembers. She folded it to about twenty-eight and a half inches, and she said "I measured twenty-seven last time." She had practiced before her testimony.

This is nowhere near the thirty-five to thirty-eight inches in length the bag would have to be to contain even a broken-down rifle. "*All* the testimony suggests quite the opposite," Folliard writes. "They did not think the bag in evidence looked like the one Oswald carried.

"But Posner doesn't give up: He's like a strike-out victim trying to reach first base when the catcher drops the ball: 'Frazier later admitted the package could have been *longer* than he originally thought: 'I only glanced at it . . . hardly paid any attention to it. He had the package parallel to his body, and it's true it could have extended beyond his body and I wouldn't have noticed it.' "[136]

Either Randle and Frazier are lying or mistaken, "or else the package Oswald carried that morning did not contain the rifle," Folliard writes. "By itself, the *complete and correct* Randle-Frazier testimony is not conclusive or definite—*either way*—as to whether Lee Harvey Oswald fired the shots with the Mannlicher-Carcano on November 22, 1963. Similarly, Posner's manipulation and misrepresentation of evidence in this matter is not conclusive for judging his entire book."[137]

Folliard comments: "A grocery-store sack approximately two feet long does not bear much resemblance to a homemade wrapper held together by tape and measuring approximately three feet long."

The Dallas police found no finger or palm prints on the sniper's nest paper bag. But the FBI claimed that they did. They found one fingerprint and one palm print, the latter at the bottom of the bag. There was a similar story with the rifle, which contained no fingerprints. Three days later, a palm print showed up at the FBI.

The Warren Commission found that the palm print was at the bottom of the bag, which, according to Posner, "concurred with how Buell Frazier and his sister, Linnie Mae Randle, testified he carried the package."[138] Randle did *not* testify to the bag being carried this way, as Folliard points out. "And of course Posner made absolutely no allusion to this testimony of *Frazier—alone—*in his earlier, *principal discussion* of the Randle-Frazier evidence on pp. 224–5. There he distorted testimony by conflating it—. . . . Frazier's 'armpit' combined with Randle's package 'not far from the ground' allows him to posit a package plenty long enough to accommodate a rifle, and to claim the testimony of two witnesses in its support.

"On page 272, Posner distorts by *omission*: not a word about an armpit, and specifically how *Frazier alone* saw Oswald with one end of the bag tucked under his armpit, the other held by his right hand. Having made his main point on pp. 224–5, about the length of the bag, Posner *qualifies* the point forty-seven pages later. On a 'technicality,' Posner could claim to be complete and accurate. After all, he has mentioned both methods used to carry the bag. And both witnesses did say Oswald gripped the bag in his right hand!

"Posner's distortions may not necessarily be deliberate, but only the result of slipshod methods and/or unfamiliarity with the issues and evidence. No matter: the book simply abounds with similar attempts to 'have it both ways.' "[139]

Posner, page 245: "*There were a good many witnesses who saw the actual shooter, or the rifle itself, and in every instance they identified the same location—the southwest corner of the sixth floor of the Texas School Book Depository.*" Folliard says that, "Posner takes pains to discredit witnesses who claimed to see more than one man near the sniper's nest, or (b) a gunman at a different window (pp. 229–231")[.140]

Posner, page 247: James Worrell looked up at the Depository after the first shot and "saw something few others did, the rifle actually fire, 'what you might call a little flash of fire and then smoke.'" Posner has nothing to say about this. On page 256, the subject is possible rifle smoke seen on the Grassy Knoll: "In addition, since modern ammunition is smokeless, it seldom creates even a wisp of smoke." Technically, Posner can't be faulted. After all he can claim that the judgment on page 256 also applies to the incident from page 247, nine pages earlier. "But is this an impartial, evenhanded, consistent, and thorough evaluation of all the evidence? Hardly. Besides, the claim about smokeless ammunition itself must be qualified," Folliard says.[141]

Under the heading of Posner as Scientist: The Medical/Ballistics Evidence, Folliard says that we are "like spectators at a ping-pong game, we're treated to a continual back-and-forth over whether President Kennedy was first struck in the *back* or in the *neck*. If the wound was in his back, then the famous 'throat wound' could hardly be a wound of exit, but virtually conclusive as evidence for at least one shot from the front of the motorcade. Even Posner gets tired of the game, and discovers a new and exquisitely precise anatomical location, the 'shoulder/neck.'"[142]

The *U.S. News & World Report* issue on Posner's book says the Warren Commission thought the bullet struck Kennedy in the *"base of the neck."* They admit that Secret Service agent Glen Bennett wrote that he saw the bullet strike *"about four inches down from the right shoulder,"* and "When (Bennett) made his notes it was not known that the President had been hit in the *rear neck/shoulder.*"[143]

It is worth repeating some of the evidence of just where that back wound was, which the FBI report said did not pass through the back. We can't repeat it enough. The FBI men, Sibert and O'Neill, wrote that "Dr. Humes located an opening which was below the shoulders" and did not exit.[144] Clint Hill, the Secret Service man who had climbed up on the trunk of the fatal limousine in Dallas as it sped off down the street after the last shots said that he "saw an opening about six inches below the neckline" at the autopsy;[145] Agent Roy Kellerman[146] and the driver of the car, William Greer, said that the wound was in the "right shoulder" which is *not at all* the "neck/shoulder."[147]

With regard to the "scientific" evidence in the case, Folliard notes that *"Science* by itself cannot be faulted for the confusion surrounding the physical evidence in JFK's murder. Ballistics analysis and forensic medicine—to name two very relevant applied sciences—have well-established methods, procedures, and documentation standards. It is reasonable to conclude that, had these methods and standards been applied to the evidence as they were meant to be applied, there would be little room for confusion or doubt over such a basic fact as the location of President Kennedy's wounds. Most disturbing is not so much the dispute over how to interpret such facts, but that the 'facts' themselves are still described with such unscientific imprecision . . . like Gerald Posner's anatomical rarity, 'the shoulder/neck.' In the absence of conclusive 'scientific' evidence about such an elementary fact, it seems that the most reasonable recourse is to go to the (next) best evidence: what people observed and reported they observed *at the relevant time*—November 22, 1963. To do this, of course, one must overcome the pseudoscientific vogue of maligning eyewitness testimony."[148]

Posner also misrepresents the size of the hole in Connally's shoulder as being 1¼"(3 cm) long. This was how long the wound was after Dr. Shaw cut away most of the area around the bullet's entrance, which he described as about 1.5 cm across. Shaw did not believe the wound was made by a tumbling bullet.[149]

Posner fails to grasp that the damage to Kennedy's shirt and tie[150] some of which may have been scalpel cuts when the clothing was cut away.

The autopsy drawing on the descriptive sheet made by Dr. Boswell has the wound some six inches down on the back, exactly where the bullet holes are in the shirt and coat, which the autopsy doctors did not see at that time. The various descriptions by Dr. Burkley and others that the wound was at the level of the third or fourth thoracic vertebra also place it well down on the back.

One cannot discuss the "single-bullet theory" without bearing in mind the above information on just how far down the nonpenetrating wound really was.

The simple truth and the simple refutation of Posner and the Warren Commission is the fact that the bullet did not penetrate the back and it was too far down on the back to come out his neck and go through John Connally. There are other refutations, such as the amount of lead that was really found in Connally (exceeding that lost from the bullet that was allegedly discovered at the hospital). Posner tries to rely on the work of one of the three presentations made by Failure Analysis, which tried to demonstrate that the single-bullet theory might be plausible, and ignores their own refutations of that theory, as discussed at the beginning of this chapter, and that fails for the reasons explained there. "It is yet another example of the author's casual approach to documentation—his disregard for the very methods and restraints of science itself."[151]

Folliard wrote, "*Case Closed* is a fatally flawed, intellectually dishonest effort. One wonders then at the adulation being heaped on it in the media and academic professions. One marvels at the obsession which the guardians of the national story bring to the task of closing off discussions of what is—in their eyes—nothing more than a thirty-year old 'aberration' in American history, an unfortunate 'interruption in our regular programming' by a lone nut who didn't want to be part of the American story anyhow. So why bother?

"To close the Kennedy case, as Gerald Posner would have us close it, is to tell the American people that a whole range of 'cases' ought to be closed: 'cases,' in other words, that are none of the American public's business; 'cases' that in dollar cost alone are sufficient to account for the entire national deficit. Like how "Desert Storm" came about, or the BCCI and savings-and-loan scandals, or how the U.S. government to this day is the major clandestine support for the international drug trade; or how taxpayers spent one million dollars a day for ten years in covert support for "death squads" in El Salvador; or maybe even the AIDS epidemic. That's why "assassination research" must be closed off.

"And that's why it must be done well."

Folliard writes, of Posner's use of Failure Analysis: "The reader is asked to trust the superior, up-to-date methods and techniques of this firm, but searches in vain for any basis for such trust—information about the company, its track record, or about what it actually *did*. Not even an address!"[152]

11. POSNER THE CUSTOM TAILOR

One of the supposed myths Posner tries to demolish is the evidence that Oswald was fluent in Russian. Posner first discusses Oswald's difficult effort to teach himself in his spare time in the service, an effort that could not compare to Berlitz or the military's Monterey school of languages.[153] He then cites a few people he talked to who were in Russia when Oswald arrived, some of whom are tainted by other interests and thus compromised. We can't trust any of this. What we *can* trust are those Russians living in the United States who knew Oswald well when he returned from Russia and found that he was so completely fluent in the language that he had no accent, and that he read, wrote, and spoke it almost perfectly.[154]

George DeMohrenschildt wrote an unpublished book about Oswald, which the House of Representatives printed.[155] In it, Oswald's closest friend in the U.S., DeMohrenschildt, an educated, aristocratic nobleman who had great respect for him and who many feel was the government's agent in watching Oswald closely, wrote that other Russians were amazed by Lee's almost perfect command of the language (Russian)." "Lee's English was perfect, refined, rather literary, deprived of any Southern accent. He sounded like a very

educated American. But to know Russian as he did was remarkable—to appreciate serious literature—was something out of the
ordinary."[156]

This is one more example of the type of *non*issue which Posner
repeatedly raises in his distortions to trick the reader and the nation. The trick lay in the fact that Posner presents Oswald when he
was first trying to learn Russian, however long it took, and ignores
the end result of the man's great effort in a very difficult language.
Oswald mastered it. The whole issue raised by Posner so he can
demolish it was never an issue in the first place, but demolishing it
makes him feel like a champion, a heavyweight who crushed a
flyweight.

SHACKELFORD'S COMMENT ON THE SHOOTING of officer Tippit deserves
to be quoted in full: "Posner accepts the official version of the
Tippit shooting.[157] He glides over contradictory evidence of Oswald
speaking to Tippit through the open passenger side window of the
police car [which was closed] by referring instead to 'the open vent
window.'[158] He cites 1:15 as the shooting time, giving Oswald plenty
of time to get there, by saying Bowley and Benavides used the police
radio 'immediately' to call in a report,[159] but Bowley, who arrived
after the shooting, reported the time as 1:10 (he looked at his watch
when he arrived).[160] This is consistent with the account of Benavides, who reported waiting 'a few minutes' before going to Tippit's
car, fumbling with the radio (he was unable to operate it), before
Bowley came over and made the call.[161] Helen Markham identified
the time as 1:06 or 1:07, as she was on the corner waiting for the
1:15 bus (four witnesses put the shooting as early as one o'clock).[162]
Posner seems to prefer the convenient version over the probable
one. He cites the Warren Commission testimony of Warren Reynolds, suggesting there would be no witness-related motive for the
January 1964 shooting of Reynolds,[163] failing to note that Reynolds's
earlier account differed from the one he gave, post-shooting, to the
Commission. He states 'there is no credible eyewitness testimony
that undercuts the evidence that Oswald was the shooter,'[164] dismissing those who gave a different description of the shooter and reported a second man with him."[165] Credible seems to be defined
as agreeing with Posner's thesis.

Shackelford writes about Posner's inadequate chapter note (p.
566) citing testimony of Ruby and of Arthur Watherwax: "Nothing
from that sentence comes from Ruby's cited testimony, leaving one
to wonder why it is cited, except to mislead the reader."[166]

Folliard points out several major conflicts in the behavior of Marina and Lee and their relationship with each other, and Folliard comments on Posner's failure to deal with it: "People do not always behave with logical consistency, yet such discordances are the exception rather than the rule. Posner makes no attempt to sort out exception from rule in the behavior patterns of Lee—and Marina—Oswald. . . . It's hard to understand how a well-informed author like Posner would not see them, be curious about them, and comment on them. . . . But the largest and strangest anomaly is this: Posner offers no political context at all for the assassination event."[167] We know how *Oswald despised both the right wing and segregation, things Kennedy worked against. How could Oswald have killed him?*

"Posner's onesidedness is also revealed in how he constantly draws attention—in a pejorative way—to the 'uncorroborated' stories of his mentally disturbed witnesses. . . . He had a chance to be equally 'right' by pointing out all his 'uncorroborated' evidence against Lee Harvey Oswald, especially Marina's. But that's a chance someone bent on 'closing the case' could not afford to take."

Posner reports Carolyn Arnold, who saw Oswald on the second floor at 12:15, as telling the FBI she didn't see Oswald at all. What she told them was that she "did not see Lee Harvey Oswald at the time President Kennedy was shot." Posner mixes elements from two different FBI reports.

Concerning Oswald's whereabouts in the time period of the assassination, Shackelford writes that "in his zeal to confirm the findings of the Warren Commission, Posner adopts some of its bad habits. An example (p. 226–8) is his summary of Oswald's movements from 11:45 A.M. until 12:30 P.M. He implies that no one saw Oswald during this period, explicitly dismissing the testimony of Carolyn Arnold. He completely ignores the testimony of Bonnie Ray Williams and Billy Lovelady, who both said Oswald asked them to send the elevator back up for him; William Shelley, who saw Oswald on the first floor about five minutes later, at 11:50; Eddie Piper, who saw Oswald on the first floor at noon; and Mary Hollies, who saw Oswald on the second floor about 12:25, the time when the motorcade was due. This doesn't sound like the Oswald whom Posner has busily building a shield of boxes on the sixth floor this entire time. He also states that James Jarman denied seeing Oswald in the first-floor lunchroom, but fails to note the testimony of his companion, Harold Norman, that 'there was someone else in there,' but he didn't remember who it was."[168] Carolyn Arnold told the FBI that she saw Oswald in the lunchroom between 12:20 and 12:25,[169] the time the motorcade was due.

12. AVOIDING THE BEST EVIDENCE

If Posner can't make his case by quoting eyewitnesses, he will find
a secondhand source whose error makes the point. He does this,
for example, when he repeats the story that police gathered "every
one of the Depository's employees on the first floor. The only one
missing was Lee Oswald."[170] Though Posner cites no source, the
story comes from Lieutenant Gerald Hill, who misunderstood what
he was told by Captain Will Fritz.[171] The police, as Martin points
out, had already taken into custody Danny Arce, Bonnie Ray Williams, and Charles Givens. Others were kept outside when police
sealed off the building, and employees had been told by William
Shelley that they could go home, as Oswald did.

As the testimony of both Roy Truly and Will Fritz makes clear,
there was no employee "roll call."[172] Joseph Ball asked Truly: "Did
you make a check of your employees afterward?" Truly responded:
"No, no; not complete." Fritz testified: "Mr. Truly came and told
me that one of his employees had left the building."[173]

Shackelford points out that Posner distorts another major fact in
the case, that several competent people gave evidence that one of
Jack Ruby's girls, Rose Cheramie, told them—state police Lt. Francis
Fruge[174] and Dr. Bowers—before the assassination that the President
was going to be killed.[175]

Posner wrote that "Dr. Victor Weiss, a treating physician, told
investigators that he did not hear her say anything about the assassination until November 25." Even Dr. Weiss told the HSCA that Dr.
Bowers told him Rose Cheramie "stated before the assassination
that President Kennedy was going to be killed."[176] Posner simply
ignores Louisiana State Police Lt. Fruge and others who heard the
statements prior to the assassination.

13. "EXCLUSIVE" NEW EVIDENCE

Posner says that Dr. Bill Midgely "has never before spoken publicly."[177] This is another mind game, as Midgely's account is in Dr.
Charles Crenshaw's book, *Conspiracy of Silence.*

Shackelford, in his exhaustive commentary on Posner, points out
endless errors, including material dealing with the photographs and
films, such as stating that he was publishing for the first time a photo-

graph of Oswald taken in the New Orleans courthouse. "It is in fact a frame from the Johann Rush WDSU-TV film footage which has appeared in a number of videotapes, and Rush published it himself."

14. HAVING IT BOTH WAYS

Folliard combed through Posner's opus and found the following additional examples of errors: On page 225 there is an unqualified assertion that *"The FBI discovered the bag contained microscopic fibers from the blanket with which Oswald kept his rifle wrapped in the Paine garage."* "'Case closed?'" Folliard asks. "Flip to page 272, where we find that the fibers 'were too common to be linked exclusively to that blanket.'"[178]

Posner wants us to trust the autopsy photos. One of the pictures shows an entrance wound in the back, below the shoulders, yet Posner also wants us to believe the bullet entered in the "shoulder/neck" or the "rear neck/shoulder." Posner's version agrees with the drawing done for the Warren Commission, but contradicts not only the autopsy photo but the autopsy face sheet, the eyewitnesses, and the holes in Kennedy's coat and shirt. The lower location, however, doesn't fit well with Posner's trajectory analysis.

"Fifty-six pages of discussion and a nine-page illustrated appendix cannot obscure how Posner sidesteps all this by *evading the key starting point*—the location of Kennedy's back wound. Hence, the whole analysis is rooted in a premise contradicted by the weight of evidence," Folliard writes.[179]

Posner dismisses the account of the police car at Beckley by arguing that Earline Roberts [Oswald's landlady] made up the story,[180] but accepts her account that he got his jacket, saying it was 'to hide the revolver.'"[181]

PETER DALE SCOTT

Peter Dale Scott, professor of English at the University of California at Berkeley and a former Canadian diplomat, has studied the Kennedy case since the murder. In his area of study in the case, "deep politics,"¶¶ his is the best mind ever to investigate that aspect. In the November/December 1993 issue of the *San Francisco Review of*

¶¶*Deep Politics and the Murder of JFK*, Peter Dale Scott (University of California Press: Berkeley, Los Angeles, London, 1993).

Books, Scott took Posner to task. Compared to Scott, Posner is a little boy in short pants, and as Scott says, Posner's greatest problem is bringing a lawyerly approach to the case, pleading one side and ignoring any evidence that might contradict what he wants to say.

This is the view of the rest of us who know this evidence and the witnesses Posner talks about. He has repeated the worst sins of the Warren Commission, the House Committee, and some of the other critics of those bodies.

Scott says that aside from the "cranks, ideologues, paranoid obsessives, charlatans, and a clairvoyant," lawyers and scholars are the two special types of people attracted to study the case. "From the outset there have been reasons of state to close the case; and from the outset there have been glaring problems with the evidence that have kept it open. If anything has become more clear about the case since the Warren Report, it is that officials of many government agencies lied, sometimes repeatedly, to maintain the Commission's conclusions. Congressional committees established that FBI agents lied about Oswald's visit to the Dallas FBI office before the assassination, and that CIA officials gave false statements (even within the Agency) about CIA surveillance of Oswald at the Cuban and Soviet embassies in Mexico City."[182]

Scott says that *Case Closed* persuades uninformed readers that Oswald committed the crime alone, "but to those who know the case it is also evidence of an ongoing cover-up. For Posner often transmits without evaluation official statements that are known to be false, or chooses discredited but compliant witnesses who have already disowned earlier helpful stories that have been disproven. He even revives a wild allegation which the Warren Commission rejected, and reverses testimony to suggest its opposite."[183]

And, as we have seen, Posner's book was given tremendous approval in the mainstream press and by the national media, whereas anything to the contrary was closed out at that same moment.

Posner is being credited, even by the Warren Report critics, with some perceptive comments, which Scott points out: that our books and research are not flawless, and that there are more questions about the physical and medical evidence that may not be answered by the critics. Posner insists, for instance, that the connection between David Ferrie and Oswald is not proven.

Posner repeats stories that even the Warren Commission rejected. He uses Marina's story that she tried to prevent Oswald from shooting Nixon, which the Warren Commission threw out as having "no probative value."

"But my complaint is about the national media pundits who (like

Tom Wicker) have hailed this book as 'thoroughly documented' and 'always conclusive.' My complaint even more is with prominent academics who (like Professor Stephen Ambrose) have hailed it as 'a model of historical research.' The case will certainly never be closed as long as the media tout such misrepresentations as the proper answer to the critics.''[184]

SOME OTHER COMMENTS BY THE AUTHOR

Posner writes about Dr. Guinn's neutron activation analysis for the House Committee, which tested the metal found in the car and in John Connally's body to see if it corresponded to that of the bullets, but he ignores the entire issue Guinn raised when he indicated that the fragments he tested did not weigh the same as those tested in 1964,[185] or the fact that Guinn was connected to those tests also. What we have is a case of substituted fragments, following a general pattern of substitution in the evidence.

Posner takes the position that Ruby was not a gangster. The reader must decide whether or not to agree. There is far more evidence linking Ruby to the Mob and none that would lead one to believe that he never had any such ties, except for flat statements by two dubious characters, Tony Zoppi and former Assistant District Attorney Bill Alexander, that Ruby was not connected. Law enforcement in Dallas, like J. Edgar Hoover, and like America's power structure itself, had a strong interest in maintaining that there was no organized crime—while working hand in glove with gangsters. Posner does admit, however, that Ruby showed up at Parkland Hospital shortly after Kennedy was shot. This suggests the possibility that Ruby planted the bullet found there.

Posner's silliest statement is: "From conversations with others . . . it is evident that Ruby knew Earl Warren was someone prominent in government but was not sure of which position he held until Knight told him.''[186] It is silly because Earl Warren, the Chief Justice of the United States Supreme Court, was one of the most hated men in the United States. All across the South were billboards saying "Impeach Earl Warren." He was especially hated in Dallas, and it is not credible that anyone didn't know who he was when the Warren Court made school integration the law of the land. In addition, during Ruby's meeting with Warren and Gerald Ford when they came to see him in jail for a day, Ruby clearly jogged "Chief Warren's" memory when bringing up mutual acquaintances, such

as a man Warren remembered who was killed by a taxi in New
York City.

Near the end of Posner's book are some illustrations (page 479)
showing his imaginary idea of the trajectories of the bullets. He did
not bother to consult the published autopsy photograph of the back
which shows the entry in the back quite a bit farther to the left and
farther down the back. His two drawings have two different positions
for the back entry. But these are subjective judgments, and once
again we are faced with evidentiary problems that don't lead to easy
resolution. Posner mentions that the bullet splintered the vertebra,
but his drawing shows it much too low to strike any neck vertebra,
and the autopsy report mentioned nothing about it. The 1968 Clark
Panel report stated that "there is no evidence of fracture of either
scapula or of the clavicles, or of the ribs *or of any of the cervical and
thoracic vertebrae*" (emphasis mine).

Two doctors (not radiologists) think damage shows up in the X-
rays put forward by the House of Representatives, so we might have
real evidence of the evolution of the autopsy evidence and how the
different versions changed over the years. All other radiologists see
no damage even in these pictures.

Posner writes about the "backyard photos" of Oswald holding
the rifle, wearing a pistol and holding copies of *The Militant* and
The Daily Worker.[187] He does not deal with the fact that Marina told
me and numerous others that she stood with her back to the stairway we see in the background when she took the photos.[188]

Shackelford points out that Posner changed his footnote on page
108 in the paperback edition regarding *The Militant* and the backyard photograph that was sent them before the assassination from
"did not find any photo of Oswald" to "claimed not to find any
photo of Oswald," though citing testimony that gives no indication
any photo remained in the files by the time of the assassination.

Deleting the rest of his original footnote, Posner adds: "In 1993,
two former *Militant* staffers reportedly admitted that one of Oswald's backyard photos had indeed arrived at their office before
the assassination. It vanished after JFK's death." By failing, as he so
often does in the new material, to cite his source, Posner avoids
having to acknowledge that this information comes from a longtime
critic, Hal Verb. He also specifies that the photo vanished *after JFK's
death*, though Verb reported the photo was discarded rather rapidly
after it was received, seven months *before* JFK's death.

Posner relies on the credibility of a Dealey Plaza witness, Howard
Brennan, who identified Oswald as being in the sixth-floor window,
which he could see from the street.[189] All we need to know about

this crucial linchpin in the government's case is the fact that Brennan, standing in the street some distance away, only gave the police a description of the height of the alleged assassin, who was kneeling behind a stack of boxes upon which he rested his rifle, and was only barely visible. A "description" of the assassin was simply impossible.

Another of Posner's faults is his constant criticism of various critics for not dealing with matters that Posner chooses to pontificate upon. In almost all instances, his subjects have nothing to do with the particular books those critics were writing. For instance, if they were writing a book on the medical evidence, they would not particularly be interested in Oswald if at all, or vice versa. Yet Posner is the primary loser for whom the vice of selectivity causes such great mistakes.

CONCLUSION

Posner raises countless red herrings in the assassination of President Kennedy that are clearly planted in the case, and which constitute a thousand rabbit trails having little or nothing to do with the real issue: *Is the primary evidence in the case fake?* Posner's whole book tries to demolish whatever questions or counterevidence there is on innumerable points (which would take volumes to deal with) and which have already consumed a vast amount of time and the energy—and even lives—of very many investigators and researchers. Many of these questions become academic in view of the compelling evidence of forgery of the autopsy materials, which he never addresses. His entire book is a misdirection of the public away from the primary issue of *fake evidence.*

Posner wears us down while he restates the Warren Report's theory of the assassination as fact. He sidetracks any real inquiry under the guise of knowledgeable and exhaustive scholarship which has no real substance, only a paltry attempt at style. His method is therefore misleading in that he gives the illusion with this sleight of hand of having dealt with all of the questions, when he hasn't really.

Posner was undisciplined in his work: not a work of scholarship at all, but a polemic, a work of propaganda wearing the cloak of scholarship, an example of a phenomenon unfortunately all too common in that growing segment of American intellectual life which prostitutes itself to power. His book demonstrates the dismally low depths of that intellectual pit.

Is twisting history so different from a medical researcher who testifies there is no evidence tobacco causes lung cancer, a "Star Wars" scientist who signs up to help spend billions in tax money on a project he believes impossible? Or the intelligence assets in the major media, exposed years ago by Watergate journalist Carl Bernstein in *Rolling Stone*, the CIA with its "mighty Wurlitzer" of propaganda assets, men and women in every major national media outlet, transmitting selective information and disinformation to the public, unverified and sometimes totally fraudulent. There are too many famous TV anchor people who don't undertake their own serious investigations. They are just "stars" and it's all show biz.

Summing up, Martin Shackelford points out that Posner claims to have studied "all of the available evidence" on *all* aspects of the assassination before reaching his conclusions. "The sheer nonsense of this claim, given the amount of time spent researching and writing his book, plus the many personal interviews he claims to have done during that period, is self-evident. He simply doesn't acknowledge issues such as misleadingly blended testimony; avoidance of inconvenient primary sources by citing secondary sources, including Jim Moore, and his own interviews—even when they contain nothing new; careful omission of the evidentiary photos he misuses in the text; misrepresentation of the photos he cites (e.g., CE 5, the Walker photo, the Patsy Paschall film, and Jackie at Parkland), avoidance of photos which contradict his statements (e.g., Dillard, MacCammon, Reiland); selective omission of inconvenient witnesses, as in the story of Rose Cheramie, which he perpetuates in the paperback edition; perpetuation of long-dispelled myths such as the employee 'roll call' at the Book Depository; blind insistence there is no evidence of an Oswald-Guy Banister tie, etc."[190]

Folliard writes that, "Posner may be an example of my contention that *who tells the JFK story, and how they tell it* may unlock the story itself. Put another way: If you want to investigate an unsolved crime, don't focus on the question of 'Who done it?' but on *why does it remain unsolved?* Which means you investigate the investigators. One must wonder whether Posner was given a 'literary assignment,' aided with well-orchestrated mammoth publicity—another attention-deflecting operation."[191]

Oswald's personal history only becomes relevant "when and if Oswald is conclusively linked to the crime." Did he have the *means* and the *opportunity* to murder the President? ... In short, he [Posner] puts the cart before the horse. Some two hundred pages of Lee Harvey Oswald's 'personal history' lull the reader into *assuming what must be proved*—that lone nut Oswald murdered President Kennedy for motives best left to psychiatrists to explain."[192]

Posner has failed in his attempt to substantiate the Warren Report's finding of no conspiracy. His claims that Oswald shot President Kennedy are based purely on speculation and theory with facts insufficient to make a case, just as Dallas Chief of Police Jesse Curry said thirty years before. Neither the Warren Commission, the FBI, nor anyone else ever had evidence proving conclusively that Oswald did it, and Posner has come up with no more than a circumstantial case based more on style than substance. In fact, this is all *The New York Times* book reviewer, Christopher Lehmann-Haupt, far out of his depth, could come up with: "Because Lee Harvey Oswald wasn't important doesn't mean that his mind, once sufficiently twisted, couldn't conceive an important crime. By paying deserved attention to that mind, Mr. Posner has restored the balance between the perpetrator and the crime. The result is more satisfying than any conspiracy theory because at every step its explanation is clearer and more elegant."(!)[193] It eliminates *evidence!*

Apparently the *Times* assigned a literary critic to the review because it was more interested in elegance than in evidence. Their other reviewer was Stephen Ambrose, a biographer of Nixon and Eisenhower who has never written on the Kennedy case. The truth is, Posner's book is utterly inelegant.

I find this disgusting. It is a shame that a newspaper so august as *The New York Times* used a literary editor to review a book of historical investigation. This is the same sort of affliction so much of America is subject to in its intellectual life—lack of expertise available to its publishers and the media. In Canada and other French and English speaking nations the media can always draw on experts in a field to find the perspective, analysis, and peer review each manuscript or publication deserves. But not in America.

It is a tragedy that the *Times* cannot find anything more to recommend a book than its "elegant solution" to a great mystery, a solution based on *style!* The problem, as is all too often the case, is style rather than substance.

One of the crimes of the Posner/*U.S. News & World Report* joint effort to kill the truth is the following result (quoted from the latter publication's comments on Posner's book): "On issue after issue, Posner catches Stone and all the major conspiracy writers in serious misrepresentations of the evidence."[194] This is a propaganda trick, because it is Posner who misrepresents the evidence. Granted, both sides have done it, but that does not negate actual evidence showing conspiracy.

As I have said throughout my previous books, and as has been noted by a few other writers, it is totally irrational for anyone not to have fired at the car as it approached the Texas School Book Depository along Houston Street, and instead wait for it to turn the last corner, disappear beneath a big tree, and then begin firing at it as it goes away from the Depository. The reason the car was not fired upon until it had passed by the building was that it was driving into an ambush facing it on both sides of the bridge. Someone began firing from low down and behind when they had a clear shot at the car along the center lane of Elm Street, and that helped ensure the car went forward into the primary shooters.

Posner's arguments that Oswald did it are based on establishing that Oswald's background was one of violence and therefore that he *could* have done it. So could most of the people in the world, who get violent at one time or another in their childhoods or lives.

Is there anything of value in the book for the sake of history? Maybe a few small pieces of information, but the trouble is, their reporter has little credibility. The book will likely be consigned to history's dumpster and Posner and his book—like so many others— will be no more than a footnote.

Frankly, this business is a racket. It is easy enough for both critics of the Warren Commission as well as its supporters to fudge evidence and scholarship, and since I know very well what I recorded the Dallas doctors as saying, I have no doubt but that Gerald Posner took the easy way.

Kennedy, for all his faults, deserved better. Kennedy rose far above the level of those corrupted spirits who now play mind games with the mystery of his death. It's a business and a racket. That great man deserved better than what he's getting while his children still live and watch.

8

Conflicting Evidence
and What It May Mean

Every challenger for public office, especially for the Presidency, talks about a great crusade to end corruption; to obtain government clean as a hound's tooth. But experience has shown that promises are not enough. For ours is a government of men, not of promises, and some men yield to temptation.

—John F. Kennedy

I WISH TO HERE POSTULATE FOR THE FIRST TIME in print a new theory, God forbid.

About three years prior to writing this, I discerned a trail through the evidence that had a significance far beyond possible normal interpretations. The trail consisted of many serious conflicts, but it was a while before an explanation occurred to me beyond the chance that the conflicts were merely due to mistakes by witnesses and other human error.

It no longer seemed remotely rational that human error could explain how forty-two witnesses could describe wounds that are not seen in the X-rays or photographs. The reluctance of officialdom to question photographs and X-rays began to be overcome by the relentless insistence on certain facts by eyewitnesses who could not all be lying, nor did they have a *reason* to lie about such things.

But what of the fact that some of the points the witnesses insisted upon conflicted with other of their claims, such as saying that a low shot blew off the back and top of the President's head, when such a shot could not have come from a high window? Had the doctors ever said that in the first place or were they obliged to say it, made to write it in their autopsy report, made to lie on that or other points and then—being human—forgot the lie?

We get an indication of the force and coercion involved when we look at the issue of the first examinations of the photographs by the autopsy doctors themselves, in 1966 and early 1967. After the autopsy, some of the personnel were sent to Vietnam, including the Army doctor present, Pierre Finck, a foremost expert on forensics.

The fake photos, X-rays, and films were in part made to self destruct. They were created to be uncovered as fake, but not immediately. That's why they were kept secret for so long, only now to be discovered as forgeries.

ON NOVEMBER 1, 1966, just four days after the photographs and X-rays were transferred from the Kennedy family to the National Archives, Drs. Humes, Boswell, Ebersole, and Thomas Stringer, the civilian photographer who had taken the pictures at the hospital, were brought to the National Archives in Washington to inventory the photographs and X-rays. The report that flowed from this was called an "inspection" and was signed on November 10 by the four men.[1] This document states at the end that "the X-rays and photographs described and listed above include all the X-rays and photographs taken by us during the autopsy, and we have no reason to believe that any other photographs or X-rays were made during the autopsy."

Why would they need to make this statement? Why say that they have no reason to believe that there were any other pictures? The evidence is quite strong that Lieutenant Commander William Bruce Pitzer, and maybe others, took pictures and even films. Dennis David claims that he helped edit Pitzer's film.[2] Pitzer was in charge of audiovisual at Bethesda. Obviously there was concern by someone who evidently had them make the final statement in their inventory. There are reports of three photographers, including Stringer and Riebe. And I suspect that since Pitzer and others were known to have photographs, somebody was scared. Pitzer was soon found shot to death at Bethesda, and his widow was warned not to talk to me.*

*See article in the May 1995 issue of the *Fourth Decade*, by Lt. Col. Daniel Marvin, p. 16. Marvin writes:

"Late in the afternoon, on Saturday, 29 October 1966 Lieutenant Commander William Pitzer was found dead in his office at the Bethesda Naval Hospital where the autopsy on President Kennedy had been performed three years earlier. With a gunshot wound to the right temple, Pitzer's death was officially ruled a suicide, but family and friends found this verdict impossible to accept, not least of all because his widow knew better. In January 1995 Mrs. Joyce B. Pitzer told me unequivocally that she knew her husband 'had parts of the autopsy that they wanted destroyed.' She was speaking of our government wanting the autopsy photos he'd taken of JFK on 22 November 1963 destroyed. She told me that her husband 'refused to do this.' Instead of the United States Navy assisting Mrs. Pitzer to get to

The doctors and Stringer must have blurted out that some of the photographs they took (they had the photographer with them) were missing, and that the ones that remained were fake. Yet the 1966 list does not include two interior chest photographs. It does include photographs of the entry hole in the occipital region of the skull[3] that the doctors said they took, but those are missing as well. It is not clear if this is an external or internal skull photograph. The indications that the photographs were removed fairly screams from the pages one reads today, so many years later, when these men are still alive and insist the photographs of the interior wall of the back were taken through the opened chest.[4]

Within a matter of weeks, in January 1967, the Johnson administration arranged for Dr. Pierre Finck to be brought back from Vietnam and had all of the doctors again look at the photographs and X-rays at seven in the evening until midnight of January 20, making them sign a statement with regard to their inspection. They were shown the autopsy photographs and X-rays in the presence of Justice Department lawyer Carl Eardley.[5] The Department of Justice then gave them a paper to sign that said the autopsy photographs and X-rays did not alter in any way their report of the autopsy itself.[6] What did this mean, and who gave it to them to sign? Why was it happening then?

This latter document was clearly coerced, with false statements contained at the end: "The photographs and X-rays corroborate our visual observations during the autopsy and conclusively support our medical opinion as set forth in the summary of our autopsy report."[7] A paper trail was being left.

Finck's blistering anger can be felt as one reads the opening of his second day of testimony to the House Assassinations Committee, a meeting on a Sunday that he himself requested, quoted elsewhere

---

the bottom of her husband's violent death, they ruled it suicide. She knew different, but the Navy refused her access to the autopsy of her husband. Instead, she told me, 'After his death, four of the Navy Intelligence were here at the house. They told me not to talk.' She clarified that saying, 'and for 25 years I did not realy discuss this.' Even after a quarter of a century had passed, Mrs. Pitzer told me of how 'Several of the Captains and one of the Admirals told me when Livingstone was writing the book [*High Treason 2*]—to stay out of it.

"Mrs. Pitzer is worried that the Navy will take away her survivors benefit pay if she talks about this incident or asks too many questions. During my first conversation with her on 5 January 1995, Mrs. Pitzer told me 'we have wondered, if more were said about this, if my compensation might be stopped.' Joyce Pitzer is 80 years old and, I firmly believe, a very frightened woman, and a true patriot. She deserves straight answers from the U.S. Navy."

in this book. The interview was kept secret since 1978 and only just
released. After some brief remarks, the substance of the doctor's
statement begins with: "In particular I'd like to refer to the photographs shown to me, not seen in 1964, taken in 1963 at the time
of the autopsy, not seen at the time of the Warren Commission
hearings, and seen for the first time in 1967. I think that the doubts
and the controversies now arise from the fact that people used these
photographs as a basis for interpretation, saying they don't fit the
autopsy report. And that's what bothers people and that's why I
came back. . . . At the time of the autopsy, I palpated the scalp of
President Kennedy. I examined it. Outer and inner surfaces of the
scalp, and there was only one perforating wound of the scalp in
the back of the head.[8] . . . I [will] try to summarize my opinion
about this photograph, having examined the scalp myself. I don't
think there is much point in arguing about the so-called wound
seen high in the scalp, above the level of the right ear. . . . There
is not much point in arguing about this, when asked the question,
'could that be a wound of entry, is that the penetrating or a perforating wound?' for the good reason that at that level *I did not see in
the scalp of President Kennedy, a perforating wound of the scalp* [author's
emphasis]. Again, there was only a perforating wound of entry of
the scalp in the back of the President's head, and *that was the wound
low in the photograph* [author's emphasis] with a wide center in contrast to the previously described area which has a red center on the
photograph. What I'm referring to now is the wound in the lower,
lower portion of the photograph, *near the hairline, and this is what
corresponds to the perforating wound of the scalp, a wound of entry in the
back of the head, unequivocally being a wound of entry because it corresponds to the hole in the bone* [author's emphasis] I have described
with no beveling on the outer aspect of the skull and with beveling
on the inner aspect of the skull. Again, here we have to remember
the differences between what you palpate with your fingers at the
time of autopsy and what you see on a flat photograph. . . .[9] I think
it's very dangerous to, to make positive identifications on the basis
of a photograph. . . . But we should not make the photographs say
more than what they can say.[10] . . . And it bothered me, yesterday's
session bothered me very much, you know, to answer 'I don't know'
and to—I don't want to add doubts to this, and I think now I
understand why there are doubts. It's the difference between the
interpretation of photographs and the autopsy wounds, and this is
why I can help."[11]

The very next question shows Finck repeating what was said during the above. He insists, as did the other doctors, that the rear head bullet entry was low near the hairline, at or near the small bump on the head, not four inches higher where it appears in the photographs. Dr. Petty asks Finck: "The wound that you, or the item [author's comment: !!] on the photograph you point out as being representative of the area of the inshoot portion of that perforating wound is down near the hairline . . ."

"Yes."[12]

The next comment deals with a major point about the "measurements" in the photographs, in case anyone thinks that there was something scientific about the ruler being in the photographs taken at the autopsy. Finck says: "I would hesitate very much to make measurements for two reasons. . . ."

Dr. Davis: "I would agree that the ruler certainly cannot be used. Besides, it's not even in a plane, in that. . . ."[13]

The government cut this transcript off pages later in the middle of this sentence: ". . . do you think it's possible that that measurement relative to the occipital protuberance that's contained with the "[14] That's it. The sentence is left hanging in midpage, and we have no idea what was said after that

THE PHOTOGRAPHS AND THE X-RAYS seriously conflict with their autopsy report of a low entry wound. There is no large exit wound on the X-rays or in the photographs where it is described in the autopsy report.

What was going on during those weeks that caused Finck to be brought back from Vietnam, and what control did the Department of Justice exercise to gain the cooperation of the military in the matter? Lyndon Johnson was the President, and he was in a position to order the military to bring Finck back, to order the other doctors to examine the material, and to sign the paper his Justice Department prepared which said that the photos and X-rays did not change their report.

Jim Garrison's conspiracy investigation had not begun. The media revealed it on February 17, 1967,[15] so that isn't the answer for Finck's sudden trip halfway around the world in January 1967, to view some photographs and X-rays. The other doctors had previously viewed them on November 1, 1966. Of course, it's possible that the government was sitting on Garrison so closely that they knew what he was up to.

"I saw no photos of bone of entry; I thought we had photographed the outside and inside of the entry wound in skull. We remained in the Archives until midnight, having prepared a statement comparing the illustrations with our autopsy report.

"On 26 January 1967 at 1700, we met at Suburban Hospital: Humes, Boswell, Eardley, and myself. I objected to the fact that equivalents of our measurements in mm were given to the third decimal in inches! The two other prosectors agree that measurements to 1/100 inch were precise enough and that 1/1000 inch was unnecessary. The statement had been prepared by Justice Dept. We signed the statement. My conclusion is that the photos and X-rays of the autopsy of President Kennedy do not modify our conclusions stated in the autopsy report."[16] This statement can be read to mean: "The pictures are not of Kennedy, and don't change our autopsy report."

Dr. Finck met with Barefoot Sanders of the Department of Justice, one of President Lyndon Johnson's cowboys who moved to Washington when John Kennedy was replaced by the Texas crowd. Sanders and Attorney General Ramsey Clark (also from Texas) ran the JD. That Justice Department had previously been headed by Robert Kennedy, the dead President's brother, who was in great conflict with J. Edgar Hoover, and RFK was still alive when the above events transpired. Hoover's FBI, of course, was in that same Department of Justice, and Hoover, it is believed, was a linchpin in the plan to murder Kennedy.* Carl Eardley, a lawyer with the Justice Department for 35 years, supervised the examination of photos and X-rays by the doctors. Was anyone else present?

The photographs and the X-rays are the keystone of the official story. They are also the keystone of the cover-up in the assassination of President Kennedy. If they are fake, then the entire official story collapses.

What triggered Finck's sudden call to Washington then? Remember that a naval commander present at the autopsy, William Bruce Pitzer, was found shot to death at Bethesda Naval Hospital on the day, October 29, 1966, when the autopsy photographs and X-rays were transferred from the Kennedys' control to the National Archives.[17] Four days later, November 1, Humes, Boswell, Ebersole, and Stringer were asked to inventory the pictures. Until then no one from the autopsy had seen the photographs, and no one had seen the X-rays since the night of the autopsy. Although theoretically under the control of the Kennedy family, they had been in the National Archives the whole time.

---

*See Mark North's *Act of Treason*, Carroll & Graf, 1991.

*   *   *

THE TEXAN PRESIDENT, Lyndon Johnson, had an Attorney General—
Ramsey Clark—also from Texas, who then convened a panel to
examine the photographs and X-rays. That occurred on February
26–7, 1968, and was undoubtedly stimulated by the Garrison affair,
though it was explained this way by Russell Fisher, M.D., of Baltimore, who headed the Clark Panel: "In 1968, the book *Six Seconds
in Dallas* [by Josiah Thompson] was about to appear, and in it the
original autopsy was discussed at some length. Clark became concerned about some statements he'd seen in the proofs of the book
as to whether or not things had indeed *been* missed at the original
autopsy. He decided to get a panel of people together to look at
it, independently of all other investigations. . . . The result of this
panel review was that we found some minor errors in the protocol,
such as the description of the site of the entrance wound as being
just above the external occipital protuberance, whereas, in fact—if
you *measured* its location—it was some 10 centimeters *above* the external occipital protuberance."[18] This statement, revealing such a
wide discrepancy in the placement of the rear head entry wound,
went by everyone for ten more years. Dr. Boswell told the HSCA
that it was *his* letter to Clark that brought about the Panel. Did
Boswell tell him photos were false or missing?

One might also ask how come the Attorney General had the
proofs of a book that so concerned the political existence and suc-
cess of his boss, as well as the murder that installed that boss, Lyndon Johnson, in the office of President?

What comes through with devastating finality, with devastating
truth, is that they *knew* long ago that the autopsy pictures and X-
rays were fake. The X-rays were not what were seen the night of
the autopsy, and the photographs were wildly at variance with both
the findings of the autopsy and the personal observations of all
those who saw the body.

In addition, there was nearly precise corroboration for the exact
appearance and position of the large head wound in a number of
drawings by the people at the autopsy, **especially a drawing made by
FBI agent Francis X. O'Neill—with what was seen in Dallas.**

But what was the trail I spoke of above? What did it mean?

The autopsy doctors compounded their lies to make the whole
thing appear preposterous to those who truly think it through. That
was their way of telling us they had a gun to their heads, were
under military orders. Giving us a too-heavy, 1500-gram brain and
a liver far too small are examples. Pretending that the brain they

later examined was the same brain that came with the body was a
lie. Claiming that they had evidence of a bullet passing through the
neck from the back is an out-and-out lie, since they found no damage to the bones of the neck or that the bullet perforated the back.

I will give the doctors this credit: There is no out-and-out lie with
the key portion of what they wrote early in the autopsy report:
"The second wound *presumably* [author's emphasis] of entry is that
described above in the upper right posterior thorax. . . . The missile
path through the fascia and musculature cannot be easily probed.
The wound *presumably* [author's emphasis] of exit was that described by Dr. Malcolm Perry of Dallas in the low anterior cervical
region." Perry, of course, had described it as an "entrance wound,"
not an exit wound. The doctors at the autopsy officially did not
even know it was there. "When observed by Dr. Perry the wound
measured 'a few millimeters in diameter,' however it was extended
as a tracheostomy incision and thus its character is distorted at the
time of autopsy." The two wounds were then thought to be connected because there was a bruise in the apex of the right pleural
cavity and lung. Such a bruise is normal in body trauma.

The key paragraph in the autopsy report comes near the end; it
describes the path of the bullet that hit Kennedy in the back "and
made its exit through the anterior surface of the neck. As far as
can be ascertained, this missile struck no bony structures in its path
through the body."[19] Earlier in the report, the doctors make it clear
what their *presumptions* are with regard to the path of the missile.
Then it became an out-and-out lie: a presumption converted to fact.

In the space of two sentences, the doctors essentially tell us the
lie they are being forced to say and then in the next sentence tell
us it has to be a lie because no bullet can pass through that way
without striking bone. They were saying it was magic.

THEY LIED WHEN THEY HAD TO, but just as quickly told us the truth,
such as the position of the low rear head entry, because those who
made them lie did not think of everything, did not realize then
that the bullet could not come from the sixth-floor window. Sometime later when it dawned on the cover-up people that they had
made a mistake, they convened their panels of experts and produced their fake pictures and simply wrote the doctors off as having
made a grossly incompetent mistake, continuing to use the other
findings of the doctors where and when it suited them in spite of
the fact that their own discreditation of the doctors served to destroy whatever was left of the official story.

Drawings made by persons present at the autopsy of President Kennedy at Bethesda Naval Hospital. Note that the outlines and position of the large defect in the back of the head is essentially identical to the placement and description given by the Dallas witnesses. This means that the wound was not altered during transit, as popular mythology has maintained. These drawings were made for interviews with the House Select Committee on Assassinations.

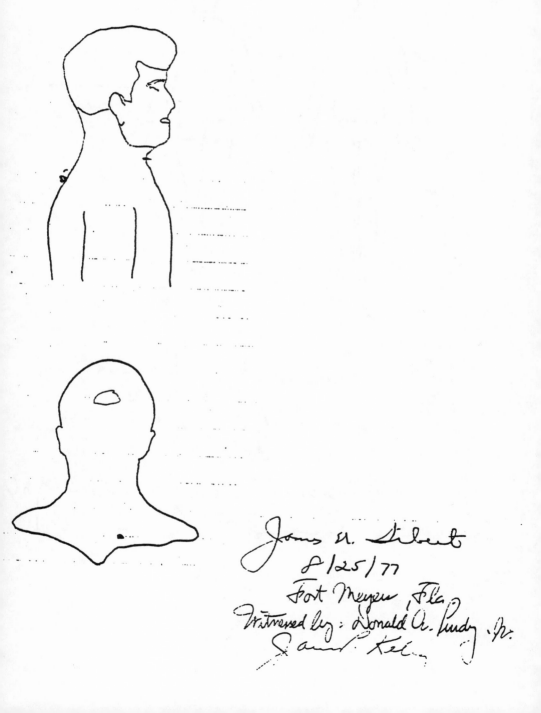

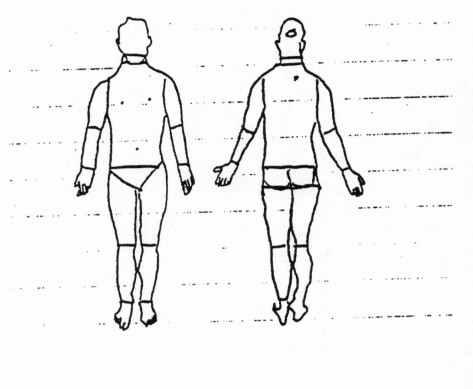

James M. Sibert
8/25/77
Fort Meyer, Florida
Witnessed by: Donald A. Purdy, Jr
James C. Kelly

000662

Jan 12, 1977

Thomas Evan Blau

Reviewed by — D. A. Purdy, Jr.

Jim Couzelman

FRONT side g dots

BACK p.ket

1 2 3 4 5 6 7 gm cm mgms   SCAR

8-24-77

Witnessed by   Donald A. Purdy, Jr.

Jackson, Miss.

8/24/77.

Roy H. Kellerman
St. Petersburg, Florida

Witnessed by: D. A. Purdy, Jr.

James Kelly

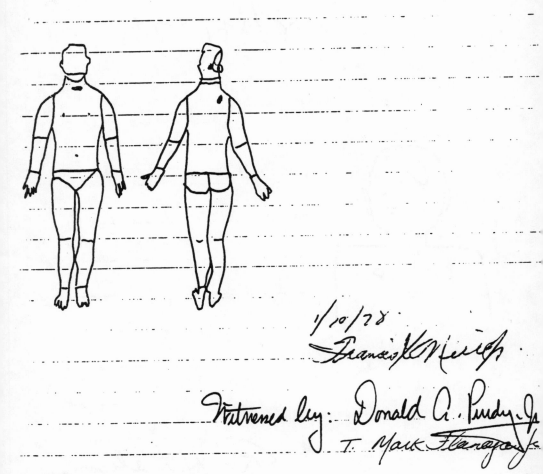

1/10/78

Francis K. Weir

Witnessed by: Donald A. Purdy, Jr.
T. Mark Flanagan, Jr.

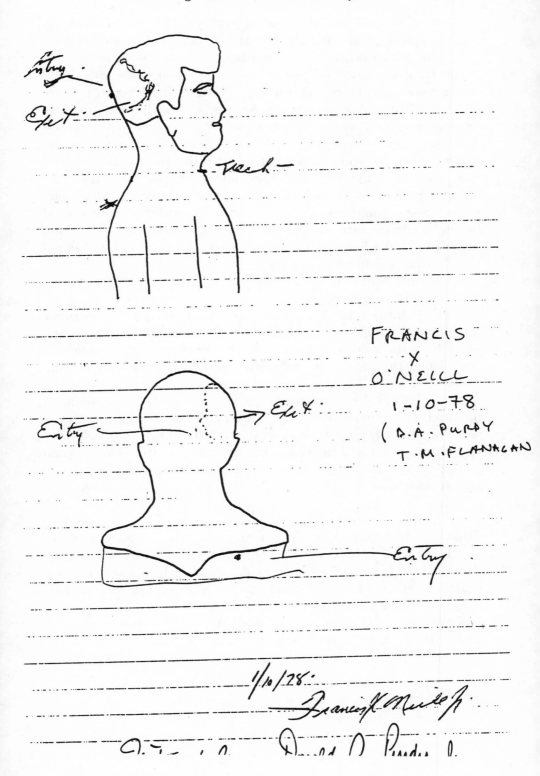

Many of the doctors and federal agents who were made to lie were in contact with one another and discussed the case, in spite of orders not to do so. There had been an attempt to isolate witnesses from one another, just as researchers had done with them. There were so many conflicts in the evidence that I began to wonder if the FBI, police, and Secret Service agents who were so close to what happened *knew* there was a conspiracy. They had been made to lie or fabricate evidence, so they switched evidence, substituting materials—faked photographs for faked photographs, altering the films, switching the rifle and the bullet (CE 399) and the fragments—trying to alert us—and failing that, posterity, to what happened. Some could say the conflicts in the evidence were caused by the incompetence of the plotters, but nobody could be that stupid. True, the lies lasted thirty years without detection, but sometime *someone* would guess the truth.

It was otherworldly—that is—so surreal as to be completely void from our life experience.

Autopsy doctors, federal agents, police, all acting from an inner urgency and integrity, left a trail for us to follow, a trail so fantastic as to be unbelievable, yet the only real answer to the riddles—a trail left in the face of overwhelming power so great that no one could say a word.

And what was the chain of evidence of the most obviously faked or switched materials? Hoover's FBI grabbed the ballistics evidence and the Secret Service took possession of the photographs, X-rays, and all other autopsy materials first produced at the Navy hospital autopsy, *after* the photographs were developed at the Navy photo labs at Anacostia.[20]

THE RESULT IS WHAT THE NATION and its officials have not yet faced: *There is no case left for the lone assassin theory* because of the discrediting of the autopsy doctors by Johnson's Ramsey Clark Panel, the HSCA, Posner, and *The Journal of the American Medical Association.*

Nevertheless, we must listen to what the doctors have really said. The difficulty is in sorting that out.

SOME OTHER CONFLICTS

The Minox Spy Camera. This camera was found by the Dallas police in Ruth Paine's garage among Oswald's possessions. Oswald possessed some of the photographs from it. The FBI changed the listing of the camera to that of a Minox light meter, and brought great pressure to bear on the Dallas police to accept this. They did not. Why? Michael Paine, a man with a possible intelligence background, later claimed it was his, but he could not identify the locations where the photos were taken.[21]

The Bullet Cross Section on the Outer Table of the Skull: The Ramsey Clark Panel stated that there was a bullet fragment on the *outside* of the skull, measuring 6.5 mm across, on the back of the head near the cowlick 1 cm away from where they thought the entry was (4 inches higher than in the autopsy report). The existence of this fragment on the X-ray led the Panel to believe that the entry must be close to it, though not visible in the X-ray, and not where the doctors had placed it in the autopsy report. Dr. Mantik's lengthy examinations of the actual X-rays in the Archives indicate that the bullet fragment is in fact *inside* the skull and against it. It would seem impossible for the fragment to be outside the skull and not be noted in the autopsy report. If it was inside, *it had to come from in front,* so the only explanation is that it was covered up. The doctors must have mentioned it at the autopsy table for the FBI men to have written it up in their report, as they did.

But how could there have been bone in that area? The fragment near the cowlick would be on the intact skull just left of the large defect on the right side and rear of the head extending low down into the occipital area. The FBI report mentions a fragment in that general area but it is not in evidence and not in the autopsy report. It "appeared to be at the rear of the skull at the juncture of the skull bone." This location in itself is very vague, granted, but the position on the X-ray is far clearer. It seems clear that the doctors were shut up about it, which tends to corroborate Mantik's findings that it's on the *inside* of the skull, and therefore very strong evidence of a frontal shot. It is likely *impossible* to be on the "outer table" of the skull, and therefore that description was meant to alert us.

Saying that the fragment was on the *outer table* of the skull may be another clue left on this trail, when it is actually *inside* the skull and against it, proof of a bullet from in front. Those in an official position never dared speak the truth.

Did Oswald commit any of the crimes attributed to him? After all the huffing and puffing of Posner, the Warren Commission, and the House Committee, it certainly doesn't look that way. No one can prove that he did anything at all connected with the assassination. The case against him was never more than circumstantial; there was no hard evidence of any criminal act.

The Autopsy Photographs. The film from the cameras was taken by the Secret Service agents present, and was then taken several days later to the Anacostia Naval base where the photographs were developed. Mark Crouch claims that James K. Fox, the Secret Service agent who took the film to Anacostia, told him that some days after it was developed, a number of the pictures were burned at Secret Service headquarters in Washington. Certainly quite a few of the photographs known to have been taken have never been seen and are clearly missing.

Why did the Secret Service take one part of the evidence, and the FBI take the other? The FBI displaced the Dallas police in the case. None of these people trusted each other, and some were undoubtedly suspicious that one of the other agencies had something to do with the murder.

The X-rays. The X-rays developed at the autopsy were also taken into custody by the Secret Service. Jerrol Custer told me that Dr. John Ebersole asked him to tape bullet fragments to bone fragments the next day and take X-rays of them. Ebersole obtained access to the X-rays at the National Archives a few weeks later and drew two pencil lines on them, saying he was taking measurements for a "bust."[22] The pencil lines can still be seen. Ebersole told House Committee investigators: "I realized that those were the lines that I drew at the White House Annex, and I think that more than any other reason made me want to come here to clarify for you that those were not any attempts by any ballistics experts to show pass of bullets."[23] This flatly contradicts speculations by some doctors that one or both of the lines show bullet trajectories.

Ebersole further explains the pencil lines as follows, though this is the only place in his transcript which is badly fractured with missing words and an unintelligible word transcribed: "On no. 2 specifically, this is a line that I made to identify definitely the lower line running from the *naison* [author's emphasis. This word might have been *horizon*. It is then followed by a blank space of approximately 12–15 characters, and then a period]. There is a second line at the angle to that first one which I also made. The attempt here was to get a line from the high point of the forehead back to the occipital."[24] We assume he means the entry on the back of the head. "And that was for the purpose of, as you understood it—at the sculptor's request?"

"As I understood this was information that might be of use to a sculptor in making a bust."

Bullet fragments were removed from behind the "high point of the forehead," and the X-rays showed a trail of metal dust back to the occipital entry, exactly along the line Ebersole drew, clearly defining a trajectory.

The Walker house photograph. The original photograph did not have a hole cut into it which removed the license plate of a Chevrolet parked in the driveway of General Edwin Walker's house, allegedly found in Oswald's possession.[25] The photograph turned up in official custody with the license plate cut out so that the owner of the car could not be identified.

The Films. As I have argued in my last books, the Zapruder film seems to show much or all of the President's brain emerging from the right front of his head and hanging on his face, just after the fatal head shot. This is impossible for the reason that a few moments later the President was seen at Parkland Hospital by numerous witnesses who saw no damage whatsoever to his face. *I believe the film was doctored and leaked out to researchers so that it could give the impression of a shot from behind* which appeared to cause massive damage to the front of the head. The film, therefore, corroborates what people think they see on the X-rays, under the guise of claiming to show a shot from in front.

The blob is *not* a flap hanging down over the face, as our study in the National Archives proved.[26] It is made to look like the President's brain is sticking straight out from the right eye. This never happened. Also, it's an anatomic impossibility intended to be another clue that the film was otherwise altered.

It is also clear that the film showed different events when it was first seen, as opposed to later on. Witnesses described events which are no longer present in the Zapruder film, such as the limousine stopping cold during the shooting.

The entire film is a kind of animation, where images have been moved conveniently from one part to another if events happen too soon or too late for the official story. Images may have been re-moved entirely. The film may have been "stretch-framed" also, which makes a sequence last longer than it really took, if shots were too close together, for instance. The nearly stopped fatal car was speeded up by removing every other frame in that sequence.

The Bronson film, similarly, contains intrinsic conflicts. Bronson insisted that he was unable to capture the assassination sequence itself, and did not get his movie camera going until Jackie was on the trunk of the limousine, because he was taking snapshots with a Leica camera from a block away. Yet, the film shows the car passing down Elm Street, apparently through nearly all of the shooting, which conflict with his own published snapshots. In addition, the FBI report of the film states that it does not show the TSBD, yet we see it in the present film.

The Nix film shows evidence of alteration, and Orville Nix in-sisted that it had been changed. The serious conflicts in the above films fit the pattern of alteration and substitution found with the other evidence in the case.

CONCLUSION

Forgery and faked evidence is the only way to explain the many conflicts in the evidence. The JFK case does not come together the way a normal criminal case does, unless it is seen in the light of faked and planted evidence.

One could easily get the idea that Admiral Burkley was steering the autopsy toward a one-gunman-from-behind conclusion. He did not tell the doctors that there had been a tracheostomy performed, and this would indicate that he either did so deliberately, assumed they figured it out, or was drunk, in shock, or incompetent. He also didn't tell them that there had been a shot from in front that hit the President in the throat. Boswell says that he didn't know about the tracheostomy, and yet we have a statement from Dr. Robert Livingston that he told Humes that there had been a bullet wound from in front. The wound appears from the left side to be obviously that of a tracheostomy incision and not a bullet exit wound, but that is not so obvious in the photograph with a view straight down (more or less) on the neck, and known as the "Stare of Death" photograph. The cut is radically retouched to look like a ragged exit wound. Many people have been bamboozled by this picture to think the trach was therefore extended and the body altered.

Tampered with, perhaps, but not altered to fool the camera. The pictures were simply retouched or faked.

9

Conclusion

I believe a strong America is one that leads the free world, not just because we are the richest or the strongest or the most powerful, but because we exert that leadership for the cause of freedom around the globe. Because we act as well as react, because we propose as well as oppose, because we have earned the respect of our friends as well as the respect of our enemies, and because we are moving on the road to peace.

—John F. Kennedy

THIS BOOK ESTABLISHED FOR THE FIRST TIME a clear picture of the true nature of the assassination of President Kennedy by proving that the evidence in the case used to back up the official story is fake. In addition, the entire case used to frame Lee Harvey Oswald was fake.

We proved that all of the principal visual and scientific evidence and the ballistics evidence is fake.

Specifically, we demonstrated that the images on the autopsy X-rays and photographs are not authentic, and the fabrication of key facts in the autopsy report itself. The X-rays covered up a large hole on the right rear side of the President's head, and the photographs did the same. We proved that the hole in the back of the head is demonstrated from the testimony both from Parkland and Bethesda, and from official reports and interviews. That hole indicates a shot from in front of the President and explains why such an effort was made to cover it up. The Dallas doctors were unjustly accused of being mistaken.

I presented the vehement testimony of the autopsy doctors protesting the autopsy photographs and X-rays. That testimony shows that the doctors themselves did not believe the photographs were of Kennedy, and that they were altered and the wounds moved. Their observations were not mistaken either.

Over a period of fifteen years I have shown that the position of the small entry wound in the back of the head cannot be where it is claimed to be in the photographs and X-rays and that the Parkland doctors, who uniformly denounced the autopsy photographs, were correct in their observations as to the large hole in the back of the head. I was the first person to obtain their opinion of the autopsy photographs.

We have shown that there was no evidence that a bullet passed through Kennedy and reached Connally, and that it did not perforate the wall of Kennedy's chest or his neck.

I have shown that the Zapruder film is a massive hoax and was used to cover up the timing of the shots, where they happened on the street, where they came from, where the limousine was, and what it was doing. The exposure of this film and the alterations to it demonstrate how massive the conspiracy was and how close to the government the conspirators had to be. If the original of the film went to the FBI, as it should have, it can be assumed that those responsible for it at that point know where and how it was forged, or to whom it was given who then forged it. The original, though, may have been grabbed by the conspirators before the FBI (or *Life*) got what they thought was the original.

Those connected to the film come from intelligence agencies and perhaps the FBI, and that the film was used to hypnotize the nation and the world while attention was directed away from what was wrong with the film and what it really showed, some of which the conspirators, in their haste, missed.

We know that Lee Harvey Oswald was a creature of the government and that he was bought and paid for by the FBI in Dallas.

We have shown conclusively in this book, and my last two, that the body of the President was not altered between Parkland Hospital and the autopsy at Bethesda Naval Hospital. The large wound in the back of the head was identical.

We have shown that the House Select Committee on Assassinations lied and covered up what the autopsy doctors tried to tell them. Granted, the House stated that the doctors did not agree with the placement of the entry hole in the back of the head, but they kept from us the reasons why and the insistence of the doctors that the photographs and X-rays were wrong. Obviously, the HSCA did not dare reveal this, so they sacrificed the credibility of the doctors. *The Journal of the American Medical Association* superficially tried to restore the doctors' credibility while actually pounding the lid on their coffin, not realizing that they were printing proof from the doctors that the photographs and X-rays were false. Or maybe *JAMA* did know and maybe that's why they did what they did to discredit the doctors on another level.

I have shown that there was a trail left throughout the evidence by law-enforcement police and FBI agents and the autopsy doctors, showing that they were forced to fabricate, plant, or steal evidence, and they switched and otherwise placed evidence in the case which shows that they were trying to sabotage the conspirators in ways too subtle for the killers to know.

This book and my last book, *Killing the Truth*, show that the assassination had to have come from very powerful people in Texas up to and including Lyndon Baynes Johnson, the man who succeeded Kennedy as President, and J. Edgar Hoover, the Director of the FBI.

I have shown, along with other critics, that Gerald Posner's book *Case Closed* was not convincing. He did not interview some of those whom he claimed to have interviewed, distorted much other evidence in the case, and ignored many facts which disproved his theories.

SOMETIME WE WILL HAVE TO SEE the handling of the questions in the death of John Kennedy and those who deal with it in the public media and among the Warren Commission critics—and some other matters in our society—as a reflection of the generally low level of scholarship, criticism, and intellectual integrity in the U.S. today.

There is a slavish acceptance of "authority" by those who perceive of the messengers as having unquestionable credibility. Yet, what we are getting is the product of large bureaucracies with all the failings of the bureaucratic phenomenon. In fact, it is all rather barbaric and ignorant.

We don't blame people for looking at what any amateur investigator brings forward in this case with a wary and jaundiced eye. The hoaxes did a vast amount of damage: body theft and body alteration, the Warren Report and lone assassins, phony acoustical tapes, faked official evidence, Russian spies and Mafia hit men, Secret Service agents accidentally shooting the President in the head, and so on and so on.

The tragedy of this case, among many, is that whatever evidence is offered will be instantly countered, watered down, neutralized with someone else's opinion, theory, or false evidence. It never ends. The game is to motivate someone to come forward with a credible piece of evidence, who at the same time has to claim that the official evidence is authentic. The new research often carries with it inherent contradictions that are the seeds of its own destruction, and the bottom line has been to authenticate false evidence at all costs. An example are the arguments that two shots to the head can be proven provided the autopsy materials are accepted as genuine—don't seem to be in fact provable. They appear to be scientific, but fail for other reasons. I hope these theories prove out somehow.

In 1993, there was a massive attempt by the media to permanently bury the case. At that very moment, we tried to publicize an announcement of the biggest break in the thirty years since that terrible crime occurred. Dr. David Mantik had found, with the use of hard science, that the X-rays in the National Archives had been tampered with in some way.

We were unable to get the message out. In the face of such a monolithic wall of opposition, one might ask if we should have waited until the enemy shot their load. We thought that if this country was truly free, our announcement would have contributed to the debate, and there would have been many who would be glad to hear from us.

But no, the media were not going to let us speak. The Reuters wire story was not carried by any significant American newspaper. This all added up to massive news control in the U.S. The editors across the country who made the decisions were either like a herd of lemmings going over the cliff, or they were in league with a massive conspiracy to kill the truth in the fall of 1993.

The media are the intermediaries between those who have investigated the assassination and the public, between readers and cops, between those who should think the most about political murders, and the critics, commissions, and committees who looked into it. But the media have failed in their response. The media have sometimes crossed over and attempted to investigate the killing themselves, but with mixed results. In 1993, they rallied around a recasting of the Warren Report in Gerald Posner's book and attempted to close the case through sheer propaganda alone—but at that very moment a discovery was made in the National Archives that forever broke the case— in spite of all of the power trying to close it.

Until 1968, some of the media had kept a fairly open mind about the case even after the report issued by the Warren Commission. The official story was not fully accepted in 1963–64, but *Life, The New York Times*, and others began to buy the official story after 1966. New Orleans District Attorney Jim Garrison's prosecution of Clay Shaw for the murder seemed to turn the media away from conspiracy evidence by 1968. The reasons for this: the failure of the press to have available enough information from the autopsy, including the X-rays and the photographs, and the failure to obtain extensive interviews with the medical witnesses, who were forbidden to talk to reporters. (There were a few exceptions.) In addition, no one really grasped that if internal domestic forces overthrew the administration, they would have to fake all of the evidence in the case, and if so, no one grasped what was entailed in faking that evidence. Had the media thought in those terms, they might have got on the track of clues left by those forced to cover up the murder.

Dorothy Kilgallen was perhaps the only famous reporter who went after the case in a big way and believed in a conspiracy, but she was being spoon-fed information by Mark Lane, and soon died—murdered—as her biographer Lee Israel believes.[1] Later, in 1967, the *Saturday Evening Post* published a major article questioning the case, but this seemed to begin the process of channeling the energy of those who still believed in conspiracy toward the "Mafia did it" scenario, an insupportable thesis in view of the overall evidence of a faked case, and preplanning at a high level, not necessarily of government agencies. Higher than that.

The mystery then devolved to amateur researchers like myself, untrained, as were the media, in criminal investigation. It is unfortunate that some of the leaders among the critics actually had criminal backgrounds or criminal character of a serious kind. Those who could have done something about this case—sensing the real character of those critics who needed the JFK case to give them a high profile (and immunity from prosecution for their scams)—did not act. Even the best investigative reporters were turned away by the complexities of the evidence. It is too clear to many reporters that many of the critics of the Warren Report use the JFK case for publicity. The case gives these opportunists a visibility that helps advertise their businesses or professions. Reporters know about these "critics" and so don't take them seriously. It's the public that loses to the publicity seekers. Serious work gets lost in the shuffle.

Worse, many authors have hopelessly confused the truth in the public's mind by putting their own twist on the facts. There are so many interpretations of issues that the hard facts become lost in a mountain of detail. Each critic often has his own agenda—his own special interests—and too often common sense is ignored.

The inability of the media to see through the massive distortions in recent anticonspiracy and proconspiracy publications reflecting the poor level of criticism and scholarship in the U.S. does not excuse this situation.

THE KENNEDY ASSASSINATION CASE has been a political football. The game is played with frame-ups, smears, and slander from both Warren Commission critics and apologists. The same rules apply to politics as well as history. Even John Kennedy is slandered today. His place in history is attacked and his reputation sullied so that many more people will not care what happened to him.

The media have seemed to want to promote more violence and a crime-ridden society than they do truth and a peaceful country. There are *quite* prominent people in the media who cannot admit that they might be wrong. People with no real investigative ability are then set to work in this case with little better ability or even worse than the amateur investigators who have carried the ball for the last thirty years.

What I have experienced at their hands would be enough to destroy most normal people. And the struggle to get out the truth as I have discovered it has been a murderous one.

Some of you may be aware that I have opposed the principal critics, and some of the chapters in my last book, *Killing The Truth*, expose something of what they are really like. I only regret that I had to pull my punches and not discuss some of their gross criminality, blocking of the evidence, and deliberate well-planned operations smearing, slandering, and derailing competent investigators by some of those who led this case for the past thirty years.

The naked propaganda efforts of the major news media will never restore faith in our institutions. Only the truth will, and that is what I hope you found in this book.

WHO PERPETRATED THIS CRIME? Take a good long look at the power that was arrayed in Dallas and throughout Texas in 1963.

Texas controlled much of American affairs prior to World War II as a result of its oil-based economic clout. The Rockefeller family's money came from the East Texas oil fields, and this was another means of controlling our affairs. The Rockefellers were too liberal for the radicals, so they had to be roped in, compromised, and controlled. Everybody was. President Eisenhower was installed by the Texas oil men.

Kennedy could not be controlled. Perhaps the underlying reason for wanting him dead was race hatred. Kennedy was the greatest hope that the black man had, and he was considered a "nigger lover," like President Franklin Delano Roosevelt and his wife.

A coalition of conservative Republicans and Texas Democrats came together in an alliance of the Texans and the Eastern Establishment, of Lyndon Johnson and J. Edgar Hoover, of the Far East Section and the Western Hemisphere Division of the CIA, high-

ranking military officers and military intelligence, Secret Service
agents and the United States Navy, Dallas law enforcement and
Texas Department of Public Safety and the Dixie Mafia, good bed-
fellows all.

Yet, these people all knew each other. They knew who they could
use, too, those whom they needed but who were kept unwitting. At
the lower end, the conspirators were related or close allies. At the
top, they had been in the OSS and military service together. To
this day the Pentagon, the NSA, the DIA, and the Dallas FBI closely
monitor developments in the case, watching those who go into the
National Archives and reporting on them.

THOSE BILLIONS OF DOLLARS HELD PRIVATELY in Texas can fund medical clinics and other projects that will buy the help of people and
dishonest physicians needed to cover up not only the murder of
John Kennedy but other crimes.

The main evidence involving Lee Harvey Oswald actually appears
to exonerate him, and so we have to ask why there is such an
enormous lie intended to frame him with this crime. We have to
examine the official story and who brings us the message that he
did it. No matter how you cut things, you can't get Oswald in that
window. In addition, there were no fingerprints on the weapons,
no proof they had been fired, no powder burns on his face. The
shots from the window were all but impossible.

THERE IS ANOTHER LEVEL of cover-up in this case. That cover-up is
also connected to what really lies behind the murder. "I'm afraid we
were misled," attorney and former assassination researcher Vincent
Salandria told Gaeton Fonzi, a journalist and investigator for the
House Assassinations Committee. "All the critics, myself included,
were misled very early. I see that now. We spent too much time
and effort microanalyzing the details of the assassination when all
the time it was obvious, it was blatantly obvious that it was a conspiracy. Don't you think that the men who killed Kennedy had the
means to do it in the most sophisticated and subtle way? They chose
not to. Instead, they picked the shooting gallery that was Dealey
Plaza and did it in the most barbarous and openly arrogant manner.
The cover story was transparent and designed not to hold, to fall
apart at the slightest scrutiny. The forces that killed Kennedy
wanted the message clear: 'We are in control and no one—not the
President, nor Congress, nor any elected official—no one can do

anything about it.' It was a message to the people that their Government was powerless. And the people eventually got the message. Consider what has happened since the Kennedy assassination. People see government today as unresponsive to their needs, yet the budget and power of the military and intelligence establishment have increased tremendously.

"The tyranny of power is here. Current events tell us that those who killed Kennedy can only perpetuate their power by promoting social upheaval both at home and abroad. And that will lead not to revolution but to repression. I suggest to you, my friend, that the interests of those who killed Kennedy now transcend national boundaries and national priorities. No doubt we are dealing now with an international conspiracy. We must face that fact—and not waste any more time microanalyzing the evidence. That's exactly what they want us to do. They have kept us busy for so long. And I will bet, buddy, that is what will happen to you. They'll keep you very, very busy and eventually, they'll wear you down."[2] (As quoted in Fonzi's important and fine book, *The Last Investigation.*)

The secret *does* lie in some of the details, but Salandria is fundamentally correct in much of what he says. I have been familiar with the feelings Salandria expressed in the above statement since before he first published those ideas, and his words are quoted in *Killing The Truth.* But we have to stay at it, as Kennedy admonished. That meant digging in the dirt of the details. The case became incandescent as those details finally led to some that were "case-breaking."

WE HAVE TO VIEW THE ASSASSINATION of John F. Kennedy within the larger context of politics: as a front for the powerful forces that manipulate things. We don't want to fall into the pit of ultranationalism. Nationalism has its place, but it must not be the overriding factor in the conducting of world affairs today.

Kennedy's accomplishments were the nuclear test ban treaty with the former Soviet Union, forcing the removal of the missiles from Cuba without bloodshed, holding the line against a national debt, and so on. Perhaps his greatest achievement was moving this nation forward into the future, instilling hope in not only Americans but the whole world. This nation was stagnant in 1960. A better word for it is *somnolent.* Kennedy inspired all of us from every persuasion, and it was not mere demagoguery. Even the economy cannot function without confidence, and Kennedy gave us confidence. I was a young writer then of artistic turn of mind, and Kennedy made art and culture important in this nation in a way it had not been for a very long time. He gave us beauty and grace and loveliness. His speeches and press conferences were thrilling to everyone all over the world. Although he was aristocratic in bearing, he was down-to-earth and natural with whomever he was with or in whatever situation he found himself. The crew on his PT boat in World War II loved him and ultimately owed their lives to him. (One night he swam, towing one of them by a strap clenched in his teeth, for five miles in dangerous enemy waters.) He was always funny, and we loved that. We knew we were going to get a laugh. He had grace under pressure. Kennedy had the wonderful and intangible qualities of brilliance, intelligence, and power. He had a strong presence, and all of these things you felt in his company or even across the airwaves. He became the hope of the world. Just being himself was his greatest accomplishment. We were all in the company and service of the king, and he inspired love. For the world to suddenly realize that it could stand down from the long period of the Cold War, the Great Depression, World War II, the Korean War, and the daily terror of potential atomic and hydrogen bomb warfare that began in 1931 and continued without letup for thirty long years, ruining an entire generation—that was the most important hope of all, and it was not a vain hope. His assassination set us back for another full generation and plunged us literally into chaos for a decade.

The movie *JFK* piqued interest in the assassination in the minds of a lot of young people, but it also gives them the wrong impression on some matters, and its emphasis on Jim Garrison's story detracts from the real evidence of conspiracy. It led to a backlash and the attempt to shut the whole thing up, just as Jim Garrison's prosecution became a circus and a distraction in the late sixties. The real research and evidence was buried. Both may have been a second level of cover-up.

Young people have to keep their eyes open. There are many "critics" and "researchers" who may have a hidden agenda. They use some valid evidence, problems, and conflicts in the evidence to gain credibility with the rest of us, and then mislead with fantastic theories and rearranged or altered facts and evidence. Those fantastic theories also lead to backlash, and certainly turn off those with authority or power who then do nothing about any real evidence of conspiracy. Nobody can have the time to endlessly sort through the mountain of evidence in the case to determine what is real and what is false, or meaningless if true. My books are an attempt to at least set the history straight.

Always keep in mind that the cover-up of JFK's murder depended upon the false accusation and the murder of an innocent man: Lee Harvey Oswald; even the murder of Officer J. D. Tippit. Whoever killed Tippit or was pointed at him that day made it sure that Oswald would be convicted of the assassination of Kennedy after he was dead.

The assassination of Kennedy was *political,* and that fact means that the evidence itself is politicized. The control and interpretation of that evidence therefore becomes political. Unless we understand this, we cannot ultimately understand either the evidence or the larger nature of why the assassination occurred. It happened because much more powerful people were giving us the message that *the government doesn't have the power.* The murder was a deadly stroke against moderate liberalism. It opened the door to rule by extremes of Left and Right. The Center was demolished.

GEORGE O'TOOLE CLOSED HIS BOOK, *The Assassination Tapes,* with this statement: "The events in Dallas caused a special kind of sickness in our land: the covering up of the assassination brought the big lie to America. The Warren Report was not the first instance in which the United States government lied to the American people, but it was the first case of massive public lying in our times, and it marks the point at which we stopped believing what we were told. The credibility gap has become an American idiom.

"Bad times have come to our country, and one is moved to look backward and ask where we went wrong. There can be no single answer to that question: there are too many different currents in the flow of human history. But the assassination of President Kennedy marks the point at which we took leave of the truth. Unless we find and fix this thing, we will never put ourselves right. We must reopen the case."[3]

LET US NOT FORGET the assassinations of Martin Luther King and Robert Kennedy and the attempt to kill Governor George Wallace. These were terrible and heinous crimes from which we still have not recovered a generation later. Our whole political history was changed as a result.

Let us not forget the numerous other souls who were killed or who died strangely during that period, starting with three of the four lawyers and reporters who met in Jack Ruby's apartment with his roommate, George Senator, during that fateful weekend in November 1993. No matter what anyone says, there were just too many deaths for them all to be coincidence or accidents. Just too many deaths in view of the sort of thing that happens often in Texas, always a place that breeds great violence and holds human life cheaply. A place where troublesome people are simply burned out or have their cattle poisoned. Waco is one more symptom of the disease, of the violence of the place.

In Dallas especially, and its surrounding satellite towns, lived many radicals from the far right. These people represented a grave threat to America. Many of them, like General Edwin Walker and General Charles Willoughby, McArthur's chief of staff and a long-time intelligence operative (a man born in Germany who was known to be a fascist while he served with McArthur during the war) were extreme radicals, apparently not afraid to use violence to serve their ends. A group of people like this in the Dallas area, though not necessarily this specific group, had the capability of taking out a President. Of assassinating John Kennedy. Many of the Dallas police had been or were members of the Ku Klux Klan.

Shortly after John Kennedy died, the grace, culture, and beauty he stood for in a sense above anything else was smashed beneath Lyndon Johnson's insensitive cowboy boot with his commitment to a war almost without end in Vietnam, a war we could not win in any case. We had nothing but puppets and weaklings after that. Under the Nixon White House that followed, we experienced a greatly intensified and expanded war and the "Berlin Wall" as it was known in the White House itself. The aura of neo-Nazi senti-ment and actions frightened everyone who knew about it, and so antagonized the press that the resignation of Nixon became assured as soon as the Watergate burglary was perpetrated by his men. Set up, perhaps, yes. But that fascistic element was the bottom line of the battle that raged behind the scenes for the soul of this nation. Foreign policy and all the superficial distractions of the presidency were cast aside for the overriding purpose of ridding this nation of what almost might have been. The establishment of radical right-wing power in America didn't last for long, masked as it was in the liberal facade of Johnson's Great Society, because soon we suffered twelve years of do nothing-know nothing Republican government that oversaw the wrecking of the nation's financial and economic base and the impoverishment of our treasury. It was *deliberate*.

The Ku Klux Klan, radical States' Rights Parties, Minutemen, John Birchers, White Citizens Counsels, and neo-Nazi or fascist fringes sought to control our destiny. They sought to control the destiny of a great nation through the threat of violence, just as events like the "Kristallnacht" or Night of the Broken Glass, in

Germany in the thirties, when the windows of Jewish shops were smashed, and other constant examples of violence and marches by uniformed radicals intimidated the large center majority of law-abiding citizens everywhere.

This is what we have to stand against. We have to stand against the cover-up of *any* state crime. Everything has to be out in the open in our political life. That goes for Waco and for the Randy Weaver case.

The Branch Davidians had to remain on their land in Waco for five years to obtain title, by court order. They had only 20 days to go when they were burned out. Somebody wanted them out of there, but you haven't heard this in the news yet. That's how things are done in Texas.

The murder of John Kennedy was a vast and terrible crime. Most of us will never forget his true place in history and the price of John Kennedy and all of us paid for it.

I look forward to an America that will not be afraid of grace and beauty. . . .

John Kennedy said that. Think why he had to say it. We were and remain a brutal nation, getting worse, glorifying violence every moment on television and in the movies. This has become a brutal and barbaric land of glorified and extended violence and a subconsciously terrorized population. The public is diverted with bread and circuses like ancient Romans. The money needed for research and development, health and capital investment is blown away on sports, entertainment, booze, tobacco, and drugs. They want it this way, and it always worked this way. Even now, the pot is being stirred in our country, with drugs and sports and rock and roll the deadly mix. It's all deliberately set loose, like the dogs of war.

There once was a time in Camelot. . . .

APPENDICES

APPENDICES

Daryll Weatherly

A New Look at the "Film of the Century"

WHEN THE KENNEDY ASSASSINATION becomes a large-scale media controversy again, as it inevitably will, we can expect to see the familiar Zapruder film images of President Kennedy and Governor Connally being shot. The public will once again be exposed to the idea that they are watching the assassination.

They will, of course, only see a film of the assassination, not the actual event. I question whether the film in any way resembles the reality.

There are things in this film that I think should be addressed by the various experts who have studied it—maybe before they write another word about bullet trajectories.

At the risk of seeming to take a step backwards, I will mostly confine my comments to the printed frames that appear in Volume 18 of the Warren Commission exhibits. Historically significant work has been done with superior versions of the film, such as the LMH copy which Josiah Thompson studied (but was not allowed to publish) in 1967 for his book *Six Seconds in Dallas*. The advantage of the Warren Commission pictures is that they are more readily available for study, and they show both the main parts of the frames and the underexposed, but still useful, areas between the sprocket holes. Because of limitations on this book's ability to reproduce the pictures, this article should be read with either the Warren Commission volume or copies of the relevant slides handy.

It might be useful to briefly review some of the published studies of the film in order to become acquainted with the terminology used. One of the main points of contention is the timing of non-fatal shots (including possible misses), and there is no unmistakable indication on the film of when Kennedy was first hit. So indirect methods such as "blur analysis" (also called jiggle analysis) and "tracking analysis" came into use. Both of these were based on the premise that a startle response to the sound of shots would likely have caused Zapruder to shake the camera.

"Blur analysis" refers to the fact that a sudden motion of a camera during exposure causes little spots or highlights in the field of vision to become streaks, due to a change in the camera's position during the time that the shutter is open. Such streaks can also occur when an object being photographed is in motion itself during the exposure, or if both the camera and an object in the field of vision are moving.

Physicist Luis Alvarez gave a good description of this phenomenon in an article in the *American Journal of Physics*. Alvarez illustrated blurring by comparing Zapruder frames 227 and 228. He wrote:

"I noticed a striking phenomenon in frame 227 (when compared with 228). All the innumerable pointlike highlights on the irregular shiny surface of the automobile were stretched out into parallel line segments, along the '8 o'clock—2 o'clock' direction.

"To appreciate the significance of the streak, one must remember that each frame of moving picture film is not an instantaneous snapshot, but a time exposure that lasts about one-thirtieth of a second [Alvarez is making an estimate specific to this type of camera]. For a point of light on the car to be spread out into a streak on the film, the optical axis of the camera must have an angular velocity relative to the line joining the camera and that point of light."[1]

Tracking refers to the panning motion of a photographer following a moving object with a motion picture camera. Smooth panning motion, which keeps the object of interest in the center of each film frame, is errorless tracking. A *tracking error* is any departure from smooth panning motion, which would have the effect of causing the object of interest to move from place to place in successive frames.

CBS made use of blur and tracking analysis for its four-part special on the assassination in 1967. Alvarez cited the "simplified and not too convincing" presentation given to his work as a reason for writing his 1976 article.[2] Josiah Thompson, in *Six Seconds in Dallas*, criticized CBS's presentation on the grounds that blurs and tracking errors occur throughout the film, and CBS was selective in interpreting some as responses to shots.[3]

The House Select Committee on Assassinations (HSCA) conducted both a blur and a tracking analysis and published both in the appendix to its 1979 report.[4] Its conclusions were compromised by a need to coordinate information in the film with an alleged sound recording of the shooting, and by the same selectiveness shown in the CBS study.

A notable feature of these studies is that they kept information compartmented. The lengths of the blurs were considered significant, but not their directions, or how the streaks on moving figures compared to those in the background. The relation between the streaks and tracking errors was not explored.

In what follows, I will try to combine the separate features—background streaks, streaks in the motorcade figures, and tracking. Instead of asking whether they were caused by camera motions due to shots, I will ask whether they could have been caused by camera motions at all.

The first twenty or so frames that are reproduced in the Warren volume show the motorcade moving slowly down Elm Street. A few are somewhat fuzzy, and in particular in frames 182 and 184 the images of the car, occupants, motorcycle patrolmen, and follow-up car are somewhat blurred. Small highlights on the car appear as streaks pointing in the direction that it was moving. In frame 184 where these little streaks occur, they seem to extend about half of the distance that the car moves between frames. Since the streaks correspond to movement while the shutter was open for that frame, it is possible to estimate the time of exposure as about half of the frame-to-frame interval, or about 27 milliseconds. This is close to Alvarez's estimate of 1/30 of a second (33 milliseconds).[5] For most motion picture cameras, the maximum time of exposure is just under half of the frame-to-frame interval.

Note that the above estimation is possible because the background in frame 184 is not streaked at all, indicating that the camera motion was stopped for that frame, and so the only cause for streaking of highlights on the car would be the car's own motion. There are quite a few frames in which the tracking motion is practically stopped, or in which it follows the car with no deviation, and in either case the streaks which are seen somewhere in the frame can be compared with the frame-to-frame motion.

In frame 191, the background is streaked, as it also is in frames 190 and 192. The sequence 189–192 features a *tracking advance,* panning motion that moves somewhat ahead of the limousine. Since the camera motion is from left to right and slightly upward, small light spots in the background are recorded as streaks from right to left and slightly downward. Highlights on the moving figures, the cars, and people in the motorcade are also streaked, but differently due to their motion against the background. This actual motion is down Elm Street, left to right and somewhat downward, and when added to the background motion, produces the diagonal streaks that are seen.

The streaks, of course, are visible, and the actual motion of the cars could be deduced from them by noting the difference between the background streaks and the streaks on the vehicles. If you've ever taken a physics course and remember graphically adding and subtracting vectors, this is what I'm talking about.

Now consider frame 194. Between 193 and 194 there is a reversal of the tracking motion; the camera seems to have moved to the left, and one could expect part of this movement to have occurred while the shutter was open for frame 194. Indeed, there is a substantial difference between the actual motion of the vehicles and the streaks which occur on highlights, and the difference corresponds to the apparent camera motion.

But there is a missing element—the camera movement is not represented by any streaking of the background figures (or the foreground figures of the sign and the people standing on the north side of Elm St.). These figures appear almost the same as they are in frame 193. Small highlights are visible as little points of light. They should be substantially blurred if, as the streaks in the motorcade figures indicate, the shutter was open during part of the leftward jump.

This, I think, is a composite scene with at least two elements. The images of the people and vehicles in the motorcade could not have been put on film at the same instant in time as the foreground and background figures, not unless the entire motorcade made a sudden synchronized leap toward the south side of Elm Street.

I want to be completely clear on what is being cited as the evidence of forgery. The sharp appearance of the background does not, itself, conflict with the leftward camera movement. Taking only the background into account, one could merely conclude that this motion ended before the shutter opened for frame 194. The conflict is between the appearance of the background and the appearance of the motorcade figures, whose streaks, taking into account their actual motion, indicate that the leftward (and downward) camera movement continued while the shutter was open. The two parts of the frame indicate two different things.

Frame 195 should be compared closely to 194. The motorcade figures in frame 195 appear almost exactly as they do in 194, and even have the same blurs—"8 o'clock to 2 o'clock blurs," as Alvarez would call them. Yet the background and foreground in 195 are highly blurred, very different from what we see in frame 194. This phenomenon occurs again and again in the film—one part of the scene changes substantially from one frame to the next, while another remains essentially the same.

The next three frames are not particularly noteworthy. Frame 197 is blurred all over, so much so that it has no informational value.

Now look at frame 199. Between 198 and 199 there is a camera movement to the left, and between 199 and 200 there is little or no camera motion. If the shutter were open (for frame 199) during some part of the 198/199 camera movement, then one would expect streaks in the background. They aren't there—even tiny highlights in the background are recorded as small points of light.

So according to internal information in the background images, the camera was essentially stationary during the exposure of frame 199. One would expect, then, that highlights on the motorcade figures would be recorded as little streaks pointing in the direction of their actual motion down Elm St. They are, in fact, recorded as streaks running from lower left to upper right (8 o'clock to 2 o'clock again), which is decidedly not in the direction of actual motion.

Giving this frame the maximum benefit of the doubt, we could interpret the streaks in the motorcade figures as arising from either of two camera motions. "Subtracting" the known motion of the cars gives, in each case, a vector representing the expected streaks in the background.

There is, in fact, no streaking of the background highlights, nothing even approaching the expected appearance. As with 194, we have two parts of the frame indicating two different things about what the camera was doing while the shutter was open. Once again, the scene seems to be a composite.

There are various methods of filming composite scenes. Conceptually, the simplest method is the use of "traveling mattes."

In composite matte photography, a piece of film is exposed several times, with opaque shapes, called mattes, blocking off part of the film for each exposure. For still photography, mattes can be cutouts, painted pieces of glass, or inserts in the camera aperture.

Traveling mattes, used in motion picture composites, are pieces of high-contrast film that record images either as clear or opaque black. The matte images are made by projecting the original scene(s) onto an animation table, tracing or drawing the desired matte shapes, and photographing those shapes using high-contrast film. (This part of the procedure is called "rotoscoping.")

The desired composite images are then created by running raw film through an optical printer two or more times, each time accompanied by a traveling matte that will allow only the desired part of each original film to be copied.

This highly condensed description does not do justice to the complexity of the process, and the reader should consult a source on animation methods.*

To return to the Zapruder film, frames 200 and 202 feature a leftward and slightly downward apparent camera motion, and the streaking of the motorcade highlights seems consistent with this in frame 201. There is a slight indication of streaks in the background (look at the rows of holes in the background wall). In frame 203 the camera movement is back toward the right, and slightly upward, and the streaks are about what one would expect. The description of frame 205 is similar to that of frame 201.

In frame 206 there is no streaking of any highlight. According to what we see in the background, the camera seems to have been motionless while the shutter was open. According to what we see on the moving figures, the camera was following the motorcade without any tracking error. Unless this is a composite scene, it would appear that the motorcade was moving very slowly or was even stopped at this point. In frame 207, the motorcade figures look exactly as they do in frame 206, apart from being shifted against the background. The background itself has little streaks pointing in the direction of the vehicles' motion, exactly what one would expect from errorless tracking of a *moving* motorcade.

I think it is possible to assert that the film has been altered here, without saying exactly what was done. If frame 206 is not a composite, then several adjacent frames must have been edited out in order to obscure the very slow speed of the motorcade.

There is a notable feature of the sequence of frames from 196 to 206. In the odd-numbered frames, the vehicles and occupants are blurred, usually enough for highlights to become little streaks. The degree of blurring can be seen clearly by looking at the area between the sprocket holes, where one sees not streaks but two separate images of each highlight.

These separate images or "echoes" come about, I think, because the "claw," which advances the film between exposures, briefly obstructs the path of light to this area. Since the sprocket area receives light just after the shutter opens, and again just before it shuts, one sees only the two ends of the streaks. In later frames of the film,

---

Basic Animation Techniques by Brian G. D. Salt or *The Technique of Special Effects Cinematography* by Raymond Fielding (chapters 5 and 8 especially).

the background is a smooth, grassy area and it is possible to make out the dividing line between the main part of the frame and the darker, less exposed sprocket area. In frame 406, which is very blurred and which has a small tree in the sprocket area, with many highlights, one can see many blurs with missing middle segments.

The even-numbered frames 196 through 206 have, for the most part, sharp images of the motorcade figures, and what streaks there are, are not long enough to be split into distinct points in the sprocket area (a possible exception is frame 202). The blurry and sharp images of these figures seem to be shuffled together like cards.

I am convinced that the sequence of frames from 194 to 207 contains some composite scenes, and that the corresponding frames of the original Zapruder film were both different in their content and greater in number. I can only keep an open mind about what was in those original frames.

It may be that the film once showed Kennedy visibly and unambiguously hit by a shot before he went out of view behind the freeway sign. This would force the official reconstruction into uncomfortable arguments, such as a shot through the oak tree. Deleting some frames would break up the continuity of Kennedy's movements and, to some extent, disguise his reactions.

Removal of frames would also create jumps in the apparent motion of the limousine, and this would have to be compensated for by the creation of new frames to serve as filler. In a cinematic movie, each new frame would probably be a double exposure of the frames immediately preceding and following the edit. The blurred appearance of a double-exposed frame would help restore the illusion of continuous motion. This technique could not be used for a film that would be subjected to frame-by-frame analysis, but the same effect could be achieved by transplanting blurred images of the motorcade figures into existing frames.

In proposing this possibility, I do not mean to disregard the opinions of researchers who assert that Kennedy can indeed be seen reacting to a hit during this interval. Nor do I think it necessarily wrong to point out the blurs in frames such as 194 as evidence of a shock wave or neuromuscular reaction by Zapruder to the sound of a shot. Some researchers have spent hundreds of hours studying copies of the film in motion or still form, and it may be that they correctly interpret material which has been made as obscure as possible.

A sequence of blurred frames produced by one big lurch could provide the motorcade images for composite frames. This would also explain why all the blurs on these figures have the same general lower left to upper right orientation.

To an animator faced with the problem of obscuring Kennedy's reactions to an early shot, the Stemmons Freeway Sign appearing in many Zapruder frames would be a potential aid. Since the sign hides Kennedy for a sequence of frames, it is legitimate to ask whether it appears higher or wider in the film than it really was.

This question has been raised by researcher Chuck Marler, citing notes by Dallas County surveyor Robert West that give the height and position of the sign. Newcomb and Adams, in their 1974 manuscript, assert that the sign has been retouched in the film.

It is easier to ridicule such an idea than to disprove it. The sign may have been repositioned within a few days of the assassination. Newcomb and Adams point out that a photograph taken from the concrete pedestal a few days after the assassination shows the sign in a different position from where it appears in the film, but an early repositioning might innocently explain that discrepancy.

Any scheme to move the sign's image within the film would have to be carried out before the *Life* magazine assassination issue went on sale on November 26. Some of the frames showing the sign were published. No frame between 166 and 216 was published, so the alteration and compositing done to those frames need not have been done in such short time.

I think frames 221 and 228 should be studied closely, as they may contain a focal anomaly. The image of the sign in both frames is very sharp (look at the edges). The two standing figures in the near background on the right side are fuzzy, apparently due to progressive defocus, and yet the far background is very sharp in both frames.

Frame 227 has the motorcade figures highly blurred in the "8 o'clock" direction, exactly as Alvarez described, and there is not blurring of the background, which he did not mention. As with frames 194 and 199, I think this simply represents an impossibility. This is the part of the film where many researchers think Connally was hit, or Kennedy hit for the second time. The blurred frame 227 could cover up for one or more that were removed. Thompson, in his critique of the CBS study, singled it out as an example of the blur that CBS chose to ignore.[6]

Take a look at frames 302, 303, and 304. By examining details on the car, we can see that the tracking is smooth between 302 and 303 and there is a small lag between 303 and 304 (the tracking lag continues to about frame 306). In 302, the background figures of

Jean Hill and Mary Moorman are quite blurred from side-to-side motion, and yet in 303 they are not blurred at all. I want to emphasize that this is not a focal effect—you can see some streaks in these two figures in 302 and their appearance is definitely due to motion.

One is forced to conclude that the camera was nearly motionless while the shutter was open for frame 303, or else the background figures would be as blurred as they are in 302. Yet, if the camera *was* motionless, there should be streaks of highlights on the car, and there are none. Even if you accept that the camera could track normally before frame 303, stop when the shutter opens, then start tracking again as soon as it shuts, the lack of blur on the motorcade is still impossible to account for.

Similar comments apply to the sequence 308 to 311. In 308 the figures of Moorman and Hill are highly blurred, and again it must be attributed to motion (note the "echo" of Hill, who is now in the sprocket area). In 309 and 310 they are suddenly sharp. Between 308 and 309 the foreground hardly changes at all. (This is best verified by looking at the strip of 308 that appears at the top of 309, if you use the Warren evidence volume. The focus is slightly different in these photos of slides of movie frames.) There is a small tracking lag between 308 and 309, but how can it cause no change in the foreground if it causes such a large change in the background? And why is there no dramatic change from frame 309 to frame 310, when a similar (slight) tracking lag occurs between those frames?

The sharp background images in 310 become highly blurred in frame 311 (note the echo in the sprocket area again), and once again there is little or no streaking in the foreground in either frame. Once again there is a small change in tracking, an advance this time, but nowhere near enough of a change to account for what happens to the background.

From frame 313 to 314, there is an advance in tracking. Accordingly, the background figure—the woman ("Raggedy Ann") seen running toward Elm St.—is very blurry. Suddenly, in 315, this background figure is sharp, even though the tracking from 314 to 315 has been steady. Furthermore, this figure becomes blurry again in 316, even though there has been a lag in tracking since 315.

I think a number of frames have been removed from the fatal shot sequence. The purpose was to take out material too indicative of a frontal head shot or several head shots, and possibly to make the limousine appear to have been moving faster.

The removal of frames would create an appearance of a sudden change in speed at whatever point the editing started. The lack of a really large blur on the motorcade figures leads me to believe that composite frames were created to cover any such lurches in the limousine's motion. This would account for the lack of a blur in frames 303, 309, and 310.

I don't think that the depiction of Kennedy's head wound in the frames that follow (333 and 334 in the Warren volumes, 335 and 337 in the House Committee report) can be real. The top of the head, the right side of the face, and the entire forehead seem to be missing, and that just is too contrary to the existing medical testimony. The wound described in the autopsy report was not even remotely like that, nor is there any eyewitness description from Parkland Hospital in Dallas of such a wound.

Having reached the end of the most readily accessible Zapruder frames (those in the Commission and HSCA volumes) I must admit to a strong impression that many of its depicted scenes are simply paintings. Certain images in the Commission volume suggest this to me, such as the car emerging from behind the sign, and both Kennedy and his wife in frames 323 and 337.

Jackie's face in some of these frames, 335 and 337 especially, looks like a cartoon caricature of a shocked expression. I would have kept it to myself, had the author of this book, Harrison Livingstone, not independently mentioned it. What is depicted is so horrible that people simply resist looking closely at these frames, or don't question what they see if they do look.

Detailed examination of the very clear slides in the National Archives convinced me that there is a great deal of material that has been painted and then incorporated via rotoscoping into a photographic scene. This procedure is in fact simpler than the compositing of purely photographic material.

Before dismissing this utterly, the reader should consider the vast amount of visual material to which Americans are exposed which is either heavily retouched photography or completely painted scenes. Most people will readily accept such pictures as photographs (in advertisements, for instance) of real objects, even when the paintings do not altogether resemble what they are supposed to depict. Advertisements often contain subliminal messages that the mind may not consciously recognize, or which are flashed for only an instant.

THE FILM AS A PROPAGANDA WEAPON

In almost every assertion made by those who popularize the Zapruder film as "proof" of conspiracy, there is a contradictory or
self-negating element. The insistence that the film proves a shot
from the front, when instead there appears to be a huge frontal
exit wound, is a perfect example. Calling the film the "clock of
the assassination," while showing versions that incorporate stretch-
framing or other cinematic gimmicks, is another.

The biggest lie told about the film is that it is the single most
important piece of evidence in the case, when it is not possible for
any artifact to have such importance. No matter what the film
shows, it cannot tell us why the President was murdered, or what
changed in American life and politics that day.

It has never really mattered what the Zapruder film showed. In
the immediate aftermath of the assassination, all that the authorities
needed was to be able to credibly assert that they knew what had
happened. Possession of a film of the shooting, and presentation
of a few frames to the public, was enough.

When the public lost faith in the Warren Report (if it ever had
faith), the film was used as a distraction, to turn the discussion of
the murder of John Kennedy into the puzzle of Dealey Plaza, an
elaborate and never-ending game.

We humans have an unfortunate tendency to believe what we are
told. We are told that the Zapruder film is the "Kennedy Assassination Movie," and big and famous Hollywood directors buy this propaganda—and sell it to us, the "Best Evidence," and "The Film of
the Century." So what else could it be? Perhaps a plaything, a little
toy to occupy the child in us all.

UNITED STATES SECRET SERVICE
TREASURY DEPARTMENT

U.S. NO. 13-8 (Revised)
MEMORANDUM REPORT
(7-1-50)

60C

ORIGIN Chief's Office	OFFICE Detroit, Michigan		FILE NO. CO-2-34030
TYPE OF CASE	STATUS	TITLE OR CAPTION	
Protective Research	Closed - Detroit	LEE HARVEY OSWALD	
INVESTIGATION MADE AT	PERIOD COVERED		
Detroit, Michigan	12-6-63		
INVESTIGATION MADE BY			
SAs William R. Skiles and Robert R. Lapham			

DETAILS

SYNOPSIS

Earl Ruby interviewed relative to
alleged photographs portraying
President Kennedy's head wounds.

(A) INTRODUCTION:

This case originated upon receipt of an Office Memorandum from Inspector
Thomas Kelley, Dallas, dated December 5, 1963, which requests interview of
Earl Ruby relative to photographs portraying President Kennedy's head wounds.

(B) GENERAL INQUIRIES:

Earl Ruby was personally interviewed on December 6, 1963, at Cobo Cleaners,
18135 Livernois, Detroit, Michigan, by Special Agents William R. Skiles and
Robert R. Lapham. Ruby was aware that this information had been furnished this
Service by his sister and was entirely cooperative throughout the interview.

Ruby stated that during the evening of December 1, 1963, he received a
long-distance telephone call from an old friend, Mike Shore of Los Angeles, who
said he had been conferring with one Billy Whitfield, the writer of the Caryl
Chessman murder story, relative to the possibility of writing a story on Jack
Ruby. Shore also mentioned to Earl Ruby that he had information on some photographs, but he would not elaborate because he said the subject was too "hot"
to talk about on the phone. It was agreed that Earl Ruby would leave for Los
Angeles immediately.

Ruby said he arrived in Los Angeles the following day, and at that time he
was met by Shore and Whitfield, after which they discussed the possibility of
writing a story concerning Jack Ruby. During the conversation, Whitfield said
that he was told by one Peter Moss, a writer for the Saturday Evening Post

STRIBUTION	COPIES	REPORT MADE BY		DATE
Chief ✓	Orig.			12-6-63
Dallas	2 cc's		IAL AGENT	
(Air Mail)		APPROVED		DATE
Detroit	2 cc's		460	
Los Angeles	2 cc's		460	12-6-63
		SPECIAL AGENT IN CHARGE		

(CONTINUE ON PLAIN PAPER)   U. S. GOVERNMENT PRINTING OFFICE   16—61809-4

UNITED STATES GOVERNMENT

602 *Memorandum*

TO : Director, FBI (105-82555)   DATE: March 26, 1964

FROM : Legat, Ottawa (163-364) (P)   CONFIDENTIAL

SUBJECT: LEE HARVEY OSWALD
IS - R - CUBA

ReBulet March 19, 1964.

Enclosed are six copies of a letterhead memorandum dated March 26, 1964, in captioned matter. Two copies of this memorandum which has album of photographs attached are for dissemination to the President's Commission at the Bureau.

Extra copies of the enclosed memorandum and thisletter are furnished in the event the Bureau desires to furnish them to Dallas.

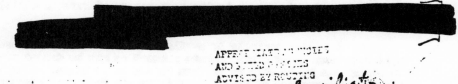

APPEAL MATTER TO VIOLET
AND SETTLED OFFICES
ADVISED BY ROUTING
SLIP(S) OF *declassificate*
DATE 7/14/77 FBI

Encs. 6
4 - Bureau (1 - Dallas
1 - Liaison direct)
1 - Ottawa
MLI:MEG
(5)

AGENCY *Dallas (Lt. FHAI & all....)*
REQ. RECD
DATE FORW 4-8-64
HOW FORW *reg*
BY *JMS:*   REG-20 105-82555- 302

EX-101

ENCLOSURE

Classified by 2040
Exempt from GDS, Category 1
Date of Declassification Indefinite 7/13/77

CONFIDENTIAL

JLR:MR:al
5/6/63

MAY 7   1964

Mr. J. Edgar Hoover
Director, Federal Bureau of Investigation
Department of Justice
Washington, D. C.   20535

Dear Mr. Hoover:

This Commission has been making a careful study of the
various motion picture films taken at the scene of the assassination.
In this project we have had the valuable assistance of members of
your Bureau, particularly Inspector James R. Malley, Inspector Leo
Gauthier and Special Agent Lyndal A. Shaneyfelt. As a result of the
information obtained from these films the Commission would like the
cooperation of your Bureau in the performance of certain additional
investigation at the scene of the assassination.

I will personally be available to supervise this work and
will have such other staff members present as may be deemed necessary.
We would hope to be able to perform this work in Dallas on May 18 and
May 19. The purpose of this letter is to set forth the steps which
we feel are necessary to properly complete this project.

I. PROBABLE RANGE WITHIN WHICH THE FIRST TWO SHOTS OCCURRED

Our examination of the Zapruder films indicates that
Governor Connally was hit at some point prior to frame 240. (All
references to frames in the Zapruder films are on the basis of a
numbering system worked out with FBI personnel who have been working
on this project.) Doctors familiar with the Governor's wounds
concluded that after frame 236 his body was not in a position to
have received the wound from a projectile fired from the sixth floor
southeast corner window of the Texas School Book Depository Building.
The Governor feels he was hit at approximately frame 230; some members
of our staff feel that it could have been as late as 240. There is
general consensus, however, that it could not have been later than
240. Governor and Mrs. Connally also testified that the Governor
was hit by the second shot.

cc: Mr. Rankin
     Mr. Redlich
     Mr. Willens

2

The FBI laboratory examination of the Zapruder camera established that it operates at a speed of 18-1/3 frames per second. Weapons experts have testified that the minimum time required to operate the assassination weapon is 2-1/4 seconds. It would appear, therefore, that a minimum of 41 frames would have to elapse between the first and second shots (18-1/3 X 2-1/4).

The Commission is aware that it is impossible to determine the exact point at which the first two shots were fired. We request the following on-site investigatory steps, however, in order to determine whether it was possible for a person located in the sixth floor southeast corner window of the TSBD building to fire two shots at the Presidential car, the second of which occurred no later than frame 240:

(1) A point should be marked on the road corresponding to frame 199 on the Zapruder film, which is the last point at which the assassin could have fired from the window and still have been able to fire again by frame 240. A car should be photographed on this spot from the point where Zapruder was standing so that this photograph can be compared with frame 199 to make certain that the location is accurate. This should be done with the Zapruder camera, which has been retained for this purpose. A Polaroid should also be used for immediate comparison.

(2) After a car has been placed at this point on the road it should be photographed from the assassination window to determine whether the assassin had a clear shot at the occupants of the rear seat, with particular reference to the tree which at some point blocks the view from this window.

(3) If the car had not passed the tree at frame 199, when viewed from the window, the car should be moved forward to the point at which there is a first clear view from the window and photographed at this point from both the window and from the place where Zapruder was standing so that we may determine what frame in the Zapruder film corresponds with this location.

(4) If the car has in fact passed beyond the tree at frame 199, it should be moved back to the point where it first cleared the tree and photographed from the window and the Zapruder location to establish the corresponding frame reference.

(5) The car should also be placed at the point where there is the last clear shot before it goes behind the tree and photographed from the window and the Zapruder location to determine the frame reference at this point.

3

(6) All the above points should be mapped on a survey. Actual distances should be measured on the ground between these various points. Trigonometric readings should be taken to determine the distances from these various points to the assassination window and the surveyor should also determine the angle with the horizontal which is made when a line is plotted from each of these points to the assassination window.

II. PROBABLE LOCATION OF THE THIRD SHOT

Unlike shots one and two, the third shot has been fixed at a particular frame in the Zapruder films (frame 313), as well as a particular frame in two other films (frame 24 of the Nix film and frame 42 of the Muchmore film). A car should be placed at the point which we believe to be the approximate location corresponding to these frames and then photographed from the point where the three cameramen were standing to establish the accuracy of this location. Distances should be measured from this point to the various points described in part I and angles and distances established between this point and the assassination window. The car should also be photographed at this point from the assassination window to establish the view which the assassin had when he fired the third shot.

III. PLOTTING TRAJECTORIES FROM THE RAILROAD OVERPASS

From each of the ground points established in parts I and II trigonometric readings should be taken from a point on either end of the overpass to chart the path which a bullet would travel if fired from those points on the overpass to the rear seat of the car. It should be determined whether a bullet could reach the rear seat without hitting the windshield, and the angle with the horizontal which would be made by a bullet fired from these points to a car located at each of the points on the ground as determined in parts I and II.

A copy of this letter has been sent to Chief Rowley of the Secret Service with a request that the Secret Service provide such assistance in this work as the Commission and your Bureau may require. The Secret Service has furnished the Commission with photographs, surveys and measurements which we have used in our examination of the films and which will no doubt be useful to your Bureau in completing this project.

We would like your Bureau to make all necessary arrangements for this project. Members of the Bureau assigned to this project should contact either Mr. Norman Redlich or Mr. Melvin Eisenberg of the Commission staff if additional information is required.

Sincerely,

J. Lee Rankin
General Counsel

MEMORANDUM

FROM RG 272 Series 12
INV 1 or 1.1

May 12, 1964

From a
Carbon

TO: Mr. J. Lee Rankin

FROM: Arlen Specter

SUBJECT: Agenda for On-The-Site Tests at Dallas

I. Objectives

    A. The precise positions on Elm Street of President Kennedy and Governor Connally should be determined where they were when:

        1. Frame 199 was photographed by Zapruder;

        2. Frame 225 was photographed by Zapruder;

        3. Frame 240 was photographed by Zapruder;

        4. Frame 313 was photographed by Zapruder.

    B. The precise positions on Elm Street of President Kennedy and Governor Connally should be determined and the corresponding frame number on the Zapruder film should be ascertained where:

        1. Oswald would have had his first clear shot at President Kennedy after President Kennedy emerged from behind the tree.

        2. Oswald would have had his first clear shot at Governor Connally after Governor Connally emerged from behind the tree.

        3. Oswald would have had any clear shot through the tree.

        4. Oswald would have had his last clear shot at President Kennedy before President Kennedy went behind the tree.

    C. A determination should be made whether the wounds on President Kennedy or Governor Connally could have been caused by a shot fired from the Triple Underpass.

- 2 -

II. Preparatory Steps Before Departing for Dallas

A. Arrange to simulate the car to be used so that its dimensions correspond with the President's car. To that end, Inspector Ke has been requested to ascertain the following measurements:

1. The height from the ground to the seat of the President's car without any automatic elevation of the seat which corresponds to the positioning of the seat at the time of the assassination.

2. The height of the back rest on the President's seat so that we may determine how much of the President's back was exposed.

3. The dimensions of the jump seat, including:

   a. the distance between the right edge of the right jump seat to the right door.

   b. the distance between the back of the right jump seat and the front of the President's seat.

   c. the height of the jump seat from the floor.

   d. the height of the jump seat on the President's automobile from the ground.

Intention to have Humes look at the pictures

B. Construct a dummy with the measurements of the President's body so that it may be positioned in the precise location where President Kennedy sat. Inspector Malley of the FBI is arrangir to have such a dummy prepared. I suggest that Commander Humes mark the points of entry and exit of the neck wound and the point of entrance of the head wound when he reviews the x-rays and photographs of the autopsy.

III. Proposed Measurements, Calculations and Photography

A. The precise location of President Kennedy should be ascertained at each position itemized in I above, with linear measurements from the center of the intersection of Elm and Houston Streets.

B. The precise location of Governor Connally should be ascertained at each position itemized in I above, with linear measurements from the center of the intersection of Elm and Houston Streets.

- 3 -

C. The angle of declination should be calculated from the position where we believe Oswald held the rifle to the points of entry on President Kennedy's back and head at the positions specified in I.

D. The angle of declination should be calculated from the position where we believe Oswald held the rifle to the points of entry on Governor Connally at the positions specified in I.

E. The distances should be ascertained of all the possible shots considered in C. and D. above.

F. Motion pictures and still photographs should be taken of all the positions specified in I. from:

    1. the view through the Oswald rifle.

    2. the place where Zapruder stood.

IV. Necessary Personnel, Equipment and Facilities

A. Under your supervision, this project should be handled by the same people who worked on these problems during the numerous viewings of the films and slides:

    1. Inspector James R. Malley, Inspector Tom Kelley, Inspector Leo Gauthier, SA Lyndal L. Shaneyfelt and SA John Joe Howlett should be present.

    2. Norman Redlich and I should be stationed interchangeably at the window and on the street.

B. We should have a surveyor available to make the calculations and measurements and provide the necessary trigonometric readings. To that end I have asked Inspector Malley to obtain the services of Robert Jones who has worked with the Secret Service on this project before.

C. We should have a 6-foot, 2-inch man available to simulate Governor Connally.

D. Governor Connally's clothing should be taken to be worn by the man sitting in his position.

E. We should have available at the Texas School Book Depository Building a room for showing the movies and slides. Inspector Malley advised that it can be arranged without difficulty.

David W. Mantik, M.D., Ph.D

69780 Stellar Drive · Rancho Mirage, CA 92270 · (619) 324-4591 · FAX (619) 324-7931

June 16, 1995

Letters to the Editor
Journal of the American Medical Association
515 North State Street
Chicago, Illinois 60610

Re: JFK autopsy evidence in
  "Dennis Breo's Reply"
  JAMA, May 24/31, 1995
  Vol. 273, No. 20, p. 1633

Dear Editor:

I have reviewed the JFK autopsy X-rays and photographs at the National Archives on seven occasions, most recently three hours ago. I have viewed the photographs in stereo and have made many hundreds of point by point measurements on the X-rays. Neither Dennis Breo, nor *JAMA*'s editor George Lundberg, have ever bothered to visit the Archives -- not even once. To a large Chicago audience in 1993 Lundberg admitted that he is not an expert in this matter -- and Breo is not even a physician. Unfortunately, what Breo regards as evidence is too often obfuscation. The unadulterated data are as follows.

The throat wound.

The pathologists officially neither saw -- nor even knew about -- this supposed exit wound while they were at the autopsy. So what Breo describes as autopsy evidence is purely hearsay and could not even be used in court! Instead, only Parkland medical personnel claim to have seen this wound. In transcripts of his CBS interview at Parkland Hospital, Dr. Malcolm Perry, who performed the tracheotomy, described this wound three times as an entrance wound. He described the wound as pencil sized and circular -- critical pieces of data that Breo has never disclosed in any of his articles. Dr. Charles Carrico, who assisted Perry, described a small, "penetrating," and "even, round wound." Dr. Ronald Jones stated: "The hole was very small and relatively clean-cut as you would see in a bullet that is entering rather than exiting from a patient." Dr. Robert McClelland stated, "...but we are familiar with wounds. We see them everyday -- sometimes several a day. This did appear to be an entrance wound." Nurse Margaret Henchcliffe told the Warren Commission that she had never seen an exit wound like this. In fact, none of the Parkland personnel described this as an exit wound. But Breo persists in claiming that only the pathologists, who never officially saw it (nor even a photograph of it), are the only ones qualified to make such a judgment. To parody Breo, this is why we have autopsies!

The back wound.

Breo claims that this wound was the corresponding entrance for the supposed exit wound in the throat. I personally spoke with Dr. John Ebersole, the sole radiologist at the autopsy, who was never contacted by Breo. He advised me unequivocally (on tape) that the back wound was at the level of T4. When we spoke he was a practicing radiation oncologist, which is also my specialty. Because cancers must be precisely targeted in radiation therapy, this is the one specialty in which specific and precise correlation between external and internal anatomy is critical. If anyone could make this correlation it would be someone like Ebersole. As further confirmation of this site, the autopsy diagram shows the wound at about this level and Admiral George Burkley's Death Certificate specifically describes the wound at T3. It is simply impossible for a bullet to go steeply downward (presumably from the sniper's nest), entering at T3 or T4, and then exit at a traditional tracheotomy site. By their own admission, the pathologists could not pass a probe into the chest cavity from this back wound. Furthermore, they confess that they never did trace this wound from front to back; they only theorized that the bullet transited. Although Breo finds "conspiracy theorists" distasteful, lone gunman theorists are admired, even when the primary evidence (the body itself) is available and is not properly examined. To parody Breo, this is why we have autopsies!

The skull wounds.

The best evidence for a skull entry wound was at a site near the right external occipital protuberance (EOP), just inside the hairline. Here the pathologists discovered a beveled, partially circumferential defect. This was further confirmed by a corresponding hole in the scalp. If this entry site is granted, as seems reasonable, then there is no explanation for the array of 30 - 40 metal fragments widely scattered across the skull vertex, more than 10 cm above the pathologists' entry site! Neither the Warren Commission nor the House Select Committee on Assassinations (HSCA) had the courage to ask the pathologists to relate this distant debris to an entry bullet. Only an option the pathologists did not consider (at least not officially) -- a second bullet to the head -- can explain this debris. Despite Breo's obeisance to the evidence, he seems oblivious to this entire issue.

There is no longer any question that the right parietal-occipital skull was blown out. In an HSCA document released in 1993, pathologist J. Thorton Boswell described the large skull defect as extending all the way to the bullet entry site near the EOP. He has also confirmed this recently (on tape) to Dr. Gary Aguilar. Such a far posterior defect is entirely consistent with the official notes of all the Parkland physicians who commented on this question. In addition, the official autopsy report uses the word "occipital" in describing the large skull defect, and all these descriptions closely match the diagram published by the Warren Commission. Such a large posterior defect was strong evidence to the Dallas medical personnel (and even to many autopsy personnel) for a frontal bullet. Furthermore, the apparent trail of metallic debris at the skull vertex projects backward into the sky -- well above the highest rooftops around Dealey Plaza. This apparent trail, however, could easily be consistent with a second head shot from the front (most likely when the head was tilted backward), a possibility not officially considered by the pathologists. In fact, they have never explained this metallic debris -- nor were they ever queried about its curious location. Despite Breo's self-proclaimed reverence for the evidence, one can only wonder if he glanced at even poor quality prints of the X-rays.

Summary.

We must choose. We can either accept the theorizing of the pathologists on an unobserved chest transit wound and we can ignore the vertex trail of bullet debris and we can disregard the large parietal-occipital skull defect, all of which Breo is content to do -- or we can do what Breo obstinately refuses to do, i.e., look at the evidence with an open mind and arrive at an informed opinion. Not only many Dealey Plaza witnesses, including numerous occupants of the Presidential and follow-up limousines, but even the medical evidence itself strongly supports shots from the front. Breo's original unfamiliarity with -- and continued gross indifference to -- Dr. Charles Crenshaw's presence in Trauma Room One on November 22, 1963, is only further confirmation of his persistent and willful ignorance in the murder of President John F. Kennedy. One can only speculate on the motivations for such myopic behavior.

With some astonishment,

David W. Mantik

David W. Mantik, M.D., Ph.D.

P.S. I am no longer an AMA member.

cc: Marc S. Micozzi, M.D., Ph.D.
National Museum of Health and Medicine
Washington, D.C. 20306-6000

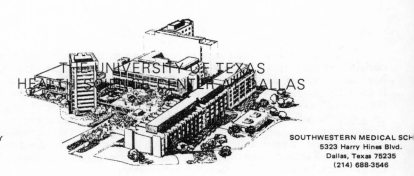

DEPARTMENT OF SURGERY
Division of Urology
Paul C. Peters, M.D.
  Professor & Chairman
Terry D. Allen, M.D.
  Professor

SOUTHWESTERN MEDICAL SCH
5323 Harry Hines Blvd.
Dallas, Texas 75235
(214) 688-3546

August 7, 1979

Mr. H. E. Livingston
30 West 25th Street
Baltimore, Maryland 21218

Dear Mr. Livingston:

I have marked an "X" on the picture which more accurately depicts the wound, although neither is quite accurate in my opinion. There was a large hole in the back of the head through which one could see the brain.

Sincerely yours,

Paul Peters

Paul C. Peters, M. D.
Professor and Chairman
Division of Urology

PCP:pl

THE UNIVERSITY OF TEXAS
SOUTHWESTERN MEDICAL CENTER
AT DALLAS

Paul C. Peters, M.D.
Ashbel Smith Professor of Urology

Department of Surgery
Division of Urology

April 17, 1995

Mr. Harrison Livingstone
3025 Abell Avenue
Baltimore, MD 21218

Dear Mr. Livingstone:

I returned to work today, having been ill the past three weeks with mycoplasma pneumonia, and found your letter waiting for me. I am sorry you are upset. I have never openly criticized by name any of the many authors who have spoken to me during the past 30 years regarding the assassination of President Kennedy. I would like to state again what I saw.

At the time of President Kennedy's autopsy, I saw only the hole in his neck in front and the large hole in the occipitoparietal area, estimated about 7 cm., on the right side. That is all I ever said I saw. Even when I went to view the autopsy 25 years later, at the request of NOVA, and they showed me a picture of the occipital area of President Kennedy's head and had the hair parted to indicate the so-called hole of entry in the skull, I told them I could not tell if it was a hole in the skull from the photograph and would have had to stick my finger through the hole in the skull to see if it was a through-and-through wound. I did not see the entry wound in the back of the neck or upper shoulder which resulted in the exit wound in the front of the neck (which I did see). Certainly, none of us attending President Kennedy at the time picked up his head. Dr. Jenkins has said that he did feel the wound on the right side in the upper shoulder as he was positioning President Kennedy's head to improve the airway. I have no idea whether the autopsy pictures which they showed me at the Archives were the real ones or not. When I asked them at the Archives if I could see the brain itself, they said the brain was unavailable. I did think the cerebellum was injured at the time. However, Dr. Lattimer told me that when he viewed the autopsy soon after the assassination, the cerebellum was not torn and was intact beneath its cover, the tentorium. When I did view the brain photographs, as presented to me at the Archives, I did see that the cerebellum was indeed depressed on the right side compared to the left. You are quite correct that the wound in the front of the neck, which Dr. Perry enlarged slightly to do the tracheostomy, was assumed by us to be a wound of exit. We no doubt were influenced by subsequent discussions by the people from Bethesda and the Warren Commission.

In summary, I believe everything I told you initially when you came to visit me, I would say again today. I have tried to present this to you as it appeared to me that day and not to confuse it with the many texts and newspaper articles that have appeared since the assassination.

Sincerely yours,

Paul C. Peters

Paul C. Peters, M.D.
Ashbel Smith Professor of Urology
Former Chairman, Division of Urology

PCP:pl

From
Report of SA Robert P Gemberling
11/30/63 Dallas, Texas

(CD 5) This is the entire content relative to shot distances.

Commission Document #5, pages 117-118

CD-5

FD-302 (Rev. 3-3-59)

FEDERAL BUREAU OF INVESTIGATION

Date _____ 11/29/63 _____

1

SA JOHN JOE HOWLETT, U. S. Secret Service, Dallas, advised that with the aid of a surveyor and through the use of 8 millimeter movie films depicting President JOHN F. KENNEDY being struck by assassin's bullets on November 22, 1963, HOWLETT was able to ascertain that the distance from the window ledge of the farthest window to the east in the sixth floor of the Texas School Book Depository Building, 411 Elm Street, to where the President was struck the first time in the neck was approximately 170 feet. He stated this distance would be accurate within two or three feet. The distance from the same window ledge to the spot where President KENNEDY was struck in the head by the assassin's bullet was approximately 260 feet. Mr. HOWLETT stated that Secret Service Agents, using the 8 millimeter film had been unable to ascertain the exact location where Governor JOHN B. CONNALLY was struck.

SA HOWLETT advised that it had been ascertained from the movies that President KENNEDY was struck with the first and third shots fired by the assassin, while Gov. CONNALLY was struck with the second shot. SA HOWLETT stated the window referred to above was the one from which the shots were fired and faces south.

on ____ 11/29/63 __ at _ Dallas, Texas _____ File # _ Dallas 89-43 _____
ROBERT M. BARRETT
by Special Agents _and IVAN D. LEE/sl _____ 117 ___ Date dictated _ 11/29/63 ____

This document contains neither recommendations nor conclusions of the FBI. It is the property of the FBI and is loaned your agency; it and its contents are not to be distributed outside your agency.

[handwritten] guest Harry Livingstone, room 133

U,E,7 - BC-USA-KENNEDY-XRAYS,   11-18 0492 -
BC-USA-KENNEDY-XRAYS
  JFK X-RAYS ARE FAKE, RADIOLOGIST CHARGES
      By Jeanne King
      NEW YORK (Reuter) - A radiologist charged on Thursday that
skull X-rays taken at the autopsy of President John Kennedy were
altered to hide the possibility that a second gunman had taken
part in the assassination.
      Dr David Mantik, a radiologist and physicist from the
Eisenhower Medical Center in Rancho Mirage, California, said the
X-rays ``were abnormal'' and altered in such a way as to
disguise the direction that the bullet entered Kennedy's skull.
      Speaking at a Manhattan news conference sponsored by the
author of a new book charging a cover-up in the assassination,
he said a great white patch had been superimposed on the X-rays
to hide the possibility that a bullet had entered the skull from
the front.
      Conspiracy theorists have long argued that Kennedy was
fired at from both the Texas School Book Depository and from a
grassy knoll near Dealy Plaza.
      The official Warren Commission investigation said there was
no evidence of a second gunman and that the shots were fired by
Lee Harvey Oswald from a sixth-floor window at the school book
depository.
      Most other scientists accept the X-rays as genuine.
      Mantik said he examined the X-rays with a sensitive light-
measuring instrument using a technique called optical
denistometry three weeks ago.
      He said the instrument measures the transmission of
ordinary light through selected points of the X-ray film.
      Mantik said he became suspicious of the large white area
where the missing bone should have been because he had never
seen such a phenomena. The measured light was a thousand times
the maximum seen in any other X-ray, he said.
      The radiologist said white areas on any X-ray always
represents denser tissues, such as bone.
      ``What someone did in taking the X-rays of Kennedy during
the autopsy was to put a great white patch on the back of the
lateral X-ray to cover up the hole, which is why the area is so
extraordinarily white,'' Mantik said.
      ``To see a big hole like that implies that a bullet came in
from the front, not the back and is indicative that a second
gunman shot Kennedy.''
      ``The X-rays are composites. There's no doubt about it,''
he concluded. ``The way they faked the X-rays was similiar to
what happens when you double expose film using two different
images.''
      Jerrol Custer, an X-ray technican at Bethesda Naval
Hospital in 1963 responsible for taking and then developing the
X-rays, told the same news conference that the official skull X-
rays are not the X-rays he took that night.
      He said that he was instructed by his superior, Dr James
Ebersole, to tape bullet fragments to pieces of bones and to
take X-rays of them.
      Custer now believes the X-rays were used to help make the
composites or double-exposures.
      The news conference was called by Harrison Edward
Livingstone, who has written three books on the Kennedy
assassination, including a new one, ``Killing the Truth.''

o9446^ nyc--
    r-nbx
1^AM-NY---JFK-Conspiracy,520<
^Doctors Offer New Claims of JFK Autopsy Coverup<
^BY RICHARD PYLE=
^Associated Press Writer=
        NEW YORK (AP) _ Three doctors offered evidence Thursday purporting t
show that autopsy photos of President John F. Kennedy were faked, but their
claim was all but ignored by news media evidently weary or wary of JFK
conspiracy theories.
        Harrison E. Livingstone, a Baltimore author who believes a cabal of
powerful Texans and the FBI were behind the murder of Kennedy, called the
news conference to buttress the theories as outlined in the latest of his
three books on the subject.
        Describing himself as ``David versus Goliath,'' Livingstone charged
that ``the most powerful forces in the media'' have tried in the past year
to shut down the ongoing public debate over Kennedy's death on Nov. 22,
1963.
        ``After this 30th anniversary, it will be dead. So we are in an uphi
struggle,'' he said.
        That was apparent on Thursday, as only a handful of reporters, most
them for foreign news organizations, showed up for the detailed, 90-minute
presentation at a midtown hotel.
        Livingstone conceded that he had a credibility problem after a simil
news conference a year ago turned rancorous. But he said he came this time
``with more backup,'' meaning the three doctors and a former naval lab
technician who made the autopsy X-rays at Bethesda Naval Hospital.
        While the ``second gunman'' theory is not new, they contended that t
autopsy pathologists were under what Dr. Robert Livingston, of San Diego,
called ``explicit non-medical control,'' and that the official photos are
fakes that conceal the fact that Kennedy was shot twice from the front,
rather than from behind by Lee Harvey Oswald.
        Author Livingstone claims that the overall decisions were made by a
senior Air Force officer who was present in the autopsy room. That officer,
he says, was the brother of the mayor of Dallas, and had been fired by
Kennedy from a security job.
        Dr. Gary L. Aguilar of San Francisco said that for the official autc
photos to be authentic would require that all but one of 42 witnesses, many
of them doctors, described the head injury incorrectly. That ``defies
belief,'' Aguilar said.
        Dr. David Mantik, a radiologist from Rancho Mirage, Calif., said he
recently conducted ``optical density'' tests on the photos in the National
Archives, finding that they were ``composites'' that blocked out the large
exit wound and positioned a bullet fragment to suggest a shot from the
rear.
        Mantik said that when he asked the autopsy radiologist, Dr. John
Ebersole, about this, Ebersole refused to answer his questions. Ebersole
died recently of cancer, he said.
        Livingston, who worked for the National Institutes of Health at the
time and is now a professor emeritus of neurosciences, said that when he
heard news reports about a throat wound on Nov. 22, 1963, he considered it
such a ``matter of utmost importance'' that he phoned the doctor who was to
perform the autopsy, to alert him to it.
        He said that during the conversation, the latter broke off, saying '
can't talk with you any longer. The FBI won't let me.''

Gary L. Aguilar, MD
909 Hyde Street, #530
San Francisco, California 94109
(415)775-3392 FAX - (415) 563-4453

May 19, 1994

Henry Cohen
Federal Bar News and Journal
Federal Bar Association
1815 H. Street N.W., #408
Washington, D.C. 20006-3697

Dear editor,

Mr. George Costello's excellent article on Gerald Posner's *Case Closed* brought to mind unsettling experiences I've had exploring Posner's work. Mr. Posner mentioned, in support of his contention that Mr. James Tague was hit by a fragment from the first of three shots, that Tague reported in a 1992 interview that he did not know which of the three shots hit him.[1] As recently noted by Harold Weisberg in his new book, *Case Open*,[2] however, Tague told the Warren Commission that he was not hit by a fragment from the first shot. I called Tague on 4/30/94 and he told me the same thing he told the Warren Commission. Tague thus not only flatly contradicts Mr. Posner's reconstruction of the shooting, he revealed that Posner misrepresented Tague's views which have been consistent over three decades. Moreover, Tague also told me that he has never spoken with Mr. Posner, though the implication of three references in *Case Closed* is that Posner did speak with him on two successive days.[3]

Mr. Posner dismissed Rose Cheramie's remarkable clairvoyance that JFK was to be killed in Dallas by cla   iming that the witness to Cheramie's statements, Dr. Victor Weiss, reported that Cheramie only mentioned this after Oswald's death. This is flatly untrue, which Mr. Posner must know from the work of the 1978 House Select Committee on Assassinations (HSCA) which reported, "[According to Dr. Weiss] Dr. Bowers allegedly told Weiss that the patient, Rose Cheramie, had stated before the assassination that President Kennedy was going to be killed..."[4] Moreover, Mr. Posner certainly knowingly neglected to mention another unassailable, HSCA-cited witness, Louisiana State Police lieutenant, Francis Fruge. He reported Cheramie made the prediction directly to him two days before JFK's murder.[5]

Mr. Posner cited the testimony of Renatus Hartogs, the psychiatrist who examined Oswald as a teenage truant, arguing that Hartog's findings suggested a violent potential.[6] The Warren Commission dismissed Hartogs's testimony when an examination of his original report revealed the opposite conclusion. In fact, the Commission concluded, "Contrary to reports that appeared after the assassination, the psychiatric examination did not indicate that Lee Oswald was a potential assassin, potentially dangerous, that his 'outlook on life had strongly paranoid overtones,' or that he should be institutionalized."[7]

On November 17, 1993, before the Committee on Government Operations House of Representatives, Mr. Posner reported that he had interviewed two of JFK's pathologists, James Humes, MD and J. Thornton Boswell, MD.[8] Posner testified that they confirmed to him that they had changed their minds about the original location they had given for JFK's skull wound. In their 1963 autopsy report[9], and again in 1992 interviews published in the Journal of the American Medical Association, both pathologists claimed the bullet entered JFK's skull "to the right and just above" the base of the rear of the skull, near the external occipital protuberance.[10] Mr. Posner informed the U. S. Congress that the pathologists told him that they had erred -- the wound was 10-centimeters higher, at the top rear of the skull. On March 30, 1994 I called both Drs. Humes and Boswell. Both physicians told me that they had not changed their minds about JFK's wounds at all. They stood by their statements in JAMA, which contradict Mr. Posner. Startlingly, Dr. Boswell told me that he has never spoken with Mr. Posner.

While one is naturally loath to question the good faith of any author, especially one nominated for the Pulitzer Prize, Mr. Posner seems to be begging even Warren Commission loyalists to question his.

Truly,

Gary L. Aguilar, MD
Chairman, Department of Surgery, Saint Francis Memorial Hospital, San Francisco
Assistant Professor of Ophthalmology, Stanford University Medical Center
Assistant Professor of Ophthalmology, University of California, San Francisco
Member, Board of Directors, San Francisco County Medical Society
Member, American Medical Association
Member, California Medical Association

---

[1] Posner, Gerald, *Case Closed*, p. 325. New York: Random House, 1993.

[2] Weisberg, Harold, *Case Open*, p.149. New York: Carroll and Graf, 1994.

[3] Posner, Gerald, *Case Closed*, p. 553, refs 31, 32 &33. New York: Random House, 1993.

[4] Appendix to Hearings before the Select Committee on Assassinations of the U.S. House of Representatives (HSCA) V.10:200-201.

[5] HSCA V.10:201-202.

[6] Posner, Gerald, *Case Closed*, p. 12 - 13. New York: Random House, 1993.

[7]Report of the President's Commission on the Assassination of President John F. Kennedy (Warren Report). Washington, DC; US Government Printing Office; 1964, p. 379.

[8] Hearing before the Legislation and National Security Subcommittee of the Committee on Government Operations House of Representatives, One Hundred Third Congress, First Session, November 17, 1993, p.112-113. Washington, D.C., US Government Printing office, 1994, ISBN 0-16-043551-X.

[9]Report of the President's Commission on the Assassination of President John F. Kennedy (Warren Report). Washington, DC; US Government Printing Office; 1964, p.543 (St Martin's Press edition).

[10] Breo DL. JFK's death-the plain truth from the MDs who did the autopsy. JAMA 1992; 267:2797.

NOTES

Introduction

1. Harrison E. Livingstone, *Killing the Truth*, p. 114.
2. Michael L. Kurtz, *The Crime of the Century*, p. 82; Cyril H. Wecht and Robert P. Smith, "The Medical Evidence in the Assassination of President John F. Kennedy," *Forensic Science*, vol. 3, (1974) 105–28. Wecht calls reports of a frontal entry in the throat "erroneous." He implies that the FBI report saying the bullet in the back had "no point of exit" is wrong. Wecht says that Kennedy's back wound and that of Connally came from a position "considerably further west" in the Texas School Book Depository. He thinks that Kennedy's wound came from a lower floor than that which struck Connally (p. 126). This kind of analysis is preposterous.
3. *Newsweek*, November 22, 1993, p. 67.
4. Ibid.
5. *Newsweek*, Ibid. p. 99.
6. John Stockwell, *The Praetorian Guard* (Boston: South End Press, 1991), p. 175.
7. Jonathan Vankin, *Conspiracies, Cover-ups and Crimes* (New York: Paragon House, Dell edition, 1992), p. 232. "Top Censored Stories of the Past Ten Years," *Utne Reader*, March–April 1994, p. 72.

1. The Official Story

1. Warren Report, *New York Times* edition, p. 504, third from last paragraph.
2. WR, *NY Times* edition, p. 103.
3. WR, *NY Times* edition, p. 104.
4. CE 585, 18 H 262.
5. CE 883, 17 H 901.
6. Ibid, p. 101.
7. WR, Government Printing Office edition, p. 19.
8. WR, *NY Times* edition, p. 503.

9. Ibid. p. 502.
10. Report of Dr. Pierre Finck to General Joseph Blumberg, February 1, 1965, p. 4; *Killing the Truth*, H. E. Livingstone, pp. 43, 71–72; *High Treason 2*, H. E. Livingstone, pp. 148–57, 254, 284–95, 233–38, 293–95.
11. WR, p. 21.
12. *The Dallas Morning News*, James Ewell and Suzanne DuBeau, June 24, 1980.
13. Jesse Curry, *JFK Assassination File*, p. 61.
14. Carlos Hathcock in *Police Sniper* by Craig Roberts (NY: Pocket Books, 1993), p. xxvii.

2. The Fake Autopsy Photographs from the Secret Documents

1. Associated Press story, *Baltimore Sun*, May 27, 1993.
2. Gary Aguilar, M.D., "John F. Kennedy's Fatal Wounds—The Witnesses and the Interpretations From 1963 to the Present," October 1993, unpublished manuscript.
3. 7 HSCA 115.
4. Gary Aguilar, M.D., unpublished manuscript, *JAMA and JFK—Politics vs. Science*, 1993, p. 17.
5. 1 HSCA 310–11.
6. Gary Aguilar, M.D., unpublished manuscript, *JAMA and JFK—Politics vs. Science*, p. 8.
7. HSCA Record Number 180–10093–10429, Agency File No: 002070, August 17, 1977, Purdy, Donald A., Jr., Subjects: Harper, Jack C.; Cairns, A.B.; Bone fragments; Evidence, Medical; Burkley, George; Humes, James J.
8. 7 HSCA 23; *High Treason 2*, pp. 90, 100, 138, 245, 300, 314, 318, 322, 327–28, 333–34; *Killing the Truth*, 269–88.
9. HSCA Record Number 180–10093–10429, Agency File No: 002070, August 17, 1977, Purdy, Donald A., Jr., Subjects: Harper, Jack C.; Cairns, A.B.; Bone fragments; Evidence, Medical; Burkley, George; Humes, James J., p. 11.
10. Ibid. p. 12.
11. Ibid. p. 16.
12. 7 HSCA 253 and other examples listed in the chapter "From the Secret Documents: Conflicts in the Autopsy."
13. Ibid. pp. 11–12.
14. Report of Andy Purdy, HSCA, August 7, 1978, HSCA File No. 180–10077–10107, Agency File No. 010574.
15. Ibid. p. 12.
16. Ibid. p. 15.
17. Ibid. p. 15.
18. The color version was printed for the first time in the supermarket tabloid, the *Globe*, December 31, 1991, p. 12, along with several other of his autopsy photographs; and again on page 84 of Groden's *The Killing of the President*, Viking, 1993. Statements by the publisher that the publi-

cation of the color autopsy photographs was for the first time in the Viking book is of course false, along with nearly every other statement in their ad.

19. HSCA Memorandum of interview with Dr. J. Thornton Boswell, August 11, 1978, p. 2.
20. HSCA interview with Dr. Pierre Finck, March 11, 1978, pp. 111–12.
21. HSCA interview with Dr. Pierre Finck, March 11, 1978, p. 84.
22. HSCA interview with Dr. Pierre Finck, March 11, 1978, p. 89.
23. Ibid. pp. 89–90.
24. HSCA interview with Dr. Pierre Finck, March 11, 1978, p. 104.
25. HSCA interview with Dr. Pierre A. Finck, March 12, 1978, p. 2.
26. Ibid. pp. 3–4.
27. HSCA Record No. 180-10093-10429, Agency File No: 002070, August 17, 1977, p. 8.
28. Ibid. p. 6.
29. Ibid. p. 7.
30. Ibid. p. 9.
31. Ibid. p. 10.
32. Ibid. p. 12.
33. 7 HSCA 246.
34. HSCA interview with Dr. John Ebersole, March 11, 1978, p. 62.
35. HSCA interview with Dr. John Ebersole, March 11, 1978, p. 63.
36. Ibid. p. 63.
37. Ibid. p. 64.
38. HSCA Memorandum of interview with Dr. J. Thornton Boswell, August 16, 1977, p. 7.
39. HSCA August 12, 1977, interview with John Thomas Stringer, dated August 17, 1977, p. 11.
40. HSCA interview with Roy Kellerman, August 24, 1977, p. 7.
41. HSCA interview with Roy Kellerman, August 24, 1977, p. 8.
42. HSCA interview with Dr. Pierre Finck, March 11, 1978, pp. 105–6.
43. HSCA August 12, 1977, interview with John Thomas Stringer, dated August 17, 1977, p. 11.
44. HSCA August 12, 1977, interview with John Thomas Stringer, dated August 17, 1977, p. 11.
45. HSCA August 12, 1977, interview with John Thomas Stringer, dated August 17, 1977, p. 12.
46. Ibid.
47. Ibid.
48. Ibid. pp. 13–14.
49. Ibid. p. 16
50. HSCA August 12, 1977, interview with Dr. J. Thorton Boswell, August 16, 1977, p.11.
51. 7 HSCA 253.
52. HSCA interview with Dr. James J. Homes, August 17, 1977, p.7.
53. HSCA interview with Dr. George Burkley, August 17, 1977, p. 5.
54. HSCA interview with Dr. Pierre Finck, March 11, 1978, p. 85.
55. HSCA August 12, 1977, interview with John Thomas Stringer, dated August 17, 1977, p. 10.

56. HSCA August 12, 1977, interview with John Thomas Stringer, dated August 17, 1977, p. 11.

57. Sibert & O'Neill FBI report of the autopsy, November 26, 1963.

58. HSCA August 12, 1977, interview with John Thomas Stringer, dated August 17, 1977, p. 11.

59 Ibid. p. 16.

60. HSCA August 12, 1977, interview with John Thomas Stringer, dated August 17, 1977, p. 14.

61. HSCA interview with Admiral Calvin Galloway, May 17, 1978, p. 1.

62. Harrison E. Li

63. I cannot reveal the several sources I have for this, and I'm not sure it is accurate, but see *Killing the Truth,* p. 511.

64. Letter of David Stern, M.D., April 20, 1994, to the author.

65. Secret Service document, December 6, 1963, File No. CO-2-34030, SAS William R. Skiles and Robert Lapham.

66. See the following stories on Liggett in the *Dallas Morning News*: July 7, 1972, p. 1A: "Firemen Find Two Dead In Club."; February 11, 1974, p. 1A: "Body of Divorcee Found in Burning Apartment"; February 12, 1974, p. 1A: "Two Fire Murders Probed"; March 27, 1974, p. 9B: "Woman Left For Dead In Beating"; March 28, 1974, p. 16A: "Suspected Attacker to be Questioned"; March 30, 1974, p. 1F: "Police Probing Beating Deaths"; February 15, 1975, p. 11C: story on death of John Melvin Liggett. There are corresponding *Dallas Times-Herald* stories to go with these.

67, *Dallas Morning New*: Dan Watson, March 27, 1974, p. 9B: "Woman Left For Dead In Beating"; March 28, 1974, p. 16A: "Suspected Attacker Questioned."

68. James Ewell, *Dallas Morning News,* July 7, 1972, p. 1A: "Firemen Find Two Dead in Club."

69. Obituaries on death of Jay Robert "Bert" Peck, Dallas papers July 5–8, 1969, stories, obit, and photo.

70. *Dallas Morning News,* February 15, 1975, p. 11C

3. The Reenactments and the Trajectories

1. 5 H 144.

2. Interview of Daryll Weatherly with Robert West, January 11, 1995.

3. Fort Worth *Star-Telegram,* April 14, 1978; *The Continuing Inquiry,* May 1978, p. 5.

4. Martin Shackelford note to the author, January 22, 1995.

5. CE 298, pp. 14–15.

6. Warren Report, pp. 110, 115.

7. Secret Service memorandum to Chief, and from Inspector Kelley—Dallas file # CO-2-34030, December 5, 1963, bearing Secret Service Control number 418.

8. Explanation of Film Sequences Reconstructing the Assassination of the President. Commission Record 87, Secret Service control number 233.

9. 17 H 899, Exhibit 879.
10. CD 298, pp. 14–15.
11. CD 5, Archives copy, pp. 116–17.
12. CD 298, p. 11.
13. Ibid. p. 17.
14. 24 H 539, CE 2109.
15. Interview of Daryll Weatherly with Robert West, January 11, 1995.
16. *Murder From Within*, Newcomb and Adams, p. 120.
17. LBJ Library, discussion of J. Edgar Hoover and Lyndon Johnson, November 29, 1963, tapes and transcript.
18. CBS News, November 23, 1963, transcript; Newcomb and Adams, p. 60; Richard Trask, *Pictures of the Pain*, radio broadcast: p. 87, TV broadcast: p. 89. The CBS Radio broadcast description of the Zapruder film by Dan Rather from a transcript from the Richard E. Sprague papers, Special Collections Division, Georgetown University Library; source for the transcript of the TV broadcast is an article by Gary Mack in *The Continuing Inquiry*, August 22, 1980, pp. 3–4.
19. Ibid.
20. 17 H 571.
21. *Ft. Worth Star-Telegram*, April 14, 1978.
22. 5 H 138–42.
23. Letter of Chuck Marler to the author, November 18, 1994.
24. Chuck Marler, "Questioning the Warren Commission's Evidence in JFK Assassination Reenactment," p. 4, November–December 1994.
25. Ibid. p. 5
26. Shown on the cover of *The Continuing Inquiry*, June 1983, published by Penn Jones, Jr; shown in Trask, *Pictures of the Pain*, p. 350, and in Weisberg, *Whitewash II*, p. 247. These show twelve pairs of traffic lines.
27. Chuck Marler, early draft of "Questioning the Warren Commission's Evidence in JFK Assassination Reenactment," December 1994.
28. Ibid. p. 3.
29. Discussion with Daryll Weatherly, January 3, 1995.
30. WR 105–9.
31. Newcomb and Adams, p. 135.
32. Interview with Daryll Weatherly and Robert L. West, January 11, 1995.
33. Newcomb and Adams, p. 136.
34. Letter of Chuck Marler to the author, December 16, 1994.
35. Separate discussions with Chuck Marler, Daryll Weatherly, and the author, October–November 1994.
36. 3 H 444.
37. Letter of Chuck Marler to the author, December 16, 1994.
38. Chuck Marler, early draft of "Questioning the Warren Commission's Evidence in JFK Assassination Reenactment," December 1994. p. 6.
39. Ibid. p. 7; 5H 144.

4. The Forged Autopsy X-rays and Dr. David Mantik's Historic Findings

1. Letter of G. M. McDonnell, August 4, 1978, p. 2; HSAC Record No. 1801007710118; Agency File No. 010585.
2. David Mantik, "Optical Density Measurements Of the JFK Autopsy X-rays and A New Observation Based on the Chest X-Ray," unpublished, November 18, 1993, pp. 1–2.
3. Ibid. p. 2.
4. Ibid. p. 2.
5. Note appended to a letter of the author to David Mantik, M.D., March 23, 1994.
6. Mantik's note attached to this paragraph, April 6, 1994.
7. Ibid. pp. 2–3.
8. Ibid. p. 3.
9. David Mantik, "Optical Density Measurements Of the JFK Autopsy X-rays and A New Observation Based on the Chest X-Ray," unpublished, November 18, 1993, p. 4.
10. Ibid. p. 4. Also *JAMA* of May 27, 1992, p. 2798.
11. Ibid. pp. 4–5.
12. 7 HSCA 254.
13. 7 HSCA 254–5.
14. 7 HSCA 254–5.
15. Mantik, p. 5.
16. Howard Roffman, *Presumed Guilty*, 1975, p. 109.
17. Mantik, pp. 5–6.
18. Dr. Gary Aguilar to Dr. Robert Artwohl, Prodigy, December 15, 1992, 7:17 A.M.
19. Clark Panel Report, *Maryland State Journal of Medicine*, March 1977, p. 74.
20. 7 HSCA 254.
21. David Mantik, public talk on "Optical Density Measurements of the JFK Autopsy X-rays, November 18, 1993, p. 1.
22. 7 HSCA 249; see also pp. 698, *Killing the Truth*.
23. 7 HSCA 254.
24. Dr. Robert Artwohl, Prodigy, to John McAdams, September 25, 1993.
25. Dr. Randolph Robertson to Keith Preston, Prodigy, May 11, 1993, 9:16 P.M.
26. Note to the author, March 1994.
27. Dr. Randolph Robertson, Prodigy, May 12, 1993, 1:59 P.M.
28. 7 HSCA 115.
29. 7 HSCA 125.
30. Daryll Weatherly, *The Investigator*, October–November 1993, p. 24.
31. 7 HSCA Addendum D, p. 222.
32. Daryll Weatherly, *The Investigator*, October–November 1993, p. 16.
33. Ibid. p. 17.
34. David Mantik, M.D., letter to the author, January 16, 1995.
35. Weatherly, p. 17.
36. Ibid. p. 18.
37. Ibid. p. 19.
38. 7 HSCA Addendum D, p. 222.
39. Weatherly, p. 20.

40. Ibid.
41. Exhibit F-323, 1 HSCA 153–76.
42. 1 HSCA 166–67, 170.
43. 7 HSCA 45.
44. Weatherly, p. 21.
45. 7 HSCA Addendum D, p. 222.
46. Weatherly, p. 21; 7 HSCA pp. 228–30.
47. 7 HSCA pp. 217, 219.
48. Weatherly, p. 22; 7 HSCA 219.
49. Weatherly, p. 22.
50. Weatherly, p. 22.
51. 7 HSCA 223.
52. 7 HSCA 228–30.
53. Weatherly, p. 23.
54. 7 HSCA 254–55.
55. 7 HSCA 255.
56. 7 HSCA 256.
57. 7 HSCA 218, 221.
58. Ibid. p. 221.
59. 7 HSCA 217–21.
60. Weatherly, p. 23.
61. HSCA interview with Dr. John Ebersole, March 11, 1978, p. 14.
62. Ibid. p. 15.
63. Ebersole interview with Art Smith, *The Continuing Inquiry*, July 1978.
64. HSCA interview with Dr. John Ebersole, March 11, 1978, p. 4 and elsewhere.
65. Harrison E. Livingstone, *High Treason 2*, chapter on Jerrol Custer.
66. 2 H 353.
67. HSCA interview with Dr. John Ebersole, March 11, 1978, p. 16.
68. Ibid. p. 17.
69. HSCA interview with Dr. John Ebersole, March 11, 1978, p. 31.
70. HSCA Memorandum of interview with Dr. J. Thornton Boswell, August 16, 1977, p. 7.
71. HSCA Memorandum of interview with Dr. J. Thornton Boswell, August 16, 1977, p. 10.
72. Harrison E. Livingstone, *High Treason 2*, p. 192.
73. Harrison E. Livingstone, *High Treason 2*, p. 201.

5. The Hoax of the Century: Faking the Zapruder Film

1. *Six Seconds in Dallas*, Josiah Thompson, Berkley Medallion paperback, p. 7.
2. Ibid. p. 9.
3. FBI report, December 4, 1963, SA Robert Barrett, File No. DL 89-43.
4. See p. 367 of the author's *High Treason 2*, and Professor Phil Melanson's "Hidden Exposure: Cover-Up and Intrigue in the CIA's Secret Possession of the Zapruder Film," *The Third Decade*, November 1984.

5. Letter of Richard Bartholomew to the author, January 4, 1995, on his interview with Erwin Schwartz, November 21, 1994.

6. 7 H 575.

7. All information from Erwin Schwartz is from his nephew, researcher Richard Bartholomew, and was given to the author over a period of one and a half years.

8. Phil Melanson, *The Third Decade*, November 1984, p. 15; *High Treason 2*, p. 371.

9. Melanson, Ibid. p. 15.

10. Ibid. p. 16.

11. Ibid. p. 19.

12. Ibid. p. 16.

13. Letter of Richard Bartholomew to the author, January 4, 1995, on his interview with Erwin Schwartz, November 21, 1994.

14. Ibid.

15. Ibid.

16. Quoted in Richard Trask, *Pictures of the Pain*, Yeoman Press, Danvers, Mass., p. 80; FBI Memo file #62-109060-1094, November 23, 1963, and December 31, 1963, obtained by FOIA by Richard Trask; U.S. Secret Service memo from Forrest Sorrels, # CO 2-33-030, January 22, 1964.

17. Stolley's history of the *Life* acquisition of the film is contained in both an article in *Esquire*, "What Happened Next?" November 1973, pp. 134–35; 262–63; statement of George Hunt, managing editor, *Life* (cited in Josiah Thompson, *Six Seconds in Dallas*, Berkley edition, 1976, pp. 217–18; and Stolley in *Entertainment Weekly*, January 17, 1992 (Time Inc.). See also Zapruder testimony in 7 H 569–76; FBI report of agent Robert M. Barrett, December 4, 1963.

18. Newcomb and Adams, *Murder From Within*, p. 155.

19. Discussion with the author, December 20, 1994.

20. 5 HSCA 693 for the record of the film being loaned to HSCA.

21. Letter of Doug Mizzer to the author, December 12, 1994.

22. Letter of Doug Mizzer to the author, December 12, 1994.

23. *The Village Voice*, March 31, 1992.

24. Source: Martin Shackelford letter to the author, December 31, 1994.

25. Daryll Weatherly, letter to the author, March 26, 1994.

26. Ibid.

27. Roy Madsen, *Animated Film—Concepts, Methods, Uses* (New York: Interland Publishing Inc., 1969), pp. 163–65; see also Brian G. D. Salt, *Basic Animation Stand Techniques*, (Oxford, England: Pergamon Press Ltd., 1977), with a photo of the rotoscope, p. 28.

28. Ibid.

29. Newcomb and Adams, pp. 115–16; "Closing Arguments that the Zapruder Film has been Altered," Chuck Marler, November 1994, to the author.

30. Newcomb and Adams, p. 117.

31. *Killing the Truth*, p. 334. I need to correct two sentences on that page dealing with the hole behind the head: the incorrect sentences read: "Greer turns back toward the front at frame 316. There is a very clear picture of Greer turned to his right at 317." This last sentence meant

that he had turned enough that his head was now ninety degrees from forward, faced directly right. The first sentence should read: "Greer starts his turn back toward the front at frame 316." Greer continues to turn and completes his turn forward by 320.

32. FBI document dated December 4, 1963, File # DL 89-43, Special Agent Robert M. Barrett, and File # 7; *Whitewash II*, Harold Weisberg, p. 184.
33. 7 H 576.
34. 7 H 572.
35. *Six Seconds In Dallas*, Josiah Thompson.
36. Letter of James W. Altgens to Doug Mizzer, November 21, 1994.
37. Letter of Doug Mizzer to the author, December 12, 1994.
38. Doug Mizzer, first draft of an article written at the author's request, November 17, 1993.
39. 2 H 138–39.
40. Letter of Doug Mizzer to the author, September 24, 1992.
41. Also quoted in Richard Trask, *Pictures of the Pain* (Mass: Yeoman Press), p. 80; FBI Memo file # 62-109060-1094, November 23, 1963 and December 31, 1963, obtained by FOIA by Richard Trask; U.S. Secret Service Memo from Forrest Sorrels, # CO 2-33-030, January 22, 1964.
42. Letter of Doug Mizzer to the author, April 6, 1994.
43. Letter of Doug Mizzer to the author, April 7, 1994.
44. Ibid.
45. FBI report, Siebert and O'Neill, November 22, 1963.
46. CBS national broadcast, November 23, 1963; *The Continuing Inquiry*, July 1977, p. 2.
47. Dan Rather with Mickey Herskowitz, *The Camera Never Blinks: Adventures of a TV Journalist*, p. 125.
48. Letter of James W. Altgens to Doug Mizzer, November 21, 1994.
49. CBS News, November 23, 1963, transcript; Newcomb and Adams, p. 60; Richard Trask, *Pictures of the Pain*, radio broadcast: p. 87, TV broadcast: p. 89. The CBS Radio broadcast description of the Zapruder film by Dan Rather from a transcript from the Richard E. Sprague papers, Special Collections Division, Georgetown University Library; source for the transcript of the TV broadcast is an article by Gary Mack in *The Continuing Inquiry*, August 22, 1980, pp. 3–4.
50. Ibid.
51. Newcomb and Adams, p. 120. Also see *Modern Cinematographer*, June 1969, pp. 566–67.
52. *Killing the Truth*, pp. 313–19.
53. Interview of Perry Adams and Fred Newcomb with Douglas L. Jackson, who was not deposed by the Warren Commission.
54. Newcomb and Adams, p. 121.
55. 7 H 571 (it is not too clear just where the filming started or if he stopped the camera after the lead motorcycles, then started it again); CD 7, p. 12 (FBI report of December 4, 1963).
56. CBS News, November 23, 1963.
57. 7 H 571.
58. CBS News, November 23, 1963.
59. Newcomb and Adams, p. 122.

60. Newcomb and Adams, p. 135.
61. 7 H 576.
62. Letter of James W. Altgens to Doug Mizzer, November 21, 1994.
63. CD 87, p. 434.
64. Fred Newcomb and Perry Adams, *Murder From Within*, unpublished manuscript, p. 62.
65. 7 H 518.
66. 19 H 467.
67. 7 H 518.
68. CD 897, p. 17; 22 H 837.
69. 6 H 225.
70. Charles Roberts, *The Truth About the Assassination*, p. 17; and Newcomb and Adams interview with Senator Yarborough.
71. 3 H 289.
72. Interview of Fred Newcomb and Perry Adams with Billy Martin, *Murder From Within*, p. 63.
73. 7 H 486–87.
74. Ibid.
75. 6 H 165
76. CD 5, pp. 66–7.
77. 7 H 534–35.
78. 6 H 231–33; CD 205, p. 311.
79. 7 H 571.
80. *Fort Worth Star-Telegram*, April 14, 1978.
81. Report of Pierre Finck to Brigadier General Joseph Blumberg, February 1, 1975, Otis Historical Archives, National Museum of Health and Medicine, Armed Forces Institute of Pathology, Washington DC, 20305, Blumberg Collection, about page 15 from start of notes (in WC section of his notes). There are no page numbers.
82. *Newsweek*, December 2, 1963.
83. Chuck Marler, "Questioning the Limousine's Speed On Elm Street," *The Fourth Decade*, May 1994, p. 19.
84. Letter of Martin Shackelford, January 26, 1995, to the author.
85. 6 H 233.
86. 3 H 266.
87. 3 H 221. The limousine swerving to the left would improve the line of sight of anyone firing from the Grassy Knoll.
88. Chaney interview November 22, 1963, as broadcast on "Thou Shalt Not Kill," CFTR-Radio, Toronto, May 1976.
89. 7 H 440.
90. 7 H 487.
91. Trial of Clay Shaw, New Orleans, 1969, as reported in Penn Jones, Jr., *Forgive My Grief III*, p. 53; Harrison E. Livingstone, *High Treason*, p. 19 hardback, p. 22 in paperback.
92. *Dallas Morning News*, November 22, 1963.
93. Martin Agronsky, "Interview With John B. Connally at Parkland Hospital," CBS, November 27, 1963.
94. Newcomb and Adams interview with Billy Martin.
95. Ibid., with Douglas L. Jackson.

Notes

Notes   **411**

96. 3 H 266.
97. Newcomb and Adams interview with Joe H. Rich, *Murder From Within*, p. 71.
98. *Dallas Morning News*, November 23, 1963, Section 1, p. 2.
99. UPI's book *Four Days*, p. 16.
100. Newcomb and Adams, *Murder From Within*, p. 71, with the list of witnesses and their Commission and other testimony in note 102, page 96.
101. Gerald Posner, *Case Closed*, p. 234.
102. *Time*, November 29, 1963, p. 23.
103. Newcomb and Adams, p. 113.
104. Richard Trask, *Pictures of the Pain*, p. 128.
105. This testimony is enumerated in Newcomb and Adams's *Murder From Within*, pp. 72–3. Here are the cites: Newcomb and Adams's interview with Marrion L. Baker; Officer Harkness 6 H 309; Reporter Robert Baskin, *Dallas Morning News*, November 23, 1963, p. 2; Secret Service agent John D. Ready, CE 1024, 18 H 749; *Newsweek*, December 2, 1963, p. 21.
106. Ibid. p. 114.
107. 7 H 562, CE 2003 (p. 213), 2508, Decker Exhibit 5323 (p. 481). Hudson may have misspoke himself here, and not meant that the Stemmons sign replaced the Thornton sign.
108. Newcomb and Adams, p. 113.
109. Chuck Marler, *The Fourth Decade*, May 1994, p. 20.
110. Chuck Marler, *The Fourth Decade*, May 1994, p. 19.
111. Measurements by the author and Marco Miranda, and mathematics by Daryll Weatherly, 1994.
112. Report, HSCA, pp. 46–47.
113. Josiah Thompson, *Six Seconds in Dallas*, p. 375.
114. Ibid.
115. 5 H 160.
116. Ibid. p. 377.
117. Fort Worth *Star-Telegram*, April 14, 1978; *The Continuing Inquiry*, May 1978, p. 5.
118. Ibid.
119. Livingstone, *Killing the Truth*, p. 339.
120. Richard Burgess, *The Fourth Decade*, September 1994, p. 6.
121. Letter to the author, December 18, 1994.
122. Ibid., letter to the author, December 18, 1994.
123. Richard Burgess, *The Fourth Decade*, September 1994, p. 7.
124. Livingstone, *High Treason 2*, p. 366, middle. I seem to be the first person to note or write about this.
125. Burgess, *Fourth Decade*, September 1994, p. 7.
126. Ibid.
127. Timothy Cwiek, *The Third Decade*, July 1987, p. 19.
128. Sitzman reported this to Professor Josiah Thompson on November 29, 1966. Richard Trask reports it from the transcript in his *Pictures of the Pain: Photography and the Assassination of President Kennedy* (Danvers, MA: Yeoman Press, 1994), p. 73, and see footnote 4, p. 148, in that book.
129. Ibid. p. 148.

130. Trask, p. 75.
131. Trask, p. 76. On p. 74 Trask identifies the photo as taken by Johnny Flynn of the *Dallas Morning News.*
132. Matthew Smith, *JFK: The Second Plot* (Edinburgh, Scotland: Mainstream Publishing Company, 1992), p. 124.
133. 4 H 410.
134. Letter of Bill O'Neill to Martin Shackelford, 10/24/94.
135. 6 WC 184, and Trask, p. 74.
136. Trask, pp. 73–4; O'Neill phone call and letter to Martin Shackelford.
137. See also a chapter in *Unsolved Texas Mysteries* by Wallace O. Chariton, Charlie Eckardt and Kevin R. Young (Dallas: Wordware Publishing, 1991).
138. O'Neill letter to Shackelford. Referring to the "Badge Man" location— about the same distance—Sitzman stated "the blast of a high-powered rifle would have blown me off that wall." Shackelford writes in his footnote that "she did allow, however, that a shot could have been fired from 'farther down, closer to the overpass . . . or maybe they were using silencers.' "
139. "William Greer's Impossible Head Turn," by Chuck Marler, *The Fourth Decade*, November 1994, p. 42.
140. "William Greer's Impossible Head Turn," by Chuck Marler, *The Fourth Decade*, November 1994, p. 42.
141. Letter of Chuck Marler to the author, November 18, 1994.
142. "Closing Arguments that the Zapruder Film has been Altered," by Chuck Marler, to the author, November 1994.
143. Phil Melanson, *The Third Decade*, November 1984, p. 20.

6. From the Secret Documents: Conflicts in the Autopsy Evidence

1. 7 HSCA 249.
2. May 29, 1992.
3. William Manchester, *Death of a President*, p. 398.
4. Ibid.
5. HSCA interview with Dr. Robert F. Karnei, August 29, 1977, p. 4.
6. HSCA interview with Lt. Richard Lipsey, January 18, 1978, p. 2.
7. Harrison E. Livingstone, *High Treason 2*, p. 269.
8. HSCA interview with Francis X. O'Neill, January 10, 1978, p. 1.
9. Affidavit of James W. Sibert, October 24, 1978, p. 2.
10. HSCA interview with Dr. J. Thornton Boswell, August 16, 1977, p. 2.
11. Ibid.
12. HSCA interview with James Curtis Jenkins, August 24, 1977, p. 3.
13. *High Treason 2*, p. 231.
14. Ibid. p. 232.
15. HSCA Memorandum of interview with Dr. J. Thornton Boswell, August 16, 1977, pp. 8–9.
16. HSCA interview with Dr. Pierre Finck, March 11, 1978, p. 77.
17. HSCA Memorandum of interview with Dr. J. Thornton Boswell, August 11, 1978, p. 2.
18. Report of Dr. Pierre Finck to General Joseph Blumberg, February 1, 1965, p. 4.

19. HSCA interview with Dr. Pierre Finck, March 11, 1978.
20. Report of Dr. Pierre Finck to General Joseph Blumberg, February 1, 1965, p. 4.
21. Report of Dr. Pierre Finck to General Joseph Blumberg, February 1, 1965, p. 20.
22. Report of Dr. Pierre Finck to General Joseph Blumberg, February 1, 1965, pp. 20–21.
23. HSCA Memorandum of interview with Dr. J. Thornton Boswell, August 11, 1978, p. 2.
24. 7 HSCA 181–94.
25. HSCA interview with Dr. J. Thornton Boswell, August 16, 1977, pp. 2–3.
26. HSCA memorandum of interview with Dr. J. Thornton Boswell, August 16, 1977, p. 4.
27. HSCA interview with Dr. Pierre Finck, March 11, 1978, p. 109.
28. HSCA interview with Dr. Pierre Finck, March 11, 1978, p. 110.
29. HSCA interview with Francis X. O'Neill, January 10, 1978, p. 3.
30. HSCA interview with Jan Gail Rudnicki, May 8, 1978, pp. 2–3.
31. Harold Weisberg, *PostMortem*, p. 236 (Testimony of Pierre Finck, 2nd day in the Clay Shaw trial in New Orleans), pp. 4–5.
32. Reports of the Dallas doctors from the Price Exhibit, Warren Commission, and their testimony, 6 H; Livingstone, *High Treason 2*, p. 146; see also the Medical Encyclopedia at the end of *Killing the Truth* (Livingstone) under "Scalpel Cuts In Upper Chest," p. 724.
33. Charles Wilber, p. 189; Harrison E. Livingstone, *High Treason 2*, p. 198.
34. Harrison E. Livingstone, *High Treason 2*, p. 210.
35. HSCA interview with Roy Kellerman, August 24–25, 1977, p. 3.
36. Warren Report, autopsy report, *New York Times* edition, p. 501.
37. Harrison E. Livingstone, *High Treason 2*, pp. 210–11.
38. HSCA taped interview with Thomas Evan Robinson, January 12, 1977, p. 1.
39. HSCA interview with Richard Lipsey, Doc No. 014469, p. 4.
40. HSCA interview with Dr. John Ebersole, March 11, 1978, p. 19.
41. HSCA interview with John Ebersole, M.D., March 11, 1978, p. 60.
42. HSCA interview with John Ebersole, M.D., March 11, 1978, p. 26.
43. Ibid. p. 26.
44. HSCA interview with Dr. John Ebersole, March 11, 1978, p. 64.
45. 7 HSCA 257.
46. Harrison E. Livingstone, *Killing the Truth*, p. 114.
47. Autopsy Report, *New York Times* edition, p. 503. The handwritten autopsy report is reproduced in Harold Weisberg, *PostMortem*, pp. 509-23.
48. HSCA Memorandum of interview with Dr. J. Thornton Boswell, August 11, 1978, p. 2; p. 4 of the longer report of the interview.
49. HSCA interview with Dr. Pierre Finck, March 11, 1978, pp. 73–74.
50. State of Louisiana v. Clay Shaw, p. 34.
51. Harrison E. Livingstone, *High Treason 2*, p. 222.
52. HSCA Interview with John Ebersole, March 11, 1978, p. 41.
53. HSCA interview with James Curtis Jenkins, August 24, 1977, p. 5.
54. Livingstone, *High Treason 2*, p. 237.
55. Livingstone, *High Treason 2*, p. 293.

56. CBS Memorandum of Robert Richter to Les Midgley, January 10, 1967. Source: Roger Feinman.

57. Letter of Roger Feinman to Congressman John Conyers, November 16, 1993.

58. 2 H 361.

59. Report of Andy Purdy, HSCA, August 7, 1978, HSCA File No. 180-10077-10107, Agency File No. 010574.

60. HSCA interview with Francis X. O'Neill, January 10, 1978, p. 2.

61. HSCA August 25, 1977, interview with James W. Sibert, August 29, 1977, p. 2.

62. HSCA interview with James W. Sibert, August 25, 1977, p. 5.

63. Affidavit of James W. Sibert, October 24, 1978, p. 4.

64. HSCA interview with Francis X. O'Neill, January 10, 1978, p. 4.

65. Affidavit of James W. Sibert, October 24, 1978, p. 2.

66. Harrison E. Livingstone, *High Treason 2*, p. 179.

67. First revealed by the author: Livingstone, *High Treason 2*, Karnei chapter, confirmed by Dr. Lawrence Altman, *New York Times*, Science section, October 6, 1992, and by *JAMA*, October 7, 1992, pp. 1737.

68. HSCA Memorandum of an Interview with Dr. J. Thornton Boswell, August 11, 1978, p. 2.

69. HSCA Memorandum of interview with Dr. J. Thornton Boswell, August 16, 1977, p. 4.

70. HSCA interview with Dr. John Ebersole, March 11, 1978, p. 42.

71. HSCA interview with Roy Kellerman, August 24, 25, 1977, pp. 3–4.

72. HSCA August 25, 1977, interview with James W. Sibert, p. 3.

73. HSCA interview with Roy Kellerman, August 24, 25, 1977, pp. 3–4.

74. HSCA interview with Jan Gail Rudnicki, May 8, 1978, p. 3.

75. Affidavit of Francis X. O'Neill, November 8, 1978, p. 3.

76. Ibid. p. 4

77. 2 H 93.

78. 2 H 103.

79. 7 HSCA 15–16.

80. HSCA interview with Captain James H. Stover, May 11, 1978, p. 2.

81. HSCA interview with Paul O'Connor, June 28, 1978, p. 2.

82. *High Treason 2*, pp. 209–10.

83. HSCA interview with Dr. Pierre A. Finck, March 12, 1978, p. 4.

84. Weisberg, *PostMortem*, pp. 512, 515.

85. The handwritten autopsy report is reproduced in Harold Weisberg, *PostMortem*, pp. 509–23; 515.

86. HSCA interview with Dr. John Ebersole, March 11, 1978, p. 6.

87. HSCA interview with Dr. John Ebersole, March 11, 1978, pp. 53–55.

88. HSCA interview with Dr. John Ebersole, March 11, 1978, p. 8.

89. HSCA interview with Dr. Robert E. Karnei, August 29, 1977, p. 2.

90. 7 HSCA 8.

91. HSCA interview with Chester H. Boyers, April 25, 1978, p. 2.

92. HSCA interview with Dr. Robert F. Karnei, August 29, 1977, p. 2.

93. HSCA August 12, 1977, interview with John Thomas Stringer, dated August 17, 1977, p. 10.

94. Testimony of Dr. Pierre Finck, State of Louisiana vs. Clay Shaw, p. 52.

95. HSCA (Andy Purdy) interview with Dr. J. Thornton Boswell, August 17, 1977, pp. 1–2.

96. Ibid. p. 2.

97. Ibid. pp. 5, 11.

98. HSCA (Andy Purdy and Jim Kelly) interview with Robert F. Karnei, August 23, 1977, p. 1.

99. HSCA interview with Francis X. O'Neill, January 10, 1978, p. 6.

100. Livingstone, *High Treason 2*, p. 219.

101. Affidavit of Francis X. O'Neill, November 8, 1978, p. 3.

102. Harrison E. Livingstone, *High Treason 2*, p. 220.

103. HSCA August 12, 1977, interview with John Thomas Stringer, dated August 17, 1977, p. 13.

104. Ibid. p. 13.

105. HSCA interview with Admiral Calvin Galloway, May 17, 1978, p. 2.

106. HSCA interview with James Curtis Jenkins, August 24, 1977, p. 10.

107. HSCA Memorandum of interview with Dr. J. Thornton Boswell, August 11, 1978, p. 2.

108. HSCA interview with Dr. J. Thornton Boswell, August 16, 1977, pp. 2–3.

109. HSCA interview with Dr. Pierre Finck, March 11, 1978, pp. 73–4.

110. HSCA interview with James W. Sibert, August 25, 1977, p. 5.

111. Affidavit of James W. Sibert, October 24, 1978, p. 3.

112. Affidavit of Francis X. O'Neill, November 8, 1978, p. 3.

113. HSCA interview with Dr. Pierre Finck, March 11, 1978, pp. 73–4.

114. Ibid.

115. HSCA interview with Dr. John Ebersole, March 11, 1978, pp. 10, 42.

116. Ibid. 42–5.

117. HSCA Memorandum of interview with Dr. J. Thornton Boswell, August 16, 1977, p. 5.

118. Harrison E. Livingstone, *High Treason 2*, p. 195.

119. HSCA interview with Dr. Pierre Finck, March 11, 1978, p. 78.

120. Harrison E. Livingstone, *Killing the Truth*, p. 114.

121. HSCA interview with Dr. John Ebersole, March 11, 1978, p. 52.

122. HSCA interview with James W. Sibert, August 25, 1977, p. 5.

123. HSCA Memorandum of interview with Dr. J. Thornton Boswell, August 16, 1977, p. 5.

124. Sibert and O'Neill report, November 26, 1963.

125. HSCA Memorandum of interview with Dr. J. Thornton Boswell, August 11, 1978, p. 2.

126. HSCA interview with J. Thornton Boswell, August 17, 1977, p. 3.

127. HSCA interview with Lt. Richard Lipsey, January 18, 1978.

128. The *Baltimore Sun*, November 25, 1966, pp. A1, A8. This is the reporter, Richard H. Levine, talking, and does not relate to the evidence very well. Overall, the article seems to distort the evidence to get the result they wanted.

129. Ibid.

130. 7 HSCA 292–318.

131. HSCA Memorandum of interview with Dr. J. Thornton Boswell, August 17, 1977, p. 8.

132. Harrison E. Livingstone, *High Treason 2*, p. 198.

133. HSCA interview with Chester H. Boyers, April 25, 1978.
134. HSCA Memorandum of interview with Dr. J. Thornton Boswell, August 16, 1977, p. 8.
135. HSCA Memorandum of interview with Dr. J. Thornton Boswell, August 17, 1977, p. 12.
136. HSCA interview with Dr. Pierre Finck, March 11, 1978, p. 115.
137. Ibid. p. 117.
138. HSCA interview with Dr. John Ebersole, March 11, 1978, p. 20.
139. HSCA interview with James Curtis Jenkins, August 24, 1977, p. 4.
140. HSCA interview with Dr. John Ebersole, March 11, 1978, p. 52.
141. Harrison E. Livingstone, *High Treason 2*, p. 195.
142. HSCA interview with James W. Sibert, August 25, 1978, p. 4; Affidavit of James W. Sibert, October 24, 1978, p. 2.
143. HSCA interview with Francis X. O'Neill, January 10, 1978, p. 6.
144. HSCA interview with Dr. Robert F. Karnei, August 29, 1977, p. 5.
145. HSCA interview with Lt. Richard Lipsey, January 18, 1978, pp. 4, 6–7.
146. 7 HSCA 20, ref. no. 95.
147. Ibid.
148. Report of Dr. Pierre Finck to General Joseph Blumberg, February 1, 1965, p. 19.
149. 2 H 368–69.
150. 7 HSCA 256–57.
151. Letter of Roger Feinman to Congressman John Conyers, November 16, 1993, p. 6.
152. HSCA Memorandum of interview with Dr. J. Thornton Boswell, August 11, 1978, p. 2.
153. Interview of David Mantik with Dr. John Ebersole, as related to the author, 1993.
154. HSCA interview with Tom Robinson, January 12, 1977, pp. 6, 9, and see discussion p. 11.
155. HSCA interview with Dr. Pierre Finck, March 11, 1978, p. 119.
156. HSCA interview with Dr. John Ebersole, March 11, 1978, p. 39.
157. HSCA Memorandum of interview with Dr. J. Thornton Boswell, August 17, 1977, p. 4.
158. HSCA interview with Lieutenant Richard Lipsey, January 18, 1978, p. 9.
159. HSCA interview with Lieutenant Richard Lipsey, January 18, 1978, p. 4.
160. HSCA Interview with Richard Lipsey, January 18, 1978, pp. 4, 6–7.
161. 2 H 103.
162. WR 541, 16 H 981.
163. 2 H 361.
164. HSCA interview with Thomas Evan Robinson, January 16, 1977, pp. 7–8.
165. HSCA interview with Dr. Pierre Finck, March 11, 1978, p. 116.
166. Ibid. pp. 75–76.
167. HSCA interview with Dr. John Ebersole, March 11, 1978, p. 53.
168. Ibid. p. 52, line 11.
169. Harrison E. Livingstone, *High Treason 2*, pp. 189–90.
170. HSCA interview with Dr. Robert F. Karnei, August 29, 1977, p. 6. Also see pp. 5 and 7.
171. Harrison E. Livingstone, *High Treason 2*, p. 195.

172. HSCA interview with Roy Kellerman, August 24, 25, 1977, p. 5.

173. HSCA interview with Jan Gail Rudnicki, May 8, 1978, p. 3.

174. HSCA interview with James Curtis Jenkins, August 24, 1977, p. 5.

175. Harrison E. Livingstone, *High Treason 2*, p. 303.

176. HSCA interview with James Curtis Jenkins, August 24, 1977, p. 13.

177. HSCA interview with James Curtis Jenkins, August 24, 1977, pp. 14–15.

178. HSCA interview with Dr. John Ebersole, March 11, 1978, pp. 3, 5, 9.

179. Gil Delaney, *Lancaster Intelligencer-Journal*, and the *Philadelphia Inquirer*, March 10, 1978; and in an interview with Art Smith, March 28, 1978. The month of March seemed to be the time for Ebersole to plant that bit of disinformation, unless he was trying to tell us something too strange for us to imagine.

180. Discussion of David Mantik, M.D., and the author, June 4, 1994.

181. HSCA interview with Dr. John Ebersole, March 11, 1978, pp. 4–5, also pp. 51–2.

182. Ibid. p. 9.

183. Interview with Harrison E. Livingstone, October 14, 1990.

184. Interview with Harrison E. Livingstone, October 29, 1990.

185. Harrison E. Livingstone, *High Treason 2*, chapters devoted to Rudnicki and Custer.

186. HSCA Memorandum of interview with Dr. J. Thornton Boswell, August 11, 1978, p. 2.

187. HSCA Memorandum of interview with Dr. J. Thornton Boswell, August 16, 1977, pp. 5–6.

188. HSCA interview with Dr. John Ebersole, March 11, 1978, p. 4; also page 52, line 11; p. 53, line 11.

189. HSCA interview with James W. Sibert, August 25, 1977, p. 6.

190. Affidavit of James W. Sibert, October 24, 1978, p. 4.

191. Affidavit of Francis X. O'Neill, November 8, 1978, p. 5.

192. HSCA interview with Francis X. O'Neill, January 10, 1978, p. 6.

193. HSCA interview with Admiral Calvin Galloway, May 17, 1978, p. 2.

194. HSCA interview with James Curtis Jenkins, August 24, 1977, p. 11.

195. Pierre A. Finck, *Military Medicine*, "Ballistic and Forensic Pathologic Aspects of Missile Wounds. Conversion between Anglo-American and Metric System Units," June 1965, p. 555.

196. *High Treason 2*, p. 210.

197. HSCA Memorandum of interview with Dr. J. Thornton Boswell, August 11, 1978, p. 2.

198. Harrison E. Livingstone, *High Treason 2*, p. 189.

199. HSCA interview with Dr. Robert F. Karnei, August 29, 1977, p. 5.

200. HSCA interview with Dr. J. Thornton Boswell, August 16, 1977, pp. 3–4.

201. 6 H 361, 375.

202. Report of the Ramsey Clark Panel, 1968, *Maryland State Medical Journal*, March 1977, p. 77.

203. *High Treason 2*, p. 210.

204. Affidavit of Francis X. O'Neill, November 8, 1978, p. 6.

205. Harrison E. Livingstone, *High Treason 2*, p. 162.

206. Affidavit of James W. Sibert, October 24, 1978, p. 3.

207. Sibert and O'Neill report, November 26, 1963, p. 4.

208. HSCA interview with Dr. John Ebersole, March 11, 1978, p. 57.
209. HSCA interview with Dr. John Ebersole, March 11, 1978, p. 47.
210. Ibid. p. 48.
211. HSCA interview with Dr. James J. Humes, August 17, 1977, p. 7.
212. 2 H 103.
213. HSCA Interview with Dr. Pierre Finck, No. 013617, p. 80.
214. Letter of Roger Feinman to Congressman John Conyers, November 16, 1993, p. 8.
215. HSCA interview with Richard Lipsey, January 18, 1978, p. 6.
216. Harrison E. Livingstone, *Killing the Truth*, p. 188.
217. Ibid. See also *Killing the Truth* by the author, pp. 69, 174. The conference in Dallas where Jenkins spoke was June 3, 1992.
218. HSCA interview with Thomas Evan Robinson, January 12, 1977, p. 7.
219. HSCA interview with Thomas Evan Robinson, January 12, 1977, p. 7.
220. HSCA interview with Thomas Evan Robinson, January 12, 1977, pp. 11–12.
221. Report of Dr. Pierre Finck to General Joseph Blumberg, February 1, 1965, p. 19.
222. *RT Image*, August 31, 1992, p. 7.
223. Harrison E. Livingstone, *High Treason 2*, interview of May 20, 1991.
224. Associated Press article, June 1, 1992.
225. Affidavit of Francis X. O'Neill, November 8, 1978, p. 4; and HSCA interview with Francis X. O'Neill, January 10, 1978, p. 3.
226. 7 HSCA 262.
227. Report of Dr. Pierre Finck to General Joseph Blumberg, February 1, 1965, p. 2.
228. Warren Report, *New York Times* edition, p. 501.
229. HSCA interview with Dr. John Ebersole, March 11, 1978, p. 3.
230. Gary Aguilar, M.D., prodigy post, December 4, 1992; and discussions with Dr. David Mantik and the author, 1994. Mantik's interviews with Ebersole were November 2, 1992 and December 2, 1992.
231. Burkley's death certificate HSCA Record Number 180-10109-10383, Agency File No. 002631 November 23, 1963 p. 2, National Archives.
232. HSCA interview with Dr. Pierre Finck, March 11, 1978, p. 78.
233. Harrison E. Livingstone, *High Treason 2*, chapter on Floyd Riebe.
234. HSCA interview with Chester H. Boyers, April 25, 1978.
235. HSCA interview with Jan Gail Rudnicki, May 8, 1978, p. 3.
236. HSCA interview with James Curtis Jenkins, August 24, 1977, p. 4.
237. Harrison E. Livingstone, *High Treason 2*, O'Connor chapter, and *Killing the Truth*, p. 69.
238. Harrison E. Livingstone, *Killing the Truth*, Bowron chapter, and photograph with her notation that it is not Kennedy's back.
239. Affidavit of James W. Sibert, October 24, 1978, p. 2.
240. 2 H 143.
241. Affidavit of Francis X. O'Neill, November 8, 1978, p. 4.
242. Sibert and O'Neill report, November 26, 1963, p. 4.
243. Affidavit of James W. Sibert, October 24, 1978, p. 2.
244. HSCA August 25, 1977, interview with James W. Sibert, p. 3.
245. HSCA interview with Francis X. O'Neill, January 10, 1978, p. 8.

246. HSCA interview with Francis X. O'Neill, January 10, 1978, p. 3.
247. HSCA interview with Lt. Richard Lipsey, January 18, 1978, pp. 3–4.
248. HSCA interview with Chester Boyers, April 25, 1978, p. 3.
249. HSCA interview with James Curtis Jenkins, August 24, 1977, p. 15.
250. HSCA interview with Dr. John Ebersole, March 11, 1978, p. 58.
251. Ibid. pp. 58–59.
252. HSCA interview with Dr. John Ebersole, March 11, 1978, p. 61.
253. Sibert and O'Neill FBI report, November 26, 1963.
254. HSCA interview with Dr. Pierre Finck, March 11, 1978, p. 120.
255. Martin Shackelford, note to the author on the manuscript, March 14, 1994, p. 8.
256. HSCA interview with Lieutenant Richard Lipsey, January 18, 1978, pp. 3, 4, 8, 9. The intervening pages describe the wounds that he saw.
257. HSCA interview with James W. Sibert, August 25, 1977, p. 7.
258. HSCA interview with Francis X. O'Neill, January 10, 1978, p. 6.
259. HSCA interview with James Curtis Jenkins, August 24, 1977, p. 7.
260. Ibid. p. 5.
261. Ibid. p. 7.
262. HSCA interview with James Curtis Jenkins, August 24, 1977, p. 12.
263. Ibid. p. 12.
264. HSCA interview with James Curtis Jenkins, August 24, 1977, pp. 14–15.
265. HSCA interview with James Curtis Jenkins, August 24, 1977, p. 13.
266. Ibid.
267. 7 HSCA 253.
268. HSCA interview with Francis X. O'Neill, January 10, 1978, p. 6.
269. HSCA interview with Dr. J. Thornton Boswell, August 16, 1977, p. 3.
270. HSCA interview with Dr. John Ebersole, March 11, 1978, pp. 25–26, 29.
271. HSCA interview with Dr. John Ebersole, March 11, 1978, p. 29.
272. HSCA Memorandum of interview with Dr. J. Thornton Boswell, August 16, 1977, p. 7.
273. HSCA interview with Dr. John Ebersole, March 11, 1978, p. 25.
274. HSCA interview with Dr. John Ebersole, March 11, 1978, pp. 25–26.
275. Pierre Finck, *Military Medicine*, "Pathologic Aspects of Missile Wounds," June 1965, p. 555.
276. HSCA interview with Thomas Evan Robinson, January 16, 1977, p. 10.
277. HSCA interview with Dr. John Ebersole, March 11, 1978, p. 33.
278. HSCA interview with Dr. John Ebersole, March 11, 1978, pp. 33–34, 35.
279. Note to the author on this manuscript.
280. HSCA interview with Dr. John Ebersole, March 11, 1978, pp. 33–34, 36.
281. Ibid.
282. Ibid. p. 38.
283. HSCA interview with James W. Sibert, August 25, 1977, pp. 4–5, and Sibert's affidavit, October 24, 1978, p. 5.
284. HSCA interview with Francis X. O'Neill, January 10, 1978, p. 5.
285. HSCA interview with Chester Boyers, April 25, 1978, p. 3.
286. HSCA interview with Francis X. O'Neill, January 10, 1978, p. 7.
287. HSCA interview with Jan Gail Rudnicki, May 8, 1978, p. 3.
288. Harrison E. Livingstone, *High Treason 2*, pp. 229, 246, 290.
289. HSCA interview with Thomas Robinson, January 12, 1977, pp. 3, 4.

290. Ibid. p. 4.
291. Ibid. p. 8.
292. Ibid. pp. 4–5.
293. Ibid. p. 6.
294. HSCA interview with Richard Lipsey, January 18, 1978, p. 4.
295. Ibid. pp. 3, 4.
296. *Six Seconds in Dallas,* Josiah Thompson, Berkley Medallion edition, paperback, p. 64.
297. Duffy and Ricci, *The Assassination of John F. Kennedy,* p. 286; Testimony of Dr. Paul Peters, 17 H 31, BAR page 2; testimony of Dr. Robert McClelland, 17 H 33, 36; *Los Angeles Times,* Robert Donovan, November 23, 1963; *Best Evidence,* David Lifton, footnote page 42.
298. HSCA interview with Thomas Robinson, January 12, 1977, p. 6.
299. HSCA interview with Richard Lipsey, January 18, 1978, pp. 6, 8–9.
300. HSCA interview with James Curtis Jenkins, August 24, 1977, p. 11.
301. Harrison E. Livingstone, *High Treason 2,* p. 246, interview of July 14, 1991.
302. Harrison E. Livingstone, *High Treason 2,* p. 229, interview of October 8, 1990.
303. Affidavit of James W. Sibert, October 24, 1978, p. 4.
304. HSCA interview with Dr. Pierre Finck, second day, March 12, 1978, pp. 3, 12, 7, 8.
305. WR, *New York Times* edition, p. 502.
306. HSCA interview with Dr. Pierre Finck, March 11, 1978, p. 90.
307. HSCA interview with Dr. James J. Humes, August 17, 1977, p. 8.
308. 7 HSCA 246–47, also 260 and elsewhere in the panel interview.
309. HSCA interview with Chester H. Boyers, April 25, 1978.
310. HSCA Memorandum of interview with Dr. J. Thornton Boswell, August 16, 1977, p. 6.
311. 7 HSCA 248.
312. HSCA Memorandum of interview with Dr. J. Thornton Boswell, August 16, 1977, p. 9.
313. 7 HSCA 260.
314. HSCA interview with Dr. Pierre Finck, March 11, 1978, p. 78.
315. HSCA interview with Dr. Pierre Finck, March 11, 1978, p. 81.
316. Ibid. p. 82.
317. 7 HSCA 246 (inshoot below the EOP), 254 (inshoot above the EOP).
318. HSCA interview with Dr. Pierre Finck, March 11, 1978, p. 82.
319. Ibid. p. 83.
320. Ibid. p. 88.
321. Dr. David Mantik to the author on the manuscript.
322. HSCA interview with Dr. John Ebersole, March 11, 1978, p. 18.
323. Harrison E. Livingstone, *High Treason 2,* p. 193.
324. HSCA interview with Roy Kellerman, August 24, 25, 1977, p. 5; 2 H 81.
325. HSCA Memorandum of interview with Dr J. Thornton Boswell, August 16, 1977, p. 7.
326. HSCA interview with Dr. John Ebersole, March 11, 1978, p. 28. Also see page 18 when he is first asked the question.

327. Discussion with Dr. David Mantik, Rancho Mirage, California, January 19, 1994.
328. Discussion between the author and David Mantik, M.D., June 4, 1994.
329. HSCA interview with Dr. Pierre Finck, March 11, 1978, p. 88. See also the next page.
330. 7 HSCA 254, 256, 260–61.
331. Harrison E. Livingstone, *High Treason 2*, p. 193.
332. HSCA interview with Dr. Pierre Finck, March 11, 1978, p. 125.
333. HSCA interview with Dr. Pierre Finck, March 11, 1978, p. 125. Note also on page 126 Purdy tries again to get Finck to recognize the "red spot" as an entry wound.
334. HSCA interview with Dr. Pierre Finck, March 11, 1978, p. 127.
335. 7 H 261.
336. 2 H 352.
337. Report to General Joseph Blumberg by Dr. Pierre Finck, February 1, 1965, "Summary," around p. 18 (pages are not numbered).
338. Finck report to General Joseph Blumberg, 1 February, 1965, p. 2.
339. 7 HSCA 260.
340. HSCA interview with Dr. Pierre Finck, March 11, 1978, pp. 79–80.
341. Harrison E. Livingstone, *High Treason 2*, p. 198.
342. HSCA interview with Francis X. O'Neill, January 10, 1978, p. 5.
343. Sibert and O'Neill report, November 26, 1963, p. 3.
344. HSCA August 25, 1977, interview with James W. Sibert, p. 2.
345. 2 H 353.
346. Discussion with David Mantik, M.D., June 5, 1994.
347. HSCA interview with Roy Kellerman, August 24, 1977, p. 3.
348. Conversation with Dr. David Mantik, January 19, 1994.
349. HSCA interview with Dr. Pierre Finck, March 11, 1978, p. 123.
350. Ibid.
351. 7 HSCA 248.
352. Personal notes of Pierre Finck to General Joseph Blumberg, February 1, 1965, p. 2.
353. 2 H 353.
354. Harrison E. Livingstone, *High Treason 2*, p. 192.
355. Report of Dr. Pierre Finck to General Joseph Blumberg, February 1, 1965, p. 2.
356. Report of Dr. Pierre Finck to General Joseph Blumberg, February 1, 1965, p. 3.
357. 7 HSCA 253.
358. Interview of Dr. Gary Aguilar and Dr. James Boswell, March 2, 1994.
359. 7 H 253; 249 bottom.
360. 7 HSCA 249.
361. 7 HSCA 253.
362. HSCA interview with Dr. John Ebersole, March 11, 1978, p. 3.
363. 7 HSCA 253.
364. 7 HSCA 253.
365. *JAMA*, p. 1750, October 7, 1992.
366. 7 HSCA 249.

367. HSCA Memorandum of interview with Philip C. Wehle, August 19, 1977, p. 2.
368. Ibid.
369. HSCA taped interview with Thomas Evan Robinson, January 12, 1977, p. 1.
370. Ibid. p. 4.
371. Harrison E. Livingstone, *High Treason 2*, pp. 579–81.
372. HSCA August 25, 1977, interview of James W. Sibert, p. 3.
373. HSCA interview with Francis X. O'Neill, January 10, 1978, drawings on last pages.
374. Affidavit of James W. Sibert, October 24, 1978, p. 2.
375. Report of Dr. Pierre Finck to General Joseph Blumberg, February 1, 1965, p. 2.
376. Pierre A. Finck, *Military Medicine*, "Ballistic and Forensic Pathologic Aspects of Missile Wounds. Conversion between Anglo-American and Metric System Units," June 1965, p. 551.
377. HSCA interview with Jan Gail Rudnicki, May 8, 1978, p. 2.
378. HSCA interview with James Curtis Jenkins, August 24, 1977, p. 4.
379. Humes, 2 H 354.
380. Ibid.
381. Harrison E. Livingstone, *High Treason 2*, pp. 196–97.
382. Ibid. p. 197.
383. Harrison E. Livingstone, *High Treason 2*, p. 197.
384. 2 H 352.
385. HSCA interview with Dr. John Ebersole, March 11, 1978, p. 20.
386. Sibert and O'Neill FBI report, November 26, 1963.
387. Sibert and O'Neill FBI report, November 26, 1963.
388. WR autopsy report, p. 502, *New York Times* edition.
389. HSCA interview with Dr. John Ebersole, March 11, 1978, p. 5.
390. 2 H 141.
391. Gil Delaney, *Lancaster Intelligencer-Journal*, March 10, 1978. This was just prior to his interview on the way down to Washington the next day.
392. 7 HSCA 124; 246 and elsewhere in the Panel interview with Humes and Boswell as they try to figure out where the bone went. See Dr. Lawrence Angel's drawings, 7 HSCA 230.
393. 2 H 354.
394. HSCA interview with Dr. John Ebersole, March 11, 1978, p. 19.
395. HSCA interview with Dr. John Ebersole, March 11, 1978, p. 5.
396. Note to the author.
397. HSCA interview with Dr. John Ebersole, March 11, 1978, p. 22.
398. HSCA interview with Dr. John Ebersole, March 11, 1978, p. 22.
399. Ibid. p. 23.
400. Ibid. p. 24.
401. Report of Dr. Pierre Finck to General Joseph Blumberg, February 1, 1965, p. 18.
402. WR, *New York Times* edition, p. 502.
403. 7 HSCA 13; HSCA interview with Dr. Humes, August 17, 1977, p. 7.
404. HSCA interview with Dr. George Burkley, August 17, 1977, p. 6.

405. HSCA interview with Doctors Harper and Cairns, August 17, 1977, pp. 1–2.
406. 7 HSCA 123.
407. 7 HSCA 123.
408. 7 HSCA 110.
409. 7 HSCA 116.
410. Harrison E. Livingstone, *High Treason 2*, p. 198.
411. Affidavit of James W. Sibert, October 24, 1978, p. 4.
412. Harrison E. Livingstone, *Killing the Truth*, pp. 75, 79, 298, 300, 302, 697.
413. Harrison E. Livingstone, *High Treason 2*, p. 580.
414. HSCA taped interview with Thomas Evan Robinson, January 12, 1977, pp. 2, 5.
415. Warren Report, autopsy report, *New York Times* edition, p. 502.
416. 7 HSCA 259, Dr. Petty.
417. HSCA interview with Dr. Pierre Finck, March 11, 1978, p. 91.
418. Little sawing by Humes, 2 H 354; report of Dr. Pierre Finck to General Joseph Blumberg, February 1, 1965, p. 2.
419. HSCA interview with Dr. Pierre Finck, March 11, 1978, p. 79.
420. HSCA interview with Roy Kellerman, August 24, 25, 1977, p. 5.
421. Harrison E. Livingstone, *High Treason 2.*
422. Ibid. p. 241. There is extensive discussion of the brain in the chapter on James Jenkins.
423. Ibid. pp. 195–96.
424. HSCA interview with James Curtis Jenkins, August 24, 1977, p. 9.
425. Harrison E. Livingstone, *High Treason 2*, Chapter 11, pp. 225–26.
426. Discussion with Dr. Robert Livingstone and the author, January 20, 1994.
427. Livingstone, *High Treason 2*, p. 293.
428. HSCA interview with Dr. Pierre Finck, March 11, 1978, p. 106.
429. HSCA August 12, 1977, interview with John Thomas Stringer, dated August 17, 1977, p. 15.
430. HSCA Memorandum of interview with Dr. J. Thornton Boswell, August 11, 1978, p. 2.
431. HSCA interview with Chester H. Boyers, April 25, 1978, p. 4.
432. HSCA Memorandum of interview with Dr. J. Thornton Boswell, August 16, 1977, p. 5.
433. HSCA Memorandum of interview with Dr. J. Thornton Boswell, August 16, 1977, p. 11.
434. HSCA interview with Dr. Robert F. Karnei, August 29, 1977, pp. 6–7.
435. HSCA interview with Dr. George Burkley, August 17, 1977, p. 5.
436. HSCA August 12, 1977, interview with John Thomas Stringer, dated August 17, 1977, pp. 13, 15.
437. HSCA interview with Chester H. Boyers, April 25, 1978, p. 4.
438. Report of Dr. Pierre Finck to General Joseph Blumberg, February 1, 1965, p. 4.
439. HSCA August 12, 1977, interview with John Thomas Stringer, dated August 17, 1977, p. 15.
440. HSCA interview with Captain James H. Stover, May 11, 1978, p. 2; 7 HSCA 25.

441. 7 HSCA 31–33.
442. HSCA Memorandum of interview with Dr. J. Thornton Boswell, August 16, 1977, p. 5.
443. HSCA interview with Dr. George Burkley, August 17, 1977, p. 5.
444. This history is told in 7 HSCA 23–25.
445. HSCA interview with Dr. George Burkley, August 17, 1977, p. 5.
446. HSCA interview with Admiral Calvin Galloway, May 17, 1978, p. 3.
447. HSCA interview with Dr. Robert F. Karnei, August 29, 1977, p. 4.
448. HSCA interview with James Curtis Jenkins, August 24, 1977, p. 8.
449. HSCA Memorandum of interview with Dr. J. Thornton Boswell, August 11, 1978, p. 2.
450. HSCA interview with J. Thornton Boswell, August 16, 1977, p. 4.
451. Harrison E. Livingstone, *High Treason 2*, p. 238 (Jenkins); p. 277 (O'Connor).
452. HSCA interview with Dr. Robert F. Karnei, August 29, 1977, p. 3.
453. HSCA interview with Jan Gail Rudnicki, May 8, 1978, p. 3.
454. HSCA interview with John Stringer, Document No. 013617, p. 4.
455. HSCA interview with Thomas Evan Robinson, January 12, 1977, p. 3.
456. HSCA interview with Dr. Pierre Finck, March 11, 1978, pp. 71–72.
457. HSCA interview with Dr. Pierre Finck, March 11, 1978, p. 72.
458. Harrison E. Livingstone, *High Treason 2*, chapter 12.
459. HSCA interview with Thomas Robinson, January 12, 1977, p. 3.
460. Ibid. p. 9.
461. HSCA interview with James Curtis Jenkins, August 24, 1977, p. 8.
462. HSCA interview with Francis X. O'Neill, January 10, 1978, p. 5.
463. HSCA interview with James Curtis Jenkins, August 24, 1977, p. 8.
464. 7 HSCA 15.
465. HSCA interview with Paul O'Connor, June 28, 1978, p. 1.
466. William Manchester, *Death of a President*, p. 294.
467. Outside contact report with Roy H. Kellerman, December 1, 1978; with William Greer, December 4, 1978.
468. HSCA interview with Thomas Evan Robinson, January 16, 1977, p. 10.
469. 7 HSCA 255.
470. HSCA interview with Dr. John Ebersole, March 11, 1978, p. 10.
471. Note of Andy Purdy, August 29, 1978, HSCA File No. 180-10076-10316, Agency File No. 011099.
472. HSCA interview with Dr. Pierre Finck, March 11, 1978, p. 129.
473. Livingstone, *Killing the Truth*, p. 114.
474. Warren Report, *New York Times* edition, p. 504.
475. Livingstone, *High Treason 2*, p. 294.
476. Report of Dr. Pierre Finck to General Joseph Blumberg, February 1, 1965, p. 20.
477. Statement of Drs. James Humes, J. Thornton Boswell, Pierre Finck, prepared by the Department of Justice, and signed January 17, 1967.
478. As per the drawing of January 18, 1978, that Richard Lipsey made for House investigators.
479. Statement of Drs. James Humes, J. Thornton Boswell, Pierre Finck, prepared by the Department of Justice, and signed January 17, 1967, pp. 3–4.

480. HSCA interview with Dr. Pierre Finck, March 11, 1978, p. 129.

481. Boswell's drawing is mentioned by Andy Purdy, Mark Flanagan, and Jim Kelly in their HSCA interview of Francis X. O'Neill, January 10, 1978, p. 6; also in O'Neill's affidavit of November 8, 1978, p. 5.

482. 7 HSCA 181.

483. Livingstone, *High Treason 2*, p. 260.

484. Ibid. pp. 215, 216, 220.

485. Livingstone, *High Treason 2*, p. 162.

7. **Posner's** *Case Closed*

1. *New York Times Book Review*, February 2, 1992.

2. *Extra!* November/December 1994, p. 14.

3. Jim Folliard, "Gerald Posner Closes the Case," *The Fourth Decade*, November 1993, vol. 1, no. 1.

4. Jack Sirica, *Newsday, Alta Vista Magazine*, September 26, 1993.

5. Ibid.

6. *U.S. News and World Report*, August 30, 1993, p. 62.

7. Gerald Posner, *Case Closed*, p. xi.

8. Harrison E. Livingstone, *Killing the Truth*, p. 228.

9. Harrison E. Livingstone, *Killing the Truth*, p. 211.

10. Harrison E. Livingstone, *Killing the Truth*, p. 207.

11. Jeffrey Frank, *The Washington Post Book World*, October 31, 1993, p. 4, review of Fonzi, Scott, and Posner.

12. Patricia Holt, the *San Francisco Chronicle*, September 5, 1993, p. R 2.

13. *On the Money* TV program, July 31, 1993, Brian Banmiller, host.

14. Posner, p. 226. The rifle expert is Cortlandt Cunningham, 2 H 252.

15. American Bar Association, "Trial of the Century," August 10, 1992; Livingstone, *Killing The Truth*, firearms chapter, p. 232.

16. Credibility of: 12 HSCA 527–35, 540, 552–54, 557–59, 567–69, 578, 581, 587–95, 603-6, 609, 615–16, 620-26, 631, 636, 639–41. See also the entire index for Nosenko in the *Master Index to the J.F.K. Assassination Investigations* by Sylvia Meagher and Gary Owens, p. 279. The latter index is difficult to obtain and is out of print.

17. Posner, p. 348.

18. Meagher, *Accessories After the Fact*, p. 349; O'Toole, *The Assassination Tapes*, p. 216. See also 5 H 242–43.

19. Gary Aguilar, M.D., discussion with the author, April 5, 1994, and letter of May 19, 1994, to Henry Cohen of the *Federal Bar News and Journal*, Federal Bar Association.

20. *Dateline: Dallas*, November 1993, p. 9.

21. Livingstone, *High Treason*, p. 266; *High Treason* cites Summers, *Conspiracy*, pp. 295–96.

22. Peter Dale Scott, *The San Francisco Review of Books*, November/December 1993.

23. *Dateline: Dallas*, November 1993, p. 9.

24. Peter Dale Scott, *The San Francisco Review of Books*, November 1993, p. 2.

25. Report HSCA 149.

26. Peter Dale Scott, *The San Francisco Review of Books*, November 1993, p. 2.

27. Posner, p. 361.
28. Posner, p. 355.
29. Report HSCA 151; Livingstone, *High Treason*, pp. 130, 243, 273–74.
30. Scott, p. 2.
31. Ibid. p. 2.
32. Report HSCA 243 (26).
33. WC memorandum from Norman Redlich, February 28, 1964.
34. Folliard, "Gerald Posner Closes the Case," *The Fourth Decade*, November 1993.
35. 3 H 217; Posner, pp. 12–13.
36. Jim Folliard, "Gerald Posner Closes the Case," *The Fourth Decade*, November 1993.
37. Warren Report, p. 379.
38. Sylvia Meagher, *Accessories After the Fact*, p. 244.
39. Folliard, p. 14.
40. Folliard, p. 15.
41. Martin Shackelford, *The Investigator*, December 1993, p. 11.
42. Renatus Hartogs and Lucy Freeman, *The Two Assassins*, (New York: Thomas Y. Crowell Company, 1965).
43. Jim Folliard, "Gerald Posner Closes the Case," *The Fourth Decade*, November 1993; James W. Clarke, *American Assassins*, pp. 5–12.
44. Ibid.
45. Posner, p. 314.
46. Ibid.
47. 6 H 40.
48. Gerald Posner, p. 291; interview with Dr. Marion Jenkins, March 10, 1992.
49. Gerald Posner, p. 291; interview with Dr. Marion Jenkins, March 10, 1992.
50. Gerald Posner, *Case Closed*, p. 312.
51. WR, GPO edition, p. 530 (Appendix VIII), CE 392.
52. 7 HSCA 286–87.
53. *American Medical News*, November 24, 1978.
54. Posner, p. 313.
55. 6 H 51.
56. Aguilar, unpublished manuscript, October 1993, p. 10.
57. Gary Aguilar, M.D., discussion with the author, April 5, 1994, and letter of May 19, 1994, to Henry Cohen of the *Federal Bar News and Journal*, Federal Bar Association.
58. *The New York Times*, May 26, 1992, p. C3.
59. Interview with Dr. Charles Carrico, March 8, 1992; Posner, p. 311.
60. 3 H 361.
61. Posner, p. 312.
62. 7 HSCA 302; interview with Andrew Purdy, January 11, 1978.
63. Aguilar, unpublished manuscript as above.
64. Posner, p. 311.
65. Harrison E. Livingstone, *High Treason*, pp. 31, 44, 46; The *Boston Globe*, June 21, 1991, p. A 23, and their raw data which I placed in the JFK Library in Boston.

66. Dr. Richard Brooks Dulaney to Ben Bradlee, Jr., and reported in Livingstone, *High Treason* (Berkley paperback), p. 460; p. 397, Conservatory Press edition. *Boston Globe* investigation, 1981. I placed their raw data in the JFK Library, Boston. *Globe* article of June 21, 1981.
67. Ibid.
68. Ibid.
69. Ibid. p. 30 (paperback); p. 25 hardback.
70. Aguilar, unpublished manuscript on the wounds, p. 19.
71. Aguilar, p. 19.
72. Warren Report, p. 518, CE 392 (17 H).
73. Shackelford, *The Investigator*, August–September 1993, p. 17.
74. Posner, p. 251.
75. Posner, p. 334, paraphrasing Dr. Piziali. See also *Killing the Truth*, pp. 215–16 for the actual text of Dr. Piziali's presentation.
76. Posner, p. 258.
77. Posner, p. 245 footnote.
78. West and Rush, "Confirmation of the Single Bullet Theory," 1992.
79. Roy Vaughan, Livingstone, *High Treason*, pp. 202–3.
80. Roy Vaughan v. Mark Lane, National General Pictures Corporation, General Cinema Corp. of Texas and Penn Jones, Jr., United States District Court for the Northern District of Texas, Dallas Division, Civil Action No. CA 3-74-58-E, January 23, 1974.
81. Peter Dale Scott, *The San Francisco Review of Books*, November–December, 1993, pp. 3–4, citing Posner, p. 225.
82. Ibid.
83. Sylvia Meagher, *The Texas Observer*, "The Curious Testimony of Mr. Givens," 1971 (exact date unknown).
84. Ibid.
85. Peter Dale Scott, *The San Francisco Review of Books*, November–December, 1993, p. 4.
86. Posner, p. 227.
87. Posner, p. 227.
88. Peter Dale Scott, *The San Francisco Review of Books*, November–December, 1993, p. 5.
89. Posner, p. 98.
90. Posner, pp. 272–73.
91. Posner, pp. 289, 305.
92. Posner, p. 302.
93. Michael Baden, M.D., and Judith Adler Hennessee, *Unnatural Death*. (New York: Ballantine Books, a division of Random House, 1989), p. 11.
94. Posner, p. 294 footnote.
95. Shackelford, *The Investigator*, August–September 1993, p. 13.
96. Shackelford, *The Investigator*, August–September 1993, p. 18.
97. Dr. Roger McCarthy (Failure Analysis), "Trial of the Century," American Bar Association, 1992; and in *Killing The Truth*, firearms chapter; Shackelford, in *The Investigator*, August–September 1993, p. 14.
98. Posner, p. 335.
99. Shackelford, *The Investigator*, August–September 1993, p. 22.
100. Posner, p. 474.

101. Posner, p. 477.

102. Shackelford, p. 23.

103. The Dillard and Powell photographs show the windows.

104. Martin Shackelford, *"Case Closed: Lee Harvey Oswald and the Assassination of JFK* by Gerald Posner: A Preliminary Critique," *The Investigator*, August–September 1993, p. 5.

105. Posner, pp. 272–73.

106. Shackelford, *The Investigator*, pp. 11–12.

107. Posner, pp. 467–68.

108. Posner, p. 273.

109. Shackelford, *The Investigator*, August–September, p. 12; see note 167 for list.

110. Posner, p. 283; Rusty Livingstone, Dallas Police Crime Lab, at 1992 Chicago Midwest Third Decade Conference.

111. Dr. Roger McCarthy (Failure Analysis), at the American Bar Association's "Trial of the Century," 1992, and in Livingstone's *Killing The Truth* (1993).

112. Posner, p. 144 footnote.

113. Palmer, HSCA testimony; Shackelford, *The Investigator*, p. 6.

114. James DiEugenio, "Clarifying the Clinton Incident," p. 14, *Back Channels*, vol. 3, no. 3.

115. Posner, pp. 182, 187–88.

116. December 4, 1992, letter of W. David Slawson to Amanda Rowell, as published in the appendix of *Killing The Truth*, p. 621, Appendix E; and in *The Investigator*, No. 2, p. 7.

117. Posner, p. 188.

118. Posner, pp. 195–96.

119. Posner, p. 304 footnote.

120. 7 HSCA pp. 13–14.

121. 7 HSCA p. 193.

122. 7 HSCA pp. 192–3; letter of Pierre Finck to General Joseph Blumberg, February 1, 1965.

123. 7 HSCA pp. 188–94, with the rules for autopsy preceding this from pp. 181–88.

124. 7 HSCA p. 193.

125. Livingstone, *High Treason 2*, p. 303.

126. Livingstone, *Killing The Truth, JAMA* chapter.

127. Livingstone, *High Treason 2*, p. 121.

128. Livingstone, *High Treason 2*, p. 186.

129. James Folliard, "Gerald Posner Closes the Case," October 1993.

130. Folliard, "Gerald Posner Closes The Case," p. 2.

131. Ibid.

132. 2 H 225–50; Meagher, *Accessories After The Fact*, pp. 55–57.

133. Ibid.

134. Folliard, p. 4.

135. Posner, p. 225.

136. Posner, p. 225.

137. Folliard, p. 8.

138. Posner, p. 272.

139. James Folliard, unpublished manuscript, p. 9.
140. Folliard, p. 9.
141. Folliard, p. 10.
142. Posner, p. 288; Folliard, p. 10.
143. *U.S. News & World Report*, August 30–September 6, 1993, p. 90.
144. Siebert and O'Neill FBI report of November 26, 1963, p. 4.
145. 2 H 143.
146. 2 H 103.
147. 2 H 127.
148. Folliard, p. 11.
149. *Killing the Truth*, pp. 173, 175.
150. Posner, p. 288 footnote.
151. Folliard, p. 12.
152. Folliard, p. 12.
153. Posner, pp. 64–65.
154. Livingstone, *High Treason*, pp. 113, 139, 163–64; 12 HSCA 153, 171.
155. 12 HSCA 69.
156. Ibid. 153, 171.
157. Posner, p. 273–74.
158. Posner, p. 274.
159. Posner, p. 275 footnote.
160. CE 2003, p. 11.
161. Henry Hurt, *Reasonable Doubt*, p. 142.
162. Ibid. p. 144.
163. Posner, p. 277 footnote.
164. Posner, p. 278 footnote.
165. Shackelford, *The Investigator*, August–September 1993, pp. 12–13.
166. Shackelford, *The Investigator*, August–September 1993, p. 17.
167. Folliard, p. 15.
168. Martin Shackelford, *The Investigator*, August–September 1993, p. 8.
169. Weisberg, *Photographic Whitewash*, pp. 210–11; *The Dallas Morning News*, November 26, 1978, p. 13a, story by Earl Golz; Anthony Summers, *Conspiracy* pp. 108–9.
170. Posner, p. 272.
171. Hill, 7 H 59.
172. Truly, 7 H 382–3.
173. Fritz, 4 H 206.
174. Summers, *Conspiracy*, pp. 591–92, note 83; Hurt, *Reasonable Doubt*, pp. 411–12.
175. Posner, p. 446.
176. 10 HSCA 200–201.
177. Posner, p. 287.
178. Ibid.
179. Folliard, p. 12.
180. Posner, p. 268 footnote.
181. Shackelford, *The Investigator*, p. 11.
182. Peter Dale Scott, *The San Francisco Review of Books*, November–December 1993, p. 1.
183. Ibid.

184. Peter Dale Scott, *The San Francisco Review of Books*, November–December 1993, p. 5.
185. 1 HSCA 561–62; Livingstone, *High Treason*, pp. 60, 64, 102, 200, 331.
186. Posner, p. 388 footnote.
187. Posner, p. 107 footnote 2.
188. *High Treason 2.*
189. Posner, pp. 245–48.
190. Memo of Martin Shackelford, September 4, 1994, on the "corrected" paperback version of Posner's *Case Closed.*
191. James Folliard letter to the author, December 12, 1993.
192. Folliard, "Gerald Posner Closes The Case," p. 2.
193. Christopher Lehmann-Haupt, *The New York Times*, September 9, 1993. The *Times* also had a review by Geoffrey Ward, author of the script for the PBS special *The Kennedys*, which also dismissed some of the new proconspiracy books.
194. *U.S. News & World Report*, p. 68.

8. Conflicts in the Evidence and What They May Mean

1. Harold Weisberg, *PostMortem*, pp. 565–73.
2. Livingstone, *High Treason 2*, pp. 556–57.
3. # (15), # (17) p. 5 (p. 568, *PostMortem*). & # (44) p. 8.
4. 7 HSCA 253; the photographer who took them, John Thomas Stringer: HSCA Record Number 180-10093-10429, Agency File No: 002070, August 17, 1977, Purdy, Donald A., Jr., Subjects: Harper, Jack C.; Cairns, A. B.; Bone fragments; Evidence, Medical; Burkley, George; Humes, James J., p. 16.
5. Pierre Finck, notes made 10 February 1967 and typed by him in Brussels on Sunday, 26 February 1978, regarding his review of the autopsy photographs and X-rays at the National Archives, January 20, 1967.
6. January 20, 1967, inspection of Drs. Humes, Boswell and Finck, signed January 26, 1967; document published by Harold Weisberg, *PostMortem*, p. 575.
7. Examination of photos and X-rays, January 20, 1967, report signed January 26, p. 5; *PostMortem*, p. 579.
8. HSCA interview with Pierre Finck, March 12, 1978, p. 2.
9. Ibid. pp. 3–4.
10. Ibid. p. 6.
11. Ibid. p. 9.
12. Ibid. p. 9.
13. Ibid. p. 10.
14. Ibid. p. 12.
15. Rosemary James and Jack Wardlaw, *Plot or Politics*, pp. 33–34.
16. Pierre Finck, notes made 10 February 1967 and typed by him in Brussels on Sunday, February 26, 1978, regarding his review of the autopsy photographs and X-rays at the National Archives, January 20, 1967.
17. *High Treason*, pp. 50–52, 83, 92, 124; *High Treason 2*, 556–59; *Killing the Truth*, 76.

18. *Maryland State Medical Journal*, March 1977, pp. 65–66.
19. WR, *New York Times* edition, p. 504.
20. 7 HSCA 23 (5).
21. Earl Golz, in the *Dallas Morning News*, June 15, 1968 (*The Continuing Inquiry*, July 1978, p. 16); August 17, 1978 (*The Continuing Inquiry*, August 1978, pp. 6–7). See also *First Day Evidence* by Gary Savage, pp. 207-15.
22. HSCA interview with John Ebersole, March 11, 1978, p. 67.
23. HSCA interview with Dr. John Ebersole, March 11, 1978, p. 67.
24. HSCA interview with Dr. John Ebersole, March 11, 1978, p. 17.
25. George O'Toole, *The Assassination Tapes*, p. 114; see the photograph published in Jesse Curry's book, *JFK Assassination File*, p. 113, of the evidence found in Ruth Paine's house.
26. Doug Mizzer, Daryll Weatherly, David Mantik, M.D., and the author in the National Archives, June 1994, observation of the slides.

9. Conclusion

1. Lee Israel, *Kilgallen*, Dell, 1980, Epilogue, p. 395. See also the long section on John Kennedy's murder and Kilgallen's relationship with Jack Ruby, chapter 27, p. 357.
2. Gaeton Fonzi, *The Last Investigation*, 1993, pp. 28–29.
3. George O'Toole, *The Assassination Tapes*, p. 243.

Appendix. A New Look at the "Film of the Century" by Daryll Weatherly

1. Luis Alvarez, "A Physicist Examines the Kennedy Assassination Film," *American Journal of Physics*, September 1976, Vol. 44, No. 9, pp. 813–27.
2. Ibid. p. 814.
3. Josiah Thompson, *Six Seconds In Dallas*, pp. 374–75.
4. HSCA Vol. VI, pp. 15–32.
5. Alvarez, supra, p. 815.
6. Thompson, supra, p. 375.

BIBLIOGRAPHY AND AUTHOR INDEX

JOURNALS, ORGANIZATIONS, BOOKSELLERS
& ARCHIVES

COPA, or **Coalition on Political Assassinations,** Inc., is the newest organization (January 1994). COPA was set up in Washington after extensive dissatisfaction expressed in Dallas with ASK. Primary movers are Jim DiEugenio, Dan Alcorn, John Judge, Cyril Wecht, and John Newman. A newsletter is planned, along with regular meetings to discuss evidence, political action, publicity, and other efforts. COPA is an umbrella organization bringing together the efforts of several groups and organizations. Write c/o P.O. Box 772, Washington, DC, 20044. COPA claims (in 1994) to be only interested in lobbying the JFK documents Review Board set up by Congress for the release of documents being withheld by agencies. But its separate organizations have differing agendas, and many on its board do not like or agree with each other. It will be interesting to see who wins the power struggle within it, and what it ends up doing. It certainly should not attempt to speak for the research community as a whole. COPA has moved into a position of immediate power in the case, and considering the various lightweights and disinformation specialists (along with some good people) involved with it, should be watched carefully.

AAR, or **Association of Assassination Researchers,** set up by Doug Mizzer, Harrison E. Livingstone, and a number of others to counter COPA. This is planned as a grassroots research organization and is not intended for the former leadership to use to blow their horns and misdirect the JFK case. Interested people should write AAR at P.O. Box 7149, Baltimore, MD 21218. Membership is free.

AARC, or the **Assassination Archives and Research Center** was founded in 1984 by Bernard Fensterwald, Jr., and Jim Lesar, two Washington attorneys who have long had an interest in political assassinations. Fensterwald once served as speechwriter and campaigner for his Harvard classmate, John Kennedy. He was also the lawyer who represented Watergate burglar James McCord when McCord cracked the cover-up through his famous letter to Judge John Sirica. He and Lesar both represented James Earl Ray, the alleged assassin of Dr. Martin Luther King, Jr., in his attempts to get a trial. Lesar has handled most of the Freedom of Information Act litigation for those seeking records on the assassinations of President Kennedy, Senator Robert F. Kennedy, and Martin Luther King, Jr. The AARC is a unique and valuable repository of information on political assassinations and related matters, such as intelligence activities and organized crime. It is also a contact center for authors, researchers, and members of the media, and many of them have donated their own manuscripts and research materials to the AARC. Fensterwald provided virtually all the financial support for the AARC until his death in April 1991. As a result, the AARC's very existence is now threatened and it is urgently in need of financial support. Contributions are tax deductible and may be sent to: The AARC, 918 F St., N.W., Washington, DC 20004. The AARC's new president is Jim Lesar. Annual membership is twenty-five dollars, but large contributions are needed.

BOOKS

For new and used or hard-to-get books on this case and related matters, the following stores are recommended: The Last Hurrah Bookshop, 937 Memorial Avenue, Williamsport, PA 17701, Tel: (717) 327-9338; M & A Book Dealer, P.O. Box 2422, Waco, TX 76703; The President's Box Bookshelf, P.O. Box 1255, Washington, DC 20013, 703-998-7390; Cloak and Dagger Books, 9 Eastman Avenue, Bedford, NH 03102, 603-668-1629; and for new copies of *Farewell America*, call Al Navis at 416-781-4139—Handy Books, 1762 Avenue Road, Toronto, ONT, M5M 3Y9, Canada.

The Conspiracy Museum, R. B. Cutler, director, the KATY Building, 110 S. Market Street, Dallas, TX 75202. Tel: (214) 741-3040; Fax: (214) 741-9339.

The **JFK Assassination Information Center** in Dallas has closed.

JOURNALS

THE INVESTIGATOR is devoted to assassination and allied research, and now the best of the journals. Published by Gary Rowell, editor, 1529 Elizabeth, Bay City, MI 48708. Four dollars per issue, and twenty-four dollars for one year (six issues). This is turning out to be the best of the magazines which provides a forum for research in Kennedy's assassination.

PROBE, a periodical containing mostly hard news and developments in the case. Author Jim DiEugenio is the chairman, and Kathy Cunningham, Gary Aguilar, David Mantik, Doug Carlson, Edwin Lopez, and Gaeton Fonzi are some of the board members. Subscriptions c/o Jim DiEugenio, CTKA, 2139 N. Vine Street, Hollywood, CA 90068. Phones are (213) 463-6792; twenty-five dollars per year. Basically a gossip column.

DATELINE: DALLAS was published by the JFK Assassination Information Center. No longer published.

THE FOURTH DECADE, which was known as **THE THIRD DE-CADE,** A Journal of Research on the John F. Kennedy Assassination, is published by Professor Jerry Rose at the State University College, Fredonia, NY 14063. Twenty dollars for one year, thirty-six dollars for two years, and fifty dollars for three years. Single issues are four dollars. *The Fourth Decade* published too much amateur material which disinforms, but has considerably improved.

BACK CHANNELS, A Quarterly Publication of Historical and Modern Espionage, Assassination and Conspiracies. Editor: Peter Kross; $4.50 per issue; Kross Publications and Research Services, P.O. Box 9, Franklin Park, NJ 08823.

PROLOGUE: Newsletter of the Committee for an Open Archives. Editor: John Judge; twenty-five dollars or more to Committee for an Open Archives, P.O. Box 6008, Washington, DC 20005. An informative newsletter containing articles on numerous subjects of interest to researchers.

PREVAILING WINDS is a good source of reprints. Contact Prevailing Winds Research, P.O. Box 23511, Santa Barbara, CA 93121. Tel: (805) 566-8016. Write for Catalogue/Reader (two dollars).

JFK HONOR GUARD: A magazine devoted to keeping alive the case of the assassination of John F. Kennedy. Published by Deanie Richards. "In general only members' material is printed." Fifteen dollars for the first twelve issues. Write to P.O. Box 3724, Akron, OH 44314.

DALLAS, '63, c/o Chris Mills, 76 Main St., Burton Joyce, Nottingham, England, NG14 5EH. Tel: (0602) 314018.

LOBSTER, edited and published by Robin Ramsay, 214 Westbourne Avenue, Hull, HU5 3JB, U.K. (Tel: 0482-447558). Appears in June and December each year.

ECHOES OF CONSPIRACY, 1525 Acton St., Berkeley, CA 94702. (Paul Hoch) A journal of assassination research published by Paul Hock, which is basically no longer functioning, except occasionally, and issues appear infrequently.

THE CONTINUING INQUIRY (TCI). Journal of assassination research, monthly, created by Penn Jones, Jr. No longer published.

COVER-UPS: Larry Dunkel (aka Gary Mack). A journal of assassination research. No longer published.

WHO'S WHO IN THE JFK ASSASSINATION, AN A-TO-Z ENCYCLOPEDIA, Michael Benson, Citadel Press, Carol Publishing Group, 1993. Useful reference work, and probably the best.

ENCYCLOPEDIA: THE ASSASSINATION OF PRESIDENT JOHN F. KENNEDY: A COMPLETE BOOK OF FACTS by James Duffy, edited by James Waller, Thunder's Mouth Press, 1992. This is a reference work for the beginner.

ABBREVIATIONS USED FOR CITATIONS

3 H 67: Vol 3. p. 67 Appendix or Hearings of the Warren Report.

3 HSCA 422: Vol 3. p. 422 Appendix to the Report of the House Select Committee on Assassinations, or Assassinations Committee. 12 vols. JFK; 13 vols. King.

WR: Warren Report *New York Times* edition used here unless otherwise stated.

Report—Report of the Assassinations Committee. Also Bantam, 1979.

CD= Commission Document.
CE= Commission Exhibit.

Investigation of the Assassination of President John F. Kennedy, GPO, U.S. House of Representatives Select Committee on Assassinations, 1976–78.

Final Report on the Select Committee to Study Governmental Operations with Respect to Intelligence Activities, U.S. Senate, 1976. Recommended reading.

Report to the President by the Commission on CIA Activities Within the United States (the "Rockefeller Commission"), also Manor Books, New York, 1976.

SICROFA—Senate Intelligence Committee Report on Foreign Assassinations, *Alleged Assassination Plots Involving Foreign Leaders*. Recommended reading.

BOOKS

Ashman, Charles. *The CIA-Mafia Link*. New York: Manor Books, 1975.
Bishop, Jim. *The Day Kennedy Was Shot*. New York: Funk & Wagnalls 1968; Bantam, 1969.
Blair, Joan and Clay. *The Search for JFK*. New York: Berkley, 1976.
Blumenthal, Sid, with Harvey Yazigian. *Government by Gunplay: Assas-*

sination Conspiracy Theories From Dallas to Today. New York: Signet, 1976. Recommended reading.

Bowart, William. *Operation Mind Control: Our Secret Government's War Against Its Own People.* New York: Dell, 1978. Recommended reading.

Brown, Walt. *The People v. Lee Harvey Oswald.* New York: Carroll & Graf, 1992. *Treachery In Dallas.* New York: Carroll & Graf, 1995.

Buchanan, Thomas. *Who Killed Kennedy.* New York: Putnam, 1964; London: Secker, Warburg, 1964; New York: MacFadden, 1965.

Callahan, Bob. *Who Shot JFK? A Guide to the Major Conspiracy Theories.* New York: Simon & Schuster, 1993.

Canfield, Michael, with Alan J. Weberman. *Coup d'Etat in America: The CIA and the Assassination of John F. Kennedy.* New York: Third World Press, 1975.

Cameron, Gail. *Rose.* New York: Berkley, 1971.

Christic Institute. *Inside The Shadow Government,* 1988, The Christic Institute, 1324 North Capitol Street NW, Washington, DC 20002: (202) 797-8106; $15.

Collier, Peter and David Horowitz. *The Kennedys: An American Drama.* New York: Warner Books, 1985.

Crenshaw, Charles A., with J. Gary Shaw and Jens Hansen. *JFK: Conspiracy of Silence.* New York: Signet, 1992.

Curry, Jesse. *JFK Assassination File,* 1969, American Poster and Printing Co. Inc., 1600 S. Akard., Dallas, Texas 75215.

Evica, George Michael. *And We Are All Mortal.* University of Hartford, 1978, $7.95 plus $1 for postage and handling. University of Hartford, 200 Bloomfield Avenue, West Hartford, CT 06117.

Fall, Bernard B. *The Two Vietnams: A Political and Military Analysis.* New York: Praeger, 1963; revised in 1964.

Fensterwald, Bernard. *Assassination of JFK by Coincidence or Conspiracy?* New York: Zebra Books, 1977. Committee to Investigate Assassinations (C. to I.A.). Recommended reading.

Flammonde, Paris. *The Kennedy Conspiracy: An Uncommissioned Report on the Jim Garrison Investigation.* New York: Meredith, 1969.

Fonzi, Gaeton. *The Last Investigation.* New York: Thunder's Mouth Press, 1993. About how the HSCA failed—by its only field investigator.

Ford, Gerald R., with John R. Stiles. *Portrait of the Assassin.* New York: Simon & Schuster, 1965.

Fox, Sylvan. *The Unanswered Questions About President Kennedy's Assassination.* New York: Award Books, 1965 and 1975.

Galloway, John. *The Kennedys and Vietnam.* New York: Facts On File, Inc.

Garrison, Jim. *A Heritage of Stone.* New York: Putnam, 1970; Berkeley, 1972. Recommended reading for all Americans. *On The Trail of the Assassins,* Sheridan Square Press (Institute for Media Analysis), 1988.

Golz, Earl. *The Earl Golz Collection.* Two bound volumes of the newspaper stories on the assassination of Kennedy by Earl Golz from 1970–1982. Forty dollars total for both volumes, from Earl Golz, 3816 S. Lamaar Blvd, apartment 607, Austin, TX 78704. An important series of articles.

Goodwin, Doris Kearns. *The Fitzgeralds and The Kennedys.* New York: Simon & Schuster, 1987.

Haley, J. Evetts. *A Texan Looks At Lyndon. A Study in Illegitimate Power.* Palo Duro Press, 1964; P.O. Box 390, Canyon, TX.

Hepburn, James (pseudonym, author unknown, but thought to be French Intelligence and American sources according to former FBI agent William Turner). *Farewell America.* Frontiers Publishing Company 1968, Vaduz, Liechtenstein, Printed in Canada and Belgium, but this is a fictitious publishing company. Available from Al Navis, Handy Books, Toronto. Recommended reading; a very important book. The book was written by someone with an intimate knowledge of the CIA and the United States.

Hill, Jean and Bill Sloan (listed under Sloan's name first). *JFK: The Last Dissenting Witness.* Pelican, Gretna, LA, 1992.

Hinckle, Warren and William Turner. *The Fish is Red.* New York: Harper and Row, 1981.

Hougan, Jim. *Spooks, The Haunting of America—The Private Use of Secret Agents.* New York: William Morrow, 1978. Recommended reading. *Secret Agenda.* Random House, 1984; Ballantine, 1985.

Hurt, Henry. *Reasonable Doubt.* New York: Holt, Rinehart and Winston, 1986.

Joesten, Joachim. *Oswald: Assassin or Fall Guy?* Marzani and Munsell, 1964.

Jones, Penn, Jr. *Forgive My Grief* vols I–IV. Rt 3, Box 356, Waxahachie, TX 75165. Recommended reading. Most out of print now, but volumes can be obtained from the AIC in Dallas.

Kantor, Seth. *Who Was Jack Ruby?* New York: Everest, 1978; *The Ruby Cover-Up.* New York: Kensington Books, 1992. Republication of *Who Was Jack Ruby?* with new material.

Kennedy, Rose. *Times to Remember.* Garden City, NJ: Doubleday, 1974.

The Kennedy Years. Text by *The New York Times.* New York: Viking Press, 1966.

Kirkwood, James. *American Grotesque: An Account of the Clay Shaw-Jim*

Garrison Kennedy Assassination Trial in New Orleans. New York: Harper Perennial, 1992. Simon and Schuster hardcover, 1970. Highly recommended overview of the Garrison debacle.

Kritzberg, Connie. *Secrets From the Sixth Floor Window.* Undercover Press, $11.95, P.O. Box 703026, Tulsa, OK 74170-3026.

Lincoln, Evelyn. *My Twelve Years With John F. Kennedy.* New York: David McKay, 1965; Bantam, 1966.

Livingstone, Harrison E. *High Treason.* The Conservatory Press, (1989) $24.45 for new hardbacks, including postage and handling: P.O. Box 7149, Baltimore, Md 21218; Mass Market pocketbook: Berkley Publishing Group, New York, 1990. *High Treason 2,* Carroll & Graf, New York, 1992; Trade paperback, 1993. *Killing the Truth.* Carroll & Graf, New York, 1993; Trade paperback, 1994.

Manchester, William. *The Death of a President: November 20–25, 1963.* New York: Harper & Row, 1967; Popular Library, 1968.

Marchetti, Victor and John D. Marks. *The CIA and the Cult of Intelligence.* New York: Knopf 1974. Recommended reading.

Marks, John. *The Search For the Manchurian Candidate.* New York: Times Books, 1979. Recommended reading.

Martin, Ralph G. *A Hero For Our Time—An Intimate Study of the Kennedy Years.* New York: Macmillan, 1982; Fawcett Crest, 1983.

Meagher, Sylvia. *Accessories After the Fact: The Warren Commission, the Authorities, and the Report.* New York: Bobbs-Merrill, 1967; Vintage, 1976. Recommended reading.

Melanson, Philip H. *Spy Saga: Lee Harvey Oswald and U.S. Intelligence.* New York: Praeger, 1990. Praeger was a famous (and documented) CIA front, so their publication of this book is of interest in itself.

Milan, Michael. *The Squad: The U.S. Government's Secret Alliance With Organized Crime.* New York: Shapolsky, 1989.

Subject Index to the Warren Report and Hearings and Exhibits. New York: Scarecrow Press, 1966: Ann Arbor, Michigan University microfilms 1971.

Miller, Tom. *The Assassination Please Almanac.* Chicago: Henry Regnery Co. 1977. A reference of sorts to people, and events.

Moyers, Bill. *The Secret Government: The Constitution in Crisis,* 1988, Seven Locks Press, P.O. Box 27, Cabin John, MD 20818; (301) 320-2130; $9.95 plus postage and handling.

Newman, John M. *JFK and Vietnam: Deception, Intrigue and the Struggle for Power.* New York: Warner Books, 1992. *Oswald and the CIA.* New York: Carroll & Graf, 1995.

North, Mark. *Act Of Treason: The Role of J. Edgar Hoover in the Assassination of President Kennedy.* New York: Carroll & Graf, 1991.

Noyes, Peter. *Legacy of Doubt.* New York: Pinnacle Books, 1973.

O'Donnell, Kenneth P., David F. Powers, and Joe McCarthy. *Johnny, We Hardly Knew Ye.* New York: Little, Brown, 1970.

Oglesby, Carl. *The Yankee and Cowboy War.* Mission, Kansas: Andrews and McMeel, 1976.

Oliver, Beverly with Coke Buchanan. *Nightmare in Dallas.* "The Babushka Lady." Starburst Press, 1994, P.O. Box 4123, Lancaster, PA 17604.

Oswald, Robert, with Myrick and Barbara Land. *Lee: A Portrait of Lee Harvey Oswald.* New York: Coward-McCann, 1967.

O'Toole, George. *The Assassination Tapes: An Electronic Probe Into the Murder of John F. Kennedy and the Dallas Cover-up.* New York: Penthouse Press, 1975.

Palamara, Vincent Michael. *The Third Alternative—Survivor's Guilt: The Secret Service and the JFK Murder,* 1993, unpublished, available from the author for twenty-five dollars. Recommended reading. Write Vince Palamara, 484 Hoodridge Drive, Apt. D3, Pittsburgh, PA 15234.

Popkin, Richard H. *The Second Oswald.* New York: Avon Books, 1966.

Prouty, L. Fletcher. *The Secret Team: The CIA and Its Allies in Control of the United States and the World.* New York: Prentice Hall, 1973. Recommended reading, a very important book.

Roffman, Howard. *Presumed Guilty.* Fairleigh Dickinson University Press 1975; Associated University Presses, Inc. Cranbury, New Jersey, London England. An important book.

Russell, Dick. *The Man Who Knew Too Much: Richard Case Nagell and The Assassination of JFK.* New York: Carroll & Graf, 1992.

Rust, William, J. and the editors of *U.S. News & World Report. Kennedy In Vietnam.* New York: Scribner's, 1985. Also a Da Capo Press paperback.

Salinger, Pierre. *With Kennedy.* New York: Doubleday, 1966.

Sauvage, Leo. *The Oswald Affair: An Examination of the Contradictions of the Warren Report.* Cleveland: World Publishing Co., 1966.

Savage, Gary. *JFK, First Day Evidence, Stored Away for Thirty Years in an Old Briefcase, New Evidence Is Now Revealed by former Dallas Police Crime Lab Detective R. W. (Rusty) Livingston.* Monroe, LA: The Shoppe Press, 1993.

Scheflin, Alan W. and Edward Upton, Jr. *The Mind Manipulators.* Paddington Press Ltd., 1978. Recommended reading.

Scott, Peter Dale. *Deep Politics and the Death of JFK.* University of California Press, 1993. I recommend this book to every interested student of the assassination of JFK. Scott is the best scholar at work on the relationships and politics of the murder. His work lacks the forensic underpinnings that establish conspiracy, but by the time Scott finishes constructing a circumstantial case, he has proved it. *Crime and Cover-Up, the CIA, the Mafia, and the Dallas-Watergate Connection,* Westworks 1977 P.O. Box 2071, Berkeley, CA 94702. Recommended reading.

Scott, Peter Dale, Paul Hoch, and Russell Stetler. *The Assassinations, Dallas and Beyond: A Guide to Cover-Ups and Investigations.* New York: Vintage Books, 1976. Recommended reading.

Schlesinger, Arthur. *A Thousand Days: John F. Kennedy in the White House.* Boston: Houghton-Mifflin, 1965. *Robert Kennedy and His Times.* New York: Ballantine Books, 1985.

Sculz, Tad. *Compulsive Spy: The Strange Career of E. Howard Hunt.* New York: Viking, 1974.

Sloan, Bill. *JFK: Breaking the Silence,* 1993, Taylor Publishing Company, 1550 West Mockingbird Lane, Dallas, TX, 75235. A collection of interviews and discussions of twelve major witnesses in the Kennedy assassination. Hard to corroborate, but interesting nonetheless.

Sorensen, Theodore C. *Kennedy.* New York: Harper & Row, 1965. *The Kennedy Legacy.* New York: New American Library, 1970.

Summers, Anthony. *Conspiracy.* New York: McGraw Hill, 1980. Reprinted by Paragon House, 1989 (Some material added.) Recommended reading. *Official and Confidential: The Secret Life of J. Edgar Hoover.* New York: Putnam, 1993.

Thompson, Josiah. *Six Seconds in Dallas: A Microstudy of the Kennedy Assassination* (revised). New York: Berkley, 1967, 1976. Recommended reading; an important book, though it contains some silly ideas with respect to the wounds. It's also out of print.

Thornley, Kerry. *Oswald.* Chicago: New Classics House, 1965.

Trask, Richard B. *Pictures of the Pain: Photography and the Assassination of President Kennedy.* Danvers, Mass.: Yeoman Press, 1994. Perhaps the best book to ever bring together the visual evidence in the assassination.

Turner, William and John G. Christian. *The Assassination of Robert Kennedy—A Searching Look at the Conspiracy and Cover-Up 1968–1978.* New York: Random House, 1978. Recommended reading.

Vankin, Jonathan. *Conspiracies, Cover-Ups And Crimes, From JFK to the CIA Terrorist Connection.*

Weissman, Steve. *Big Brother and the Holding Company: The World Behind Watergate.* Palo Alto: Ramparts Press, 1974. Recommended reading.

Wilber, Charles. *Medicolegal Investigation of the President John F. Ken-*

nedy Murder. Charles C. Thomas, Publisher, Springfield, Illinois. Very important study, but the author wrote Livingstone admitting that he missed the main point of the head wounds.

Wise, David, and Thomas B. Ross. *The Invisible Government: The CIA and U.S. Intelligence.* New York: Vintage, 1974. Recommended reading. *The Espionage Establishment.* New York: Random House, 1967; Bantam, 1968. Recommended reading.

Wofford, Harris. *Of Kennedys and Kings: Making Sense of the Sixties.* New York: Farrar, Straus, and Giroux, 1980.

Woods, John R. II. *J.F.K. Assassination Photos: Comprehensive Listing of the Photographic Evidence Relating to the Assassination of President John F. Kennedy*; self-published, limited edition, looseleaf, 1993, $100, c/o John R. Woods II, P. O. Box 472182, Aurora, CO, 80047. This book also functions as a catalog and is valuable.

Zelizer, Barbie. *Covering The Body.* University of Chicago Press, 1992.

Zirbel, Craig I. *The Texas Connection: The Assassination of John F. Kennedy.* TCC Publisher, 1991 (self-published) The Texas Connection Company, 7500 E. Butherus Dr., Scottsdale, AR 85260, or phone (602) 443-3818. FAX (602) 948-8206. Maintains LBJ and others in Texas were involved in the assassination.

There are many other books on the subjects of assassination and intelligence, and about Kennedy, but those above are the most important. The appendix to the report of the Assassinations Committee is crucial to study the case, but only twenty sets were printed for libraries and the public.

INDEX

Purvis, Tom, 72, 75

Rackley, Virginia, 149
Randle, Linnie Mae, 316–20
Random House, 283, 286, 313
  see also *Case Closed* (Posner)
Rankin, Lee, 122
Rather, Dan, 66–67, 76, 142, 143, 145, 149, 150, 169
Rear head entry, HSCA autopsy interviews on, 236–49
Red mist, in Zapruder film, 127–28, 131–33
Reed, Edward F., 222
Reenactments, 18, 52–78
  Bronson film, 61, 62–63, 129, 144, 354
  car used by, 75, 76
  of December 1963, 55, 59, 63–65, 67–68, 70–71, 73, 74, 75
  FBI's Commission Document 298 and, 54–61, 70, 76–78
  late hit to Connally and, 65–67
  May 1964 Warren Commission, 52, 65, 71–76
  Muchmore film, 127–28, 129, 132, 154, 175
  Nix film, 61–63, 127, 129, 136, 137, 138, 141, 154, 354
  Oliver film, 62, 70
  placement of shots and, 68–70
  Stemmons Freeway sign and, 155
  see also Zapruder film
Reiland, Ron, 306
Reynolds, Warren, 324
Rich, Joe H., 152
Richter, 196
Riebe, Floyd, 46, 47, 224, 336
Rifle, 15
  Oswald's fingerprints on, 15–16
  placement of shots from, 60, 68–70, 74–75, 76–78
  shots from two different directions from, 158
  single shot from, 198–199, *see also* Single-bullet theory
  into Texas School Book Depository, 316–20
  three shots from, 16, 18, 26–27, 54, 60–61, 70, 76–78, 152, 198–99
  two shots from, 137–38, 142–43, 198
  see also under Bullet; Trajectory analysis

Riley, Joseph, 264
Rivera, Geraldo, 127
Roberts, Earline, 327
Roberts, Ray, 149
Robertson, Randy, 264
Robinson, Thomas, 114, 191, 210, 213, 221–22, 233, 236–38, 254–55, 257, 264, 271, 272, 273, 299
Rodgers, Joshua, 80
Rogers, Lillian, 123
Rose, Dr., 40
Rotoscoping, of Zapruder film, 129–31, 159, 168
Rowell, Gary, 29–30, 99
Rowland, Barbara, 170–71
Ruby, Earl, 48
Ruby, Jack, 21, 48, 294, 305, 307–8, 313, 326, 329–30, 365
  FBI and, 8
  organized crime and, 123, 291–92
Rudnicki, Jan Gail, 189–90, 198, 214, 216, 224, 235–36, 256, 271
Rush, Johann, 307, 327
Rydberg, Harold, 231

Salandria, Vincent, 362–63
Sanders, Barefoot, 36, 196, 277, 340
Saturday Evening Post, 48, 121, 360
Schwartz, Erwin, 116, 117, 118–19, 120–21, 122–23, 172
Schweiker, Richard, 289–90
Scott, Peter Dale, 288, 290, 291–92, 307–11, 327–29
Secret documents, 4–5, 24
  autopsy photographs from, 28–51
  see also House Select Committee on Assassinations, autopsy interviews of
Secret Service, 16–17, 18, 71, 175, 177
  at autopsy, 197, 203, 271
  autopsy photographs and, 352
  bullet entry hole and, 211
  cover-up and, 69
  December 1963 reenactment and, 55, 59, 63–65, 67–68, 70–71, 73, 74, 75
  getting into car, 154
  Hunt and, 116
  placement of shots and, 69
  shots from, 146, 148–49
  Zapruder film and, 116–17, 118, 119, 120–21, 122, 126, 168
  see also Greer (Secret Service